Dostoevsky's Democracy

Ivan Kramskoi, The Contemplator (1876). Courtesy of the Kiev Museum of Russian Art, Ukraine. Photo courtesy of James L. Rice.

Dostoevsky's
⁓Democracy

Nancy Ruttenburg

PRINCETON UNIVERSITY PRESS   PRINCETON AND OXFORD

Library of Congress Cataloging-in-Publication Data

Ruttenburg, Nancy.
Dostoevsky's democracy / Nancy Ruttenburg.
p.   cm.
Includes bibliographical references and index.
ISBN 978-0-691-13614-1 (hardcover : alk. paper)
1. Dostoyevsky, Fyodor, 1821–1881—Political and social views. 2. Dostoyevsky, Fyodor,
1821–1881—Criticism and interpretation. 3. Democracy in literature. 4. Russia—Politics
and government—1801–1917. 5. Serfdom—Russia—History. I. Title.
PG3328.Z7P673 2008
891.73'3—dc22   2007047143

British Library Cataloging-in-Publication Data is available

This book has been composed in Galliard

Printed on acid-free paper. ∞

press.princeton.edu

Printed in the United States of America

1 3 5 7 9 10 8 6 4 2

For the remarkable Greg Lowry

Contents

∼

Acknowledgments

~

Dostoevsky was my earliest literary love. His name was for me synonymous with literature itself, literature was synonymous with religion, and religion was inseparable from the conviction that politics was a matter of ethical rather than pragmatic action. To read Dostoevsky as I first did, naively, was to be inhabited by the voices of his characters, by their ideas and their passions. These voices elicited the widest spectrum of emotional-intellectual response: I felt the full, craven hilarity of the Underground Man's preparations to walk down the street without yielding his place to other passers-by; I was stunned by the crisis of forgiveness contained in Ivan Karamazov's story of a landowner's brutal murder of a peasant child. In the interim between my adolescent reading and my writing of this book, Bakhtin has made the Dostoevskian voice a familiar concept even to those who have never read Dostoevsky. But I was fortunate to have encountered this body of literature without the theoretical armature with which we learn to shield our naked minds from the power of verbal art. The experience of carrying Dostoevsky's voices as I did over so long a time was deeply formative. The opportunity to write *Dostoevsky's Democracy* has been, first and foremost, an attempt to reflect on that experience.

I've been extremely grateful for the support of Hanne Winarsky, my editor at Princeton University Press. Friends and colleagues who had worked with her had encouraged high expectations, all of which she has exceeded. Rita Bernhard has been a considerate and patient copyeditor whose suggestions have improved the manuscript. I've been very fortunate, too, in my readers for the Press: one who has remained anonymous, and the other, Caryl Emerson, who revealed herself as a Press reader by initiating a remarkable conversation about Dostoevsky that I hope will continue.

Dostoevsky's Democracy began as a lengthy dissertation chapter that was then set aside while I pursued its ideas in the context of American colonial through antebellum literature and culture. Thanks to the excellent mentoring of my dissertation directors, William Mills Todd III, the late Jay Fliegelman, and René Girard, my Russian chapter stood me in good stead when I returned to it years after it was written. I wish I could have presented this book to Jay Fliegelman to show him how much of what he taught me carried over to the Russian side of my work.

I'm grateful to my colleagues in the Department of Comparative Literature for the generosity they've shown me since I came to NYU in 2001, for their much appreciated reception of this book, and for the atmosphere of warm collegiality and intellectual stimulation they provide every day. Special thanks are due to Richard Sieburth, Tim Reiss, Misha Iampolski, and Mark Sanders whose engagement with the book has been deeply gratifying. Susan Protheroe is, in the most positive sense, a great facilitator. In the Slavic Department, Eliot Borenstein heroically read the entire manuscript on his PDA, Anne Lounsbery unstintingly offered her services as an astute reader similarly fascinated by Russian-American entanglements, and Ilya Kliger cheerfully facilitated long-distance negotiations with the Russian-speaking bureaucracy. They have never complained about the number of "quick emergency question" emails I continue to send them. My remarkable research assistants—Bella Grigoryan, Mariano Siskind, Dmitry Kiyan, Adrienne Ghaly, and Monika Konwinska—buoyed me up with their discernment, patience, and initiative. Special thanks to Spencer Keralis for drawing my attention to the painting by Alphonse Mucha reproduced on the cover of this book.

In 2005–2006, New York University provided me with a year free from the responsibilities of teaching and chairing so that I could complete this study. I am grateful to Deans Richard Foley and Edward Sullivan for their generous advocacy and support of faculty research.

For welcoming me (back) into the Slavic discipline by inviting me to present portions of this work, I'm especially grateful to Cathy Popkin, Eric Naiman, Irina Paperno, Svetlana Boym, and Susan McReynolds. I benefited from the valuable feedback of audience members at their respective institutions: the Columbia University Seminar on Slavic History and Culture; the Slavic Colloquium at the University of California, Berkeley; Harvard University's Humanities Center in conjunction with the Davis Center for Russian and Eurasian Studies; and the Slavic Department at Northwestern University. The University Seminars at Columbia University generously helped cover publication costs for this book. Svetlana Boym kindly included my essay "Dostoevsky's Estrangement" in her special issue on estrangement for *Poetics Today* 26:4 (Winter 2005), where Meir Sternberg proved to be an exacting and therefore invaluable reader of my work in progress. I am grateful to the journal's publisher, Duke University Press, for giving me permission to reprint that article, a portion of which appears in revised form in Part 1 of *Dostoevsky's Democracy*. Deborah Martinsen has been a generous friend and interlocutor who encouraged me to present work at the International Dostoevsky Society conference, first in Geneva and then in Budapest. I found a real fellow traveler in James L. Rice, who contacted me as I was putting the finishing touches on the manuscript. Our ensuing correspondence has been a delight, and his work has been a revelation. I have been honored by Dale E. Peterson's support for my work and been inspired by his.

The following colleagues and friends outside the field of Slavic studies have generously read portions of work in progress and given me the benefit of their perspectives: Margaret Cohen, Diana Fuss, Anne Higonnet, Sharon Marcus, David Bates, Lorna Hutson, and Leslie Kurke. Victoria Kahn, whose work on literature and politics has been so inspiring, generously helped me navigate through several difficult passages. I have enormously appreciated the conversation and the friendship of Rochelle Gurstein, Barbara Fehrs, Lisa Considine, Bia Jaguaribe, Nan Goodman, and Karin and Kenny Sanders.

Certain friends contributed so directly and importantly to this work that the finished product is unthinkable without them. I met Sharon Cameron, a brilliant reader of American literature and theorist of "impersonality," not long after she had begun to work on Dostoevsky. It's humbling to realize how much she has taught me about him and other matters of mutual interest. Ross Posnock, the witty evangel of immaturity, adopted me into his circle of family and friends when I first moved to New York and, more than anyone else, made it seem like home. Annie Janowitz has kept me in true for several years with her communiqués, both hilarious and profound, which refresh me every day by letting me see our world through her sparkling eyes. Sam Otter has long served as my confidant and mentor, the dignity of whose office has over the years proven happily compatible with all manner of high silliness, of which I have an inordinate need. Because his is even more inordinate and because he is the soul of generosity, Jeff Knapp read *Ferdyduke* even though I refused to read *The Golden Bowl*. Through his great capacity for intellectual companionship, he disentangled what had seemed fatal conceptual knots, and the book is a better one for his help. Dori Hale's faith in me and this project has been not just a life raft, but one equipped with a little outboard motor, a nice canopy for shelter from the elements, and all the fixings for a really great cup of coffee and some tasty snacks. Her generosity, manifested in her extraordinarily insightful readings of my work and much else besides, is simply without parallel.

In writing these acknowledgments, I've struggled to give credit where it's due by distinguishing the intellectual, professional, and personal gifts bestowed on me by friends and colleagues as I wrote this book. In truth, as Jay Fliegelman taught me and affirmed through his life and work, the intellectual and the personal are not legitimately separable. Our intellectual endeavors and obsessions are at the core of who we are and how we live, and in no domain is that fact clearer—as Jay well knew—than it is in the family. Here, the difficulty is to acknowledge that for which no words adequate to one's gratitude exist. My brothers and their families, Bruce Ruttenburg and Kathy Pickering, Phillip Ruttenburg, Susan Reed Ruttenburg, and Ben, Katy, and Sam sustain me daily with their love, not necessarily on the phone. My son Hart Lowry has brightened my life with his comic brilliance and, inseparable from it, his uncanny powers of discernment. He has in so many ways taught me that laughter is always where the meaning is and the hope. My daughter Michela Lowry would disapprove if I told her how much I value her friendship. She would say, rightly, that a daughter is not a friend, but more and other than a friend. Yet what better word than friend to convey, beyond maternal pride, my admiration for her remarkable insight, her commitment to social justice, her unsentimental powers of feeling? I honor both my children in dedicating this book to their father, the source of our profound content, separately and together, Greg Lowry.

Introduction

∾

Can something that has no image appear as an image?
[Mozhet li mereshchit'sia v obraze to, chto ne imeet obraza?]
—F. M. Dostoevskii, *The Idiot* [1]

The Image of the Beast

Just as he was preparing to write the penultimate book of his last novel, *The Brothers Karamazov*, and suffering from poor health, F. M. Dostoevsky received an invitation to address the Society of Lovers of Russian Literature at their June 1880 celebration of the poet Alexander Pushkin. The significance of this three-day event was by no means confined to what it purported to be: an occasion to bring together the nation's most prominent writers, artists, actors, journalists, editors, and intellectuals to pay tribute to a celebrated poet of an earlier generation. Instead, as with all such events in nineteenth-century Russia where there was no question of freedom of expression, the literary fête would also provide a platform for public discussion of urgent social and political matters in the guise of literary commentary and interpretation. This occasion, however, was distinctive from its inception for making participants feel, as one expressed it, like "citizens enjoying a fullness of rights."[2] Speakers were not made to submit their addresses to the censor for advance review; indeed, the government of Alexander II, which had offered to pay the expenses of invited guests, made no attempt to control the planning, execution, or reception of the festivities. One journalist enthused that "in these festivities everything was the public's: public initiative, public participation, public thought, and public glory." The boldness of the planning and acquiescence of the authorities testified to a collective desire for "freedom of thought, freedom of the press, a greater scope for society's independent activity in the name of the state and the public good," proving, when all was said and done,

> that Russian society does not exist only in the imagination but in living reality; that there is cement in it that connects it all together into one inspired mass; that it has matured and grown into manhood; that it thinks, and can grieve, and be conscious of itself; that it counts freedom of expression as one of its natural, inborn needs; and that, via its literature, it has earned itself its diploma.[3]

The expressive latitude permitted first to the organizers and then to the press to cast the event as "epoch-making" was especially remarkable given the volatile political climate.[4] Only months later, in March 1881, the tsar would be assassinated by the revolutionary terrorist group the People's Will, six weeks after Dostoevsky's own death from complications of emphysema.[5] Alexander II, the "Tsar-Liberator," had been extolled for the reforms he initiated soon after his coronation in 1855, particularly the emancipation of the serfs in 1861.[6] Despite precautions taken in the planning and execution of the reforms, they generated social and political unrest across the class spectrum and, with the concomitant rise of a non-noble intelligentsia, anticipated the proliferation of radical thought and activity throughout the 1860s and 1870s.[7] The romantic utopian socialism of the 1840s—the "crime" for which Dostoevsky himself had suffered a decade of Siberian exile (from 1849 to 1859), four of those years in a hard-labor camp—metamorphosed in the 1860s into the revolutionary socialisms which by 1870 had advanced far beyond the Moscow and St. Petersburg intelligentsia and into new demographic, geographic, and ideological terrain.[8]

At issue for radicals of whatever stripe, from the populists who spearheaded a "back to the people" movement to the nihilists ambitious to organize terror cells among those same people, was the nation's unconditional liberation from its subjection to the autocratic state. They shared with liberals and conservatives an obsession with divining the significance of the Russian common people (*narod*) for the realization of their own political aspirations. To do so required the resolution of two related, and perpetually open questions: first, who, precisely, were the people and how could they be known? And, second, what part, if any, might they play in identifying and then helping Russia fulfill its world-historical destiny in relation to the West? These questions begged many others. Did "the people" signify all Russians regardless of class or only the common mass, the vast majority, whose illiteracy, poverty, and (for many) enslavement had kept them innocent of the Europeanization which had long marked the identity of the upper class? In the wake of emancipation, would a viable and genuine Russianness (*narodnost'*) manifest itself to embrace these extremes, and under whose direction would the rapprochement of the classes occur? Was it wishful thinking to imagine that a people largely sunk in poverty and barbarism might nevertheless possess an indigenous culture, almost entirely unknown to the elite but whose expressive forms were inherently worthy of broader attention? Could such a people play any but a subaltern's role in a world consecrated to modernity, and would their inclusion in *narodnost'* doom the upper classes to assume a diminished role on the world's stage? Or, on the contrary, might the unknown culture of the common people contain the new word destined to bring world culture forward, resurrected from the cultural morbidity which modernity—secularism, individualism, and materialism—all but guaranteed?

Notwithstanding the variety of responses to these questions posed by radical, liberal, and conservative members of the educated class about the identity and destiny of the Russian people, opinion tended to fall into one of two camps. The Westernizers felt that, since the time of Peter the Great, Russia's sole option, for better or worse, had been to embrace its cultural colonization by Europe and commit the nation to adapting and perfecting all aspects of its culture. They confronted the Slavophiles, those who felt that the nation's survival depended on its recognizing and developing indigenous resources of cultural power. At the same time they condemned Europeanization for emasculating Russian culture by substituting foreign forms for its genuine cultural virility whose source lay in the common class, despite their having been cast into the oblivion of perpetual labor. Westernizers imagined that the Europeanized educated elite would eventually succeed in raising the illiterate masses to their level so that Russia might take its place in the family of (Western) nations. Slavophiles prophesied that the common people would lead Russia in pronouncing a "new word" to a moribund West, delivering it from modernity and to a universal (post-national) spiritual truth. Both camps based their programs and prognoses in some more or less theoretical portrayal of the Russian common people who, despite the emancipation and the attention it brought, could still be viewed as "the mysterious God of whom one knows practically nothing."[9]

The Pushkin celebration was not conceived as offering some respite from this long-ripened and acrimonious dispute. On the contrary, the burning question to which it was consecrated in the minds of the festival's organizers and participants was whether Pushkin was to be enshrined as the national poet in whose work one might find both the word of national reconciliation and the new word through which Russia would convert Europe to a higher level of global cultural existence. Thus the fête, anticipated to be epoch-making, did not disappoint; one commentator compared its cultural-historical significance to that of Russia's Christianization in the late tenth century or to Westernization by Peter the Great in the early eighteenth.[10] Dostoevsky was asked to give the second of two keynote speeches. The first was given by that other literary lion, I. S. Turgenev, his ideological opponent since the mid-1860s when Dostoevsky began to develop views on Russia's national-spiritual preeminence that ran counter to Turgenev's Europhilism. In his address, Turgenev lauded Pushkin's accomplishment but refrained from crowning him the national poet as Shakespeare was undeniably the national poet of England or Goethe of Germany. He based his judgment not on a failure of Pushkin's poetic merits per se—quite the reverse, he had provided Russian literature with a poetic language and a range of character types—but to the vagaries of his reception over the decades since his death in 1837, suggesting that, however talented Pushkin may have been, his time had not been ripe. In contrast to Turgenev's modulated enthusiasm, Dostoevsky unhesitatingly, ringingly, and, as many testified, "prophetically" pronounced Pushkin the national poet on the grounds, elaborated previously in *Diary of a Writer* entries, that although of the nobility, this poet had been "a man who was reincarnated by his own heart into the common man, into his essence, almost into his image."[11] Moreover, Pushkin had recognized that only through literature could the feat of his "reincarnation" be transferred to the nation at large through the creation of "a whole series of positively beautiful Russian types he found among the Russian people," in comparison with which our "many experts on the people among our writers [are] merely 'gentlemen' who write about the people."[12] According to a multitude of accounts, Dostoevsky's speech was greeted with hysterical adulation. Joseph Frank attributes his success to the fact that his Russian messianism and exalted view of the people would have harmonized with the sentiments of the "vast majority" of his audience: in other words, unlike Pushkin in Turgenev's estimation, Dostoevsky's time was, indeed, ripe.[13]

Dostoevsky elaborated on the claims presented at the fête in the August 1880 issue of *Diary of a Writer*, the sole issue he would produce that year, by framing the text of the Pushkin speech with two polemical essays, the "Explanatory Note Concerning the Speech on Pushkin" and a four-part reply to a critique of his speech published in the liberal daily *Golos* (*The Voice*) by a professor and historian of law, A. D. Gradovsky. In this trio of essays, the problem that I call "Dostoevsky's democracy" emerges, not with the power and complexity it had exhibited previously (it had been a focus of the writer's work since his return from Siberian exile on the eve of emancipation) but yet with the concision and pathos of a valedictory address. The problem of Dostoevsky's democracy is fundamentally a problem of perception which had led even "our democrats"—those among the educated class who believe most earnestly in the apotheosis of the people—to betray them. "Why in Europe," he thus writes, "do those who call themselves democrats always stand for the people, at least base themselves on them, but our democrat [*nash demokrat*] is more often than not an aristocrat and in the final analysis almost always plays into the hand of those who suppress the people's strength and ends by lording it over them?" (*PSS* 26: 153/1302). The elite's betrayal of the people is inevitably self-defeating, since, as Pushkin had been the first to track and record in "Eugene Onegin" and elsewhere, the former's existence had been "sickly" and abnormal since they had torn themselves from and elevated themselves above the people. This ultimately fatal malaise could be

remedied only by embracing the "people's truth," premised on the acquisition or recovery of "faith" in that truth (*PSS* 26: 129–30/1271–72).
In the dialogical manner with which we are now familiar, Dostoevsky's
representative of the elite in his essay responds by protesting in all sincerity
that this popular truth, despite the best efforts of members of the upper
class, had remained entirely invisible to them. In its place, they see "only
an unworthy, barbaric mass which must be forced merely to obey" (*PSS*
26:135/1279). The hypothetical exchange of views elicits from Dostoevsky not a statement of the people's sublime truth but rather the prosaic
truth of his elite speaker who regretfully, but without remorse, insists that
"we didn't encounter this spirit of the people and didn't detect it on our
path," and for a very good reason: "we left it behind and ran from it as
fast as we could." Why flee beauty, truth, national reconciliation, spiritual
and social health? Because when we look at the people, say the elite, "we
see an inert mass [which we have] to re-create and refashion," a mass "low
and filthy, just as they've always been, and incapable of having either a
personality or an idea" (*PSS* 26: 134–35/1277–78).

The Pushkin speech which immediately follows is dedicated to a refutation of the prosaic truth of the elite in the form of a hypothesis concerning
the three stages of Pushkin's development. Dostoevsky's claim is that they
led the poet to embody unerringly the elusive popular truth in a series of
positively beautiful Russian types he found across the class spectrum. In
his subsequent response to Gradovsky's critique of the speech, large excerpts of which he includes in the body of his essay, Dostoevsky interjects
a dose of realism into his defense of the people and their truth: "But let's
allow, let's allow that our people are sinful and rude, let's allow that they
still bear the image of the beast"—illustrated by some lines from a popular
song: "the son rode on his mother's back / with his young wife in
traces"—and again, "But let's allow, in spite of everything allow that in
our people are brutality and sin" (*PSS* 26:152/1300). The hint of acquiescence in the repetition conveys his distress; as always in Dostoevsky, we
find no foregone conclusions. He offers several rationales for the people's
crude behavior: that all subject peoples behave so and the Russians may
not be as bestial as most; that the elites are to blame for bestializing by
enslaving the people; and so forth. But his most compelling argument for
the existence of the people's truth, paradoxically because to entertain it at
all requires a sustained act of faith, refers not to a weakness of character
or will on the part of the elite or the people but to a peculiar problem of
vision in which both are equally inveigled.

Invoking his experience as a political convict in a Siberian hard-labor
camp almost thirty years earlier, a member of the educated elite forced to
live cheek-by-jowl with hostile peasant-convicts, Dostoevsky asserts that

there are among the people not just crude and bestial sinners or mindless non-entities but "positive characters of unimaginable beauty and strength, whom your observation still hasn't touched." He continues:

> There are these righteous ones and sufferers for the truth—do we see them or don't we see them? I don't know; to whom it is given to see, will, of course, see and comprehend them, but who sees only the image of the beast, will, of course, see nothing. (*PSS* 26:153/1301)

Here is the answer not to the problem of the people, but to that of the problem's longevity. Twenty years after the emancipation, twenty years during which both traditionalists and revolutionaries passionately declared their commitment to its full (rather than merely official) realization, the problem of the people remained not just unresolved but poorly conceptualized and therefore inadequately articulated. The malaise of the deracinated Russian elite had been personified in the strong characters of Pushkin and Gogol; the malaise of the bestial Russian people had been expressed in literary or polemical caricature, enshrined in specimens of folk literature, or sentimentalized in attempts to translate the folk character and milieu into a contemporary literary idiom such as the novel. Meanwhile, the popular truth, embodied by the unimaginably beautiful—that is, culturally invisible and aesthetically unrepresentable—people, remained abstract and unspecified: in attempting to embrace it, one all too often found oneself embracing a phantom, or worse, a projection of one's own pathology. Dostoevsky's democracy, as we will see, entails the development of an aesthetic based less on his vision of the people than of an uncanny cultural blindness which continued to obscure the image of the people and which, precisely because all are blind, no one even suspects. Although we find the most powerful elaboration of Dostoevsky's democracy and the aesthetic to which it gives rise in the first of his great novels, *Notes from the House of the Dead* (1861), the primary focus of this book, the problem is perhaps most concisely formulated, and with specific reference to the character of "the democrat," in *The Idiot* (1868) to which I now briefly turn.

The *Ne To* and the "Democrat"

In the spring of 1868, having finished the first part of his novel *The Idiot*, Dostoevsky wrote a letter to Apollon N. Maikov from Geneva in which he asks his trusted friend ("perhaps my only friend!") to stand as godfather to his first child, Sonia, born a month earlier (*PSS* 28 [II]: 279/282). He describes the powerful and novel sensations of parental love and the equally intense feelings of anxiety arising from a sudden inability to write, threatening to delay submission of his novel and thus repayment of his significant debt to his publisher. His only chance of meeting his deadline is to write the novel's second part in eighteen days. But this seems unlikely: he describes his sleeplessness and the consequent exacerbation of his epilepsy; his wife's physical and emotional stress before and after their child's birth; their pending eviction because of the baby's crying, and their desperate need to find new living quarters with extremely limited financial resources. He discusses his anxiety over his dependents left behind in Russia—his stepson, Pasha, who has not written to congratulate him on the birth of Sonia and may not have contacted his editor, as Dostoevsky had urgently requested; and the wife of his deceased brother who had also failed to acknowledge the baby's birth. He laments that the state of his finances has forced him to live abroad, away from Russia, the source of his inspiration. The tenor of the letter then changes as he writes about Russia itself and its "enormous regeneration under our current great sovereign," Alexander II: "Here abroad, I have conclusively become with respect to Russia a perfect monarchist" (*PSS* 28 [II]: 281/283). Only the tsar, Dostoevsky claims, managed to accomplish things in Russia, "simply because he is the tsar. In Russia the people have given and will give their love to every one of our tsars and in the end they believe only in him. For the people, this is mysterious, holy, sacramental."[14] The Russian Westernizers, however, were blind to this truth; having taken pride in grounding themselves not in a sentimental attachment to tradition, but in facts, "they've overlooked the most important and greatest fact of our history": "that our constitution is the mutual love of the monarch for the people and the people for the monarch" (*PSS* 28 [II]: 281, 280/283).

This unconditional faith in the sovereign at which Dostoevsky claims to have arrived—induced, perhaps, by his involuntary exile and painful nostalgia for Russia—is accompanied by unambiguously hostile observations of all aspects of Western culture and its Russian sympathizers in this and other letters from the late 1860s during which he conceived and wrote *The Idiot*.[15] He is particularly incensed by the Russian monarchy's political opponents living voluntarily or otherwise in exile. His utopian socialism of the 1840s, for which he spent a decade in Siberian exile, seems completely eclipsed.[16] He excoriates the moribund worldliness of the Roman Catholics, the self-contradictions of Protestantism, the vulgarity and stupidity of the Germans, the despicable mediocrity of the Swiss republic, and the pettiness of Western bourgeois culture generally. He denounces the Westernizers, that "unfortunate class of little smart-asses [*umniki*] uprooted from the soil," and all Russian liberals as "poor wretches," "nonentities," "garbage, bloated with self-love," and "turds" (*PSS* 28 [II]: 280, 259, 282/283, 275, 285).[17] He lumps Turgenev together with Herzen and all the other "stupid little liberals and progressives [*liberalishki i progressisty*]" as "obscenely vain," "shamelessly irritable, mindlessly proud"; taken together, they represent the "cursed dregs of what is obsolete and retrograde" (*PSS* 28 [II]: 210, 259/254, 259). These characterizations of liberals and progressives and their beliefs, not surprisingly, make a strong appearance in the novel on which Dostoevsky worked so intensively during these months. They appear in a refracted (dialogic, rather than monologic) way, voiced by various characters, some of whom have little if any claim to the reader's uncritical acceptance. Nevertheless, the valence of liberal and radical ideas in the novel, and their association with the extremes of socialism and nihilism, seems clear, with one exception: despite Dostoevsky's appreciation of monarchism, the term whose meaning remains uncertain, in part because it is foregrounded as such, is "democrat."

In the final part of *The Idiot*, Dostoevsky's famously failed attempt to portray a "wholly beautiful man," the title character, Prince Myshkin, is accused five times of being a "democrat" (*demokrat*).[18] Initially somewhat comical, the scenes of accusation become increasingly dire, yet neither the political nor the characterological significance of the epithet, and thus its explanatory value in relation to the novel's tragic denouement, ever materialize. Far from helping to explain the rationale for tragedy—Rogozhin's murder of Nastasia Filippovna and Myshkin's return to imbecility—it remains unclear (despite the tone of disapproval with which it is pronounced) if to be a "democrat" is in any substantial sense a good or a bad thing. Lizaveta Prokofevna Epanchina, the comically and perpetually distressed mother of one of the two women the Prince loves and the first in the novel to denounce him as a "democrat," wonders, "Was the prince good or not? Was the whole thing good or not? If it was not good (which was unquestionable), what precisely was not good about it? And if it was good (which was also possible), then, again, what was good about it?" (*PSS* 8:421/507).[19] The question, she feels, is urgent and demands immediate resolution, "yet not only was it impossible to resolve it, but poor Lizaveta Prokofevna could not even pose the question to herself with full clarity, try as she might." As she struggles to articulate her own objections to Myshkin's reputed interest in her daughter Aglaia, the word "democrat" incorporates everything that makes him unquestionably bad yet possibly good. "First of all there was the fact that 'this wretched princeling is a sick idiot, second of all he's a fool, who neither knows society nor has any place in society: to whom can he be shown, where can he be tucked in? He's some sort of impermissable democrat, without even the least rank,' " and yet "at the same time something stirred in [her] heart which suddenly said to her: 'And what makes the prince not the sort you want?' " Lizaveta Prokofevna's objection to the prince as "some sort of impermissable democrat" is, finally, one made "against her own heart" (PSS 8:421/507, 508).

The unspoken summary condemnation, however inexact and inadequate a description of Lizaveta Prokofevna's potential son-in-law, stands, as Myshkin intuits in the second scene of accusation. This occurs at the Epanchins' engagement party for Aglaia, prematurely arranged by her mother who has become impatient with her own doubts. On this occasion, Myshkin is to be presented to "high society" for the first time, a social circle, Aglaia frets, to which her own family, "people of the middle circle, as middle as can be" despite their wealth and social respectability, do not belong: she condemns the event in advance as "ridiculous" (*PSS* 8:435/525). But the explicit focus of her fear about appearing ridiculous is Myshkin's propensity to "start talking," to introduce lofty subjects of conversation, which she forbids in advance (*PSS* 8:436/526). Despite this prohibition and his own anxious dream that he would nevertheless speak somehow inappropriately in an effort "to convince [the guests] of something," at the party Myshkin talks uninhibitedly, inspired by his increasing delight with the guests' elegant civility, which he "took at face value, for pure, unalloyed gold" (*PSS* 8:437, 445/527, 537). Myshkin is inspired, that is, by a kind of optical illusion of class which leads him in this scene to see aristocratic vanity as candor, cynicism as naïve friendliness, and conventional politesse—"tact and cunning"—as the warmest sincerity.[20] His "eyes shining with rapture and tenderness," his heart filled with "the warmest and sincerest gratitude to someone for something," he " 'starts talking' " when one of the party's dignitaries tells him that he remembers the prince as a child and was a distant relation of his late guardian (*PSS* 8:448, 449/540, 541). This distant connection, just short of kinship but imbued with its pathos, provides Myshkin with a platform and referent for what has been building into a groundless emotional ecstasy, "out of all proportion to the subject of the conversation" (*PSS* 8:448/541). When he learns from the dignitary that his guardian, Pavlishchev, had converted to Roman Catholicism before his death, he becomes distraught and delivers an impassioned monologue on the sinister attraction of Roman Catholicism for educated Russians who have lost their instinct for religious truth along with their connection to the common people, but whose Russianness is evident in their continuing thirst to believe in something higher.

In this monologue, Dostoevsky puts in his hero's mouth his own "personal and long-standing" conviction that only the advent of the Russian Christ could defeat the power of Roman Catholicism—an "unchristian faith" worse than atheism, a faith which had led those mourning "the lost moral force of religion" first to socialism and then to the violence of nihilism (*PSS* 8:450, 451/543, 544).[21] But even before he had derived the weighty and therefore inappropriate topic of religious truth from what the dignitary had intended as an item of gossip, Myshkin had already begun to speak strangely to him. By then his conversation was marked by the kind of tittering self-abasement mixed with a seemingly inadvertent denigration of the character of his lofty interlocutor typical of another character who voices some of Dostoevsky's own beliefs: the crudely learned, often drunk, and always half-cocked Lebedev.[22] A shameless busybody entirely without personal allegiance and therefore ever-present, Lebedev functions as a go-between among the various social classes who collectively produce the novel's tragic plot. With the conscientiousness of the scandal monger whose practice is an art form (unlike Myshkin, Lebedev's equal in abetting scandal but who does so inadvertently, out of a principled reluctance to recognize social hierarchies), Lebedev draws social lessons for the prince's benefit from his facilitations of forbidden contact, based on a *reductio ad absurdum* of social principles. While informing Myshkin that he enabled the rivals for the prince's attention, Aglaia and Nastasia Filippovna, to exchange letters, for example, he conspicuously leaves out the women's names, referring to them instead in a coded terminology which he explains to the prince: "one of them I designate by the name of 'person' [*litsa*], sir, and the other only as 'personage' [*personazha*], for humiliation and for distinction; for there is a great difference between the innocent and highly noble daughter of a general and a . . . kept woman, sir" (*PSS* 8:439/529). When Myshkin rents a room in Lebedev's dacha in Pavlovsk, it becomes the site of motley gatherings where "persons" and "personages" encounter each other with naked antagonism in ways impossible in more public venues. The opportunity to vent their mutual outrage enables some unmediated communication and even friendships, but finally produces a greater entrenchment of class positions. The constant chaos of social mixing when rules of decorum no longer apply and which so fatigues him at Lebedev's elevates for Myshkin the charm of the elegant manners and easy mutual understanding of the Epanchins' guests.

In his conversation at the party, it becomes clear that, for the dignitary, Pavlishchev's conversion to Catholicism spells his abandonment of "his service"—his abandonment, that is, of the conventional life of "a man of good family, with a fortune, a gentleman-in-waiting" (*PSS* 8:449/542).[23] The unseemliness of the conversion rather than its meaning disturbs the dignitary. To comment on the meaning, as Myshkin does, extends and exacerbates this unseemliness. The effect is amplified when the prince, trembling with enthusiasm, prophesies before the Epanchins' astonished guests the advent of the Russian God as "a mighty and righteous, wise and meek giant [rising] up before the astonished world, astonished and frightened" (*PSS* 8:453/546).[24] As Aglaia foretold in the earlier scene when she forbade him to "start talking" at the party, Myshkin, declaiming and gesticulating, then breaks her mother's expensive Chinese vase. In the wake of this accident, in an excess of gratitude toward the guests for not taking offense at his clumsiness, Myshkin proceeds, with characteristic earnestness, to tell the assembled dignitaries court jester's truths in the guise of confession. As himself a member by birth of that class of "our foremost people, the elders, the ancient stock," Myshkin insists that he felt driven to acquaint himself with the Epanchins' guests.

> I've always heard so much more bad than good about you, about the pettiness and exclusiveness of your interests, about your backwardness, your shallow education, your ridiculous habits [. . .] I had to see for myself and become personally convinced: is it actually so that this whole upper stratum of the Russian people is good for nothing, has outlived its time, has exhausted its ancient life, and is only capable of dying out, but in a petty, envious struggle with people . . . of the future, hindering them, not noticing that it is dying itself? (*PSS* 8:456–57/550–51)

That it is "actually so" the dignitaries "sarcastically" deny, and Myshkin goes on to insist that the guests' gracious sincerity (which the narrator has thoroughly debunked) disproves in and of itself "that in society everything is a manner, everything is a decrepit form, while the essence is exhausted." Nor does he stop at characterizing (albeit in the mode of vigorous denial) his interlocutors as members of a moribund and (in the mode of joyful approval) a "ridiculous" class (*PSS* 8:457/551).[25] Beyond these unintentional insults to the guests' collective amour-propre, he also poses damaging rhetorical questions about individuals: given the story he had told so artlessly, for example, can Prince N. really be "a . . . dead man, with a dried-up heart and talent?" (*PSS* 8:457/551). Myshkin does not spare himself in this scene of unseemly exposures: as the guests try to soothe and silence him, he insists on speaking even though his ridiculous "gesture" compromises and even "humiliates" his idea, and even though—as Dostoevsky had claimed of himself—"I have no sense of measure either" (*PSS* 8:458/552).[26]

The breaking of the vase signals the shift in Myshkin's address to the Epanchins' guests from a polemical to a confessional tone. As this confession proceeds, it is increasingly marked by what M. M. Bakhtin calls the "sideward glance," the speaker's anticipatory acknowledgment of that which he imagines others are about to accuse him:[27]

> Do you think I'm a utopian? An ideologist? Oh, no, by God, my thoughts are all so simple . . . You don't believe it? You smile? You know, I'm sometimes mean, because I lose my faith; today I was walking here and thinking: "Well, how shall I start speaking to them? What word should I begin with, so that they understand at least something?"

Despite Aglaia's prohibition, here Myshkin reveals that he looked forward to the party as an occasion to put forward his "word," to "start speaking."

His eagerness to have his say, along with the doubts he voices about the adequacy of his interlocutors to his word ("This I tell you, you, who have already been able to understand . . . and not understand . . . so much") and his anticipation of their condemnation of his word, make him a type of the Underground Man, as Bakhtin has powerfully described that character (*PSS* 8:458/552–53).[28] Unlike the Underground Man's narrative, Myshkin's brief confession here is not motivated by spite or cynicism, nor does his discourse betray the "vicious circle," the endless internalized polemic, of one who would refute the irrefutable: that "one's attitude toward oneself is inseparably interwoven with one's attitude toward another" (*PDP* 229, 231). On the contrary, Myshkin joyfully identifies himself with his auditors in the spirit of mutual understanding and forgiveness:

> For it's actually so, we are ridiculous, light-minded, with bad habits, we're bored, we don't know how to look, how to understand, we're all like that, all, you, and I, and they! [. . .] You know, in my opinion it's sometimes even good to be ridiculous, if not better: we can the sooner forgive each other, the sooner humble ourselves. (*PSS* 8:458/553)

It is in this manner, and not (like the Underground Man's) through a deliberately annoying or inelegant style of address, that Myshkin's speech is marked by what Bakhtin calls the reverse aestheticism of holy foolishness, which makes him "ambiguous and elusive even for himself" (*PDP* 231, 234). Intended to convert his noble auditors, to resurrect them from spiritual and cultural death, his address fails in its intent because it fails (as Myshkin recognizes) "to set an example," to assert a stable self-definition built on a stable referential word (*PSS* 8:459/553). His very sense of integrity compels the prince to give pride of place to the "contrary evaluation of oneself" which he suspects his hearers have made (*PDP* 233).

In particular, the uncertain status of the "we," and therefore of the "them," in his address to the Epanchins' guests leads Myshkin to articulate their unspoken suspicion that he is a "democrat." In the fashion of the Underground Man, he denies by anticipating the "impermissable" truth that he knows circulates among friends and detractors alike and to which he has become acutely sensitive, as he has with the epithet "idiot" itself.[29] In both cases, his denial of the epithet's truth is also an assertion of its truth:

> "You thought I was afraid for *them*, that I was *their* advocate, a democrat, a speaker for equality?" he laughed hysterically (he laughed every other minute in short, ecstatic outbursts). "I'm afraid for you, for all of you, for all of us together. For I myself am a prince of ancient stock, and I am sitting with princes. It is to save us all that I speak, to keep our estate from vanishing for nothing, in the darkness, having realized nothing, squabbling over every-

thing and losing everything. Why vanish and yield our place to others, when we can remain the vanguard and the elders? Let us be the vanguard, then we shall be the elders. Let us become servants, in order to be elders." (*PSS* 8:458/553)

Denying that he advocates indifference, a collapse of the hierarchies, Myshkin obscures the distinctions of class and ideology indicated by his pronouns, elides the difference between the secular standing of the prince and the theological standing of the elder (*starshii*), and reverses the priority of first and last, of elders and servants. Denying the desire of the one who would be first, he invokes the quintessentially democratic gesture of Jesus in Mark 9:35. In an agony of self-consciousness, having just proclaimed himself not the destroyer but the would-be savior of his estate, Myshkin, who would preserve their authority by making them the servants of servants, has an epileptic seizure and loses consciousness.[30]

Two weeks later, the term "democrat" is applied to Myshkin for the third time. It reemerges in the wake of the fateful engagement party and the subsequent face-to-face encounter of Aglaia Epanchina and Nastasia Filippovna at which the prince, crucified between his romantic and spiritual inclinations, appears to "choose" the latter. That the prince is a democrat is part of a general evaluation of Myshkin's character concocted by "several serious gossips." The epithet then circulates "over almost the whole town and even its environs." No longer an unspoken or intuited accusation, the epithet is now the staple of a communally produced narrative, "embroidered with scandals" involving "many well-known and important persons," and intended to make sense of the fact that "a certain prince [. . .], having caused a scandal in an honorable and well-known house, and having rejected the daughter of that house, already his fiancée, had been enticed away by a well-known tart." This narrative circulates through all classes of Pavlovsk society in the form of "one and the same story" but in "a thousand different versions" of the same "irrefutable and graphic facts" about Myshkin: he is "a young man, of good family, a prince, almost wealthy, a silly fool, but a democrat [*durachok, no demokrat*], and gone crazy over modern nihilism which was discovered by Mr. Turgenev, barely able to speak Russian," and so on. (*PSS* 8:476/573–74). As the story goes, the "democrat" is first and foremost a dissembler, like a fabled French atheist who had gone to the trouble of being ordained simply in order to proclaim publicly the inauthenticity of his ordination. Myshkin's version of the French atheist's trampling of the pieties had been to use the Epanchin party as a forum at which "to proclaim his way of thinking aloud and in front of everyone, to denounce the venerable dignitaries, to reject his fiancée publicly and offensively, and, while resisting the servants who were taking him out, to smash a beautiful Chinese vase."

Although he loved the general's daughter, he had rejected her solely out of nihilism and for the sake of the immanent scandal, so as not to deny himself the pleasure of marrying a fallen woman before the whole world and thereby proving that in his conviction there were neither fallen nor virtuous women, but only free women; that he did not believe in the social and old distinction, but believed only in the "woman question." That, finally, a fallen woman, in his eyes, was even somewhat higher than an unfallen one. Though some aspects of the story were murky, "there remained not the slightest doubt that the scandalous wedding would actually take place" (*PSS* 8:476–77/574).

The novel's narrator reproduces the anecdote about Myshkin, "a fool, but a democrat," not as an absurd rumor and not as the unvarnished truth but because of its advantages as explanation: it is "graphic" (*nagliadnyi*)—its import is clear, it can be seen without obstacle, and therefore grasped immediately and without difficulty, if not necessarily believed. Its clarity rather than its truth is what recommends the "graphic anecdote" to the desperate narrator as a solution to a narrative impasse he finds otherwise impossible to surmount. The communally produced, "strange, rather amusing, almost unbelievable" account, the narrator insists, should not be considered a "digression" from a story that has become untellable. Nor, on the other hand, does it contain some otherwise unavailable insight into the prince, his motives and beliefs; its illogic—on the "woman question," for example—is a familiar absurdity, reminiscent of the novel's self-styled nihilists who have convinced themselves that they have the "right" to steal from Myshkin. Instead, the narrator offers it in the absence of any other way to take his readers from the engagement party for Aglaia and Myshkin to the wedding planned for Nastasia Filippovna and Myshkin two weeks later—he offers it, that is, simply because it delivers us to the fact of the prince's wedding to Nastasia which, at this juncture, although baffling to everyone, including the narrator, is "indeed appointed" (*PSS* 8:477/575). In the absence of the narrator's own explanation and out of his reluctance to fabricate one, the graphic anecdote serves not as substitute explanation (we are never supposed to accept it at face value) but for its purely structural advantage as "a direct and immediate continuation of the story" (*PSS* 8:476/573).

Yet, the question intrudes itself: In what sense can an absurd fabrication, no matter how opportune and even if sanctioned by the community, be considered a direct and immediate continuation of the story? Where is its principle of continuity located if not in the logic—or at least the plausibility—of its details? Because the individual details of the graphic anecdote in its several versions are patently false and even far-fetched, it can only be the reiterated characterization of the prince as fool and democrat that bridges the gap for a mystified community between the engagement party for one woman and the wedding plans for another. The "democrat" of the anecdote is first and foremost he who allows such things to happen and such stories to be told, stories that cohere around a bewildering motive, inscrutable and therefore unrepresentable. The graphic anecdote serves as direct and immediate continuation of the story, then, not simply because it offers a trumped-up narrative to bridge the informational abyss but because the narrative it offers features precisely this unrepresentability in its central formulation. The conceptual difficulty is highlighted, moreover, by the oppositional rather than complementary conjunction joining its paired terms—"a fool, *but* a democrat." The phrasing suggests that although the terms are incompatible, both are improbably operative in the prince's character, and this foundational improbability is metonymically replicated in each of the anecdote's constitutive assertions. The narrative, both the graphic anecdote collectively produced by the gossips and the larger narrative in which it is embedded and used as connective material, thus sustains the centrality of the epithet "democrat." Produced by the narrator's odd *crise de confiance* and the communal judgment of the prince, the narrative carries the epithet forward as a simultaneously absurd and authoritative explanation for the novel's escalating tragic tension, suspending its meaning along with the questions of goodness or badness, truth or falsity with which it is surrounded.

Evgeny Pavlovich Radomsky, Myshkin's urbane and amiable rival for Aglaia's attention, embellishes the community's indictment, to which the narrator tells us he had "perhaps contributed," with his psychological diagnosis of the prince's motives (for whose insightfulness the narrator praises him twice) in the fourth and final instance in which he is branded a democrat. Myshkin's "innate inexperience," "extraordinary simple-heartedness," "phenomenal lack of the sense of measure," and "enormous, flooding mass of cerebral convictions" which the prince's "extraordinary honesty" led him to mistake for "genuine, natural, and immediate convictions": these traits of character underlay his "*conventionally democratic*" relations with Nastasia Filippovna, attributable, when all is said and done, to "the charm, so to speak, of the 'woman question.' " Despite his recognition that the prince is "strange enough not to be like all other people," which leads many to consider him an idiot, Evgeny Pavlovich judges Myshkin to have behaved "conventionally" (*PSS* 8:481/579; emphasis in original). His indictment is especially curious, because he is the only character in the novel to have aggressively sought out the prince's views on the subject of progressive reform in Russia, and to have been astonished at his unconventional responses.

On that occasion, upon Myshkin's arrival in Pavlovsk, Evgeny Pavlovich raised the subject of Russian liberalism. He maintained (and Dostoevsky's own views of the late 1860s are again clearly audible) that Russian liberalism was deeply fraudulent: unlike his Western counterpart, the Russian liberal attacked not just the "existing order of things," but "the very essence of our things," "the things themselves" and not merely "their order." The Russian liberal, that is, denies and even hates "Russia itself"— he "hates and beats his own mother"; liberalism, he argues, a Western phenomenon fatally embraced by "the former landowners (abolished) and the seminarians," contains the seed of Russia's self-destruction (*PSS* 8:277/335).[31] The liberal reform on which Evgeny Pavlovich especially wished to sound Myshkin out was the jury trial, established in 1864 along with open courts by Alexander II's judicial reforms.[32] In particular, he wanted to ask Myshkin's opinion of an infamous case in which the jury acquitted a man who had murdered six people on the basis of his defense attorney's argument that the "environment"—the murderer's poverty— was responsible for his crime. For the lawyer and those who acquitted his client, such an argument exemplified "the most liberal, the most humane and progressive" reasoning, but Evgeny Pavlovich condemns it as a "perversion of notions and convictions" that had become generally accepted (*PSS* 8:279/337).

Asked for his opinion, Myshkin agrees, and adds that he had recently spent time in prisons and become acquainted with some inmates. The difference between these convicts and the liberals "whom Evgeny Pavlych has begun speaking about" is that even "the most inveterate and unrepentant murderer still knows that he is a *criminal*, that is, in all conscience he considers that he has done wrong, though without any repentance. And every one of them is the same," whereas the latter, those ostensibly influenced by liberal theories of crime and punishment, "do not even want to consider themselves criminals and think to themselves that they had the right and . . . even did a good thing" (*PSS* 8:280/339). I return to this conversation in part 2 of this study (section 4). At this juncture, it is worth noting that Myshkin's response, which Evgeny Pavlovich purposely elicited, is anything but "*conventionally democratic*" insofar as it condemns the abstract notion of "right" as an excuse for denying individual moral accountability.[33] Perhaps more accurately, it is anything but conventional: the prince's views are sui generis—they do not conform to those of any ideological camp, nor, as Evgeny Pavlovich observes "with astonishment," do they appear to conform to Myshkin's own tolerant response toward the would-be nihilists who in an earlier scene had maintained the "right" to fleece him (*PSS* 8:280/339). Despite his thus having elicited the prince's views just weeks earlier, in the fourth scene of accusation Evgeny Pavlovich betrays his own inability to imagine something other than a conventional—not to say muddled— explanation for Myshkin's behavior: he reiterates, for example, Lizaveta Prokofevna's vague suspicion that the prince's unaccountable behavior must somehow come down to the "woman question" (*PSS* 8:422/509). He can only revert to the hackneyed explanation concocted by the community at large that, in the management of his romantic affairs, the prince had acted on the basis of conventionally unconventional—"democratic"—theories he had impermissibly put into practice.

In his zeal to persuade the prince to give up his perverse democratic convictions, Evgeny Pavlovich rehearses the circumstances surrounding Myshkin's return to Russia. Insofar as it is factually accurate but fundamentally false, his narrative resembles the community's narrative of what had transpired at the Epanchins' engagement party. He notes the prince's sheltered upbringing in a Swiss sanitorium and his estrangement from his native country; his bookish expectations of Russia; his desire to act; his fatigue and illness; the difficult Petersburg weather; the powerful impression made by Nastasia Filippovna which elicited all Myshkin's chivalry; the beauty of the Epanchin sisters and particularly Aglaia; and, finally, his quintessentially Dostoevskian first day "in an unknown and almost fantastic city, a day of encounters and scenes, a day of unexpected acquaintances, a day of the most unexpected reality." Myshkin concedes that his experience on that fateful day had been "almost so" (*pochti chto ved' tak*) and Evgeny Pavlovich, encouraged, presses on, insisting that the prince had been wrong to think that he could love two women and wrong to expect their understanding of his love (*PSS* 8:482/580). Finally, however, despite the fact that Evgeny Pavlovich's representations are commonsensical, emotionally generous, and factually accurate, Myshkin rejects the limitations of his understanding and condemns Aglaia and Nastasia Filippovna, too, for being unable, at their encounter, to talk "about the right thing, not about the right thing at all" (*ne pro to, sovsem ne pro to*) (*PSS* 8:483/581). If he could speak to Aglaia, Myshkin insists, she would understand that "it's all not *that*, but something completely, completely different!" (*vsio eto ne to, a sovershenno, sovershenno drugoe*). Evgeny Pavlovich confirms that Myshkin is, in fact, about to marry Nastasia Filippovna, and asks, "Then how is it not that?" (*Tak kak zhe ne to?*), to which Myshkin can only reply, "Oh, no, not that, not that!" (*O nyet, ne to, ne to!*) (*PSS* 8:483/582). The pragmatic Evgeny Pavlovich is incredulous:

"How's that? So you want to love them both?"
"Oh, yes, yes!"
"Good heavens, Prince, what are you saying? Come to your senses!"
(*PSS* 8:484/583)[34]

Myshkin cannot come to his senses. Consistent with his earlier description of the state of mind of the common criminals he had interviewed in prison whose view of their crime bore no trace of progressive theory, he cannot repent or renounce his love for both women. Without remorse but with genuine sorrow, he accepts that he is to blame.[35]

The two scenes in which Evgeny Pavlovich and Myshkin attempt to come to an understanding are linked by a set of shared and interrelated themes: specific touchstones of Russian social and political reform; the perversion of convictions under the influence of theory; the acknowledgment of wrongdoing and responsibility even in the absence of remorse; and, finally, the phenomenon of the "*ne to*," or "not that." In his brilliant study of Nikolai Gogol, Donald Fanger identified the *ne to* as the "central principle" of the earlier writer's aesthetic where it signifies "a constant denial (as fact or as value) of what appears in the represented reality and in the representation itself": "varieties of displacement [in which] things are not what or where or as they should be; parts usurp the function of wholes; expectations are baffled."[36] In contrast, Dostoevsky uses the *ne to* to indicate the inadequate expression or enactment of an as-yet inarticulable or unrealizable belief, idea, or ideal. Often linked to a conventional, bookish notion, the *ne to* stands in, as a negative signifier, for that which cannot be named or performed, that for which an "image" does not yet exist. The theme of the *ne to* is powerfully present throughout the novel. It is central to Ippolit Terentyev's confessional "Explanation."[37] It makes its last shocking appearance as Myshkin sits playing cards with Rogozhin beside Nastasia Filippovna's corpse: "he suddenly realized that at that moment, and for a long time now, he had not been talking about what he needed to talk about, and had not been doing what he needed to do" (*vse govorit ne o tom, o chem nado emu govorit', i delaet vse ne to, chto by nado delat'*) (*PSS* 8:506/610; my emphasis). The *ne to* is negatively linked to the prince's propensity to "begin talking," which Aglaia had warned him against before their engagement party, not because of its impropriety (although this was the reason she gave) but because he would not be understood, confirming his reputation as an idiot. In the fourth scene of accusation, having acknowledged the plausibility of Evgeny Pavlovich's insistence that his "democratic" tendencies underwrite his anomalous views of love (such as the "incredible exaggeration" of his "compassion" for Nastasia Filippovna), Myshkin can only object that in the last analysis what motivates him is "not that" (*PSS* 8:482/581).

Although the *ne to* in the instances I have cited are associated with his reputation as "idiot" and "democrat," Myshkin had earlier in the novel used the phrase insistently in connection with a quartet of encounters he had had on his travels through the Russian provinces. In this key scene, which immediately precedes Rogozhin's attempt to kill Myshkin and the latter's first epileptic seizure, the prince, just returned from his travels, visits Rogozhin in his grim mansion. The meeting is extraordinarily fraught: they discuss Rogozhin's family history; Nastasia Filippovna, at length; the religious import of a copy of Hans Holbein's painting *Christ's Body in the Tomb* (1522) which hangs in Rogozhin's reception room and to which Myshkin responds in Dostoevsky's own words upon seeing it in Basel.[38] This leads to a discussion about religious faith, in which Rogozhin quotes a drunk man who told him that there were more atheists in Russia than abroad " 'because we've gone further than they have' " (*PSS* 8:182/ 219). Myshkin's discussion of the significance of Russian atheism at the Epanchins' party, which precedes his second epileptic seizure, echoes this comment. In response to Rogozhin's introduction of the topic of religious unbelief in the presence of Holbein's depiction of Christ's mutilated corpse, Myshkin describes the four "different encounters in two days" that he had had on his trip. The first was with an atheist, an educated man with whom he talked for hours on a train. Myshkin had appreciated the man's "rare courtesy" but was struck by the disjuncture in his conversation between the concept of disbelief and its articulation: "it was as if the whole time he was not talking about that at all" (*chto on vovse kak budto ne pro to, govoril, vo vse vremia*). This same peculiarity, the prince notes, marked other conversations he had had with atheists as well as books he had read on the subject: these were also "as if not about that at all, although in appearance it seemed that it was about that" (*sovsem budto ne pro to, khotia s vidu i kazhetsia, chto pro to*) (*PSS* 8:82; my translation, my emphases). The "that," the *to*, stands in for the positive content of religious belief which cannot be positively named but only negatively indicated by means of the demonstrative pronoun that gestures, vaguely, elsewhere. This observation by the prince, however, is itself unspeakable and, despite his efforts to express it to his learned interlocutor (as to Evgeny Pavlovich later in the novel in relation to the nature of his love), the latter understands nothing of it.

In contrast to the learned atheist's conversation, the next three encounters involve the common or "simple" people (*prostonarod'e*) and are anecdotal rather than theoretical, the first explicitly so. Myshkin learns that, at the provincial hotel where he spent the night, a peasant slit his friend's throat because he coveted his watch, and in the very act crossed himself and prayed for God's forgiveness "for Christ's sake" (*PSS* 8:183/220). Myshkin doesn't comment on the story, although it provokes hysterical laughter in Rogozhin. The second encounter is with a drunken soldier who, addressing Myshkin as "master" (*barin*), tries to sell him his tin cross for the price of a silver one. The prince refrains from judging "this Christ-seller": "God knows what's locked away in these drunken and weak hearts" (*PSS* 8:183/220). Immediately afterward, he meets a young peasant woman nursing her infant and, noticing that she suddenly crosses herself, asks her the reason. Her child had just smiled for the first time, she explains, and she realized that a mother's joy upon seeing her infant's first smile is precisely like God's joy in seeing a sinner pray. In this quartet of encounters, Myshkin represents the peasant woman's observation as the fulfillment of the hidden or elusive content of the first three: her statement, "in almost those words," the prince notes, "was such a deep, such a subtle and truly religious thought, a thought that all at once expressed the whole essence of Christianity, that is, the whole idea of God as our own father, and that God rejoices over man as a father over his own child—the main thought of Christ! A simple peasant woman!" (*PSS* 8:183–84/221).[39] The woman's successful articulation of an elusive or hidden spiritual significance, its function in the prince's narrative as the fulfillment of a meaning deferred in the first three encounters, leads the prince to raise again the problem of the *ne to* with which he had begun:

> The essence of religious feeling doesn't fit in with any reasoning, with any crimes and trespasses, or with any atheisms; there's something else here that's not that, and it will eternally be not that [*tut chto-to ne to, i vechno budet ne to*]; there's something in it that atheisms will eternally glance off, and they will eternally be talking *not about that* [*vechno budut ne pro to govorit'*]. (*PSS* 8:184/221; emphasis in original)

If the peasant woman's truth proves beyond the powers of less simple people to formulate or receive it, the prince asserts nevertheless that this truth—this "something else," which exists beyond reason, beyond sin, beyond atheism—may be seen "sooner and more clearly in a Russian heart" (*PSS* 8:184/221).

It is a lack of such vision, however, that leads the community to overlook an essential truth which the prince claims is clearly visible in the Russian heart and to embrace instead the "graphic" anecdote that proclaims him an idiot and a democrat. The communal diagnosis of the prince's behavior as following from the fact that he is a "democrat" or has "democratic" tendencies—casually associated with nihilism, socialism, liberalism, atheism, feminism, and egalitarianism—is, finally, also an instance of the *ne to*, not precisely true and not precisely false.[40] The "democrat" stands in for that which cannot be named and is, in this sense, not simply fallacious. The accusation hovers on the verge of meaninglessness yet captures something significant about Myshkin that the metonymically allied terms—all of which support more precise definition in a distinctive set of reformist prescriptions—do not.[41] The metonymic chain spawned by the "democrat" appears to reproduce the comedy of the Gogolian *ne to* wherein represented reality is endlessly undermined by comic displacements along an unexpected chain of signifiers. But whereas Gogol's comedy celebrates the ability of language to effect a "creation out of nothing" through its very plasticity, Dostoevsky's novel registers the tragic significance of the limitations of language, doomed to reiterate its *ne to* in the hope that the pathos of its repetition alone will propel speaker and writer, listener and reader, across the abyss of understanding toward which it gestures.[42] In the 1868 novel in which Dostoevsky hoped to portray a perfectly beautiful man, the "democrat" thus names an inscrutable and seemingly agentless motive that functions as a center of gravity around which the actors—persons and personages alike—unwittingly conspire to organize the events of the story. In the final analysis, whereas the epithet "idiot" describes Myshkin's beginning and his final destination, "democrat" describes the set of beliefs and subsequent actions that move him along that destined road, beliefs and actions that can be described—like spiritual truth and the simple people who complexly embody it—by nothing other than the *ne to*.

The *Ne To*, the Writer, and the People

If the anecdote, whether graphic or allusive, must be read against its own grain just to intimate (never convey) an unspeakable or impermissible truth associated with the essence of religious feeling or the true character of the democrat, still the anecdote, the story, the narrative, is what in literature we have to go by. Its light is sufficient to make shadows visible, to show that something compelling is there which, at least at that moment, cannot be clearly seen or about which a comprehensive story cannot be told or a persuasive argument made. It allows us to pose the question but disallows a decision on whether this indiscernible thing is possible or impossible, true or false, or even good or bad. Thus Myshkin's tragic end is ensured precisely by his best qualities, those which others can think to express only by the disapproving fondness contained in the epithet "democrat"—the surfeit of compassion; the inability to consider rank or class; the ability to elicit the trust of the common people (an exceedingly rare trait that Myshkin shares with Turgenev's nihilist Bazarov and that Dostoevsky denied even to the most well-intentioned elite) and to elicit the truth from those who no longer recognize it; the refusal to stand in judgment; the absolute incapacity for lying.[43] The democrat is, in a radical sense, socially incompetent because he fails to observe the stratifications and distinctions from which the social fabric itself is constructed. This is partly why there can be no political program attached to the behavior of the democrat, which is scandalous and unpredictable, and thus the opposite of programmatic. That Dostoevsky was disenchanted with liberalism, socialism, nihilism, utopianism, materialism, and utilitarianism by the late 1860s is beyond question; his objections receive their fullest expression in his novel *The Demons* (1872). The conservative turn in a populism to which he had been committed since the mid-1840s is by the late 1860s unmistakable in his correspondence and would only intensify through the remainder of his life.[44] But Dostoevsky's democracy remains a *ne to* in relation to these other, loosely allied political ideals and theories.

My aim in this book is to understand this *ne to* on its own terms by attending to its formation in the transitional period between his early work and the great novels of his maturity.[45] During this period, Dostoevsky confronted the problem of the Russian common people with particular urgency and immediacy. The consolations of the social theories which underlay his earlier political activism—and for which he suffered a decade of Siberian exile, spent partly in a hard-labor camp—withered in the face of actual, enforced contact with the common people there. Upon his return to the capital on the eve of peasant emancipation in 1861, Dostoevsky staked the resurrection of his authorial career on his insistence that an abyss divided common and elite cultures which would bedevil elite attempts to represent the Russian common people as objects of literary and journalistic inquiry. At a moment when intellectuals and other urban elites struggled to prepare bureaucratically and imaginatively for a liberated peasantry, estrangement became the cornerstone of Dostoevsky's aesthetic practice as well as his claims for the unique integrity of his authorial perspective as a noble ex-convict.[46] Instead of rendering a naturalistic portrait of the common people enhanced by the pathos of a firsthand knowledge bought dear, Dostoevsky traces in his fictionalized account of his prison experience, *Notes from the House of the Dead* (1861), a peculiar dis-integration of the narrating consciousness (the focus of part 1) which allows the common people to emerge into cultural visibility (the focus of part 2). For Alexander Petrovich Gorianchikov, Dostoevsky's fictional autobiographer and would-be guide to the world of forced labor, estrangement is revealed to be the prerequisite for knowing the peasant-other, and for acknowledging and suffering the limitations of that knowledge. One of the central claims of this study, accordingly, is that the Dostoevskian narrator familiar to readers of the great novels who dismantles the very structure of knowing and telling makes his first appearance in *Notes from the House of the Dead*.[47] Another is that the dismantling of knowledge permits something else to emerge; here, the experience and representation of an unmasterable relationship between noble self and common other, collaboratively engendered, that permits *katorga*, the forced-labor camp, to become the unlikely mise-en-scène of emancipation.

With this novel, Dostoevsky initiates his literary exploration of the *ne to* which, in *The Idiot*, refers directly, as we have seen, to the elusive significance of the "democrat." In *House of the Dead*, the *ne to* is elaborated in reference to the circumstances surrounding the noble narrator's first unmediated contact with the common people (*prostonarod'e*) with whom he must live on a footing of absolute, abject equality for the duration of his sentence. The entwined themes of the encounter with the people and the radical, even violent, unsettling of social norms connects *Notes from the House of the Dead* and *The Idiot*. The two novels thus provide a chronological framework within which to trace the development of Dostoevsky's democracy, an idiosyncratic vision of the cultural power of commonness which, though unsusceptible to any programmatic realization, motivated the aesthetic experimentation, and most notably the narratological innovations, for which the later novels are celebrated. This idiosyncratic vision subtends what appear to be his wildly vacillating ideological allegiances which have baffled all efforts to place him convincingly in any political camp during the volatile period of Russia's transition into modernity. *Notes from the House of the Dead* sends us back to the writer's state of mind in the aftermath of his arrest as a political criminal who had contemplated the overthrow of serfdom under the influence of utopian socialist thought, and chronicles his sojourn in a world that would shatter his expectations and reveal his former views of the people he had wanted to free as "optical illusion, and nothing more" (*PSS* 4:199/309).[48] *The Idiot* takes us forward, to the aftermath of that trauma; here the people's simplicity continues to baffle the would-be theorists of their culture and its significance even as the success of Russia's struggle to enter modernity seems to hinge on the entrainment of its distinctive, still elusive power. The image of the common people's power hovers on the edge of visibility but is never actualized: the *ne to* of democracy remains, then, unconsummated, the last in a series of such images initiated in *Notes from the House of the Dead*. This book is devoted to identifying these figural predecessors in his fictional autobiography and, by tracing their textual permutations, eliciting the political, aesthetic, and spiritual contours of Dostoevsky's democracy.

In *House of the Dead*, the *ne to* refers most immediately to the peculiar state of suspense in which the noble narrator Gorianchikov finds himself. Having (like Dostoevsky) lost his class privileges and suffered exile and incarceration with common criminals, Gorianchikov is to all intents and purposes dead to his former life. But having entered into the new world of the camp, he finds himself unable to enter into its peculiar existence. An "abyss" (*bezdna*) of class difference, unexpectedly profound, separates him ineluctably from the common people despite the physical intimacy in which they are compelled to live and dooms his attempts to forge solidarity despite their common misfortune. In *katorga*, he lives in suspense for the duration of his sentence, dead to his former life, unable to enter a new one, and thus neither this nor that, neither a nobleman nor a common man (*prostoliudin*), but an embodied *ne to*. The abyss of class difference which sustains his suspense is revealed in the course of Gorianchikov's narrative as the matrix of other variants of the *ne to*, those manifestations of the life of the common convicts of *katorga* which baffle his attempts to make sense of and thus enter into the life around him. Foremost among these is the phenomenon of crime which, along with the people's experience of and ability to endure pain, become for Gorianchikov the key signifiers of class difference, that which distinguishes him from the majority of those around him. Myshkin, in *The Idiot,* is able to discern something about the common people and their religiosity through the constellation of random encounters that punctuate his travels through Russia. But what Gorianchikov discerns through his own unpredictable and often uninterpretable encounters with the common convicts is less a clear apprehension of the people than of the abyss which precludes vision. Gorianchikov sees that what he had formerly seen in them had been an optical illusion of his own making: the people, too, are a *ne to.* This profound conceptual unsettling of both parties to the future reconstitution of a nation, the nobility and the people, their emergence into visibility for each other precisely as a "not that" which, though difficult to see, cannot be overlooked, occurs uniquely in *katorga* and is a prerequisite to the rebirth at issue in *House of the Dead*: not that of an individual (the narrator upon his release) but of the nation. This rebirth, too, because it lies in the future and is only uncertainly glimpsed, is the ultimate *ne to,* an image whose consummation will deliver a new Russia and a new word not yet spoken.

Part 1 of this study thus begins by de-situating the conversion hypothesis which has long dominated critical understanding of Dostoevsky's transitional decade, particularly his experience in the hard-labor camp. The conversion theory proposes that during the writer's incarceration he underwent a spiritual-ideological reversal of his former convictions which, alleviating his alienation from the peasant-convicts, revealed beneath their repellent appearance and behavior a Christian humility that he would later identify with Russianness itself. In this book, conversion remains unconsummated, suspended, and rebirth deferred. In the purgatorial space of the hard-labor camp, Gorianchikov progresses not toward triumphant rebirth but instead experiences a deepening estrangement from his environment and its inhabitants. Beyond existential crisis, the noble-convict's estrangement ultimately entails an ontological ambiguity registered in the structure of autobiographical narration itself and which arises from the unresolved question of his crime. Part 1 analyzes the tripartite structure of this first-person narration through which the attenuation of the narrating voice—Gorianchikov's desubjectification, in effect—is accomplished.

Part 2 continues this inquiry into the representation of a dis-integrating autobiographical voice from the perspective of *katorga* as a specific milieu, a chronotope delimited temporally by the sentence (*srok*) and spatially by the stockade. It is filled with stories of violence perpetrated and suffered whose significance Gorianchikov struggles in vain to interpret. Within this milieu, class and ethnic differences have been forcibly neutralized by the disciplinary imposition of an abject equality. Here,

Giorgio Agamben's concepts of "the space of exception" and "homo sacer" offer a useful alternative to the paradigm of incarceration as the scene of religious-ideological conversion.[49] The chronotope of *katorga*, the house of the dead, literalizes—makes available to the material, sociological, and historical specificities of literary representation—Agamben's philosophical analysis of the space of exception. In so doing, it revises the meaning he attributes to the irreducibility of the bare and abandoned life lived therein. In contrast to Agamben, Dostoevsky portrays *katorga* as a vital medium in which everything is fungible, from the most apparently valueless material object to identities. The exchange and even merging of identities, processes of de- and resubjectification peculiar to the house of the dead, are both conveyed through and realized in the dis-integrating consciousness of the autobiographical narrator. This ontology of crime presages that new philosophy of crime for which Gorianchikov calls by nullifying all ready-made points of view about it. At times this nullification of the given perspective suggests the revolutionary potential for a new community that fitfully asserts itself, revealing *katorga* as the unlikely mise-en-scène of emancipation. I examine this potential community or "corporation," as the peasant-convicts call it, with reference to Maurice Merleau-Ponty's concept of "intercorporeity" and Claude Lefort's adaptation of this concept in his idea of "the flesh of the political." Ultimately, however, the novel registers the tenuousness of this new order, its stubborn indeterminacy, and the tentative nature of Gorianchikov's efforts to illuminate it from within its "flesh." Part 2 concludes with an account of Dostoevsky's subsequent attempt to translate his experience of the people—Dostoevsky's democracy—into a pedagogical program, on the one hand, and into the language of the novel, on the other. The conclusion examines the fate of these attempts.

In contrast to his jeremiadic condemnation of the Russian democrat in the 1880 reply to Gradovsky cited above, Dostoevsky predicted, in his *Diary of a Writer* for April 1876, that in the very near future, the power of Russia would exceed that of the great powers of Europe "for one simple reason: they will all be weakened and undermined by the unsatisfied democratic aspirations of a huge segment of their lower-class subjects, their proletariat and their poor. In Russia, however, this absolutely cannot happen: our demos [*demos*] is content, and will become even more satisfied insofar as everything is proceeding according to a general disposition or, better yet, according to common consent" (*PSS* 22:122/452). In the next issue of the *Diary*, he expounds his claim for those who are skeptical of its truth. Russia has few remaining "opponents of democratism," he writes, and "the honesty, disinterestedness, forthrightness, and sincerity of the democratism of the majority of Russian society does not admit of any doubt."[50] In distinction to Europe, "where democratism has up until now universally declared itself only from below" because the "vanquished (it may be) upper classes are still mounting a terrible resistance," in Russia "our upper class itself became democratic [*stal demokratichen*] or, rather, of the people [*naroden*], and—who in the world can deny it?" The faltering defensiveness at the end to which Dostoevsky's readers are dialogically attuned suggests that problems remain; even so, "the temporary tribulations of the demos will certainly improve in the future under the tireless and continual influence of such enormous *principles* (for one cannot call them otherwise) *as the general democratic disposition and general consensus* among all Russian people, starting at the very top" (*PSS* 23:28/500–501; emphases in original). Fifteen years earlier, in 1861, in an article for his journal *Time*, at a moment of high expectation concerning the emancipation of the peasants, Dostoevsky would also write about the need for the upper class to "become democratic" by turning into the common people: "We must now earn the trust of the people; we must love them, we must suffer, we must transform ourselves into them completely [*nado preobrazit-'sia v nego vpolne*]." Immediately doubts arise: "Do we know how to do that? Are we capable of doing that, are we up to it?" The answer is confidently affirmative: "we are up to it and we will be up to it. We are optimists, we have faith. Russian society must unite with its native soil and partake of the popular element. It is an absolute condition of its existence; and when something becomes an essential condition, well, it seems it would get done." And then the return to doubt: "Yes, but how is it to get done?" (*PSS* 19:7–8). The purpose of this book is to discover in his fiction, anterior to the rhetoric of the correspondence and polemical writing, Dostoevsky's own understanding of what the challenge of becoming democratic really involved.

Certainly Dostoevsky himself did not emerge from the dead house suffused with good will toward the peasant-convicts. In his first letter to his brother, written after his release in 1854, he described them memorably as "a crude, irritated, and embittered people" whose "hatred for the gentry exceeds all bounds": "They would have devoured us if given the chance." Dostoevsky recalls a mutual hostility that itself reinforced the prohibition, artistically elaborated in the novel, on reflecting upon one's crime:

> "You gentry, you iron beaks, have pecked us to death. You used to be a gentleman and torment the people, but now you're the lowest of the low, you've become our brother"—that was the theme played over and over for four years. One hundred and fifty enemies who couldn't stop persecuting us, it was their favorite, a diversion, a pastime , and we were saved from despair only through indifference, moral superiority, which they couldn't fail to understand and respect, and by not bending to their will. They were always aware that we were above them. They had no conception of our crime. We ourselves kept

silent about it, and for that reason we didn't understand one another so that we had to endure every form of revenge and abuse of the gentry by which they live and breathe.

Dostoevsky's bitterness was by no means unmixed—he also remarks in this letter, in an echo of his 1849 letter to his brother Mikhail, that "people are people everywhere" and how "in prison among the thugs I, in four years, finally discerned human beings" (*otlichil liudei*). He remarks on the surprising variety of popular types, and adds, "What a wonderful people"— a people whom he suggests he "knows pretty well," and perhaps better than most (*PSS* 28 [I]: 169–70, 172, 173).[51]

Nevertheless, Dostoevsky insisted that the common people whom he encountered in *katorga* were unassimilable to any prefabricated sociopolitical vision and unamenable to any totalizing scheme no matter how ostensibly sympathetic to the peasants' plight. The resistance of this figure to assimilation or instrumentalization in the name of any overarching theory or project marks a foundational stage in the literary and philosophical conceptualization of Russian democratic subjectivity. In 1861, in a series of articles warning against the error of cultivating a "theoretical" or "armchair" love of the people, whose emancipation was formalized that year, Dostoevsky amplified on the stubbornness of estrangement, experienced as the failure to see and comprehend. "Even our best 'scholars' of the life of the people," he wrote,

> still do not fully understand how *wide* and deep the gulf dividing us from the people has become, and they don't understand for the most simple reason: they have never lived with the people, but have lived their own separate life. They will say to us that it's ridiculous to propose such reasons, that everyone knows them. Yes, we'll say, everyone knows; but they know abstractly. They know, for example, that they have lived a separate life; but if they had really known to what degree this life was separate, they wouldn't have believed it. They don't believe it even now. (*PSS* 19:7, emphasis in original)

Dostoevsky goes on to explain that even those observers who have lived with the people, even those who lived with them in their huts, eating their food, wearing their clothes, and performing their labor—those like Dostoevsky, one is compelled to conclude—had only "*looked upon*" them without seeing them, without understanding their "genuine life, the essence of the life, its heart." This abyss, this yawning gap which remains unbridged and which precludes epistemological certainty and ideological closure alike, is the primary object of aesthetic inquiry in *Notes from the House of the Dead*. It is the source of its complex investigation of the psychological, epistemological, political, and spiritual problem of estrangement, and the matrix of all unconsummated images (*PSS* 19:7; emphasis in original).[52] As such, it both enables and delimits Dostoevsky's portrait of Russian democratic subjectivity—in terms of literary practice and history, the development of a national political culture, and aesthetic ideology—with which this book is primarily concerned.

The conversion hypothesis, in denying Dostoevsky's estrangement, disregards both the aesthetic experimentation to which it drove him and the full story of the development of his ideological beliefs. In so doing, it has cast the 1850s—the pivotal decade of exile and vocational recovery—as a dramatic but ideologically moribund one, an era of high emotion met with foregone conclusions.[53] But Dostoevsky's estrangement—rendered in his literary and polemical writings of 1861 by a resolutely defamiliarized narrating self who struggles to see the common people—is worth honoring with sustained critical attention for several reasons. Acknowledging both the experience and the artistic representation of Dostoevsky's estrangement opens the possibility of recovering a more nuanced and accurate picture of the writer's ideological development. It is equally crucial to our understanding of his vocational trajectory, as well as the relationship of that trajectory to the preeminent political event of his time, peasant emancipation. Finally, his estrangement frames the central aesthetic challenge he faced from this point forward: the representation of peasant culture as that which could not be fully seen because it had not yet become culturally visible to a reform-minded elite. The exigencies of forging a representational practice which necessarily preceded its own object constituted both the formal and polemical ground for his artistic experimentation. The epistemological and aesthetic challenge of the people's commonness itself drove Dostoevsky to transcend the well-established paradigm of its sentimental celebration in literature from Karamzin to Turgenev. In the context of discussing the "simple people," Dostoevsky wrote to his brother upon his release from prison that experience had taught him to be "more afraid of a simple man than a complex one" (*PSS* 28 [I]: 172). He continued to define simplicity unsentimentally, as "the enemy of analysis" (*vrag analiza*), the ultimate estrangement, but the harbinger of emancipation nonetheless (*PSS* 23:143).

Part I

BUILDING OUT THE HOUSE OF THE DEAD

My personality will disappear.
[*Lichnost' moia ischeznet.*]
—*PSS* 28 (I): 349

~

1. "Why Is This Man Alive?":
The Unconsummated Conversion

The story of Dostoevsky's "mock execution" at the sadistic pleasure of
Tsar Nicholas I is bizarre and therefore notorious. Arrested in April 1849
for his participation in the Petrashevsky circle, a group dedicated to discussion of European revolution and the possibilities of Russian reform, specifically the emancipation of the enslaved peasantry, the twenty-seven-
year-old writer languished in the Peter and Paul Fortress until December
22.[1] On that day, after eight months of near-solitary confinement and still
ignorant of the results of an interrogation completed two months earlier,
Dostoevsky and fifteen other prisoners were roused from their cells at day-
break and brought to the Semenovsky Parade Ground in St. Petersburg.
There, assembled before a scaffold constructed in the center of the square,
they were informed that they had been condemned by the tsar to death
by firing squad.[2] Men dressed like executioners broke swords over the
heads of the kneeling prisoners in a ritual gesture signifying their "civil
execution," or "*mort civile*," their death as participants in civilian life and
partakers of its rights, which for the nobility was primarily the right of
exemption from corporal punishment.[3] The military escort then helped
the prisoners into shrouds—long, white peasant blouses and nightcaps—
in preparation for the execution itself. A priest dressed in funeral vest-
ments gave the prisoners a blessing and moved away. Three men were tied
to stakes adjacent to the scaffold and their caps pulled over their faces.
Dostoevsky stood in the next group of three. The soldiers advanced within
fifteen steps of the men at the stakes and readied their rifles to fire. In
place of the anticipated shots, however, the stunned prisoners heard the
drums beating a retreat, the rifles were lowered, the men at the stakes were
untied and their hoods removed; the tsar's aide-de-camp galloped into
the square and announced the (premeditated) imperial pardon and the
details of the prisoners' commuted sentences. The peasant blouses and
caps were removed. Another change of costume—into convict headgear,
sheepskin coats, and felt boots suitable for the long march into Siberian
exile—marked the final act of what Leonid Grossman would suggestively
call the " 'unconsummated' execution" ("*nedovershennyi*" *rasstrel*), a ritual of suspended punishment as elaborately orchestrated by Nikolai I as
a "grand stage production."[4] This last change of clothing signified for
Dostoevsky the death of his former life and the beginning of a new, unimaginably marginal existence: not only was he to live outside the privileges and protections of his class, but he was to be transported to a hard-

labor camp on the far side of the European cultural frontier beyond the Ural Mountains, a domain he would later call "the house of the dead."[5]

On returning to his cell, Dostoevsky immediately wrote to his brother, Mikhail; his letter, the last he would write for more than four years, is marked by the rapture and terror of one who had so miraculously escaped death. After detailing the terms of his sentence, he summarizes the morning's events in Semenovsky Square. Dostoevsky here describes not just the dramatic experience of the sword broken over his head signaling the termination of his social and political identity as nobleman and citizen,[6] but also an intriguing corollary to that symbolic death, the metaphorical beheading of the artist for whom writing was henceforward expressly prohibited: "that head, which created, lived the supreme life of art, which understood and was accustomed to the loftiest requirements of the mind, that head has now been cut off my shoulders" (*PSS* 28 [I]: 162).[7] In its excited and somewhat incoherent flow of urgent impressions, the letter raises a number of questions linked to that day's "unconsummated" execution of citizen, nobleman, and artist, and the nature of the rebirth such a death must engender.

In the 1849 letter to his brother, Dostoevsky explicitly characterized the mock execution as a matter of conversion, of death and resurrection: "Now, changing my life [*peremeniaia zhizn'*], I am being reborn in a new form. [. . .] I will be reborn for the better" (*PSS* 28 [I]: 164/53).[8] On the one hand, "life" survives the severing of the artist's head: "Life is life everywhere, life is within us, not in externals. There will be people around me, and to be *a man* among men [*byt' chelovekom mezhdu liud'mi*; emphasis in original] and to remain that person forever, not to lose courage and not to falter, come what may—that is what life is about, that is its purpose. I realize it. That idea has entered my flesh and blood" (*PSS* 4:28 [I]: 162/51). Yet, the severing of the head leaves the still vital flesh and blood haunted, even consumed, by that which the head had conceived but cannot bring to completion as long as writing is forbidden: "Memory remains and images which I created but had not yet fully embodied [*eshche ne voploshchennye mnoi*].[9] They will eat at me, it's true! But I still have a heart and the same flesh and blood that can also love and suffer and desire and remember, and that's life all the same! On voit le soleil!" (*PSS* 28 [I]: 162).[10] Later in his letter, Dostoevsky reverts anxiously to these images, left incompletely realized by the prohibition against writing and for that reason both disabled and disabling: "My God! How many images that are still alive, or that I will create afresh, will perish, will be extinguished in my head or will stream like poison in my blood" (*PSS* 28 [I]: 163/52). Conceived but incompletely realized or embodied, condemned to circulate internally because denied an independent textual life, the unconsummated image possesses the potential to vitiate the new life Dostoevsky anticipates: "Can it really be that I will never again take a pen in my hand? [. . .] Yes, if writing is to be forbidden, I will perish. Better to be locked up for fifteen years but with a pen in my hands" (*PSS* 28 [I]: 163/52). The unconsummated image seems to prefigure Dostoevsky's own suspended status in a future he cannot conjure up even imaginatively. The rebirth into a new life, the hope to which he clings on the eve of exile and punishment, is one he worries may not complete itself, may leave him in his new life as a man among men suspended in what we might call a *conversio interrupta,* where the process of rebirth is protracted and indefinite. The writer who anticipates a speedy and complete translation into the new life is instead arrested, not quite out of his old world, not quite into the new, and thus estranged from both.[11]

The letter of 22 December 1849, motivated by the trauma of unconsummated execution, expresses not just optimism about the unknown future but also a sharp anxiety about two related forms of suspense, aesthetic and spiritual: the unconsummated image and the unconsummated conversion. How are we to understand their relation and so understand the particular horror and challenge Dostoevsky faced at the beginning of this key transitional period as well as the ideological development it initiated? The unconsummated execution dismembered aspects of the identity of the self (nobleman, citizen, and artist) whose integration Dostoevsky assumed was requisite to the consummation of the artistic image—to its completion, embodiment, externalization. He feared that the disenfranchised, dismembered self would prove artistically barren, unable to produce an image powerful enough to live an independent life. Instead, the unconsummated image might threaten the dismembered self from within, fostering its disintegration (as a poison or some other self-consuming agent) rather than promoting its regeneration. The role it plays in Dostoevsky's anxious meditation on the possibilities of rebirth suggests that the significance of conversion during what Joseph Frank has called "the years of ordeal" is not exclusively spiritual or ideological but is, as fundamentally, an aesthetic crisis.[12] In *Notes from the House of the Dead,* Dostoevsky's autobiographical novel about his experience of exile and imprisonment published in 1861 on his return to Petersburg, the problem of conversion—a problem inseparable from the dilemma of the unconsummated image—remains suspended, the elusive object of his aesthetic inquiry rather than its transcendent achievement. It is precisely on the epistemological ground of suspended conversion that Dostoevsky situates *Notes from the House of the Dead,* our richest primary source of evidence for the writer's state of mind in this enormously important, though still mysterious, transitional period between his early and mature work.

As the expression of an aesthetic predicament with political and spiritual dimensions, conversion provides the terms of a paradox with which Dostoevsky will grapple throughout the decade of his Siberian exile and into the first years of his return to Petersburg: how is the dismembered artist to end his own suspense if he is unable to bring to fruition or consummation the artistic image through which a new world—the space of his own reintegration—might come into being? If the integrated self and the consummated image live and die together, might the unconsummated image possess the aesthetic agency to figure a new world, one to which the dismembered self feels the regenerative pull even as its form and its constitutive elements remain indiscernible? As Dostoevsky describes them in his letter, the stakes are certainly high enough to warrant considerable anxiety: if residual images produced by the old self live on to poison or consume it ("if writing is to be forbidden, I will perish"), might they also in some fashion body forth the new man and the new world where he will find his place? Can they in some way create their creator? If such formulations reverse our normative understanding of literary creation in which artists create images rather than images artists, the sense of artistic and existential suspense adumbrated in this letter prepares the ground for an unsettling of the expected grammar (subject, verb, object) of creation and, anterior to creation, of perception.

In the letter written on the eve of exile, the only certainty Dostoevsky expresses is that, for an indeterminate time and in an unknown place, both the artist and his images must exist in a kind of abeyance, suspended between death and life. There they must remain until the dismembered self of the artist has found the unlikely means to his regeneration, through a literary image which he will conceive but cannot control, to which he is held responsible even as he is held hostage. In the fictional autobiography *Notes from the House of the Dead*, the image possessed of this kind of primary agency is not that of the noble political prisoner, a first-person narrator who discovers through suffering the ideological meaning of his experience and, with that meaning, a glorious new life, "resurrection from the dead," as he problematically claims at the novel's conclusion. Instead, the central image of this text, although an image of the autobiographical self, is less an embodied character than a point of self-departure around which an otherwise scrupulously honest confessional self-representation is constructed. It is precisely this *unconsummated* image of a narrating self progressively undone as he progresses through his narrative that constitutes the aesthetic breakthrough of this novel in relation to the early works of the 1840s and which prepares the way for *Notes from the Underground* and the great novels. Moreover, only the perspective afforded by an *unconsummated* self so conceived (the focus of part 1 of this volume) preserves the integrity and force of the unrelenting strangeness of the environment (the focus of part 2) in which the reborn self must come into its own if the spiritual and ideological dimensions of conversion are to cohere with, rather than prevail over, the aesthetic.

In his monumental five-volume biography of Dostoevsky, Joseph Frank characterizes the mock execution, which initiated the transitional period between the writer's early and mature work, as "the most decisive and crucial event" in his life.[13] Dostoevsky would write about it in several venues much later in his career, most famously in *The Idiot* (1868–69); there can be no question that its shock reverberated throughout his years in penal servitude. In our primary sources of information from this period— the letter of 22 December 1849, *Notes from the House of the Dead*, and correspondence written in the years immediately following his release in 1854—it is registered in descriptions of an acute and enduring sense of vulnerability and estrangement that marked his prison experience "as a *person* among people," a man among other men. His experience, in this sense, is consonant with that of Primo Levi, who wrote about survivors like himself who "perceive in their (even by now distant) imprisonment the center of their life, the event that for good or evil has marked their entire existence."[14] As conspicuous and powerful as these descriptions are, however, and despite their aesthetically innovative structural and characterological elaboration in *House of the Dead*, the most influential critical view of Dostoevsky in this period is of a writer reconciled to his new life, perhaps as early as his fourth month in penal servitude.[15] His ability to adapt to his new circumstances, and particularly to the brutality and overt hostility of the peasant-convicts who made up a majority of the camp's inmates, implies a rapid abatement of the trauma initiated by the mock execution.[16] A key element of the reconciliation scenario is that Dostoevsky found a way to see with new eyes the peasant-convicts who tormented him. He saw that their repulsive appearance and behavior might very well conceal the living spring of a distinctive Christian spirituality, the essence of genuine Russianness rendered unrecognizable to the cultured class whose education had been based entirely on Western beliefs and values. The rhetoric of this hypothesis is drawn more or less explicitly from the discourse of conversion, and envisions a comprehensive regeneration that is at once religious, social, and ideological in its orientation. If Dostoevsky flirted with the atheism of some of his fellow utopian socialists before his arrest, his former religious convictions were restored to him by his encounter, initially so distressing, with the peasant-convicts.

What I refer to as the "conversion hypothesis," then, reads Dostoevsky's powerful estrangement from the peasant-convicts, confirmed in the memoirs of other political prisoners at Omsk, both Russian and Polish, as a painful but not protracted dialectical step. It arises from a trio of sites within

Dostoevsky's epistolary and journalistic oeuvre. The first is a letter he wrote upon his release from prison in 1854 to Natalia D. Fonvizina, who had followed her Decembrist husband into Siberian exile in 1825 and whom Dostoevsky met on his own journey eastward.[17] In this letter, he describes himself famously as "a child of this century, a child of doubt and disbelief," who had nevertheless formed for himself a "symbol of faith" which had taken root in his heart as an abiding conviction: "if someone succeeded in proving to me that Christ was outside the truth, and if, *indeed*, the truth was outside Christ, I would sooner remain with Christ than with the truth" (*PSS* 28 [I]: 176/68; emphasis in original).[18] The second site invoked to support the conversion hypothesis, an 1873 *Diary of a Writer* piece entitled "One of Today's Falsehoods," makes a similarly brief allusion to "the regeneration of my convictions" while in prison, a "story" he claims never to have told (*PSS* 21:133/290).[19] The final site, the 1876 *Diary of a Writer* entry entitled "The Peasant Marei," appears to supply precisely this still untold story more than twenty-five years after the fact.

In "The Peasant Marei," Dostoevsky tells a story of having remembered twenty-six years earlier in 1850, at a particularly difficult moment in the early months of his incarceration, a kindness done him in 1831 by one of his father's serfs when he was nine years old. This memory of a memory does indeed lend a retrospectively salvific aura to the years of penal servitude. In this powerful account, Dostoevsky writes how one night he had retreated to his bunk in a desperate fury of revulsion at the brawling peasant-convicts around him. There he was visited by a dream-memory of Marei, and "when I got down from my bunk and looked around, I remember, I suddenly felt that I could look on these unfortunates in an entirely different way and that suddenly, by some sort of miracle, all the hatred and malice in my heart had entirely disappeared [*ischezla*]" (*PSS* 22:49/355). Here Dostoevsky links the regeneration of the peasant in his eyes with his own ideological and religious regeneration; this dual rebirth of self and other occurs during the Easter celebration of Christ's resurrection from the dead. I return to a more extended discussion of "The Peasant Marei" and the conversion hypothesis in section 5 below. For now, my point is that this primary piece of evidence for Dostoevsky's state of mind in the decade of penal servitude and exile was written at a remove of more than twenty-five years. Its evidentiary value must be weighed alongside earlier literary and epistolary accounts written closer to the time of his actual experience. It seems particularly worthwhile for our purposes here to consider without prematurely foreclosing the extreme nature of the situation in which Dostoevsky found himself in December 1849 and the years immediately following, primarily because—as the conversion hypothesis itself makes clear—it is closely associated with the development of his thinking about "the people."

~

The rebirth Dostoevsky anticipates in the wake of the mock execution and on the eve of exile proves elusive; the urban intellectual eager to make a complete translation into a new life stands instead arrested on its threshold: these claims are thematically, ethically, and structurally situated at the heart of *Notes from the House of the Dead*. The text's first-person narrator, Alexander Petrovich Gorianchikov, progresses only fitfully in his quest for self-translation, limited by unanticipated and incongruous obstacles and openings on his journey into the "life beyond life" (*kromeshnaia zhizn'*), as he characterizes the world of hard labor (*katorga*) early in his account (*PSS* 4:13/14).[20] As the passage of both time and narrative inevitably lead him to the conclusion of his sentence, he comes to believe that only from a position within the prison's deepest interiority—to which, despite ten years of penal servitude, he had never acceded—might he have acquired an undistorted perspective on this world and been able to render "one clear and vivid picture" of it (*PSS* 4:220/342). Only there might he have found the answer to the fundamental question of crime, the psychology of its commission as well as the system it calls forth for its isolation and containment. Only there might he have succeeded in casting off the impediments to a true understanding of this new world and its inhabitants, largely criminals of the common class. Only from that vantage point within would it have been possible to bear witness to the significance of these criminals for Russian society, because only there would the "new word" have been revealed (*PSS* 18:35). Far from discovering this new word, however, he can claim only a series of necessarily negative victories: his insight may be said to develop only insofar as he comprehends the extent of his ignorance, the extent to which he remains the victim, not only of his lapses of memory of what transpired but primarily of his own "optical illusions" in relation to his surroundings (*PSS* 4:199/309).[21]

Because he never accedes to this interiority, the story of *Notes from the House of the Dead* is that of a man who, although eventually liberated, remains fundamentally ensnared. Written after his release, his first-person account bears witness to his continuing experience of imprisonment. This is immediately apparent from the portrait of him provided by a nameless prefatory narrator who, in an introduction, first acquaints the reader with both Gorianchikov and his memoirs. The prefatory narrator's portrait emphasizes the ex-convict's radical estrangement from society: even after his liberation he lives as an outcast (*otverzhenets*). Released into exile still a young man, he does nothing to redress the social or the "spiritual isolation" he describes as his chief torment in prison; instead, he occupies himself exclusively with the composition of his prison memoirs, his back turned both upon his future and the local society of Siberian nobility unreservedly prepared to embrace him as a member of their circle (*PSS* 4:220/

343). He dies in isolation after concluding his account with the completion of his sentence, represented as a rebirth: "Freedom, a new life, resurrection from the dead . . . What a glorious moment!" (*PSS* 4:232/361)

The irony of Gorianchikov's death—or, more exactly, the irony of his failure to bear out the promise of his claim to have emerged from the House of the Dead reborn—is lost on the reader unless he or she returns to the prefatory narrator's postscript to Gorianchikov's story with which the novel begins. In his introduction to the memoirs, this narrator characterizes the manuscript as "unfinished, and perhaps cast aside and forgotten by the author himself," and suggests that its failure to achieve closure reflects the state of its author's mental health (*PSS* 4:8/6). Describing the "one rather bulky notebook" he extracts from the mass of papers he had appropriated from the ex-convict's room after his death, he acknowledges the uneven quality of its contents but decides that it contains enough material of exceptional interest to justify its publication:

> It was a description, although a disconnected one, of the ten years in prison endured by Alexander Petrovich. In places this description was interrupted by some kind of other story, by some sort of strange, terrible reminiscences, sketched unevenly, spasmodically, as if under some sort of compulsion. I read through these passages several times, and had almost convinced myself that they were written in madness. But the prison notes—"Scenes from the House of the Dead" as he called them himself somewhere in his manuscript—seemed to me not completely without interest. A completely new world, hitherto unknown, the strangeness of some of the facts, several remarks in particular about a lost people, fascinated me, and I read with curiosity. (*PSS* 4:8/6)

For the prefatory narrator, that is, the discontinuous text, its upwelling stories disturbing what might have been the smooth flow of its narrative surface, precludes that integrity of self-presentation by which the reader is assured of the writer's reliability. Whatever Dostoevsky's contemporary audience may have thought, the text's first reader, the prefatory narrator who lays claim to being its representative reader, does not see Gorianchikov as a Virgil leading his armchair companion unscathed and enlightened in and out of the inferno.[22] The filter of doubt through which he views the former convict, and encourages the reader to view him, leads him to enumerate the text's anomalies in advance of the reader's reading. The introduction appears to impose closure on the "unfinished" text disinterestedly, objectively, in the form of the prefatory narrator's judicious conclusions concerning the degree to which Gorianchikov's narrative reflects—and thus can be explained by—his eccentric character. Our reading of *Notes from the House of the Dead* both begins and ends with this confident and urbane voice protesting its own good intentions and honest perplexity over the memoirist's impenetrability.

Clearly, in order to unseat (or, literally, one-up) Gorianchikov as narrator, the prefatory narrator need only present him as a character before he has even begun to tell his story. Unable to exist in his text as autonomous discourse, "pure voice," he emerges from the prefatory narrator's pen as an "eccentric who stubbornly avoided everyone" (*PSS* 4:7/3).[23] (The Russian is richer here: the noun, *chudak*, carries overtones of holy foolishness and is also etymologically connected with *chuzhoi*, radical otherness; the verb, *storonit'sia*, renders the image of one standing apart, reinforcing the noun and locating Gorianchikov well off the beaten track.)[24] His description of the former convict's determination "to hide himself as completely as possible from the entire world [*svet*; alternatively, from all of society]" ensures that Gorianchikov will emerge into the text, in advance of his having articulated a single word, under the sign of an unequivocal estrangement and singularity (*PSS* 4:7/5).

With a bewilderment reminiscent of the amiably obtuse employer of Melville's Bartleby, the prefatory narrator thus tells us that "there was not the slightest possibility of holding a conversation" with Gorianchikov (*PSS* 4:7/3):

> If you began to speak with him, he would look intently and extremely attentively at you; he would listen to your every word with a strict courtesy, as if meditating on it, as if with your question you had given him a riddle or wanted to elicit from him some sort of secret. Finally he would answer clearly and briefly, but to the point of weighing each word of his answer so that for some reason you became uncomfortable and were finally glad yourself to end the conversation. (*PSS* 4:6/2–3)

He additionally remarks that "after such conversations, his suffering and exhaustion were invariably apparent" (*PSS* 4:7/4). This suffering is poignantly described when the prefatory narrator, in a last-ditch attempt to break Gorianchikov's insularity, decides to pay him an unexpected visit, one of several self-confessedly "stupid and insensitive" efforts to "tempt" the latter into engagement (he comes armed with the latest books and magazines). The ex-convict looks up in horror at the intruder "as if I had caught him in some sort of crime" (*PSS* 4:7/4). His landlady, a "gloomy and silent peasant woman," describes him to the prefatory narrator as intolerant of visitors, excessively mistrustful, and almost silent for the entire three years of his tenure as her boarder (*PSS* 4:8/5). The manuscript he leaves behind at his death, the prefatory narrator finds, manifests the same radical disjointedness as his social interactions. In short, the introduction provides *Notes from the House of the Dead* with a logic of closure structured as a circularity by which its introduction is also its postscript. In its capacity as enclosure, it undermines the text it frames, in part by offering the memoir as an illustration of its own postulations about it.[25]

Here we might borrow a question from Dmitri Karamazov (if not that character's irascibility in asking it) to inquire: "Why is this man alive?" Why through numerous reprintings of *Notes from the House of the Dead* in Dostoevsky's lifetime—the introduction and the opening chapter(s) appeared four times between September 1860 and January 1862 alone— did he retain the awkward fiction of a prefatory narrator whose identification of Gorianchikov as a civil criminal indicted for his wife's murder reverts unceremoniously in the memoir proper to the autobiographical fact of Dostoevsky's own political conviction?[26] Why, upon returning to St. Petersburg after a ten-year absence in Siberia, eager to make a triumphant literary comeback at a time when the most influential critics promoted literature as a means of social and political reform, did Dostoevsky not offer *Notes from the House of the Dead* as straightforward autobiography?[27] Why open the text, so directly responsive to the call for works "with social-cultural substance," with a prefatory narrator who compromises the narrative he claims is sufficiently worthy to have been preserved for posterity because it represents "a completely new world, hitherto unknown" (*PSS* 4:8/6)? Why, when Gorianchikov ends with his ringing proclamation of victory over the Dead House, of resurrection from the dead and entry into a new life, does the prefatory narrator then assert *House of the Dead* to be unfinished, and perhaps abandoned by the author? Was Dostoevsky simply conforming to the convention of such prefatory narrators who soothe and seduce the reader with (fictional) information that pretends to authenticate the text's existence?[28] Is this fictional authentication purchased at the price of the text's credibility? And if the introduction does not represent an unthinking concession to convention (one that was in any case, by mid-century, on the wane), what are its implications— generic, semiotic, narratological, and ideological—for this text as well as for the project it initiates: the social and political resurrection of the nation through the literary raising up of the common people? What does it tell us, that is, about Dostoevsky's democracy?

Before examining these questions more closely, it is worth observing in passing that Dmitri's question—"Why is this man alive?"—may be asked with reference to at least two of the dramatis personae in *Notes from the House of the Dead* and to Dostoevsky himself. Biographically, the question arises from the mock execution, the stripping of his rights and social identity, Siberian exile, and penal servitude, all of which designate Dostoevsky, according to Giorgio Agamben's influential paradigm, as a type of *homo sacer*, a living dead man, who must live henceforth in a "state of exception" to which Gorianchikov refers as the "life beyond life." This identification is supplemented by the writer's own account in his letter written on the eve of exile of a suspended or unconsummated conversion produced by the mock execution, a transformation from the old man to the new arrested at the threshold or point of intersection of two worlds, the one to which he has officially died and the new, just as *homo sacer* inhabits a space of exception on the threshold between the sacred and secular domains but outside both.[29] (I explore the Agambenian paradigm as an alternative to the conversion hypothesis in part 2.) Textually, the question "Why is this man alive?" may be asked of the prefatory narrator of *Notes from the House of the Dead*, a seemingly superfluous figure who yet announces that the autobiographer's account of himself is flawed, that his conversion was never completed, and that he lived in the world as if in a state of exception.[30] The prefatory narrator's account thus suggests in turn that Dmitri's question may be asked of Gorianchikov, the autobiographer himself, as one who was not resurrected from the dead despite his triumphant closing claim. Additionally, as we will see, many of the text's critics have implicitly asked this question of Gorianchikov by portraying him as a superfluous and easily dismissed fictionalization of Dostoevsky, in form if not in function analogous to "the double" in his pre-Siberian (1846) novella of that name which he was reworking at the time he was writing *Notes from the House of the Dead*.[31] We can begin to untangle this knot of ontologically variable identities—Dostoevsky himself; his notion of the self that was, the self to be, and the self between these two instanciations; his epistolary self-representations; his fictional self-representations; the representations of those fictional selves by other fictional characters both within and between texts; and the selfhood critically attributed to Dostoevsky in relation to his fictional personalities—by attending first to the complex narrative structure of the dead house.

2. The Disarticulation of the Autobiographical Self

The circularity imposed on the text by the prefatory narrator, by which the ending of Gorianchikov's memoir entails a return to its postscript located in the introduction, mimics the circularity characteristic of conversion narratives. That *Notes from the House of the Dead* conforms in some respects to the narratological profile of the conversion narrative is evident in the following description included in John Freccero's discussion of St. Augustine's *Confessions*, which he identifies as the paradigm for all such narratives:

> When any narration claims an identity between the narrator or authorial voice and the protagonist, some provision must be made for their coming together. When such a narrative claims to be definitive, with a point of closure marking the coming together of author and persona, logic demands that it be a conversion narrative, a death of the self that was, whose plot is fixed for all time, and

a resurrection of a new voice, from whose standpoint the story can be told. Like the retrospective view of someone drowning, the existence of the story depends upon a survival of the crisis, yet the completeness of the story, the accuracy of the inventory, depends upon the evolution being ended.

Explicitly, Gorianchikov's *House of the Dead*, imbued as it is with the "passionate desire for resurrection, renewal, a new life" and concluding with the cry of victory at having been resurrected from the dead, invokes the conversion structure (*PSS* 4:220/342). Freccero describes the special coherence of the conversion narrative as tautological, its "central syntactic moment" ensuring the evolving identity not only of narrator and protagonist but of form and content as well:

> Conversion is both the subject matter of [the] work and the precondition for its existence. Form and content are therefore in some sense analogous, inasmuch as conversion not only is a traditional religious experience, but also has its counterpart in language, where it may be defined as that central syntactic moment in which the ending marks the beginning and the circular identity of the author coincides with the linear evolution of his *persona*.[32]

On a purely structural level, however, in itself and irrespective of the value of the evidence it provides for an unreconciled—indeed, disintegrated—personality, the prefatory narrator's initial characterization of Gorianchikov intercepts the transformational process by which protagonist and narrator "come together." The empirically available identity offered in the introduction short-circuits, as it were, the circular and spiritually coherent identity Gorianchikov claims to have achieved in his conclusion. In other words, this third voice (third in relation to Gorianchikov as protagonist and Gorianchikov as narrator), setting forth its own conclusions about the man and his manuscript, forestalls the definitive closure of the conversion narrative by challenging the integrity of Gorianchikov's self-inventory. The introduction thus constitutes a dialectical step away from the possibility of representing the integration of pilgrim and poet.[33] In his indelicate eagerness to satisfy his curiosity about the enigmatic ex-convict, the prefatory narrator takes possession of his manuscript, obliterating in advance that perspectival integrity peculiar to the conversion structure. Accordingly, through what appears a contingency of presentation, the memoir's triumphant final claim and its definitive point of closure marking the death of the self-as-protagonist and the resurrection of the self-as-narrator—represented in *House of the Dead* as the moment of liberation from the prison camp—fails to affirm Gorianchikov's spiritual rebirth.

To what degree, however, can one attribute this failure to the combined structural and characterological impact of the introduction upon the text? Does the introduction bear responsibility for or simply bear witness to the textual deformation it cites? As objective and distanced commentary, certainly, it discounts its own role in what it cites as the text's fragmentation, yet the problem of assessing that role—of determining the relationship of introduction and text—continually obtrudes itself in the temporal paradox manifested in the postscript/introduction. We may begin to analyze this relationship by noting that the prefatory narrator's attribution of the spasmodic texture of Gorianchikov's writing to his eccentricity, perhaps even his madness, is not a disinterested one. He is increasingly fascinated with Gorianchikov's singularity and has eagerly and (by his own admission) insensitively pursued him with the intention of appropriating what has eluded him: the logic of the hidden impulses and constraints governing the ex-convict's behavior, the secret of his otherness, and, relatedly, the opportunity to enter vicariously the "completely new world, hitherto unknown" of *katorga* (*PSS* 4:8/6).

The questions of the structural and characterological impact of the introduction on the memoir and of the prefatory narrator's relationship to the memoirist encourage us to attend to the way in which the latter represents his own response to the acute physical and psychological stress of life in *katorga*, so prominently thematized in *House of the Dead*.[34] As we will see, the distinguishing characteristic of Gorianchikov's self-presentation is that the motive of conversion arises and develops within, rather than in opposition to, the antagonistic mode of estrangement. In the process of syncretizing estrangement and conversion, he produces—beyond an ethnography of the peculiar life of the hard-labor camp—what we might call a phenomenology of *katorga*: a record of the individual and collective impact of the constituent elements of his environment on the narrator's consciousness.[35] More immediately to the point, his representation of his own psychological state will bear on his ideological speculation on the meaning of crime, which he expresses axiomatically as a conviction, acquired through great personal suffering, that to understand the phenomenon of crime the nobleman must be turned, "actually and in fact," into one of the common people (*PSS* 4:198/308).[36] As we will see, although Gorianchikov encounters criminals of his own estate in prison, he focuses on those outside his circle of class and ethnic privilege; his remarks on the elusive philosophy of crime are thus linked throughout his memoir to a novel ethics of class difference which Dostoevsky will continue to develop through his *Diary of a Writer* and the great novels. I explore this ethics of class difference in reference to crime at greater length in part 2.

Gorianchikov's self-representation is marked both thematically (in his own ruminations and observations) and structurally (that is, as if unconsciously) by his experience of psychosocial disarticulation, where the components of his own class identity (and assumptions about the ethical valence attached to that identity) become unstrung and he struggles, with varying success, to keep it intact. To this degree, his self-representation is consonant with the prefatory narrator's representation of him. Gorianchikov responds to his unremittingly hostile environment on three distinct experiential levels, structurally deployed as three complexly related levels of autobiographical narration. Of these three levels, he privileges two—which I call the first and third narrative levels—and presents them according to the sequential and recuperative logic of conversion. The first narrative level records in gripping detail the traumatic strangeness of prison life which undermines not only his former values and beliefs but even the degree to which he comprehends himself as a social being with a coherent role in social life. Entirely cut off from his former life as a nobleman and landowner, he represents himself on this first level as existing in a state of oppositional solitude, in the new world of *katorga* but not of it, utterly estranged from those around him and thus as disarticulated from the social body as he reportedly is after his release. In this respect, Gorianchikov realizes the psychosocial dismemberment Dostoevsky had feared in the wake of the mock execution and the ceremony of civil death. As Gorianchikov represents it (especially in part 1 of *House of the Dead*), his estrangement is an effect of his enforced intimacy with the peasant-convicts whose inner "essence" (*sushchnost'*) he cannot penetrate, in part because he is thoroughly excluded from their milieu. Despite his physical proximity, he feels that his insight remains limited to "outward appearances" which, throughout his incarceration, "torment" him with an "inexpressible anguish" because he knows them to be "optical illusion, and nothing more" (*PSS* 4:197, 199/306, 309). His perpetually raw experience of the radical otherness of the peasant-convict and prison life, to which he claims he was never reconciled, produces the phenomenological impact (and ethnographic value) of much of the description of the convicts, their customs, and their milieu.[37]

Eventually, however, Gorianchikov learns to understand his extreme isolation as a means toward his own reconception, one that ultimately encompasses the reconception of his class through the resurrection of the Russian common people (*prostonarod'e*) from civil or social death. The third narrative level, which emerges distinctly in the novel's second part as a recuperative discursive shift from description to analysis, is deployed in the conscientious elaboration of an ideology of conversion, a principled strategy for reconceiving the self by yoking the spiritual destinies of the educated and common classes.[38] Conversion informs Gorianchikov's exhortation to the educated class (his readership) to divest themselves of all "given ready-made points of view [on] crime and its philosophy" in order to accede to the peasant's "essence," and to exchange the "optical illusion" of class prejudice for "graphic" knowledge of the common people (*PSS* 4:15, 199/16, 309). Implicitly, the reader is exhorted to turn into (or convert to) the common people, an experience to which Gorianchikov claims to have submitted involuntarily at first and only in terms of outward appearances, as a requirement of his induction into prison life. Level three thus represents the ideological fruit of a metamorphosis initially mandated and constitutes its a posteriori justification: Gorianchikov's appraisal of the ethical significance of his incarceration ends with his blessing the fate that sent him into captivity and forced him to survive his painful solitude "without which neither this judgment of myself nor this stern review of my former life would have occurred" (*PSS* 4:220/343). Let us examine in more detail the first and third narrative levels before turning to what I call the mediate level, which, although not explicitly acknowledged by Gorianchikov, is yet crucial to rendering the point of view through which the process of assimilating raw experience (the focus of level one) to ideological expression (the focus of level three) is represented.[39] As will become clear, the mediate narrative level accounts for the manifest incompleteness of this process of assimilation through what will emerge as that level's distinguishing feature, the attrition (the fragmentation and displacement) of the narrating voice—the text's ultimate representation of psychosocial disarticulation and its central unconsummated image.

Gorianchikov's psychosocial integrity is initially compromised through a traumatic process of dispossession undertaken in enforced compliance with the letter of the law. What will become the ideologically mature imperative for the nobleman to become one of the common people initially involves a transformation limited to Gorianchikov's assumption of both the convict uniform and the dreary routines of penal servitude. The shaving of his head and the donning of prison garb is accompanied by an inward revolt against the outward brutality of peasant-convict life with which Gorianchikov struggles for the duration of his sentence:

> In general this was the time of my first encounter with the people [*s narodom*]. I myself had suddenly become just as much one of the common people [*prostonarod'e*], just as much a convict, as they. Their habits, understanding, opinions, customs, became as if mine also, at least formally, according to law, although in actuality I didn't share them. I was astonished and confused. (*PSS* 4:65/93)

At this early stage, then, psychosocial disarticulation figures not as a program or a therapy but as an experience of profound disorientation that overwhelms Gorianchikov upon his entry into the Dead House. The requirement of the criminal authorities that, along with the rights belonging to his estate, the noble convict divest himself of all that outwardly distinguishes him from the common prisoner leads Gorianchikov to characterize himself in his memoirs as doubly outcast: an outcast among outcasts who were themselves "slices cut off from society" (*otrezannye lomti ot obshchestva*), forever unassimilated and unassimilable (*PSS* 4:10/9). The word he uses to describe the "uncountable number" of "the strangest surprises, the most fantastic phenomena" that continually astonish and assault him in prison is *bezdna*.[40] It both invokes and is produced by that which he identifies as the source of his deepest anguish, the profound abyss—also rendered by the word *bezdna*—between the convicts of the educated and the convicts of the common classes. This combined impact of the significances of the *bezdna* ensures Gorianchikov's painful social and spiritual isolation.

Notwithstanding his assertion of estrangement as the guiding experiential principle of *House of the Dead* (and despite the prefatory narrator's claims), Gorianchikov clearly does not remain in a state of bewilderment any more than he remains incapable of reconciling himself to his lot. He counsels the repudiation of all given, ready-made points of view on the criminal available to members of his class in order that they may understand the philosophy of crime and, in the process, the peculiar inner life of the Russian people. He chooses to deprive himself of the company of his natural allies, the noblemen-convicts, rather than fraternize with those who continue to maintain their illusions. He endeavors to put himself as far as possible in the place of the peasant-convict in order to comprehend his crime as well as his pain, even to the point of attempting to experience vicariously the psychological torment and physical sensations of corporal punishment.[41] Most important, he explicitly posits his own spiritual rebirth, with which he comes to rationalize the existential trauma of incarceration, as contingent upon his success in resurrecting the peasant-convict in the eyes of the educated class.

In effect, at the third narrative level Gorianchikov defines psychosocial disarticulation as the voluntary promotion of an objectified sense of self (in the narratological discourse of conversion, the progressive differentiation of the protagonist-self from the narrator-self) and a complementary incorporation or subjectification of the other, in this case, the peasant-convict. To this end—the objectification of the self and the subjectification of the other toward the reconception of both—he develops an ideological position on class relations in Russia whose validity he attributes to the experiential rather than the speculative, textual, or even ethical basis of his conviction. The experience in question is his painful and protracted solitude:

> However just, good, and wise [the gentleman] may be, he will be hated and despised year after year by the whole mass [of peasant-convicts]; they won't understand and, most important, won't trust him. He's not a friend and not a comrade, and although over the years he will finally get to the point where they will not insult him, all the same he will not be one of them [*on budet ne svoi*] and he will be eternally, excruciatingly aware of his estrangement and

solitude. This estrangement sometimes appears to be completely without malice on the part of the convicts, as if unconscious. He's just not one of them,
and that's that [*Ne svoi chelovek, da i tol'ko.*] There is nothing more terrible
than living outside one's own milieu [*ne v svoei srede*].

The mutual estrangement of nobleman and peasant is absolute, and yet
this circumstance itself makes imperative the nobleman's voluntary renunciation of his class identity. Gorianchikov observes that despite the fre-
quency and intimacy of the nobleman's association with the peasant—"in
the civil service, for example, in the usual administrative situations, or
even simply in a friendly way, as a benefactor and in a certain sense a father"—the former remains "divided from the common people by the profoundest abyss [*bezdna*], and this is *fully* seen only when the *nobleman*
himself, by the power of external circumstances, actually and in fact, is
suddenly deprived of his former rights and becomes one of [*obratit'sia v,*
also "to convert to," "to turn into"] the common people" (*PSS* 4:198–
99/308; emphasis in original).[42]

Insofar as it emerges as the cornerstone of his own conscientiously elaborated conversion strategy, then, it is not entirely true that his psychosocial
disarticulation victimizes Gorianchikov. To the contrary, he invests his
call for the renunciation of class identity and privilege with a terrible urgency, that of eradicating the sacrificial impulse that he designates "the
executioner" whose attributes may be found "in embryo in almost every
contemporary human being" (*PSS* 4:155/238). Disarticulation so understood becomes for Gorianchikov the necessary condition and sign of the
spiritual, moral, as well as political integrity of the self (and of the text), a
manifest contradiction of the prefatory narrator's evaluation. Only when
the educated class undertakes to pierce through the husk of its own gentil-
ity and to recognize the figure Gorianchikov identifies as the "executioner
within" will the repulsive exterior of the peasant-convict be revealed as an
optical illusion and nothing more. Ultimately, the revelation of the peasant's true nature will restore God's image to the very least of them, even
to those in the Dead House living in the eternal torment of an isolation
ensured by the profoundest abyss. Gorianchikov's conversion strategy
thus embraces and articulates all that is implied by the peasants' own designation of the convict as an "unfortunate" (*neschastnyi*) who, by virtue
of his very culpability, signifies the sacred ground on which the struggle
for redemption must be carried out.

The complexity of Gorianchikov's views on the significance and necessity of psychosocial disintegration have sustained the dominant critical
interpretation of *House of the Dead* as ultimately subordinated—despite
the cumulative power of its shocking, because largely unassimilated, detail—to a coherent vision of the redemption of Russian society told as a

nobleman's successful completion of a spiritual journey. This interpretation has received its most thorough critical treatment in Joseph Frank's analysis of the 1876 *Diary of a Writer* piece, "The Peasant Marei," as "the missing pages" of *Notes from the House of the Dead* read as a conversion narrative.[43] Such readings rely heavily on the rhetoric of conversion Gorianchikov deploys: primarily, the motifs of revelation and resurrection, and the value he ultimately finds in the isolation imposed on him by the implacable peasant-convicts for enabling his unsparing judgment of his "former life." We might add as an element of the text's conversion rhetoric the degree to which the language of turning (in Russian, words etymologically derivative of the root *vort* and its variants *vrat/brat, vorot/borot, vrashch/brashch*, etc.) permeates the text.[44]

Indeed, Gorianchikov's rhetoric of conversion amounts to a choreography of turning intended for nothing less comprehensive than the stage of the nation. The revolution (*pere*v*orot*) of sensibility which the eradication of the "executioner within" would realize depends upon the nobleman's turning into, or converting to (*obratit'sia v*) the common people. This turning must occur before the singular spiritual strength of the outcast (*ot*v*erzhenets*, one who has turned away) is irreversibly (*bezvoz*v*ratno*) depleted. The stumbling-block represented by the repulsive (*ot*v*ratitel'nyi*, that which causes a turning away) exterior and the apparent corruption (*raz*v*rashchennost'*, topsy-turviness) of the outcast demands only that the privileged class, self-divested of its prejudices, extend or turn its humane attention to (*chelovecheskoe ob*r*ashchenie*, the noun suggesting the perfect fusion of overture and response, denoting both an appeal to and a turning or conversion toward) those "upon whom the image of God has long been obscured" (*PSS* 4:91/134).

The rapprochement of the classes accomplished in this elaborate choreography of turning prefigures, then, the rapprochement of humankind and God, whose triumphant image (*obraz*) eclipses the unsightliness (*bezobraznost'*, literally, the state of being without an image) of evil. The image of God provides a transcendent referent which magnetizes meaning from otherwise absurd events: for example, the imagery surrounding the absurd death of the tubercular prisoner Mikhailov, who in his final agony could not bear the weight of the hospital gown or even his cross upon his body and yet was made to die in iron fetters, clearly evokes the death of Christ and is redeemed from meaninglessness by virtue of its very status as a sign of the sacred. Similarly, as Gorianchikov experiences it at the first and third narrative levels, psychosocial disintegration allows the process of rapprochement to take place as a progression by which the benighted self, who helplessly acquiesces in the absurdity of the prison experience, is assimilated into the enlightened self, for whom that experience is replete with significance.

To talk of progression, however, is not to talk of consummation. In fact, no point in the text marks the completed assimilation of the benighted self into the enlightened self, just as no represented event testifies to the definitive reconciliation of the classes. The "new word," in which the divided self and the divided nation alike are to be reconciled, is left unspoken; nothing confirms the eradication either of the "executioner within" or of the profound abyss dividing the classes which attests psychologically, socially, and spiritually to the vigor of that figure's sacrificial impulse. Insofar as the integrity of the *bezdna*, the insuperability of the profound abyss, obviates the integrity of the text (as a chronicle of the nobleman's spiritual journey, as an objective and controlled account of life in penal servitude in Russia in the 1850s), Gorianchikov's experience of estrangement unfolds not as a process of conversion, but as an increasingly acute amazement at the singularity of prison life, and an explicit resistance to reconciliation: "I could never reconcile myself to [this life]" (*PSS* 4:19/23). Outrage overwhelms resolution, disorientation overtakes understanding. The very tenacity of estrangement, confirmed by the prefatory narrator, Gorianchikov, and Dostoevsky himself, indicates that Gorianchikov's conviction concerning the necessity of turning into the common people does not evolve as a result of his progressive (if initially compulsory) assimilation into the peasant fraternity but, paradoxically, from his experience of remaining, to a significant degree voluntarily, outside it.[45]

The tension of *Notes from the House of the Dead* is thus an ironic tension: the literal suspense of a failed conversion narrative sustained by a voice condemned to tell the death of the self that was, yet whose reconstruction is uncertain. Hovering between being and nonbeing, significance and absurdity, Gorianchikov tells his own progressive disarticulation as tragic ethnography, that is, as an ultimately unsuccessful attempt to understand the way in which the Russian common criminal and his milieu embody a religious and cultural malaise of profound but elusive import. His purgatorial vision informs the temporal anomalousness of the novel: perpetual estrangement leads it to unfold in a continual moment of crisis, at once unnaturally prolonged and contracted, like the moments preceding the execution of the criminal condemned to death that preoccupy Prince Myshkin in *The Idiot*.[46] In the absence of the new word, Gorianchikov often speaks of the very inadequacy of his words to describe his prison experience. Far from leading him beyond all conceptual barriers to a transcendent viewpoint from which he can survey and understand his circumstances and their import, his words shadow him, no more able to penetrate the discursive confines of description and analysis than the prisoner is able to break through the confining circuit of the barracks and the work station. For this reason, the end of Gorianchikov's sentence—the only possible "central syntactic moment"—fails to redeem (that is, to confer absolute meaning upon) the time spent in completing it, epistrophically in the manner of conversion narratives, but serves only as a formal marker of the termination of its passage.

Insofar as reconciliation depends upon the availability to language of that transcendent term that binds experience to expression, Gorianchikov's words to the Word, estrangement exists in this text independent of conversion as an antithetic narratological paradigm for telling the resistance of experience to meaning. Here the working definition of estrangement exceeds its role as the feeling of alienation that accompanies the psychosocial disarticulation necessary for conversion to occur. Instead, the absence of the regenerative new word reveals estrangement to be the narrational register through which the failed or incomplete conversion process is represented. Although the crisis of inarticulateness so conceived will receive its most sustained expression in *The Idiot,* where the advent of the new word is explicitly bound up with the regeneration of all of Russian society, Dostoevsky introduces the problem here in Gorianchikov's encounter with the mystery of Russianness as incarnated in the peasant-convict.

If it is inaccurate, finally, to describe Gorianchikov as ultimately undone by insanity (the triumph of raw experience) or conversion (the triumph of ideology), and thus to describe the narrative perspective either as baffled or transcendent, precisely what narrational stance does he deploy to tell his particular experience of estrangement, and to what conceivable end? Does the absence of the central syntactic moment leave the autobiographical text without an organizational principle and without a telos? If the absence of the new word locates the narrating voice neither in the experiential nor the ideological realm, what is the character and function of that mediate zone through whose verbal offices it will struggle to achieve the transliteration of one to the other? The answers to these questions lie in determining, first, the relationship of estrangement to conversion as antithetic narratological paradigms (rather than states of mind) cooperative in this text; and, second, the particular character and function of that narrative stance which I have designated the mediate narrative level through which this relationship is articulated.

3. Opposites That Do Not Attract (the *Bezdna* and Poetic Truth) and Opposites That Do (Estrangement and Conversion)

In place of the central syntactic moment at the core of the conversion narrative where beginnings and endings, linear evolution and circular identity, coincide, *Notes from the House of the Dead* possesses a substitute structure equipped with its own tautological coherence: the *bezdna.* This is the word Gorianchikov uses to denote both the *multitude* of surpass-

ingly strange events, utterances, and personalities that shock him throughout the period of his incarceration, and the profound *abyss* of class difference which constitutes their inexhaustible source. The insuperability of
the abyss is attached to its enormity and thus to the reliability of that flow
of anomalous, often shocking events which Gorianchikov experiences as
a constant anguish. All his efforts to describe those occurrences that
assault his reason or his sensibility, every expression of his desire to understand at any cost, every iteration of the phrase "I was astonished," bears
witness to the centrality of the infernal *bezdna*.[47] It is not the case, however,
that the *bezdna* is for the process of estrangement what the central syntactic moment is for the process of conversion, namely, its teleological principle. Instead of transcendence, the *bezdna* produces a continuous dialectic
of estrangement and conversion which, as antithetic narratological
paradigms, live a "tense life" (as Bakhtin claimed for the Dostoevskian
"word") on each other's borders throughout the memoir.[48] Neither the
first nor the third narrative level, raw experience or recuperative ideology,
has the final word in *House of the Dead*.

The textual dialectic to which Gorianchikov's experience of estrangement gives rise recalls the Russian Formalist discussion of estrangement
(*ostranenie*: "making strange," "defamiliarization") as a fundamentally
anti-assimilative narrative strategy for impeding habitual, conventional,
or automatic readings.[49] The principle of resisting assimilation, central to
estrangement as a narrative strategy (and as a state of mind or a stance in
the world), would appear incompatible with conversion on two counts.
First, conversion constitutes the ideal narratological expression or the "ultimate motivational charge" for what Kenneth Burke called "the principle
of perfection," a drive he finds inherent in language itself toward all-inclu-
siveness; linguistically, perfection is the Word (or "God-term") toward
which individual words strive.[50] Second, conversion, insofar as it requires
a (transcendent) closure, often achieves the complete assimilation of experience to expression through an act of subordination; that is, a totalizing
system of signification is retroactively imposed upon experience from the
perspective of the end (of the text, the utterance, the sentence, the old
life or way of seeing). Perfection (the linguistic will to the transcendent
referent) and subordination (an after-the-fact gathering to meaning of its
would-be refugees)—these are the resources with which the conversion
narrative realizes meaning.

In the conversion narrative, the perfection principle invests the end, the
point at which "all that was to be said has in fact been said," with a special
significance as the text's central syntactic moment.[51] But saying it all
(achieving an "accuracy of inventory," reaching the endpoint of the protagonist's "evolution") may not necessarily produce meaning. To see how
this might be so, I turn to Robert Louis Jackson's important analysis of

Notes from the House of the Dead in which an act of critical subordination—the imposition of a totalizing system of signification, "poetic truth"—underwrites the redemptive meaning attributed to the text. The deployment of such totalizing concepts occurs often in Dostoevsky criticism, and they are a staple of the conversion hypothesis. By taking a close look at Jackson's critical argument, it is possible to identify the limitations of such interpretive strategies for Dostoevsky criticism generally, but especially with respect to *Notes from the House of the Dead*. Having noted the discrepancy between Gorianchikov's final words of spiritual victory and the prefatory narrator's portrayal of a tormented misanthrope, Jackson writes that the reader must be prepared "to subordinate the particular and the arbitrary, the welter of surface detail and naturalistic truth, to overall design and comprehension, that is, to an inner, poetic truth." Poetic truth, a perfectionist concept as defined by Burke, inheres in the metaperfectionism of the text's "overall symbolic design" which the individual components of experience reflect and to which they ultimately refer.[52]

Jackson takes the convict anecdote "Akul'ka's Husband" as his primary example of the redemptive efficacy of subordinating naturalistic to poetic truth. A horrifying narrative of a peasant's brutal murder of his wife, "Akul'ka's Husband" figures prominently among the convict anecdotes incorporated into *House of the Dead* because it occupies a discrete chapter almost entirely narrated by the murderer himself, the peasant-convict Shishkov. Outside the prefatory narrator's, only Shishkov's voice—with its peasant idioms and vicious irrationality—eclipses for any significant length of time the familiar and sympathetic modulations of Gorianchikov's own. Having been transferred to the prison hospital, Gorianchikov describes how one night he overheard Shishkov tell his neighbor on the ward, the equally vile peasant-convict Cherevin, the details of the crime for which he was condemned to hard labor. As the violence wreaked upon the defenseless peasant woman escalates, the reader's suffering from the unprecedented absence of Gorianchikov's mediating intelligence intensifies: in effect, the reader lies helplessly awake in Gorianchikov's cot, victimized by Shishkov because unable to ward off his discursive assault, a muted interlocuter whom the maddeningly indifferent Cherevin displaces.[53] Through Gorianchikov's consciousness and his silence, the reader takes on Akul'ka's martyrdom by taking on her voicelessness. The triple silence of Shishkov's dumb victims—reader, narrator, and character—denies the textual availability of any overriding system of meaning or accountability. By awarding it formal independence as a discrete chapter, Gorianchikov imposes a kind of textual quarantine upon "Akul'ka's Husband" that underscores its apparent independence from the ethical desire to make it signify.

While acknowledging "Akul'ka's Husband" to be a moment of "total eclipse," Jackson offers two "poetic truths" with which to convert Shishkov's naturalistic or estranged truth of the brutality of peasant life to poetic meaning. Although the "death of Akul'ka is unatoned for in the historical time and space of the story," Jackson subsumes her suffering, and "the terrible suffering of the Russian people" more generally, into "Gorianchikov's personal drama," which Dostoevsky regarded as a redemptive one and intended to "superimpose on the drama of the Russian people." Through this superimposition, on "the symbolic and mythopoetic plane, Akul'ka's death may be viewed as a sacrifice generating hope for the rescue of mankind."[54] Jackson's first poetic truth, then, redeems Akul'ka's murder, and through her martyrdom the Russian people's suffering, only insofar as the nobleman's spiritual journey metaphorically—the leap transpiring across the *bezdna* of class and gender difference—encompasses her own, and even this redemption at secondhand must be reserved for "later."[55] The assumption, then, is that the nobleman may legitimately carry out the obverse of Christ's Atonement, not dying so that the common people might live, but living so that their deaths have meaning.

The second poetic truth Jackson identifies upon which Akul'ka's death relies to redeem it from absurdity derives from "a rudimentary drama of suffering, sacrifice, death, and rebirth that finds expression in the seasonal cycle of the year." The seasonal cycle in turn provides Dostoevsky/Gorianchikov with a means of symbolically structuring his experience of the Dead House. Accordingly, Jackson argues, the chapter following "Akul'ka's Husband" indirectly redresses Akul'ka's martyrdom in its opening lines which refer to the advent of spring and the Easter season ("avec les espoirs qui levent et les puces qui se déchainent la nuit," according to Jacques Catteau's unsentimental, though perhaps accurate, description of spring in a Siberian prison-camp).[56] Moreover, Jackson argues, the promise of redemption that spring conventionally symbolizes impels the final five chapters, in a "swift movement," toward (Gorianchikov's) liberation. Thus does Akul'ka's spilt blood flow down-chapter to Holy Week. There it contributes to a "sense of catharsis" actualized as "a dramatic turning point" for Gorianchikov, who will go on to avenge Akul'ka in his own immanent triumph over death. Once again, in these arguments poetic truth seems to require that the peasant's resurrection await its realization in the nobleman's.[57]

His assertion of a symbolic link between Akul'ka's murder and Gorianchikov's rebirth enables Jackson to discover a sort of serenity in the final chapters:

> An atmosphere of subdued hope—the "second realm" of which Dante speaks—seems to pervade the last five chapters of *House of the Dead*. Summer

brings thoughts of freedom, the release of the crippled eagle, the abortive protest of the convicts, the failed escape; and all lead directly to the liberation of Gorianchikov.[58]

The events cited as leading directly to Gorianchikov's liberation, however, share a tragic failure to achieve freedom or to escape death. Indeed, the list of events suggests that Gorianchikov's liberation turns upon the continued imprisonment of his fellows. This suggests in turn that the *bezdna*—the profound abyss of class difference whose eradication, according to Gorianchikov's hard-won conviction, would lead to the eradication of the "executioner within"—constitutes the inner sacrificial truth of poetic truth. Gorianchikov bears witness to the astonishing integrity of the *bezdna* in his account of his farewell to the peasant-convicts, and reflects upon his exclusion still intact after ten years of hard labor:

> Many calloused, strong hands were cordially extended to me. Some pressed my hands like real comrades, but they were not many. Others already understood quite well that I was now becoming a completely different man from them. They knew that I had acquaintances in the town and that I would go straightaway from there to *the masters* [*k gospodam*] and would sit down beside these masters as their equal. They understood this, and said goodbye to me cordially enough and even affectionately, though not at all as they would have to a comrade, but rather as if to a gentleman. Some turned away from me and sternly refrained from answering my farewell. A few even looked at me with something like hatred. (*PSS* 4:231/360; emphasis in original)

For a number of the peasant-convicts, then, Gorianchikov's "rebirth" amounts only to a cynical reclamation of his lapsed social status. At the end of his journey, they raise the possibility that the new man emerges from the Dead House indistinguishable from the old: not Gorianchikov-poet, and not even Gorianchikov-pilgrim, but simply Gorianchikov-nobleman before his pilgrimage had even begun, or, more precisely, as if it had never been undertaken. At this point the question ineluctably arises: according to whose standards is naturalistic experience to be subordinated or sacrificed to the production of poetic meaning? Who has access to poetic truth? Most important, what relation have poetic truths to Gorianchikov's saving conviction regarding the necessity of the nobleman's turning into the common peasant? One might begin to answer these questions by examining Gorianchikov's representation of that "subdued hope" which, for Jackson, inspirits the final chapters.

To recapitulate Jackson's argument: the thematic appearance of hope in these chapters marks the inevitable ascendancy of poetic over naturalistic truth. The extravagant suffering of the Russian common people detailed in *House of the Dead* is subsumed by Gorianchikov's painfully direct experience of them which "purges" him of his "empty and abstract humanism" for which they had provided a referent (here Jackson seems to invoke Dostoevsky's former abolitionism of which he was later critical, since Gorianchikov does not evince a tendency to abstract humanism in his attitude toward his fellow convicts). Gorianchikov replaces his former abstract knowledge of *katorga* with another abstraction, poetic truth, unavailable as such to the common people but which nevertheless inspirits their suffering with redemptive significance. Jackson identifies Gorianchikov as the synapse for the transfer of redemptive significance, as the "redeemer of a lost people" whose salvation lies in the immanence of their redeemer's release. For this reason, Gorianchikov's last words (controverted by the prefatory narrator) proclaiming his victory over death may be regarded "as a metaphor for the whole accomplishment of the book: the raising of the Russian people."[59] For this reason, too, even as he narrates the tragedies of the dying eagle, the failed uprising, and the doomed escape in the final chapters, Gorianchikov reverses their tragic (naturalistic) significance by the poetic truth of his destiny and his status.

Gorianchikov's own discussion of subdued hope begins by anatomizing what Jackson neutrally designates "thoughts of spring." In a powerful passage on the effect of spring on the peasant-convicts, Gorianchikov rejects the possibility of a neutral reading of the unmistakable signs of a great underground anguish, noting the increased number and bitterness of quarrels in spring, the dreaminess and grievous sighs of those who, "in the flower of their years and strength," must crush the hope that rises within them before it crushes them (*PSS* 4:173/268). If, for Jackson, subdued hope signifies the ascendancy of poetic truth as symbolized by spring, Gorianchikov here dismisses this truth as irrelevant, because it is inaccessible or inadequate to that sector of humanity whose redemption it nominally intends. He grants that what Jackson describes as an atmosphere of subdued hope does indeed constitute *katorga*'s "most characteristic feature," but he gives hope a moral valence altogether inconsistent with Jackson's assessment. Moreover, he offers a contradictory analysis of the nature of its repression. So ubiquitous is hope in the prison, where grounds for hope are almost totally absent, that Gorianchikov contemplates a typology of prisoners based solely upon the manner in which individual peasant-convicts respond to its unbidden advent in themselves and in their comrades. Hope in *katorga* constitutes a grievous malaise, a "strange feverish impatience," an "unalleviated restlessness" and "delirium," that by virtue of its ubiquity "gave to the place an unusual aspect and character": prison hope bears witness not to the ascendancy of poetic truth but rather to the tormenting dream " about something almost impossible" (*PSS* 4:196/304).

For the "commonsensical and sober" Russian, then, all manifestations of hope must be fiercely subdued: only in the sense that all convicts observe the unspoken etiquette according to which those who suffer most from the nightmare of hope must be fiercest in suppressing its signs in others can it be maintained that hope unites the convict community (*PSS* 4:196/304). The focus of a relentless self-contempt, hope not only destroys the possibility of a community from which poetic truth may be derived and to which it confers its meaning, but it reincarcerates the prisoner in a claustrophobic self-loathing. As a cruel visitation that preys mercilessly upon the inmates, leaving them sick and sullen, as an illusion around which the prisoner comes, willy-nilly, to organize the innumerable moments of his sentence, hope is by common consent repressed with all the weapons in the convict community arsenal: psychological bullying, derision, and cynicism. Although it provokes physical and mental distress, its utter extinction leads to outbursts of uncontrolled violence and, in particular, self-destructive violence. In sum, hope is the expression of a futile dream of freedom that for the prisoner's sake must be viciously suppressed yet cannot be completely extinguished without risking an extinction of the self. Gorianchikov's emphasis in the final chapters of *House of the Dead* falls squarely on the naturalistic or observed, not the poetic or conventional, truth of hope: as he insists after analyzing the paradox of hope as the source of the prisoners' greatest anguish, "I am not playing the poet here, but am convinced of the truth of my observations" (*PSS* 4:173/268).

In an attempt to organize the "welter" of individual response to the interloper hope, Gorianchikov pursues a typology of peasant-convicts based upon patterns of response to its encroachment which, taken together, would comprise a psychology of hope in *katorga*. He finds that the prison population divides itself into the "naive chatterers" and the "silent types." The silent types divide into the "good" and "bright," and the "incomparably more numerous" "malicious" and "gloomy." When the latter choose to talk, they are "inevitably relentless scandalmongers and envious troublemakers" who elicit confessions of hope from others only for the pleasure of reviling them for their candor (*PSS* 4:196/305). The quiet and goodhearted ones divide into those who endeavor to retain confidence in their hopes by keeping silent and those few who keep silence from an utter lack of hope. From this last pool of spiritually destitute, if essentially "good" men come those who attempt murder in prison as a way of committing suicide. The convicts' thoughts of hope seem positive only insofar as they constitute the mere negative of a negative: in the House of the Dead, hope occupies the underground of the underworld. The futility of organizing its complexity, let alone assimilating it to some overarching, redemptive truth, ultimately leads Gorianchikov to renounce his effort to subordinate its diversity to any typological scheme:

Here I am, however, trying to subsume our entire prison into categories: but is this possible? Reality is infinitely diverse, compared with all, even the most subtle, conclusions of abstract thought, and it does not permit clear-cut and wholesale distinctions. Reality tends toward dis-integration [*Deistvitel'nost' stremitsia k razdrobleniiu*]. (*PSS* 4:197/306)

The concept of poetic truth condemns Gorianchikov to Akul'ka's horrifying spiritual solitude, martyred to his conscience and his class as she is victimized by her innocence and her gender. Both must be satisfied with a merely symbolic, metaphorical, or removed resurrection, a resurrection at secondhand. Like Akul'ka, whose suffering is unatoned for in the historical time and space of the novel, Gorianchikov-redeemer leaves the prison, according to Jackson, "to die in solitude, like the crippled eagle. But the symbolic significance of his liberation—and with it is linked the affirmative character of *House of the Dead*—is inseparable from the whole movement of the seasons, from winter to spring, from Christmas to Easter, from death to resurrection: 'Freedom, a new life, resurrection from the dead. . . . What a glorious moment!' " For Jackson, conversion, to which he alludes as an "impression of a continuous cycle or of circular movement," occurs even though its circuit (through which an evolved identity—of the enlightened and deluded self, the nobleman and peasant—must be achieved) is broken by the profound abyss of class difference and the displacements (as well as the inherently sacrificial metaphorical recoveries) it occasions.[60]

As a narrative attempt to render the "completeness" of a protagonist's story with which to indicate the end of his "evolution," John Freccero associates the phrase "accuracy of inventory" with the dynamics of conversion. In *House of the Dead*, however, Gorianchikov deploys it in the service of what appears a far less comprehensive goal: the cataloguing of all peasant-convict responses to a single emotion, hope. He does so, moreover, even though he makes no claim that it will provide an interpretive key with which to unlock the mysterious significance of *katorga* and its inhabitants. He acknowledges the insufficiency of his typology of peasant-convicts to encompass the "reality" of their life, yet he retains it as a more or less accurate inventory of that portion of their mental life devoted to the phenomenon of hope. These passages convey the memoirist's method. If, as he maintains, reality, and specifically the "singular" reality of peasant-convict life, tends toward atomization, fragmentation, dis-integration, then accuracy in respect to its diversity replaces "reality"—a totalizing concept related to poetic truth by virtue of its claims to a meaningful comprehensiveness—as the focus of memory and the object of writing.[61]

The necessity of this shift from reality to accuracy is mandated by the fact that the infinite diversity of peasant-convict life—by Gorianchikov's own admission, irredeemably aberrant in terms of any totalizing conceptual system, be it "reality," "poetic truth," or "humanism"—continually frustrates his efforts to reconcile himself to life in prison. In turn, his inability to reconcile himself with the life around him is linked to his exclusion from the fellowship of his fellow convicts, a circumstance that torments him beyond all the other agonies of prison life. At the beginning of an early chapter titled "First Impressions," he describes his continual state of astonishment, perpetuated by the endless flow of absurdities that daily confront him:

> I remember clearly that from the first step into this life I was struck by the fact that I seemed to have found in it nothing particularly striking, out of the ordinary, or more precisely, unexpected. It was as if I had glimpsed it all before, in my imagination, when going to Siberia I had tried to guess what fate lay before me. But soon a countless number [*bezdna*] of the most strange and unexpected occurrences, the most fantastic facts, began to arrest me at almost every step. And only later, after having lived rather a long time in the prison, did I fully comprehend how utterly exceptional, how utterly unexpected, such an existence was and I wondered more and more at it. I must admit that this astonishment accompanied me through the whole length of my sentence; I could never reconcile myself to [*primirit'sia s*] this life. (*PSS* 4:19/23)[62]

Gorianchikov's double usage of *bezdna* to signify both the abyss of class difference and the countless number of anomalies it continually generates underwrites the ubiquitous challenge to his narrative ambitions posed by the life beyond life: in this early statement of his bewilderment, he comes close to claiming that what he finally understood about this singular mode of existence was its irrepressible aberrance. The subsequent chronicle of surpassingly strange facts, personalities, and occurrences acquires a dramatic dimension through his sustained struggle to comprehend the flood of anomalies in a series of efforts either to systematize them or refer them to larger systems of meaning. It is precisely the drama of epistemological struggle that situates estrangement within a perfectionist dynamic: even as Gorianchikov concedes that reality strives toward dis-integration, he strives—by his efforts to describe each of the fragments and to describe them accurately—to make of his memory a composite signifier of and worthy witness to the essential fragmentariness (and, in this qualified sense, the reality) of *katorga*. This means that, although a totalizing grasp of reality eludes his careful documentation of the life beyond life, he still comes to embrace a program for action: his accuracy of inventory, an indefinite postponement of that moment when the meaning of all preceding moments is revealed, still leads Gorianchikov to the formulation of a saving conviction—conversion as the revolutionary eradication of the "executioner within." The itemization of fantastic facts which comprises the major narrative and mnemonic effort of *Notes from the House of the Dead* doubles as a record of that process of psychosocial disarticulation by which the nobleman is compelled by external circumstances, actually and in fact, to become one of the common people: the sole prerequisite for attempting the eradication of one's inner executioner.

This double function of accuracy allows us to claim the perfection principle for estrangement, insofar as estrangement functions as the register through which perfection/conversion is pursued. If conversion operates narratologically as the complete assimilation of experience to expression so that no "abyss" obtains between the two, so that a complete absorption of experience into meaning is achieved, an accuracy of inventory which precludes the possibility of residue, then estrangement deploys accuracy in relation to a textual excrescence, to that which remains resistant to assimilation or, theologically speaking, redemption. In other words, estrangement pursues perfection as and through an exhaustive enumeration of phenomena whose inexhaustible source is the *bezdna*, the collective name for all possible inventories, a kind of textual place-name that indicates wherein and for whom lie the semiotic (or ethnographic) and narratological challenges of representing the life of the Dead House. In this regard, *Notes from the House of the Dead* establishes the ground rules for Dostoevsky's democracy, the project that occupied him for the duration of his career: the discovery of the outwardly coarse and brutal peasant's spiritual preeminence and central role in the unfolding of Russia's redemptive mission and glorious destiny.

In itself, however, Gorianchikov's saving conviction—that the regeneration of Russian society depends upon the transformation, actually and in fact, of the nobleman into the peasant—presents him as a narrator with a singular problem. He claims that his convictions were "neither bookish nor speculative, but were acquired through reality [*ne knizhno, ne umozritel'no, a v deistvitel'nosti*], and I had plenty of time to verify them." He adds, "Perhaps henceforward everyone will realize to what extent they are true" (*PSS* 4:199/309). The implicit stipulation that for conviction to count it must be acquired through reality begs the question of Gorianchikov's ability to transmit his conviction to "everyone," and specifically to his reader in a manner "not bookish" and "not speculative." What external circumstances comparable to incarceration, with its imposition of the nobleman's physical transformation into a peasant, might conceivably compel the educated and privileged reader to undertake its spiritual equivalent? If conviction is available only to one who has been convicted "in reality"—that is, traumatically—how is the conviction of the reader to occur; in what sense might the (noble) reader of *House of the Dead* come to acknowledge him- or herself a convict? These questions are central to Gorianchikov's tragic identification of the "executioner within" as the moral pivot of his memoirs.

With such questions concerning the possibility and the means of actually convicting the reader, we arrive at the second plane on which the dialectical cooperation of estrangement and conversion occurs: not in Gorianchikov's strategy for representing the life of the prison but rather in Dostoevsky's strategy for his narrator's self-representation. Gorianchikov's self-portrait, like his depiction of the prison milieu, is built around the structural and thematic centrality of the *bezdna*, the focus of national, textual, and personal dis-integration. Just like "reality," his self-portrait "tends toward dis-integration."[63] Through his very fidelity to the principle of accuracy, this time deployed in the service of accurately rendering the full range of his response to *katorga*, Gorianchikov reveals (and this revelation is represented as occurring beyond the range of his controlling intention) the extent of his estrangement not just from the life around him but from himself. Explicitly, self-estrangement describes a level of psychosocial disarticulation distinct both from that accompanying the shock of raw experience (the first narrative level) as well as that conceived as preparatory to the conversion of the "old" man into the "new," and which generates Gorianchikov's ideology of conversion (the third narrative level). It gives rise instead to a formally disintegrative narrative level that yet mediates the process by which Gorianchikov's experience of *katorga* is assimilated into its ideological expression; in so doing, it accounts for the incompletion of that process to which the prefatory narrator points in his introduction. The mediate narrative level is, then, the narratological corollary of the phenomenology of *katorga*. It expresses that in Gorianchikov's psyche which resists reconciliation not with his environment and its inhabitants (the first narrative level) but with the ideological program of reconciliation itself as it is formulated at the third narrative level. It expresses, that is, his resistance to the central tenet of his own hard-won conviction. The mediate level of narration thus produces the autobiography's central unconsummated image: the self that has died to its former life but has not yet been born into the new.

Issuing from the unbridgeable gap between the enlightened and the deluded self (the self that knows what is to be done, and the self not yet willing or able to do it—a condition Augustine, and Paul before him, attribute to the preconverted or unregenerate self), the mediate narrative level expresses Gorianchikov's internalization of the *bezdna* that precludes his reconciliation with the life around him and thus the conversion he himself prescribes. It controverts his resurrectional claims just as surely as the *bezdna* of class difference precludes the intimately related rebirth of the nation. In place of spiritual autobiography, a conversion narrative through which he traces his development out of willful ignorance and blindness, the mediate narrative level channels a distinctly anti-transcendent, even regressive, impulse first detectable in what I describe as the attrition of Gorianchikov's narrating voice and ultimately in its eclipse. The compromised voice of the mediate level is structurally central to the text and constitutes its "inside narrative" (to borrow Melville's subtitle for *Billy Budd*). It reveals the astounding reach of self-estrangement, from Gorianchikov's only partially acknowledged capacity for self-deception to the fantastic displacement of his voice into other narrating personae. Theologically, "attrition" signifies an imperfect sorrow for one's sin, as opposed to "contrition" which indicates sorrow from love of God.[64] In Dostoevsky's narratological deployment of attrition, it signifies something analogous: an imperfect repentance for one's crime with profoundly political implications.

4. The Dostoevskian "As If": Self-Deception in Autobiography

How does one track the impact of self-deception upon the representation of the self in a first-person narrative? If the pilgrim is not yet the poet, although he claims to be, where does the reader begin to apprehend that discrepancy? One place to begin is with Gorianchikov's representations of the genesis of his estrangement, not for the purpose of questioning its authenticity but in order to understand the flexibility that self-deception, with its manifold strategies, lends the narrating voice in autobiography. In *House of the Dead*, this flexibility permits the text to eschew its own bookishness and to function as that "external circumstance" through which the reader is "actually" convicted. The key to discerning the mediate narrative level and the complex narratological dynamic peculiar to it is also the key to discerning the text's means of "actually" rather than "bookishly" convicting its reader. It requires as a first step that one suspend one's uncritical belief in the candid self-representation of Gorianchikov's voice and recognize self-estrangement as the dominant of his self-representation. In so doing, one discovers the way in which he expresses the "philosophy" of his own crime, the one subject related to his incarceration on which he never directly comments.

Despite the prefatory narrator's claim that the former convict's manuscript will acquaint the noble reader with a "new world, hitherto unknown," Gorianchikov, in an early passage appearing in the chapter "The First Month" (part of which we have already examined), explicitly denies that the world he describes was ever "unknown." He insists that, notwithstanding the feelings of astonishment and confusion that overwhelmed him at finding himself an inmate of the Dead House, "knowledge and rumor" had in fact supplied him with a certain prescience in regard to its peculiar life:

I myself had suddenly become just as much one of the common people, just as much a convict, as they. Their habits, understanding, opinions, customs, became as if mine also, at least formally, by law, although in actuality I didn't share them. I was astonished and confused, *precisely as if* I had never suspected that any of this existed and had heard nothing of it, when in fact *I had known and had heard*. But reality produces a completely different impression than knowledge or rumor. (*PSS* 4:65/93; my emphasis)[65]

In this passage, the second of two in which Gorianchikov describes his initial reaction to *katorga*, we glimpse the inauguration of a narrative stance which asserts the narrator's estrangement from that which he tells.

Juxtaposed, the two passages in which Gorianchikov describes the genesis of his estrangement offer an especially clear view of the contradictions upon which he fashions his self-representation. In the passage cited in the paragraph above, he implies that the immediate impact of the peculiar reality of *katorga* was so stunning as to nullify the intelligence with which "knowledge and rumor" had prepared him. He claims that astonishment and confusion overcame him "precisely as if" knowledge had never existed, although in fact it had. In the first of the two passages (*PSS* 4:19/23, cited on page 58, above, however, Gorianchikov not only denies possessing any prior knowledge of *katorga*, but he denies as well feeling either astonishment or confusion upon arriving there. He claims instead that all his expectations concerning *katorga* had materialized, derived not from any external resource but solely from an imaginative anticipation of what awaited him at the end of his forced Siberian march, leaving him impressed by the utter familiarity, even mundanity, of what he was seeing for the first time: it was not for a long while, he asserts, that anything struck him as unusual or unanticipated.[66]

This contradiction, however, does not mean that the statements are self-canceling. Whereas in the second passage (cited immediately above) the anomalousness of *katorga* instantly invalidates knowledge, in the first the information provided by imagination is credited only insofar as it allows him an illusory respite from the ineluctable encroachment of an ever alien reality. If, according to the first passage, reality does not immediately overwhelm him, its revelation bit by bit over an extended period (in fact, for the length of his sentence) still definitively precludes any possibility of familiarity, and thus any likelihood of reconciliation, and Gorianchikov represents this circumstance as beyond his control. Despite their contradictions, then, these two versions of his initial reaction to *katorga* offer similar sub-versions of their express claims for unpreventable, unmitigable, and continuous shock. In both passages, that is, Gorianchikov declares that astonishment and confusion (the emotions associated with his raw experience of the prison and thus characteristic of the first narrative level), far from encompassing his immediate response to the life of the

Dead House, were themselves preceded, and thus mediated, by some degree of foreknowledge. According to one sub-version, foreknowledge was supplied by outside information, albeit quickly suppressed ("precisely as if I had never suspected . . . when in fact I had known") and later declared irrelevant, and, according to another, by imagination, only temporarily permitted to forestall the onslaught of a reality fatally destructive to any sense of competence and control.

Given Gorianchikov's insistence on his foreknowledge, no matter how hastily and even justifiably dismissed, his astonishment and confusion more accurately bespeak a decision—the willful assumption of an estranged stance or posture toward the prison camp and its peasant-convict population—than an uncontrolled and spontaneous reaction.[67] Estrangement, in effect, emerges as a strategy for resisting the physical metamorphosis into the peasant-convict he is officially required to undertake, and he explicitly justifies this resistance at one point as a means of gaining the respect of the peasant-convicts. He had recognized immediately on entering the prison that his "first question" was "how to conduct myself, what stance to take before these people?" Anticipating conflict, he vows that,

> regardless of whatever confrontations there might be, I determined not to change my plan of action, which I had already partly devised at that time; I knew that it was right. To be exact: I decided that it was imperative to behave as straightforwardly and as independently as possible, and on no account to show any particular desire to get close to them, but not to reject them if they themselves wanted to be friendly. On no account to fear their threats and their hatred and, as opportunity allowed, to appear not to notice it. On no account to reconcile myself with them on certain points and not to indulge some of their habits and customs.

He resolves "in a word, not to thrust myself entirely into their fellowship" but rather to keep a part of himself in reserve, to command their respect by conforming to their own expectations of the nobility and remaining aloof (*PSS* 4:76/111).[68]

Dostoevsky's own account of the trauma of his prison experience vis-à-vis the peasant-convicts and his strategies for survival corroborates a reading of Gorianchikov's estrangement as partly a contrivance for expressing and retaining his former class identity.[69] Every iteration of the refrain "I was astonished" announces his difference from his fellow convicts (whose outstanding trait is their utter lack of astonishment), an assertion of his plight and thus his predicament as a nobleman among peasants. His perpetual astonishment offers proof of one of Gorianchikov's key claims: that life in *katorga* is harder for a noble- than a peasant-convict to bear, and that far more difficult for the former to cope with than "the change of customs, the way of life, the food, etc." is the fact that

every newcomer to the prison within two hours of his arrival becomes just
the same as all the others, begins to *make himself at home*, is the same full-
fledged member of the prison collective as anybody else. He is understood by
everybody and he himself understands everybody, he is familiar to everyone,
and everyone considers him *one of their own*. It is not so with *the well born
man*, with the nobleman. (*PSS* 4:198/307, 308; emphasis in original)

Gorianchikov's estrangement announces him as more a captive than a
convict, more a castaway than one who has turned away (*otverzhenets*).[70]
Moreover, it conveys a certain innocence, a delicacy of feeling, that paradoxically establishes for the reader his authority as a narrator because it
makes indecorous any probing of the question of his crime that the prefatory narrator had so sensationally opened. Estrangement emerges as an
"underground" resistance that, from the beginning of his sentence, allows
Gorianchikov to oppose to the life of the prison the inviolable integrity
of his own (noble) identity, of which his uncompromising and even principled astonishment and confusion are signs.

Indeed, the advantage of estrangement lies in its dual function: at the
same time that it allows Gorianchikov to represent the constant psychological stress of the offensive launched by the peasant-convicts and the life
of the camp against his (class) identity, it offers him an ever ready means
for asserting his identity in the face of that hostility. In other words, Gorianchikov's deployment of a contrived and principled estrangement makes
possible a narratological counterpoint to conversion which allows him simultaneously to tell the conversion experience as a record of his initially
enforced and arduous transformation into the peasant, and yet—with the
substitution of the conversion narrative's central syntactic moment by the
bezdna of class difference, here internalized—to defer indefinitely its consummation. Secretly subversive of what it openly proclaims and promotes—namely, the constructive destabilization of his class identity, the
ideologically sound becoming one of the common people—a strategic estrangement allows for the retention of a highly particularized, because
"never reconciled," narrative point of view. In the final analysis, it allows
for the peculiar flexibility that self-deception gives to first-person narration
(perfected in his next novel, *Notes from the Underground*) and which we
are now in a position to consider with respect to the narrative structure
of the text.[71]

Thus far we have described estrangement as the dominant of Gorianchikov's self-representation; as the register of psychological resistance
through which he pursues the spiritually antithetical goal of conversion;
and ultimately as a narrative strategy, ambiguously motivated, that permits
a distinctive, because always unreconciled, narrative perspective. If the
first narrative level represents Gorianchikov's raw experience of radical

alienation as unmediated and continuous, a constant affront and challenge to his noble identity accompanied by a mandated physical transformation into the common people; and the third level a conciliatory strategy for conversion which invests that enforced transformation with political as well as spiritual significance; then the mediate level of autobiographical narration emerges as their unacknowledged substrate, that which generates both the "spontaneous" and "considered" responses to *katorga*. The first and third narrative levels are thus not inconsistent with, but rather integral to, the mediate level's superintendence of the centrality of the *bezdna* as the structural staple of the memoirs over the whole range of its narratological and expository representations.

To discern three distinctive levels of autobiographical narration in his memoir is not to claim that Gorianchikov himself is aware of them as such or in control of their orchestration. Nor is it to claim that his positing of an estranged self permits our judging him to have undertaken his memoirs in bad faith.[72] It does suggest, however, that Dostoevsky's artistry is in evidence not so much in Gorianchikov's representation of his ideology of personal and political salvation as in his contrivance for stalling that event. His estrangement describes a point of self-departure around which an otherwise scrupulously honest self-representation is constructed. Gorianchikov is the first instanciation of the Dostoevskian narrator only partially in the know, but whose partial knowing has a psychological and correspondingly narratological significance of its own.[73] In *House of the Dead*, the strategic quality of his estrangement complicates his, and consequently our, understanding of his conversion: its role in the formulation of a policy of reconciliation and its role in resisting that policy, its character as spontaneous reaction and its character as contrivance, the extent to which it is admitted and the extent to which it is "admitted" only as knowledge Gorianchikov keeps from himself. This ambiguity accounts for the incompletion of the conversion process, textually manifested in the unwittingly ironic tension of a narrating voice ideologically committed to telling the death of the self that was, yet psychologically unprepared to reconstruct it. The gap between progressive ideology and regressive psychology, insofar as it results from a calculated estrangement with which the nobleman asserts his difference from his fellow convicts, testifies to the internalization of the *bezdna* of class difference.

The ironic tension between ideology and psychology that rends Gorianchikov's self-representation condemns him to a sort of narrator's limbo, a veritable hell, an antitype for which the Dead House in which he is physically incarcerated is the type.[74] The space between the deluded and the enlightened self condemns the autobiographer to produce a specular text which reflects not just an alien reality but also the progressive disarticulation—and even, as we will see in part 2, the desubjectification—of the narrating self.[75] Dedicated to illuminating the formerly obscure and novel world of forced labor by compiling a phenomenology of *katorga*, the memoir tropes the specular text which reflects the progress of the narrator's spiritual incarceration. Gorianchikov himself aptly diagnoses his condition in the first year of his imprisonment: the project of removing the optical illusion governing relations between the classes is hampered at the outset by a willful blindness—a refusal, he says, "to look around me," tantamount to a refusal to confront the executioner within (*PSS* 4:178/ 276).[76] In default of this self-liberating act, the narrating voice of the mediate level proclaims the triumph of self-deception and tells the story of the self's enslavement to its own illusions.

Not just his explicit ruminations about the habitual abuse of power but also Gorianchikov's commitment to the strategic defense of his class identity beg the question of his relation to his own inner executioner, and specifically whether he has failed even to acknowledge, let alone purge himself of, that figure's influence. The possibility of this failure suggests a hidden qualm: might the nobleman's principled transformation into the peasant, no matter how ideologically desirable, signify not his apotheosis but his self-obliteration? Is it possible for him to exist without the inner executioner who safeguards his class privileges? In his polemical writings of the early 1860s in the wake of peasant emancipation, Dostoevsky expressly addressed the tension between reform, on the one hand, and the fear of self-obliteration, on the other, insisting (though not consistently) that the educated class must retain the integrity of its class identity even as it merges with the common people.[77] In these articles, as in *House of the Dead*, the project of eradicating the "executioner within" intends not a self-sacrifice (not an attack on the noble class per se) but, on the contrary, a redemptive self-recovery.

The nobleman cannot be truly noble, Gorianchikov explains, will not have authority over his own emotions, until he has purged himself of the "ancestral sin": a desire and expectation that, through "habit," have become almost a need to exercise "unlimited dominion over the body, blood, and spirit" of "another creature bearing the image of God" by humiliating and degrading him (*PSS* 4:155, 154/238, 237). Whereas the professional executioner is universally loathed, the "gentleman amateur" is either entirely unnoticed or, at most, generates a bookish and abstract protest (Gorianchikov chooses to specify the amateur executioner as the "manufacturer" [*fabrikant*] and the "entrepreneur" [*antreprener*] who tyrannize over the "worker" and his family, making more obvious by its conspicuous omission the impeccable qualifications of his fellow Russian landowners [*pomeshchiki*] for the title). Even those who express uneasiness with their prerogative to exercise unlimited sovereignty over others, Gorianchikov notes, "have not all succeeded in extinguishing in themselves this need for absolute power." An inherited affliction, the prerogative of power enfeebles the will: "a generation cannot so readily tear out that which heredity has instilled in it; a man does not so readily repudiate that which entered into his blood, so to speak, with his mother's milk" (*PSS* 4:155/237). The afflicted afflict in turn; the powerful are victims of their own power. The violence of the executioner within is self- as well as other-directed.[78]

In Gorianchikov's case, the recovery of his autonomy depends on his owning the knowledge that he struggles to suppress. This includes not just what he "had known and had heard" of the life of *katorga*, but, first and foremost, the fact and the nature of the crime that landed him there. As a personification of the estranged self, the executioner within robs his host of the self-possession—the fullness of self-knowledge or, more accurately, self-acknowledgment —to withstand the transition from poet to pilgrim, protagonist to narrator. The voice that annuls what it knows in order to maintain an irreconcilable estrangement and perpetual confusion tells us, in so doing, of its commitment to self-diminution. The consequences of self-deception, that is, are not confined to Gorianchikov's abdication of knowledge about, and thus responsibility for, the reality of *katorga*. More significant, self-deception ensures that he will not be forthcoming in regard to what must be the central question of an ex-convict's memoir, the question of his crime.

Even without considering the information provided in the prefatory narrator's introduction, everything about Gorianchikov—from his diction, to his astonishment, and even to the way he struggles to persevere—indicates his intimate connection, by virtue of his nobility, with the educated reader of his time. He is Russian-born, "a nobleman and a landowner" (thus implicitly a serf owner) and committed to a code of behavior clearly at odds with the anarchic, often brutal, life of the peasant-convict (*PSS* 4:6/2). He is quick to appreciate what he regards as natural nobility, identifying it readily, for example, in the Daghestanian Tartar, Aley, whom he teaches to read from his Bible and whose eyes blaze indignantly at any injustice. It is perhaps because Gorianchikov is such a familiar and trustworthy figure, his voice characterized by a steady intelligence, equanimity, and, often, compassion, that his critical readers have historically neglected to consider the question of his crime.[79] Certainly Gorianchikov's own reticence on this point is noticeable, especially in view of the prefatory narrator's shocking assertion that he was imprisoned for murdering his young wife—shocking despite the townspeople's propensity to receive Gorianchikov as a possible suitor for their daughters and to regard him as "morally irreproachable" (*PSS* 4:6/3).

The only reluctance to discuss the topic of personal criminal history that Gorianchikov explicitly mentions refers to the disinclination of the peasant to "tell his story" (*PSS* 4:11/11). He characterizes the disturbingly unrepentant confessions—for confessions were made, despite the general consensus that "*one shouldn't* speak *about that* [*pro eto*], because to speak *about that* was not done" (*PSS* 4:12/11; emphasis in original)—as "stories [*rasskazy*] of the most terrifying and the most unnatural acts, the most fantastic murders" (*PSS* 4:15/17). Whether Gorianchikov shares the peasant's fear of an indifferent, even violent response from his listener, his reticence regarding the story of his own criminality has historically been met by his readers with tactful silence. Contemporary criticism, in particular, documents an almost gentlemanly refusal to speculate upon this suppressed, if central, question. At most, the only form of censorship conceded to have affected Gorianchikov's candor is that governmental form assumed to have inhibited Dostoevsky's. Collectively, the text's critics have averted their eyes from that which Gorianchikov himself refuses to see. We return to the questions raised by the history of the text's critical reception in the final section of this chapter. For now it suffices to observe that to forego an inquiry into the nature of Gorianchikov's crime, for whatever reason, is to acquiesce in his failure of (self-) recognition, and to yield without resistance to the dodges of a narrative voice transacting its own displacement.

In many ways, the text's representative reader is the prefatory narrator, a circumstance that returns us to the question posed at the outset of the present reading: Why is this man alive? Despite his brief and, as many have judged, extraneous appearance, the prefatory narrator exists on a number of narratological planes. In his short textual life, he insinuates himself as eyewitness, narrator, character, publisher, and, according to a number of the text's critics, editor.[80] He thus claims an existence at once extratextual and intratextual; perhaps it is this uncertain affiliation that quickens one's sense of his existential ambiguity. He both surrounds the text (with his introduction/epilogue) and penetrates it, altering the reader's perspective on its character, its action, and, ultimately, on the breadth of its political and social significance. In other words, he demonstrates a peculiar extratextual vitality that had been seen previously in Dostoevsky's work only intratextually, specifically on the characterological plane in the early novella *The Double* (1846). The prefatory narrator embodies, and thus projects as existentially independent, the voice of Gorianchikov's executioner within: herein lies the key to his nature as a double. His existence illustrates both the self-directedness of that figure's sacrificial energy as well as his distinctive modus operandi, a perfectly bloodless—because discursive—decapitation (to invoke Dostoevsky's own image of the beheaded artist on the eve of exile) or desubjectification.

The prefatory narrator's activities clearly reveal him to be a direct descendant of Goliadkin Jr. in *The Double*. In the post-Siberian work, Dostoevsky explores the political and social implications of what in the pre-Siberian work had been manipulated solely as a psychological-characterological phenomenon.[81] Denying to the world (in this case, the readership) that the spiritual and narratological journey from pilgrim to poet which *House of the Dead* chronicles had been completed, the prefatory narrator actualizes Gorianchikov's self-estrangement and then uses it to justify his usurpation of Gorianchikov's script. He foregrounds the ex-convict's less than ingenuous assumption of an estranged narrative stance toward his fellow prisoners by making the story of his own estrangement from Gorianchikov the focus of his metanarrative. Indeed, the introduction/epilogue, which tells how the prefatory narrator tried and failed to become the ex-convict's confidant, ultimately emerges as a parody (in the sense of a perverse imitation) of the text it frames, which tells how the nobleman Gorianchikov tried and failed to gain access to the psyche of the peasant-convict.[82] Both noble inquisitors—whose poorly concealed curiosity in regard to the *chudak* (the one who "stands apart") or the *otverzhenets* (the "outcast") generates the descriptions and anecdotes upon which the novelty and persuasiveness of their accounts depend—are contemptuously rebuffed by the objects of their curiosity. They are left to reiterate, always with bewilderment and regret, the details of a breakdown in communication. The prefatory narrator, however, clearly profits from this circumstance, gaining control over both the dissemination and the reception of Gorianchikov's memoirs—in other words, over the content of his memory and thus over his experience. His is the first word and the last; he aspires to have it be the final word on Gorianchikov, in the Bakhtinian sense. His urbanity identifies him as one of the "masters" whom the peasant-convicts imagine Gorianchikov rejoining after his release, yet the prefatory narrator not only fails to recognize him (he brands him a *chudak*) and not only fails to recognize the significance of his suffering, but he appoints himself his representative and judge before his readership: the prefatory narrator is, in a double sense, Gorianchikov's executor.

The prefatory narrator's judgment (or his characterization) of Gorianchikov is based largely upon the ex-convict's refusal to engage with him in conversation. Gorianchikov's disjointed mutterings in response to the prefatory narrator's friendly overtures, his terror and impotent fury at the bald attempts to figure out what makes him tick, retrospectively confirm the prefatory narrator's evaluation of entire sections of the manuscript of the *chudak* as disjointed and suggestive only of insanity. In a striking parallel, the inability or unwillingness to engage in or sustain a conversation features prominently in no less than a third of Gorianchikov's characterizations of individual peasant-convicts. Indeed, the characterizations in

House of the Dead read like a typology of inarticulateness, ranging from the utter inability or disinclination to converse (Iosif the cook, Sushilov); to the purposeful distortion of individual words (Skuratov, Luka Kuz'-mich); to "conversations" rendered nonsensical by lies (all the barracks dialogues Gorianchikov overhears at Christmas), non sequiturs (Petrov), or the utter absence of any shared intellectual or moral frame of reference between the conversants (Orlov, Almazov, Cherevin, and Shishkov). We must add to this list of discursive stalemates the perverted use of language, denunciations, incessant rumors, motiveless lies, and the "gossip, intrigue, cattiness, envy, squabbling, and malice" that torments Gorianchikov (*PSS* 4:13/14); the stunned silence of the Poprishchin-like madman who had relied on a love-smitten, but unfortunately nonexistent, officer's daughter to intercede between him and the gauntlet; and the wooden silence, bordering on idiocy, of the wanderer plucked out of the Siberian forest who even in prison lived irretrievably beyond all human community. In this regard, Gorianchikov's inarticulateness as described by the prefatory narrator resonates with (or figures as a contrapuntal anticipation of) the peasant-convicts' combined inarticulateness as reported by Gorianchikov.

Gorianchikov, in fact, stands in precisely the same relation to the peasant-convicts as the prefatory narrator to his fellow nobleman, Gorianchikov: one of a conventional—which is to say, a circumstantially imposed—symmetry or semblance that belies a profound dis-semblance in both the modern and the archaic senses of "dissemblance" as *lying* and *lacking similarity.* The parodic symmetry of introduction and text (the encounter of the nobleman with "a new world" through its representative, the *chudak*), like the apparent symmetry of deprivation uniting Gorianchikov and the peasant-convict, only throws into relief the "false relations" on which it is based. Insofar as the relationship of the prefatory narrator and Gorianchikov recapitulates that of Gorianchikov and the peasant-convict, and given the reader's willingness to take falseness for innocence and candor, we can discern a chain of misapprehensions, sanctioned in and by a paradigm of reader response which, through noble publisher, noble ex-convict, and peasant-convict, binds the Russian social body from noble-reader to peasant-read.[83] Thus does the topos of enslavement as "illusion" command its own peculiar integrity, exhibiting a remarkable extension far beyond the stockade circumscribing the House of the Dead, far beyond even the narrator's psyche as a metaphorical Dead House.

Premised upon the unquestioned assumption of his own perspective as the normative one, the prefatory narrator's activities and his functions, which we have described with reference to the character(s) Goliadkin, betray him as the first site for the displacement of the narrating voice of *Notes from the House of the Dead.* The prefatory narrator, that is, impersonates that part of Gorianchikov who complacently assumes his own probity, who considers himself to be anything but a criminal and is therefore in the camp but not of it: after all, he has spilled no blood.[84] For this reason, it is precisely the criminality of the other (by definition, the *chudak*) that intrigues him. The forfeiture of self-knowledge in relation to his own culpability allows the nobleman to hang back from the imperative conversion into the peasant even as he preaches its necessity: hence, his assumption, and thus his perception, of an unbridgeable experiential gap between himself and the peasant-convict.[85] This gap is subsequently confirmed in and perpetuated by the series of failed dialogues between nobleman-inquisitor and peasant-criminal, dialogues fatally premised upon the inquisitor's assumption of his own virtue. Insofar as he embodies the Gorianchikov who, upon the completion of his sentence, would rejoin the ranks of the noble class as if the pilgrimage in the Dead House had never been undertaken, the prefatory narrator embodies (externalizes) the peasant's worst nightmare of the nobleman, the "iron beak" who has "pecked us to death" and with whom, notwithstanding long years of cohabitation in the Dead House, the peasant refuses to shake hands (*PSS* 4:231/360).[86] As such, it is ironically fitting that, in addition to realizing the peasant's worst nightmare of the nobleman, the prefatory narrator articulates (externalizes) the intimate identity of the nobleman with his own worst nightmare of the peasant. As that part of Gorianchikov privileged to keep his distance from the welter of naturalistic truth—a distance which sustains the poetic truth proclaiming the revolutionary necessity of "actually and in fact" turning into the peasant—the prefatory narrator whispers the rumor of a new truth: that of the refined and sensitive Gorianchikov's affinity to the brutal and loutish Shishkov as a murderer who killed his wife out of jealousy in the first year of his marriage.

The interpolated story of Shishkov—unique among the text's peasant-convict narratives for having been given its own chapter ("Akul'ka's Husband—A Story") and which thus exists, as noted earlier, under the sign of a virtual textual quarantine—structurally enacts the maximal psychosocial distancing of the nobleman (Gorianchikov) who overhears the story from the peasant (Shishkov) who tells it.[87] This distancing is underscored by the fact that Gorianchikov introduces Shishkov's narrative as perhaps just a nightmare and by his failure to comment on the content of the story. These unique framing features of "Akul'ka's Husband" render the impression that Shishkov, like the prefatory narrator, has usurped Gorianchikov's first-person prerogative and temporarily taken over his textual existence. Shishkov's graphic narrative of his wife's miserable life and horrifying murder—a tale of abuse in which the peasant woman's own word, a word of forgiveness, is extinguished by salacious lies and rumors—occupies its own clearly demarcated terrain within Gorianchikov's narrative. Crude and brutal, possessed of no resources or refinements with which to inhibit the enactment of a violent impulse, so wholly mired in the squalor of peasant village life as to exist beyond the normative appeals to conscience and to honor, Shishkov is at once human and not human. But this alone does not account for his ontological ambiguity. As the prefatory narrator frames Gorianchikov's story with his introduction-postscript, launching it under the double sign of credibility/insanity, so does Gorianchikov frame Shishkov's, launching it under the double sign of reality/nightmare as he describes how he came one night to overhear the peasant's graphic tale of wife-murder as the two prisoners lie in adjacent bunks in the prison hospital. Just as the introduction-postscript constitutes a perverse imitation of Gorianchikov's ambivalent quest for intimate knowledge of the peasant, so, too, does Shishkov's narrative, "Akul'ka's Husband," make all too present the obliterated center of Gorianchikov's memoirs, the confession (or, as Gorianchikov chooses to call it, the "story") of the unspeakable crime of wife-murder.[88] Only "Akul'ka's Husband" accounts for the prefatory narrator's otherwise inexplicable claim that Gorianchikov's lucid memoir "was interrupted by some kind of other story, by some sort of strange, awful reminiscences, outlined unevenly, spasmodically, as if under some sort of compulsion. I read through these passages several times, and had almost convinced myself that they were written in madness" (*PSS* 4:8). As the prefatory narrator incarnates one significance of the executioner within, he hints at the way in which Shishkov, Gorianchikov's vulgar double, incarnates another.

5. The Narrator's Eclipse

Gorianchikov's most concentrated effort at a "graphic understanding" of crime and punishment occurs in the prison hospital, where the exchange of guards posted in the corridor outside the ward awakens him, causing him to overhear Shishkov's appalling confession. Before this event, bedridden, he had had the leisure and opportunity to conduct some pointed inquiries: "I wanted . . . to know absolutely all the degrees of sentencing and how they were carried out, all the nuances of their execution, the convicts' own view of all this; I tried to picture to myself the psychological condition of those going to punishment" (*PSS* 4:152/233–34). This last statement suggests Gorianchikov's own psychological readiness to begin the process of turning into the common peasant, a readiness actualized in another exchange, that of his convict jacket for a hospital dressing-gown, "utterly filthy" and "saturated with every possible unpleasant bodily fluid," most notably, that which oozed from the wounds of men who had run the gauntlet (*PSS* 4:135/207).

Having donned the bedjacket and entered the locked ward with its tainted atmosphere, Gorianchikov encounters five inmates who, taken together, provide him with something like a psychosocial topography of the prison hospital. His first acquaintance, his neighbor on the ward, is a young man his own age who gives him a detailed account of the hospital procedures. This Virgil, who initiates Gorianchikov into the inner circle of death within death, appears under the sign of forgetfulness: he has forgotten the fact of his crime. In this, the peasant-convict resembles Gorianchikov's fellow nobleman-convict, the punctilious Akim Akimich, described as a man without memories, who also functions as Gorianchikov's Virgil in the Dead House and who also "seemed utterly incapable of genuinely understanding his guilt" (*PSS* 4:105, 27/157–58, 34). Viktor Shklovsky observes that, despite their parting embrace, Gorianchikov describes "with hatred" his fellow nobleman, a man whose eternal excuse is that he was just following orders, and who, in Gorianchikov's typology of convicts, constitutes the sole member of that type who remain "absolutely indifferent" to the question of his guilt and its consequence: that he could not live in freedom (*PSS* 4:208, 323).[89] Likewise, Gorianchikov's hospital neighbor, a "great swindler," takes care to mention before everything else "that he was a captain's son": "He very much wanted to appear a member of the nobility or at least 'well-born.' " "Not at all stupid," this aspiring nobleman yet "with great seriousness believed himself the most honest and upright man in the world and even that he was innocent in every way, and this conviction remained with him forever" (*PSS* 4:132–33/202).

The second person to attach himself to the nobleman is Chekunov, about whom Gorianchikov immediately realizes "that he lied about everything" (*PSS* 4:133/202). Chekunov appoints himself Gorianchikov's servant, hoping to exchange his services for a few kopeks; in so doing, he immediately stirs up resentment toward the nobleman among the other convicts on the ward. One in particular, Ust'iantsev, a peasant-convict who, "in terror of punishment, had drunk up a quantity of tobacco steeped in wine, and thus had contracted tuberculosis" from which he was dying, does not conceal his contempt: "Look at the slave! He's found a master!" (*PSS* 4:133/203). Gorianchikov understands the outburst to be directed not at Chekunov, who is merely making a living, but at himself, and acknowledges that he never managed to avoid the self-appointed servants of *katorga* who "in the end completely mastered me, so that they were in reality my lords and I their servant; by my appearance it somehow came out that I was in fact a gentleman who could not get by without servants and lording it over others" (*PSS* 4:134/205). Thus, in the hospital, an ironic reversal of roles—ironic in relation to the revolutionary call to turn into the peasant—is enacted on the basis of appearance: the nobleman's appearance promotes his enslavement to his servants.

Gorianchikov's gaze comes to rest upon a patient notable not for the sufferings his burning eyes or wasted body bespeak but for the grotesque manner in which he represents his milieu in all its pathos and repulsiveness:

> I remember this nasty old fellow only because he made a certain impression on me then and in one minute managed to give me a rather complete understanding of some peculiarities of the prison ward. This little old geezer, I remember, had a terrible headcold. He sneezed constantly and that whole week sneezed even in his sleep, in volleys, five or six sneezes in a row, scrupulously saying each time: "Lord, what a punishment you've inflicted on me!"

Enthusiastically packing his nose with snuff in order to clear his sinuses more efficiently, the old man "wrinkled up his little nose . . . and the stumps of his old, blackened teeth would come into view together with his red, slobbery gums":

> When he had finished sneezing, he promptly unfolded his handkerchief, attentively inspected the phlegm abundantly deposited in it, and quickly smeared it on his dressing-gown.... This he did all week. (*PSS* 4:135/206)

What he witnesses causes Gorianchikov to shrink in revulsion from his own wrapping, and to begin "with loathing and curiosity" to examine the dressing-gown he had just put on (*PSS* 4:135/207). But unlike his initial inspection of the peasant-convict, undertaken with a similar feeling of "fearful mistrust," the dressing-gown destroys the sense of psychological distance he had until then succeeded in preserving (*PSS* 4:136/207). Even as Gorianchikov shrinks from contact with the redolent gown, crawling with lice, he shrinks from contact with the flesh of the peasant in which he finds himself enveloped, veritably robed in the pain about which he so assiduously inquires. I return to this scene in part 2.

From Gorianchikov's inspection, the dressing-gown emerges as a symbolic composite—startlingly corporeal—of the peasant's agony and affliction in all its grotesqueness of aspect. Combining the pathetic, the tragic, and the ridiculous as it combines "every unpleasant bodily fluid," it functions as a nexus of meanings that provide Gorianchikov with the key to a fearful world of pain, suffering, and forbearance. Having himself, in part by virtue of his class, avoided the gauntlet, his pores absorb the water from the broken blisters on the backs of those who endured it. He initially dons the dressing-gown with an imperfect awareness, a kind of innocence, of the act's significance and implications. By the very act of exchanging one wrapping for another, he finds he has been initiated, all unawares, into his own conviction, having actually, and in fact, been made one with the common peasant: in the dressing gown, he is in his very body.

The dressing-gown is among those objects on which a group of meanings, often paradoxical (the indignity and sublimity of human suffering, for example), converge. As a nexus of meanings, the dressing-gown mobilizes a number of signifieds and forges them into a constellated sign, dense and radiant, which illuminates the text with its manifold significance. The fetters present a similarly layered richness of meaning: their silence as they inertly encircle the leg of the martyred Mikhailov can thus be heard among the clanking of shackles in the bathhouse and on the road to the work station. Likewise, the kopek gathers to itself the redemptive significance of the benevolent village girl who begs Gorianchikov to accept a coin "for Christ's sake," of the passionate piety of the peasant-convict depositing his coveted kopek in the church collection box, and of its equivalence to an individual human soul in a prison legend. The text's oft-cited repetitiveness or circularity of structures of meaning is partly constituted by these constellated signs, through which the universe of *katorga* is transliterated.[90]

"Akul'ka's Husband" represents just such a nexus, except that here, rather than illuminating the text with meaning, convergence marks the site of the extinction of the sign's radiant center—the iconic image of Akul'ka. "Akul'ka's Husband," that is, names the ghastly "story" centrally located in the memoirs, both its main character and its narrator and, the prefatory narrator suggests, the narrator of the memoir that frames it. This perverse concentricity of "Akul'ka's Husband"— an inversion of Kenneth Burke's understanding of the "God-term" as a "Title of Titles," an ideal construct that sums up all particulars and unifies them by conferring meaning upon them—reflects the insidious threat of meaning's absorption by meaninglessness.[91] "Akul'ka's Husband" thus designates a closed system, eternally eclipsed and implosive, the black hole of the memoirs which, even as it tells the annihilation of a crime's significance in the understanding and memory of the one who commits it, threatens to engulf contiguous structures of meaning.

By its very title, "Akul'ka's Husband" (*Akul'kin muzh*) enacts the crime the story is about: the desubjectification of Akul'ka. It announces "a story" where martyr and murderer, wife and husband, struggle for entitlement to the ensuing narrative. Shishkov is named in the title only as Akul'ka's husband; Akul'ka thus delimits his identity, but in the process she loses her own, her name transformed (as is possible with Russian proper nouns) into a modifier of the noun "husband" and conforming to it in gender. Doubly denied, Akul'ka's powerlessness in life is succeeded by her powerlessness in death to break through the infernal circularity of her husband's detailed, but pointless, iteration of her murder, his discursive reenactment of her execution. In the vacuum represented by the interlocutory circuit of Cherevin and Shishkov, the ultimate infernal circularity, the horrifying details of the peasant woman's murder seem to float weightless. One might say that, in "Akul'ka's Husband," Shishkov's accuracy kills the spirit of death's inventory, for accuracy of gruesome detail is his narrative's only characteristic (as it is its only point): it emerges as the text's prime example of a perfectly executed ethnography, telling what Joseph Frank has called "the terrible savagery of Russian peasant customs," if not dispassionately, then with impeccable moral distance.[92] I return to the story of Akul'ka and explore its significance more fully in part 2.

As noted in the first section of this chapter, the lens many critics used to read *House of the Dead* was provided by the conversion hypothesis, which derives in turn from the 1876 *Diary of a Writer* article, "The Peasant Marei," in which Dostoevsky describes having had in the camp a saving memory of one of his father's serfs. The memory of Marei, he wrote, came to him at a point when the conditions of *katorga*, and particularly the unbearable proximity of the peasant, had almost completely unnerved him. In the fullest critical account of the conversion hypothesis, Joseph Frank maintains that "The Peasant Marei" provides Dostoevsky's own account of the "conversion experience" he had had while incarcerated twenty-six years earlier. Like the epistolary "conclusions of his prison-camp meditations" for which Frank had searched in vain, he describes the conversion experience as "the missing pages" of Dostoevsky's novelized prison memoirs: "It is one of the anomalies of *House of the Dead*," he writes, "that Dostoevsky does not include an account of his conversion experience in its pages."[93] He attributes this lapse to a number of hypothetical causes: fear of censorship, unwillingness to expose publicly something deeply personal, a sense that the intimate content of the conversion would detract from the "objective narrative tonality" of the novel.[94] Robert Louis Jackson also upholds "The Peasant Marei" as "a kind of prologue, or vital key, to Dostoevsky's prison work."[95] Pierre Pascal claims on its evidence that "on 24 April 1850, Dostoevsky stopped regarding his new companions with terror," and that "he suddenly felt that he could regard these unfortunates with different eyes: all hatred or rancor had disappeared from his heart."[96]

In "The Peasant Marei," Dostoevsky describes a memory he had in prison, in 1850, about one of his father's peasants who was kind to him as a child, in 1831. "The Peasant Marei" is therefore the recollection of a recollection written at two removes: the core event occurs forty-five years before the time of its narration, and the memory of the core event occurs twenty-five years earlier.[97] This recollection, Dostoevsky wrote in 1876, was epiphanic, coming at a moment when his estrangement from the brutality of his environment and its inhabitants had become insupportable. The unbidden memory of Marei begins with a recollection of a childhood "hallucination": playing alone one day in the woods, he falsely hears someone cry out that a wolf (*volk*) was spotted nearby.[98] The frightened child runs into a clearing where one of his father's peasants, Marei, is working, and Marei—notwithstanding, Dostoevsky notes, that no one was there to witness his kind treatment of the master's son and reward him for it, and notwithstanding that he could not have foreseen his liberation from serf-dom—comforts the terrified boy with a maternal tenderness, "in an empty field [where] only God perhaps saw from above" (*PSS* 22:49). Emerging from the context which memory had so unexpectedly provided, Dostoev-sky looked around him at the brawling peasant-convicts in the new light afforded by his past (involuntarily) recaptured. The unbidden return of the memory of Marei enabled him to see that the peasant-convicts' repul-sive appearance and behavior might conceal a humble and loving Christian soul; the powerfully alienating aspects of these fearful people might be assimilated to the type of peasant with whom Dostoevsky had been famil-iar in childhood. Working with William James's psychological paradigm for conversion, Frank surmises that this regeneration of the writer's child-hood convictions accompanied the collapse of his "psychic-emotive" equi-librium in response to the unendurable physical and mental conditions of life in a hard-labor camp, prominently including the unprecedented proximity to the peasant in whom he is suddenly able to see moral beauty.[99]

As fascinating as the thesis of the conversion experience and subse-quent regeneration of the writer's convictions is, it begs several literary-historical questions. What might Dostoevsky have forgotten of the origi-nal incident, as well as the memory and the scene of remembrance? What might he have added to it for aesthetic and ideological reasons attached to his ambition for his *Diary*'s intervention in the populist polemics of the mid-1870s? Why, having risked the flogging he so dreaded by keep-ing a prison notebook surreptitiously—a notebook in which he recorded instances of peasant speech—would he have failed to record an incident so radiant with saving significance, a point of meaning to which he could have returned in the midst of squalor?[100] Why would he refrain from mentioning it in his first, detailed letter to his brother, Mikhail, or featur-ing it prominently in *Notes from the House of the Dead*, his fullest account of his prison experience on which he began to work upon his release in 1854 and whose reputation was a vital one throughout his life? Ulti-mately, such considerations must persuade us to question the ideological closure that the conversion hypothesis retroactively imposes on this period of the writer's life and work.

If "The Peasant Marei" is read as an artistic rather than an autobio-graphical text, one that explicitly asks to be read in conjunction with *Notes from the House of the Dead*, an alternative ideological significance to that proposed by the conversion hypothesis is revealed. After setting the scene of remembrance—the squalor of the barracks and his fleeing to the yard, his encounter there with the Polish convict Miretsky, the Pole's attempt to bond with the Russian in hatred of "*ces brigands*"[101]—Dostoevsky suddenly observes that,

> up until today I have almost never once spoken in print about my life in *katorga*; I wrote *Notes from the House of the Dead* fifteen years ago, in the name of an invented character, a criminal, who had allegedly murdered his wife. By the way, I will add as a detail that since that time many people think about me and are convinced even today that I was exiled for the murder of my wife. (*PSS* 22:47/352)[102]

The digression serves to mark his readers' tendency to confuse Dostoevsky with his "invented character" Gorianchikov: he notes that many people assume he was punished for the murder of his wife and not for political crime (abolitionist activism), and he also points out—against a dominant critical tendency to disregard the information provided by the prefatory narrator—that Gorianchikov was punished not for political crime but for the murder of his wife. The digression, that is, calls attention to the fact that in the minds of many readers, both lay and critical, he has been made to assume aspects of his invented character's life and his invented character has assumed aspects of Dostoevsky's own; I return to this issue in section 6, below. The border between fiction and reality—the invented or dreamed or remembered and the actual—is a porous one. He then continues with his memory of sliding into remembrance:

> Little by little I really *forgot myself* and *imperceptibly submerged myself* in my memories. In all my four years in *katorga* I *ceaselessly recalled* my entire past and it seemed that in memories I was *reliving* my whole former life anew. These memories *appeared on their own*, I seldom *summoned them at will*. They would begin with some characteristic detail, often unremarkable, and then little by little it would grow into a *whole picture*, into some *strong and integral* impression. I analyzed these impressions, gave new attributes to that which had long ago been played out, and most importantly, corrected, constantly corrected: in this lay my entire amusement. (*PSS* 22:47/352; my emphasis)[103]

Joseph Frank describes this psychological process as one of "involuntary association" and establishes its closeness to the process of literary composition: such associations allowed Dostoevsky, in his distress, to "releas[e] repressed memories and thereby reliev[e] psychic blockages," and it also kept "alive his artistic faculties" by permitting him "to polish and refine scenes and characters as he might have done in writing his stories and novels."[104]

In a manner strikingly similar to this mnemonic-artistic process, Gorianchikov describes his psychological state immediately before overhearing

Shishkov's story which, as already noted, is given its own chapter in the memoirs. The physical atmosphere of the hospital ward intensifies that of the barracks: although the brawling has subsided, to be replaced by the eerie nighttime quiet of the sick ward, the sense of closeness—dim light, fetid air, inmates bored to stupefaction—remains the same and has even increased. The same unbidden materializations of mental images, part dream and part memory, arise:

> You would begin to dream, to remember the past, broad and vivid pictures would be drawn in your imagination; such details would be recalled that at another time you would either not remember or not feel so intensely as now.

Others, similarly suspended between dream and remembrance, would begin to whisper aloud tales of the former life and former self, a narrative that signified above all else that "he himself, the storyteller, was a slice cut from the loaf" (*sam on, rasskazchik,—lomot' otrezannyi*), and that past happiness had definitively receded and could neither return nor be recaptured (*PSS* 4:165/253). At just such a moment of radical estrangement, the self exists in a state of pure suspense, equally alienated from past and future. And in this moment, in which dream, memory, hallucination, and fiction cannot be firmly distinguished, it is equally impossible to distinguish self from other.[105] Gorianchikov "overhears" the narrative "Akul'ka's Husband—A Story [*Rasskaz*]," as if in "some kind of delirious dream, as if I lay in a fever and I dreamt all this in fever, in delirium . . ." (*PSS* 4:165/254; ellipses in original, marking the end of the chapter preceding "Akul'ka's Husband").

Gorianchikov's narration spills over into Shishkov's chapter, but his comments—mostly descriptions of the peasant-convict Shishkov, who for the space of the chapter will assume the narration of *House of the Dead*—are punctuated with ellipses, as if his voice were being gradually overpowered by the voice which, though in the crudest peasant accents, delivers the only sustained, plotted, and continuous narrative in the whole of the memoirs. Gorianchikov describes how one night he was awakened by the changing of guards outside the locked door of the ward. Slowly he became aware of voices whispering close by his cot and guesses that "one prisoner [had begun] to reveal to the other his entire past" (*PSS* 4:166/254). Thus memory begins, and, as with "The Peasant Marei," it begins with an aural hallucination: the faint whisper of Shishkov is the equivalent of the overheard, misheard, cry "Wolf!"—"*Volk!*" (a homonymic invocation of the German term for "the people").[106] Although Gorianchikov claims that at first the words of the "empty" and, as it were, half-conscious ("his eyes were uneasy, and at times seemed somehow dully pensive") Shishkov could barely be heard, still he notices that Shishkov digresses from that which he had set out to tell and allows himself to be sidetracked—perhaps, Gorianchikov surmises, because Shishkov notices or anticipates his audience's disinclination to attribute much importance to his narration (*PSS* 4:166/255). As Gorianchikov's ear accustoms itself to Shishkov's voice, this voice of memory—an almost exaggeratedly loathsome peasant-convict's voice[107]—hits its stride and attains its strong narrative flow, which either overcomes Gorianchikov, silencing him, or before which he allows himself to be silenced. The broad and detailed picture of the murder of a wife out of jealousy in the first year of a marriage does indeed compose itself unbidden and unanticipated. In "Akul'ka's Husband," the peasant's actions are governed not by the rule of Christ— as are Marei's, who treats his master's son lovingly although no one is there to reward him—but by a lie, a tangle of fabrication, rumor, and reputation which overpowers Akul'ka's own word, a word of forgiveness to those who have slandered her. If Dostoevsky would later urge on his readers a therapeutic merging with the people, merging here does not occur voluntarily and does not signify conversion as the birth of the "new man" and the outliving of the old.

In the chapter directly preceding "Akul'ka's Husband," after having ironically remarked that he, the nobleman, had become in *katorga* the slave of slaves eager to do his bidding, Gorianchikov expounds on the role of the executioner in Russian society.[108] This discourse follows (with a rather abrupt transition) his unsuccessful inquiry into the precise quality and feel of the flogged peasant's pain, to which I return in part 2. His thoughts on the executioner merit citing here at length:

> I don't know how it is now, but in the recent past there were gentlemen for whom the possibility of flogging a victim provided something that recalls the Marquis de Sade and Brinvilliers. I think that for such gentlemen there is something in this sensation, at once sweet and painful, that makes their hearts stop. There are people like tigers who thirst for blood. Whoever has once experienced this power, this unlimited dominion over the body, blood and spirit of a human being like himself, a creature just like himself, a brother by the law of Christ; whoever has experienced the power and the absolute possibility of humiliating with the greatest degree of abasement another creature bearing the image of God, has already involuntarily made himself powerless over his own feelings. Tyranny is a habit; it is capable of developing and finally does develop into a disease. I maintain that habit can coarsen and stupefy the very best man to the point of savagery. Blood and power intoxicate: callousness and depravity proliferate; the mind and the heart relent and in the end the most abnormal occurrences are delightful. The human being and the citizen perish forever in the tyrant, and the return to human dignity, to repentance, to rebirth, becomes almost impossible for him (*PSS* 4:154/236–37).

The growth of the executioner within—whose eradication depends upon the recognition of his presence through the offices of conscience (a "revolution," Gorianchikov notes, not so speedily accomplished)—enslaves all of society, including that society whose privileges the executioner's zeal would seem to guarantee:

> Moreover, the example and the possibility of such willfulness infect all of society: such power is seductive. The society that looks with indifference on such things is already itself polluted to its core. In a word, the right of corporal punishment given to one man over another is one of the plagues of society, is among the most potent means for the destruction within it of every incipient attempt at civil society and is the absolute foundation of its certain and incontrovertible disintegration. The professional executioner is abhorred in society, but not the gentleman-executioner. The opposite opinion has been expressed only recently, and so far only in books, abstractly. Even those who express it have not all succeeded in extinguishing in themselves this need for absolute power. (*PSS* 4:154–55/237)

He concludes: "The attributes of the executioner are found in embryo in almost every contemporary human being" (*PSS* 4:155/238). The passage is confession as well as indictment, and is the immediate prelude to Gorianchikov's description of his own psychological condition when he chanced to "overhear" Shishkov's whispered confession.

Gorianchikov's overhearing of the "story" of "Akul'ka's Husband" compels him, with his reader, to bear witness to the ritual reenactment of an innocent woman's execution. The chronotope of *katorga*, as a medium in which such stories are exchanged, emerges as a peculiar time-space continuum in which the ritual reenactment of crime through its narration occurs. Shishkov's confession, if it can be called that, reenacts the crime to which it admits—requiring another confession which is another commission requiring confession ad infinitum—insofar as he lacks any sense of having done wrong in killing or even of having erred in his judgment of his wife's behavior. His agitation in the telling signifies not remorse but simply the resurrection of his wounded pride (more than jealousy), and, inseparable from it, a desire to prove that he exclusively had the right to dispose of his wife as he saw fit without having to explain himself to anyone. The specific horror of Akul'ka's story is not just the viciousness of her murder—the stories of other vicious crimes appear in the course of Gorianchikov's memoirs—and not just the fact of her innocence, but rather an aspect of Shishkov's narration which Gorianchikov mentions as perhaps *katorga*'s greatest mystery: the absence of any sign of repentance in the convicts' confessions or "stories" of their crime. Here, this absence is invested in a speaker strongly individuated by his specific idiom. Although no more antithetical consciousness can be found in the entire cast of the memoirs—Gorianchikov claims that, both before and after over-hearing his story, he "paid little attention to him" and "did not feel drawn to take any interest in him"—Shishkov is, after Gorianchikov, its most voluble presence (*PSS* 4:166/255). Shishkov's sequestration of his act from even the most rudimentary apprehension of its moral significance permits the ritualization through repetition of an innocent's murder. Conversely, the essence of what Gorianchikov at one point calls humane self-extension, a turning or conversion toward those "upon whom the image of God has long been obscured," is to reunite an act and its meaning (*PSS* 4:91/134). As such, it is the essence, too, of that revolution in which the executioner is himself not executed but included (in a vision Ivan Kara-mazov will reject on moral grounds) in the eternal harmony at the end of time when the "murdered man [shall] rise up and embrace his murderer" (*PSS* 14:222). Barring such an act of revolutionary acknowledgment, "Akul'ka's Husband" can only signify the eclipse of significance, a quick-sand of non-possibility, a hole in the fabric that precludes the totality Gori-anchikov seeks to make of his inventory, through accuracy if nothing else.

6. Dostoevsky's Poetics of Conviction

By specifying Gorianchikov's crime as the murder of a wife out of jealousy in the first year of marriage, the prefatory narrator announces the absolute centrality of "Akul'ka's Husband" to Gorianchikov's memoirs. He hints at a fearful symmetry: as he himself personifies (and thus externalizes) Gorianchikov's executioner within whose malignity is directed inward upon the self, he announces Shishkov as the double's double, an embodi-ment of Gorianchikov's inner executioner who targets the other—the "beaten people," the "people without a tongue," the Russian people.[109] Our perception of this symmetry relies on our acknowledgment of the discrepancy between the prefatory narrator's account of Gorianchikov's crime and the latter's own. In the history of the text's reception, however, both the symmetry and the discrepancy, if they have not gone entirely unnoticed, have either been explained away as Dostoevsky's oversight or error, or have led readers to supply another symmetry in its place with inevitable and significant consequences for our understanding of the text's genre. It will be useful to review briefly each critical path in turn.

Not unlike the conversion hypothesis itself, critical attempts to explain away the contradiction between the two accounts of Gorianchikov's crime often rely on speculation. Thus, Leonid Grossman writes: "It appears that he had conceived these celebrated memoirs not simply as sketches of the Omsk prison, but in combination with another agonizing, terrifying story. According to Dostoevsky's compressed account, this exile's notebook contained the story of an unrestrained passion, of insane jealousy, of the inevitable murder of an ardently loved woman—perhaps a remote antici- pation of the story of Rogozhin and Nastasya Filippovna [*The Idiot*]." (Dostoevsky's "compressed account" of the "exile's notebook" refers to the prefatory narrator's description of Gorianchikov's manuscript which he cites.) But, Grossman conjectures, Dostoevsky abandoned this "roman- tic theme," and the text he had originally envisioned "broke up into a series of sketches with psychological studies and inserted stories."[110] Grossman's words invoke, of course, not an unwritten story or an "aban- doned" one (which is also the prefatory narrator's assumption) but the sensational story at the text's center, "Akul'ka's Husband," which Frank surmises was originally intended as "a peasant version of Romeo and Juliet and Othello." Given this characterization of "Akul'ka's Husband" (based upon the "poetic exchange between Fil'ka and Akul'ka" that redeems "for a moment, with a flash of the purest and most exalted sentiment, the ap- palling world of peasant ferocity amidst which the action is set"), it is not surprising that Frank, like Grossman, also posits the absence in the mem- oirs of some "strange and terrible reminiscences," as the prefatory narrator had described them.[111] Even when they resonate with the individual read- er's own intuitions, however, such claims beg the question of Dostoevsky's reasons for retaining these references once his plans for the novel had changed. As late as 1875, he reviewed *Notes from the House of the Dead* for republication, making several stylistic changes, dividing the text into two parts, and titling the introduction as such (*PSS* 4:278).

Although with divergent rationales, both the text's naïve first readers and a number of its most astute modern critics have responded to the problematic discrepancy between the prefatory narrator's and Gorianchi- kov's accounts of the latter's crime not by identifying Gorianchikov with Shishkov but by conflating him with Dostoevsky. The result has explicitly been to purge Gorianchikov from the memoirs. Thus, as we have seen, Dostoevsky wryly noted his readers' uncritical assumption that not the fictional Gorianchikov but he himself had been exiled to hard labor for murdering his wife.[112] The nineteenth-century reader's impulse surfaces in contemporary critical arguments for Gorianchikov's superfluity. The Soviet editors of *The Complete Works* [*PSS*], for example, propose that Dos- toevsky was constrained by the tsarist censorship to invent, and then to eliminate by "forgetting," his narrator:

> Gorianchikov, who goes to prison for the murder of his wife, is not identified with the author of the story who, as is already evident by the second chapter, is a political prisoner. Beginning with this chapter, Dostoevsky narrates (*Dos- toevskii vedet rasskaz ot sebia*), having forgotten about the narrator: he speaks about his meeting in Siberia with the wives of the Decembrists, about receiv-

ing a Bible from them, the only book allowed in prison, about meeting with "old school friends," about reading books.

The editors conclude that although "Dostoevsky introduces Alexander Petrovich Gorianchikov to the reader as the author of the *Notes*," he remains "purely conventional [*uslovnyi*]": here we see the substitution of the author for his prefatory narrator who introduces the reader to Gorianchikov as the author of the memoir (*PSS* 4:289). After listing a long series of autobiographical references found in the text, they reason that "all of this precludes our viewing Gorianchikov as an independent character" (*PSS* 4:289). Similarly, the biographer Mochulsky states: "The fiction of the narrator-prisoner Alexander Petrovich Gorianchikov cannot deceive; everywhere is heard the voice of Dostoevsky, an eye-witness of the events."[113]

At the same time, however, the editors of the *Complete Works* discuss Alexander II's grant of amnesty for political prisoners in 1856, and the concomitant easing of the censorship concerning works about prison: "It became possible to write about *katorga*" (*PSS* 4:276).[114] This observation is directly supported by the memoirs of A. Miliukov, the author of a highly favorable review of *House of the Dead* who described the circumstances surrounding the text's publication in his volume, *Literary Meetings and Acquaintances*:

> This work came out under circumstances that were quite favorable; the censorship at that time was animated by a breath of tolerance and in literature works appeared which until recently were still unthinkable in print. Although the novelty of the book, devoted exclusively to the mode of convict life, the somber canvas of all these stories about terrible evildoers and, lastly, the fact that the author himself was a political criminal who had just returned, somewhat disturbed the censor, yet this, notwithstanding, did not force Dostoevsky to deviate in anything from the truth, and *Notes from the House of Death* produced a startling impression. In the author they saw as it were a new Dante who had descended into hell, the more horrible in that it existed not in a poet's imagination, but in reality.[115]

Despite such evidence for a relaxation of the censorship, the editors as well as other influential scholars insist that its deformative power mandated Dostoevsky's contrivance and then abandonment, *in medias res*, of a narrator. Joseph Frank, rejecting the notion that Dostoevsky had some "artistic" purpose for allowing the discrepancy on the point of Gorianchikov's crime to stand, agrees with the "accepted view" that the conditions imposed by the censorship account for its perdurance. According to this view, Gorianchikov was meant to be seen as nothing more "than a convenient device." Frank notes that the contemporaneous prison memoirs of F. N. L'vov make use of a similar fictitious narrator, and that a later ex-convict memoirist, P. F. Iakubovich, had claimed that the writer does not intend that the "disguise" (i.e., the narrator) will fool the reader; rather, the idea is "to use an obvious and well-worn stereotype."[116] However, if Dostoevsky's strategy was to interpolate Gorianchikov as a transparent fiction with which to shield him from the censors and yet keep his readers in the know, the latter's conviction that he had indeed murdered his wife suggests that it grievously misfired. Frank's explanation also fails to address the question of Dostoevsky's arbitrarily assigning this particular crime to Gorianchikov. He seems to suggest that it was chosen only because the crime was so preposterous that it would immediately alert the reader to its function as transparent fiction: "It was important, above all, that the readers have no doubts about the veracity of his account; and so Dostoevsky eschewed all 'novelistic' effects, and developed his own original variation of the larger sketch forms used by the Russian writers he admired."[117] Perhaps Dostoevsky's own observations, an 1861 retort to the Utilitarian critics who attempted to sever a literary text's social message from its artistry, provide the best response to this proposition: "To what purpose then is artistry? Why, when all is said and done, write stories? Wouldn't it be simpler to write that such a fact exists among the common people, for this reason and that—it's shorter, clearer, more solid! 'And here you are still telling stories! These people must have nothing to do!' "(*PSS* 18:80).

As Frank's remarks make clear, whatever the critic's view of the role played by the Russian censorship in its formulation, the question of Gorianchikov's ontological status (is he independent of, identified with, or identical to Dostoevsky?) is related to, and indeed almost inextricable from, the critical disagreement concerning the genre of *House of the Dead*. To the degree that Gorianchikov is purged, the novel succeeds in eschewing its fictionality to achieve the authenticity of autobiography, and to the degree that he maintains a strong presence in the text, its autobiographical integrity is, for better or for worse, compromised.[118] Thus, the uncharacteristic ambivalence of the Russian critic V. A. Tunimanov: even while claiming that the text achieves an "organic fusion" of art and autobiography—both a "truthful representation" of prison life, and a "story of documentary precision [*dokumental'no tochnyi rasskaz*]"—he understands fusion as requiring the complete negation of Gorianchikov, whom he, too, says Dostoevsky "forgets."[119] The opposite assumption underlies Marius Teofilov's argument that, "in the memoir, the authorial 'I' is given from the point of view of the memoirist himself. But Dostoevsky eliminates himself as a player, eliminates his biography, his 'crime,' and the narrative loses the generic principle of the memoir."[120] Even critics who would abjure the either/or formulation of Gorianchikov/Dostoevsky; fiction/autobiography find it difficult to do so.[121] Frank insists that Dostoevsky preserves the "double perspective" of fiction and memoir, but he also argues that Dostoevsky sought to preserve an "objective narrative tonality" and was willing to curb manifestations of Gorianchikov's personality in order to do so. To regard him seriously as "the genuine narrator of *House of the Dead*" is to be forced to "charge [Dostoevsky] with unforgivable carelessness" and to "accuse" him "of allowing a disturbing clash to occur between his theme as a whole and the frame narration in which it is contained."[122] Ironically, the critical insistence on the innocence of Gorianchikov's self-representation, tantamount to his innocence of any criminality and manifested in an objectivity so absolute as to enable his elimination as the narrating subject, ultimately entails the indictment of the writer, Dostoevsky's re-arraignment.

In sum, the rhetoric of sacrifice—of superfluity, elimination, and forgetting—justified by an assumption of transparency (of Gorianchikov to his self-representation, of Gorianchikov to Dostoevsky or vice versa) is a constant of such critical speculation about the narrator's ontological status. It is likewise fundamental, within both the text and Dostoevsky's own biography, to the related assumption of the common people's transparency to the nobility's conceptions of them whose falsity as optical illusion the memoir painfully establishes. The elimination by critical fiat of the problem posed by Gorianchikov, the problem of crime, not only erases the significance of Gorianchikov's failure to acknowledge his crime, and thus his failure to repent, central to both the text's content and its structure. It also entails a dismissal—in the form of an elision—of the intimately related "inner process" by which Dostoevsky painfully transformed himself in the years between *Notes from the House of the Dead* and "The Peasant Marei" from one who could characterize the peasant-convict directly after his release as "coarse, angry, and embittered" to a champion, in a sense radically different from his pre-Siberian years, of the common people.[123] As a result, the aesthetic innovation involved in displacing into competing narratives the voice of a first-person narrator which Dostoevsky used to explore this inner transformation is similarly elided.[124] Only by ignoring or explaining away the testimony of the prefatory narrator and the uncanny similarity of Gorianchikov's and Shishkov's crimes can one emerge from *House of the Dead* imbued with the conviction that the abyss of class difference can be eradicated by an act of good will (even if that act is generated by a shock, the traumatic loss of one's privileged identity). Instead, one emerges from the narrative of the dead house with a powerful sense of the question that hangs in the balance: what epistemological and ideological value inheres in estrangement as a means of defamiliarizing one's own habitual blindness in order to see one's non-seeing—in Gorianchikov's case, to see for the first time the profundity of that obstacle to sight, the abyss of class difference?

In a brilliant study of secular confession, J. M. Coetzee helpfully redefines
the point of the undertaking: it is not so much a matter of telling the truth
about the self as it is a matter of learning "how to know the truth about
the self without being self-deceived." The truth is not given in advance
but is the elusive object of confession. Following Francis R. Hart, Coetzee
differentiates the genre into three subgenres according to the motive for
seeking the truth: memoir seeks to demonstrate the self's historicity (cultural-historical); apology seeks to realize the self's integrity (ethical); and
confession seeks to express the essential nature or truth of the self (ontological), and is thus the "subgenre of the novel in which problems of truth-
telling and self-recognition, deception and self-deception, come to the
forefront."[125] At the center of the confessions that Coetzee examines (including *Notes from the Underground*) is an abhorrent act committed by the
narrator.[126] In *Notes from the House of the Dead*, Dostoevsky orchestrates all
three motives in the triple-layered narrative structure we have examined,
such that the memoir may be correlated with the first (experiential/cul-
tural-historical) level, apology with the third (ideological/ethical) level,
and confession with the mediate (ontological) level of narration through
which the merging of Gorianchikov and Shishkov is accomplished. Coetzee's analysis of confession and the way in which it maps on to the layered
structure of Gorianchikov's first-person narrative denies the validity of the
fiction/autobiography binary, and obviates the sacrificial choice—Gorianchikov or Dostoevsky— this binary has entailed in the history of the text's
reception, making it possible to credit Dostoevsky's artistic decision to
insert such disturbing discrepancies into his novel.

The merging of Gorianchikov and Shishkov in Dostoevsky's first novel
prefigures the murderous collaboration central to his last, that of Ivan
Karamazov and the peasant-lackey Smerdiakov, and is equally indispensable to illuminating its core mystery, the mystery of crime. What does this
merging signify in the context established in this chapter of the disarticulation of the narrating subject, the subject of knowledge, hailed in Dostoevsky's time as its "Livingstone" and its "Virgil." There are two avenues for
exploring the meaning of this mutation of the narrative, one allegorical,
to which the remainder of part 1 is devoted, and the other more germane
to the pressing question of ontology negatively raised in current criticism,
to which I turn in part 2 of this volume. The latter avenue, as we will see,
requires that we shift our attention from the narrating subject, Gorianchikov, to his impenetrable object, the peasant-convict, who repels him both
socially and aesthetically, who instigates the loss of self-possession literal-
ized in the eclipse of his voice which we have tracked in this first part
of the book, and who foils his attempts to supply himself with a stable
epistemological footing while in the alien environment of *katorga*.

The critical choice to pursue an autobiographical rather than an allegorical reading of Gorianchikov's crime stands out in a text whose fictionalization of its author's experience has in other instances been recognized without undue concern or confusion. Only in this matter of the nature of the crime committed by the nobleman has the possibility of its fictive or allegorical embellishment been met with such resistance; critics who raise the issue of crime often simply refer readers to the facts of Dostoevsky's own exile and punishment for his participation in the revolutionary society of the Petrashevtsy. This critical resistance is doubly astonishing in light of Dostoevsky's well-known post-Siberian assessments of his participation in both that group and the more radical sub-circle led by Nikolai Speshnev and dedicated to revolution on behalf of, and ultimately by, the enslaved peasantry. In his later fictive, epistolary, and journalistic pronouncements on the subject of the radical agenda that he himself had once embraced—documents that critics have not hesitated to make ample use of to support the conversion hypothesis—Dostoevsky emphasized his belief that such activity, ostensibly undertaken on behalf of the peasants, constituted a grievous affront to them insofar as it signaled an ignorance of and a disregard for them as a "literate people" (as they describe themselves here) as well as a usurpation of their own preeminently religious agenda.[127] In this regard, the critics have shown themselves complicit in the nobleman's indifference to the actuality of his own criminal involvement, a willed ignorance that Dostoevsky will show (in *Crime and Punishment* and *The Idiot*) leads to a vague ideology of what might be described as the gentrification of crime.[128]

In order to regard Shishkov as Gorianchikov's double, to recognize his voice with its strange peasant accents as the final resting place for the narrator's own estranged voice, and thus its projection into that which is utterly foreign to the self-concept of the noble-speaking subject, one need not maintain that Gorianchikov had ever grabbed his wife by her long braids, jerked back her head, and coldbloodedly slit her throat. Nor need one eliminate the problem posed by the text's ambiguous representation of Gorianchikov's criminality by maintaining that its autobiographical or ethnographic integrity requires that the reader "forget" him (or, relatedly, that a redemptive reading of Dostoevsky's prison experience requires that the trauma of estrangement he suffered be "sublimated"). Such critical moves dismiss, by eliding, the intimately related inner process by which Dostoevsky painfully transformed himself in the years between his arrest and his later self-fashioning as a champion of the common people in a sense radically different from his pre-Siberian years. Additionally, to the extent that it ignores or explains away the text's explicit identification of Gorianchikov as a wife-murderer with the peasant Shishkov, this influential critical line ironically returns the common people to a cultural obscurity from which Dostoevsky's orchestration of vocal displacement had begun to draw them. In place of this sacrificial critical logic, in which either the narrator or the common people he encounters are consigned to oblivion, another possibility for understanding the relationship of Gorianchikov to Shishkov presents itself. In order to regard the vicious peasant as an embodiment of the nobleman's executioner within, who demonstrates neither recognition of his crime nor repentance for it (a mark, it is implied, of Shishkov's radical class otherness), one need only recognize in "Akul'ka's Husband" an allegorical expression of the nobleman's crime against the peasant, a crime born of willful ignorance.

As it evolved, Dostoevsky's critique of the radical agenda for revolutionary reform was that it betrayed an ignorant disregard of the peasant's own word—a policy of silencing the helpmate in the belief that one knows what is best for her: the substitution of the master's word for her own.[129] The peasant's peculiar "literacy" (*gramotnost'*)—that which expresses the distinctiveness of peasant culture and which uniquely expresses its inner life—is obliterated by the progressive's "bookishness" (*knizhnost'*), a merely theoretical knowledge betrayed by its own vulgarity.[130] Shishkov can thus be said to share with the outwardly blameless figure of the gentleman-convict a common enjoyment of "unlimited mastery over the body, blood and soul" of another, and the "unqualified opportunity to degrade another being with the utmost humiliation" by substituting, for the words of their victims, lies, fabrications, and false assumptions about the other's "true nature" (*PSS* 4:154/237). Like Akul'ka, her life erased by her unwitnessed death in the Russian *glush'* or backwoods (a word that shares its root with the verb "to muffle, to stifle, to suppress" and the adjective "deaf, indistinct, voiceless"), the peasant, through the nobleman's good offices, "disappears, is destroyed, is reduced, as it were, to nothing. But not all of a sudden, not by disappearing into the earth with thunder and lightning, but, as it were, delicately, smoothly, imperceptibly sinking into nullity."[131] Such an allegorical reading may illuminate one circumstance of the publishing history of *Notes from the House of the Dead*. "Akul'ka's Husband" was separately printed in an 1863 collection whose editor ended the confession of Shishkov not with silence, as did Dostoevsky, and not by invoking the "poetic truth" of returning spring, but with a phrase pulled from the very end of Gorianchikov's testament: "And this is just the point: who is guilty? [*To-to, kto vinovat?*]" The publishers of the collection straightforwardly placed this sentence where it would have its starkest effect, directly following Shishkov's confession. The sale of the collection was subsequently forbidden, and unsold copies were confiscated and burned (*PSS* 4:296–97).

In a sense, only the prefatory narrator survives Gorianchikov's experience to tell his tale, and what he has to tell undermines (in part, by superseding) the noble ex-convict's own conclusion: that his release was a re-birth, and he emerged from the house of the dead a new man. The prefatory narrator tells us that, so conceived, Gorianchikov's conversion was incomplete, interrupted, unconsummated. The necessity of conversion which Gorianchikov urges on his reader, in his case initially compelled by the outward circumstance of arrest and incarceration, is articulated as (and, in another sense, made possible by) his conviction that, unless the noble class voluntarily undertakes this turning, they will see an optical illusion in place of the Russian people's true essence. It is worth noting that nowhere in his memoirs does Gorianchikov claim to see this essence. Instead, he represents the intensity of his efforts to see, a striving stimulated by his hard-won realization of the profundity of his own blindness. Gorianchikov warns his reader that in the face of the tyranny of habit and the habit of tyranny, "rebirth"—and indeed that other kind of turning, "revolution" (*perevorot*)—are not so easily achieved (*PSS* 4:154, 155/237). The endurance of his own estrangement as he describes it in *Notes from the House of the Dead* bears this out. Gorianchikov sees no basis for identifying himself with Shishkov—the only other convict who stands accused of murdering his wife from jealousy in the first year of marriage—and is tempted to regard the peasant's "story" as the product of his own delirium: it is disowned, deflected, never incorporated into the narrative proper. To the degree that it remains unassimilable, inadmissible, Gorianchikov's conversion must be incomplete: as the prefatory narrator complacently concludes of Gorianchikov, "he was his own worst enemy" (*PSS* 4:6/3). The failure to own the story at the heart of his memoir leaves the image of the new man unconsummated. It is not despite but within Gorianchikov's estrangement, through the extended contrivance of self-displacement—the machinations of the self deviating from the self—that the promise of a novel regeneration must be sought.

Part II

BUILDING OUT THE HOUSE OF THE DEAD

I made a few banal comments on our so improbable salvation:
We were men sentenced to death and freed on the
guillotine's platform, wasn't that true?
—Primo Levi, *The Drowned and the Saved*

1. The Chronotope of *Katorga*

The sequential sentences Dostoevsky received on 22 December 1849 in Semenovsky Square with their two scenarios of punishment—the sentence of death commuted to exile and penal servitude—transformed his life radically in the space of an afternoon. Although the writer's death did not literally occur, one may speak of three experiential variations on it that disallow our thinking of death here as a mere figure: mock execution, *mort civile*, and the compensatory idea of conversion, death leading to rebirth, which Dostoevsky invokes in his letter to his brother on the eve of exile. In part 1 we examined the relation of the mock execution to conversion: the traumatic event does not resolve itself in the simple, if spirited, vow to be "reborn for the better" but reproduces its own distortion—its unconsummated structure—in the project of rebirth as it was enacted both ontologically and aesthetically. It generates not closure and fulfillment but a prolonged suspense, the opening up of a space between the death of the "old man" and the rebirth of the "new."

In *The Idiot* (1868), Dostoevsky famously invoked the trauma of the mock execution as the opening of an anomalous temporal space when Prince Myshkin tells the Epanchin women, on his first visit, about having met a man who had suffered the writer's fate: "This man had once been led to a scaffold, along with others, and a sentence of death by firing squad was read out to him, for a political crime. After about twenty minutes a pardon was read out to him, and he was given a lesser degree of punishment." . . . The Prince continues: "for the space between the two sentences [. . .] he lived under the certain conviction that in a few minutes he would suddenly die" (*PSS* 8:51/60).[1] This interval (*promezhutok*), Myshkin reports his acquaintance saying, was marked by an unbearable "loathing for this new thing that would be and would come presently" (*PSS* 8:52/61). The hopeless loathing of a living human being faced with imminent death, unique to capital punishment, constitutes "an outrage on the soul," as Myshkin passionately insists (*PSS* 8:20/22). Although *The Idiot* is famous for this autobiographical allusion, Dostoevsky stages the space opened up by the mock execution far more extensively in the 1861 novel *Notes from the House of the Dead*.[2] Moreover, he allows his fictional witness, the traumatized inhabitant of this space, to speak to us far more directly and amply.

The mock execution forced Dostoevsky to experience fully the terror of capital punishment without physical death; it was doubly aberrant within the terms of the Penal Code of 1845, which allowed for the death penalty only under exceptional circumstances but which expected that if those circumstances were met and the sentence of death pronounced the execution would be consummated.[3] Its inane solemnity (to which Leonid Grossman referred as Nicholas I's stagecraft) deepened its aura of the grotesque to which was superadded the mystical horror or "loathing" attending the experience of imminent death. In this lay the mock execution's extraordinary sadism.[4] The traumatic if symbolic death of *mort civile* expunged Dostoevsky's social identity through the ritual divestment of his class privileges (*lishenie prav*)—most significant, the nobleman's exemption from corporal punishment—followed by Siberian exile (he describes himself as "leaving for the wilds, deep into Asia") and incarceration in a forced labor camp (*PSS* 28 [I]: 177/69).[5] His new, radically liminal existence rendered his former position—as an up-and-coming intellectual and artist, a nobleman, a progressive, a human being among other human beings—null and void. Cut off perhaps forever from his past life, his ability to shape or even to imagine a future was severely compromised, his brave words to his brother in the letter of 22 December notwithstanding. The aporia at the heart of this exceptional state was that, although Dostoevsky had not physically died, his life along with the social and political identity attached to it no longer existed.[6] As he expressed it throughout his years in exile, he felt he had become merely "a slice cut from the loaf" (*lomot' otrezannyi*), "a stone tossed aside" (*kamen' otbroshennyi*).[7] He would give precisely these words to his first-person narrator in *House of the Dead*, Alexander Petrovich Gorianchikov, who uses such expressions to describe both himself and the peasant-convicts of the forced labor camp, *katorga*, which thus may be said to constitute a community of human fragments.

Precisely this exceptional quality of Dostoevsky's life after "death" brings to mind Giorgio Agamben's recent political-philosophical analysis of the "state" or "space of exception" and the figure who inhabits it, *homo sacer* or "sacred man," and suggests the potential usefulness of these concepts as an alternative to the vocabulary of transcendence or miraculous reconciliation for fathoming the writer's existential state and his relation to the environment of *katorga* in the aftermath of the mock execution (*HS* 9). *Homo sacer* is a figure of ancient Roman law, " 'one whom the people have judged on account of a crime' " (*HS* 71).[8] His sacredness was encompassed by this mysterious discrepancy: although not executed by the sovereign power that condemned him, he could yet be killed by anyone with impunity; moreover, though his murder would not count as a homicide or as sacrilege, he was ineligible to serve as the consecrated victim of religious sacrifice. Although the sovereign refrains from killing him, anyone else may; although anyone else may, the priest may not as part of a religious rite. His life counted only as "bare life"—a naked and anonymous life to which no extra value or significance could attach by means of any of the "sanctioned forms of execution," whether civil or religious (*HS* 102).[9] Bare life signifies not a merely natural existence ("the simple fact of living common to all living beings") but the "residual and irreducible" life of one "abandoned," cast out, and "exposed to death" (*HS* 1, 100, 109, 88).[10] Agamben proposes that this "state of exception" to which *homo sacer* is consigned by the sovereign ban is "an originary *political* structure" and the ban itself "the original political act" (*HS* 74). Nicholas I's mock execution enacts in the mid-nineteenth century just such a primitive gesture of absolute power: he subjects the members of the Petrashevsky circle to its pointless cruelty because he can.[11]

The mock execution seems, in fact, an astonishing literalization of Agamben's philosophico-historical eduction of the figure of *homo sacer* from the depths of antiquity: it performed with spectacular drama both the power and the refusal to execute. It is of a piece with Dostoevsky's actual punishment, *mort civile* as the deprivation of the nobleman's normative exemption from corporal punishment and the subsequent ejection to a zone—*katorga*, or the house of the dead—where life counts only as bare life, as life that can be killed. Dostoevsky's sentence formalized his capacity to be killed in some form of unpunished violence, "profane and banal," exercised either by the lower prison authorities (like the drunken and sadistic Major V. G. Krivtsov, who constantly threatened to have him flogged) or by his fellow inmates in *katorga* whom he described to his brother upon his release as "one hundred and fifty enemies [who] never tired of tormenting" him and his fellow noblemen-convicts (*HS* 114).[12] His autobiographical fiction of his experience of abandonment in the space of exception, *Notes from the House of the Dead*, is dedicated largely to the representation of "bare life" in its irreducibility as he and his fellow convicts lived it in *katorga*.[13] Dostoevsky regarded his experience of this life beyond life, his hard-won ability to represent it from within, as key to the successful resurrection of his post-Siberian career. Moreover, after *House of the Dead*, he continued to probe the existential, spiritual, and political significance of "bare life": from *Crime and Punishment* to *The Brothers Karamazov*, each of the great novels interrogates the significance of killing when it constitutes, as Agamben says, "neither capital punishment nor a sacrifice, but simply the actualization of a mere 'capacity to be killed' "— the essence of a social order whose credo, as Raskolnikov formulates it, is that "everything is permitted" (*HS* 114).[14]

We may say, then, that Dostoevsky's mature work is inaugurated by the chronotope of *katorga*. Specifically, through the offices of the literary text Dostoevsky literalizes what Agamben calls the space of exception by giving it poetic form as a novel chronotope, the "house of the dead," which prolongs and extends across the novel's time-space coordinates a dreadful moment that assumes the dimensions of a world, a world in which the most extreme opposites, life and death, all but coexist.[15] *Katorga* is the materialization of that space of exception to which a "living dead man," Dostoevsky as *homo sacer*, a slice cut from the loaf, a stone tossed aside, is sent to live "a bare life that has been separated from its context and that, so to speak surviving its death, is for this very reason incompatible with the human world" (*HS* 131, 100).[16] Agamben's philosophical representations of the state or space of exception and *homo sacer* have garnered significant attention from theorists in many disciplines, and the heuristic value of his concepts for thinking about the mock execution and its carceral aftermath is evident on its face.

At the same time, however, Dostoevsky's detailed literary investigation of the space of exception, invested with a material and sociological specificity absent in Agamben's work, powerfully revises a number of the latter's premises and conclusions. As the novelist represents it, the space of exception is a spiritual and psychological state, but it is also an actual penal environment inhabited by a specific outcast population. In the following two sections, I examine the challenge posed by the Dostoevskian text to two key features of Agamben's analysis of *homo sacer* and the state of exception. In the first instance, it controverts the historical legitimacy of the philosopher's restriction of focus to the Greco-Roman West as well as the teleology it underwrites that links the sovereign ban of antiquity to the Nazi lager by routing it through the development of an Anglo-French discourse on human rights in the eighteenth century. In the second instance, it revises Agamben's ontology of *homo sacer* through the reconceptualization of crime as an ontological category. Agamben's work provides an alternative paradigm to the conversion theory for understanding the significance of the mock execution and its aftermath, but Dostoevsky, most remarkably in *Notes from the House of the Dead*, emerges as a powerful shaper of that paradigm.

2. Exception, Equality, Emancipation

> "Why are we here?
> We're alive, but not human beings;
> we're dead, but not gone. Oh!"
> —*PSS* 4:246[17]

Russian political modernity may be said to begin in 1855, midway through Dostoevsky's decade of exile, with the transition from the repressive regime of the infamously autocratic Nicholas I (itself launched in 1825 by the rebellion of enlightened aristocrats known as the Decembrists) to that of the "Tsar-Liberator," the liberal and reform-minded

Alexander II.[18] To this transition we owe the irony that the crime for which Nicholas had condemned the writer to penal servitude in December 1849, his desire for peasant emancipation, had become the cornerstone of Alexander's reformist agenda and was a fait accompli when Dostoevsky returned to western Russia in December 1859.[19] The mature period of his career coincides precisely with Alexander's reign: the tsar's reforms, as is well known, released the revolutionary democratic energies of the nation's *raznochintsy* or non-noble intelligentsia whose suppression would lead in turn to the assassination of the tsar in 1881 (Dostoevsky died six weeks earlier) and to his successors' determined attempts to shore up an increasingly embattled autocracy until the 1917 Revolution.[20] That event intensified the previous century's alternation of repression and reform. Perhaps the starkest and most pertinent example is the revolutionary Provisional Government's abolition, in 1917, of the system of Siberian slave labor, *katorga*, which one historian has dubbed "the tsarist archipelago of punishment," followed by the Soviet construction of the gulag, beginning (as Alexander Solzhenitsyn insisted) with Stalin's decision to collectivize peasant agriculture in 1929.[21]

In *Homo Sacer*, Agamben makes two controversial claims about Western political modernity that resonate with this very brief sketch of Russian political modernity. The first is that democracy and totalitarianism evince a "curious contiguity"—even an "inner solidarity"—which is revealed by the rapid conversion in the twentieth century of Western parliamentary democracies into totalitarian states and "almost without interruption" their conversion back after the Second World War (*HS* 121, 122).[22] Combining the insights and limitations of Michel Foucault on "biopolitics" ("the growing inclusion of man's natural life in the mechanisms and calculations of power") and of Hannah Arendt on the genesis and structure of totalitarian states as well as her evaluation of the peculiar status of refugees, Agamben provocatively ascribes this lability of modern political forms in the West to eighteenth-century doctrines of inalienable natural rights and the development of the concept of citizenship (*HS* 119, 120):

> Declarations of rights represent the originary figure of the inscription of natural life in the juridico-political order of the nation-state. The same bare life that in the *ancien régime* was politically neutral and belonged to God as creaturely life and in the classical world was (at least apparently) clearly distinguished as *zoe* from political life (*bios*) now fully enters into the structure of the state and even becomes the earthly foundation of the state's legitimacy and sovereignty. (*HS* 127)

Agamben's second controversial claim, premised on the biopolitical significance of rights doctrine, is presented as the logical (if unforeseen) consequence of the first: "it is not the city but rather the camp that is the fundamental biopolitical paradigm of the West" (*HS* 181). The claim, then, is that the *telos* of the state of exception of antiquity, routed through the ethos of human rights codified in the eighteenth century, the age of democratic revolution, is the twentieth-century totalitarian camp. The emphasis on bare life as the ground of human equality celebrated and enshrined in the West's founding rights documents reaches its ironic apotheosis when the cosmopolitan city of twentieth-century Europe falls away to reveal the camp as *fundus* ("hidden foundation") and destination (*HS* 9). The state of exception, originally linked by the sovereign ban to a state of emergency or siege, becomes in the twentieth century the norm (*HS* 20, 168–69).[23]

Especially because Agamben himself invokes Arendt's insistence on Stalinism's "affinity" with National Socialism, the enabling role he assigns to an Enlightenment discourse of rights in the emergence of the totalitarian camp begs the question of the Soviet gulag (*HS* 148). Although there is little reason to critique Agamben's claims from the point of view of the historiography he explicitly excludes in making them, the Russian parallel demands closer consideration. In its tsarist and communist phases, Russia has shared with the West both the alternation of repressive and progressive regimes and the phenomenon of the camp—not as the culture's unthinkable *telos* but rather as a staple feature of its political life from the inception of Peter the Great's Westernizing innovations in the first quarter of the eighteenth century.[24] As there can be no question of ascribing these circumstances to the influence of a philosophy of rights inalienably inherent in our very humanity and protected by the state, we must ask what alternative notion of human equality in bare life underwrites them, and particularly the camp, as Russia's fundamental biopolitical paradigm.[25] Although a full examination of this question is beyond the scope of this book, its application to Dostoevsky's work allows us, first, to retain the chronotopic clarity of Agamben's notion of a "state" or "space of exception" while transcending its limitations, and, second, to explore the ontology and ethico-political significance of *homo sacer* which he leaves relatively undeveloped.

In Russia, bare life was inscribed in the juridico-political order most unambiguously through the laws that instituted slavery, although the practice of slavery preexisted by two centuries its codification in the late seventeenth through the first half of the eighteenth century.[26] Bare life was thus not politically neutral and belonged not to God but, with the sanction of the state, to the landowner, characterized by Alexander Herzen as "the whipper-of-men, who mixes up in his concept of property the garden plot and the peasant woman, boots and the village elder."[27] Even for those not enslaved, the "twelve million people *hors la loi*," Russia recognized no legal rights, natural or contractual, and thus there existed only the most attenuated concept of citizenship or, for that matter, the rule of law.[28] The historian Raymond Pearson writes that "the most that tsarism would entertain was the availability of 'privilege' for select groups on a class, occupational, or territorial basis":

> Literally operating as a kind of "private law," privilege was the discrimination of advantage sanctioned on the understanding that it in no way compromised the autocratic powers of the tsar and could therefore be cancelled by authority at will, unilaterally, without explanation, and without legal redress. [. . .] To the bitter end, tsarism expected and exacted unconditional duties from its subjects, offering in return only the possibility of group privilege. Little hope of "contractual rights" between sovereign and citizen was extended, and no prospect of the voluntary recognition of "natural" or "human" rights was ever contemplated.[29]

While the sanctity of bare life as such was never assumed, caste privileges, too, were always outside the law, always ad hoc, always the exemplary sovereign gesture, and in that sense, perhaps, the obverse of the sovereign ban as the "original political act" (*HS* 74). Dostoevsky discovered this firsthand when the deprivation of his privileges as a nobleman attending the punishment of *mort civile* left him with no protection from corporal punishment. The deprivation of his caste privileges was, in effect, a deprivation of legality *in toto*. His safety and relative well-being during his years of incarceration depended less on a body of law than "on the civility and ethical sense" of those prison authorities "who temporarily act as sovereign" (*HS* 174).[30]

Katorga, then, is that space of exception in which the withdrawal of caste privilege returns Dostoevsky not to a politically neutral bare life, a mere creaturely life, but to the bare life of a slave of the state, the equal of those peasant-convicts whose status as slaves did not change when they were banished to the camp.[31] In this sense, it constituted a "truly political element: neither public nor private nor sacred nor natural. The essence of political power [. . .] is the power to suspend (not apply) law and thus to produce a sphere of beings without qualities, *homines sacri*, whom every human being, insofar as he or she is alive, may be."[32] As historian Alan Wood writes, while those who suffered political death (*politicheskaia smert'*) through the practice of civil execution (*grazhdanskaia kazn'*) "were not actually killed, and continued to carry out their natural bodily functions and their unnatural enforced labours in exile, they were, to all other intents and purposes, dead men" who underwent "the harshest form of punishment in the tsarist Criminal Code."[33] This punishment was precisely abandonment in a place Gorianchikov describes as "Hell, the outer darkness," where every inmate was forced to "submit" not to the law, but to *katorga*'s "home-made rules [*vnutrennie ustavy*] and accepted customs" (*PSS* 4:12/12). The equality in question in tsarist Russia and which underwrites the emergence of *katorga* is an equality in abjection in which individuals are "actually and in fact" reducible to the status of beings without qualities.[34]

To state that *katorga* qualifies as a state of exception raises the question of its relationship to the totalitarian camps of the twentieth century which Agamben identifies as the "hidden paradigm of the political space of modernity" (*HS* 123). Many have rightly insisted that the Nazi camp in particular constitutes, in Primo Levi's words, "a *unicum*, both in its extent and its quality." For Levi, the camp's singularity lay in the fact that "never before have so many human lives been extinguished in so short a time, and with so lucid a combination of technological ingenuity, fanaticism, and cruelty." This fact constitutes an absolute limit: "the limits of the spirit, the nonimaginable, were there"—Levi's "there" is Auschwitz, an exception within the space of exception (a concept to which I will return).[35] Hannah Arendt, too, cites the uniqueness of the mechanization of mass murder, the "fabrication of corpses," which "put the victim into a permanent status of dying," and she wisely cautioned scholars to avoid the "greatest danger for a proper understanding" of the phenomenon of the totalitarian camp, "the only too comprehensible tendency [. . .] to draw analogies."[36] Although she insisted that the German camps in particular were "unprecedented," she also observed that "the road to total domination leads through many intermediary stages."[37] *Katorga*, which shares some historical and operational aspects of the totalitarian camps, Nazi and Stalinist, is clearly one such intermediary stage. There can be no question of claiming an equivalence between *katorga* and the Nazi camp. But determining more precisely its position in a continuum ending with the twentieth-century camp will reveal whether and how it figures as a hidden paradigm of Russian modernity for which emancipation, which must have seemed so distant during Dostoevsky's incarceration in the last years of Nicholas I's reign, constitutes the definitive event.

Among the features of the camp which Arendt cites as unique, the most irrefutable was their "non-utilitarian character," the "senselessness of 'punishing' completely innocent people, the failure to keep them in a condition so that profitable work might be extorted from them, the superfluousness of frightening a completely subdued population." "Laboratories in the experiment of total domination," their goal was the total "disintegration of personality" by bringing human beings, through "the permanence and institutionalizing of torture," to "the lowest possible denominator of 'identical reactions' " (*EU* 233, 236, 240). The unspeakable cruelty routinely and efficiently practiced in the German camps beyond any pragmatic consideration and the goal of genocide have no parallel in *katorga*. Other points of distinction she identifies, however, are less indisputably unique to the German camp.

For example, Arendt names the "permanent character" of the totalitarian camp as among its distinguishing features, which, as Agamben noted, gave rise to the novel paradox of "a stable exception" (*EU* 238; *HS* 170). Likewise, *katorga*, although its inmate profile may have changed from the time of its establishment by Peter the Great, was the exceptional state become a "permanent reality" (*HS* 169). The profound "unreality" of an exceptional state made permanent on which Arendt strongly insisted was equally the focus of Dostoevsky's account of estrangement in his prison memoir, as we saw in part 1, even though the experience of "unreality" was historically distinctive (*EU* 241). She also describes as unique to the camp what she found "most difficult to imagine and most gruesome to realize," namely, "the complete isolation which separated the camps from the surrounding world as if they and their inmates were no longer part of the world of the living," an isolation which promoted the destruction of "the moral personality" by making the inmates' martyrdom "senseless, empty, and ridiculous." In contrast, Arendt explicitly claims, the forced-labor camps "as well as other forms of slavery do not involve absolute segregation" (*EU* 240, 239). This difference, too, however, is a qualified one: *katorga* was, of course, completely isolated vis-à-vis the centers of cultural and political power in European Russia so that the convict, and perhaps the "political" (*politicheskii*) in particular, no matter the initial level of sympathetic appreciation for his martyrdom in his community, in Siberia felt himself completely cut off and forgotten, as Dostoevsky poignantly testified. Yet, as a kind of partial compensation, he does record instances in which prisoners came in contact with Siberian villagers, some of whom expressed a principled, because undiscriminating, regard for them as "unfortunates" (more on this below). Depending on the kind of slave labor they were forced to perform, some inmates of the Nazi and Soviet lagers also did not experience total isolation, as Levi, Solzhenitsyn, and many other survivors attest. Levi, for example, described his contact with "the world of the living" in the comparative "paradise" of the chemistry laboratory adjacent to Auschwitz where he worked for several months, and even noted the regard shown him by his immediate supervisor, the head of the laboratory.[38]

One particularly complex point that both Arendt and Agamben address is the "extrajudicial" status of the camp, which has a double referent, the first in relation to the fact of crime and the second to the status of the law. Arendt notes that the concentration camps, both historically and in their National Socialist realization, "were not penal institutions" and "their inmates were accused of no crime"; rather, they were intended to isolate "undesirable elements." (The Nazi camps, for example, were initially established for those accused of opposition to the regime, but that rationale was obsolete by the mid-1930s when no viable opposition remained.) Agamben, too, cites this history, and notes that in the Nazi case, far from being distinguished for criminal actions or behaviors, "*homo sacer* is virtually confused with the citizen" (*HS* 167–68, 171).[39] To a qualified degree, the history of the Russian camp is not dissimilar. Although not as conspicuously or consistently, from the inception of *katorga* under Peter the Great many were exiled and incarcerated without reference to criminal law—as serfs unwanted by their owners (Sushilov is just such a prisoner in *House of the Dead*) or as "victims of the personal vengeance or caprice of individual rulers."[40] Even if the criminal status of the inmate is disregarded, Agamben maintains that prison law (in contrast to "the juridical constellation that guides the camp," specifically "martial law and the state of siege") nevertheless "constitutes a particular sphere of penal law and is not outside the normal order" (*HS* 167–69). But as historians have shown, Russian convicts (and the Siberian exile population generally) were subject to severe punishments "passed and executed by the local authorities, the exile administration, and police officials without recourse to the courts."[41] Dostoevsky himself cites in his novel the existence of a "Special Class" of prisoners in his camp whose terms of imprisonment were unspecified, mentioned in the code of laws only briefly and provisionally as intended for "the most important criminals, pending the establishment in Siberia of the most severe forced labor" (*PSS* 4:60/86). Among the unforgettable portraits Gorianchikov provides is that of the sadistic executioner Zherebiatnikov, who psychologically torments prisoners going to corporal punishment by referring sardonically to the law either as mandating his brutality or as placing limits on it, which, however, prove illusory in the actual execution.[42] In sum, although he notes that prisoners from the noble class were often treated with a certain indulgence by the Siberian authorities, it was always possible to encounter "an evil man," perhaps "a senior commander somewhere remote": in that case, "the fate of an exile to whom that evil commander had taken a particular dislike would be very precarious" (*PSS* 4:211–12/329).

Despite these historical similarities in the extrajudicial functioning of the tsarist and totalitarian camps, Dostoevsky, in contrast to Arendt and Agamben, elaborates in *Notes from the House of the Dead* an alternative account of the extrajudicial significance of crime in which it is powerfully redefined as an ontological category. Gorianchikov will come to regard the ontology of crime as the fundamental enigma of *katorga*, one he can articulate but cannot solve. Although I return to an examination of this mystery in section 4 below, it is worth noting here—in the comparative context which Agamben and Arendt provide and which raises for the former the question of a Western, rights-based genealogy of the camps—that the "extrajudicial" status of crime is linked for Dostoevsky to the revelation rather than the destruction of personality. This is primarily because of Dostoevsky's enormously complex understanding of the relationship between desubjectification, on the one hand, and the assertion of personality—the individuation of humanness, the achievement of subjecthood—on the other. "Crime" is the vehicle or medium for the realization and the subsequent articulation ("story") of this relationship. To regard the destruction and assertion of personality as a simple opposition is, as Gorianchikov realizes, to succumb to an illusion, an unexamined assumption which the reality of *katorga* does not support. *Katorga*, then, is the space in which the "human" in all its minimalism, divested of qualities or values attached to an ethic of rights or an ethos of class, emerges into visibility, and in which the absolute difference between the subject and the non-subject, the perpetrator and the victim, the act of conferring and that of destroying subjecthood, does not necessarily exist. *Katorga* is the space in which the question "What is a human being?" is powerfully restaged.

Finally, as with the Nazi camps, *katorga*, a permanent space of exception, gathered and formally neutralized the differences between members of the various classes, ethnicities, and religions within Russia proper as well as the peoples of its empire. As *Notes from the House of the Dead* recorded in unprecedented detail, the space of exception of tsarist Russia fostered a peculiar culture, a cosmopolis of human fragments or *homines sacri* "forcibly conveyed here in one heap [*v odnu kuchu*], forcibly torn from society and normal life" (*PSS* 4:13, 16/14, 18). Gorianchikov exclaims, "How many different sorts of people were here! I think every province and every region of Russia had here its own representative. There were non-Russians too, and there were even some exiles from the mountains of the Caucasus." Apart from the Russians, his barracks alone includes "two Lezgians, a Chechen, and three Daghestanian Tartars," "a whole group of Poles," "our Jew," "four Old Believers," and "two or three Ukrainians" (*PSS* 4:10, 50–56/9, 71–79). His fellow nobleman-convict and self-appointed mentor in the camp, Akim Akimich, is less enchanted: "Just take a look around—what a motley crew! One comes from the army schools, the next is a Circassian, the third an Old Believer, the fourth an Orthodox peasant who's left his darling family, his children, back home, the fifth's a Yid, the sixth a gypsy, the seventh who knows what, and they've all got to live together no matter what, and get along with each other, eat from the same bowl, sleep on the same planks" (*PSS* 4:28/35).[43] *Katorga*, the "life beyond life" (*kromeshnaia zhizn'*) and the time out of time, constituted a powerful equalizing medium where the nobleman discovered, to his perpetual astonishment, that with the Russian peasant-convict, the Polish nobleman, the Jew, the Muslim, the Ukrainian, and the Chechen mountaineer, he had become "a pure and simple *corpus*," his existence merely phenomenal rather than historically significant (*HS* 123).⁴⁴

In the novel's contextual chronology of both national and personal trauma, equality in abjection precedes emancipation; in this sense, everything about the peasant-convict that estranges and baffles Gorianchikov in *katorga* must be considered, contrary to all reasonable assumptions, a potential element in a mise-en-scène of national reconstitution. However, in no way can this be taken to suggest that a story of social (if not spiritual) redemption in some sense completes or underwrites *Notes from the House of the Dead* or ameliorates the acuteness of the crisis it represents. If completion is understood as requiring the transcendence of the abyss (*bezdna*) of class difference, as the triumph of acceptance over resistance (or resistance over acceptance), then *House of the Dead* is no more complete than *The Brothers Karamazov*. In this first of the writer's great novels, the space of exception, and not its utopic overcoming, is and remains the object of representation. The relationship of Agamben's assessment of the camp to Dostoevsky's is not, then, a chiasmatic one of opposed trajectories where the philosopher traces a tragic history of the West in which the state of exception becomes the rule, whereas the novelist portrays a redemptive, non- (even anti-) Western history that shows how "the freedom and happiness of men" is put "into play in the very place—'bare life'—that marked their subjection" (*HS* 9–10).⁴⁵

Instead, Dostoevsky provides an intimate look at a historical variant of the space of exception and its inhabitant, *homo sacer*. This variant compels us to rethink Agamben's genealogy of the camp. It requires that we consider the ways in which historically the biopolitical realization of "human equality" exceeds the abstract principles of inalienable right at the heart of Western bourgeois democracy. It demands that we examine the uneasy dualism of *katorga* as an atavistic form of punishment suited to the primitive nature of Russian notions of sovereign power, on the one hand, and, in Dostoevsky's portrayal, as a paradigm of the political space of (Russian) modernity, on the other. Adapted to the Russian context, Agamben's core concepts allow us to acknowledge and evaluate Dostoevsky's actual experience of mock execution, *mort civile*, and exile to forced labor—a protracted struggle to tame with every resource provided by his intellect and his class an unmasterable encounter with the people in a state of abject equality—without the premature closure imposed by the conversion hypothesis. *Notes from the House of the Dead* confirms the link to "democracy" Agamben intuits but radically redefines it by removing the limitations imposed by the liberal (Western) rights-based model, and incorporating its more fundamental reference to a kind of power exercised not despite abjection but in tandem with it:⁴⁶ this peculiar, often unconsolidated power is glimpsed in the absence of *bios*. For this reason, the philosophical understanding of the abstract value of human life—detectable, for example, in the Russian elite's liberal-sentimental assessment of the common people which Dostoevsky comes to reject—proves irrelevant in *katorga*. Time and again, Gorianchikov must confront the fact that bare life in abjection is irreducible to those theories about it formulated at a remove, and, for that reason, his "feelings and conscience" derived from such theories (and which he eventually dismisses as "aphorism") and with which he initially hopes to prepare himself for his encounter with bare life prove irrelevant to the experience (*PSS* 4:69/99). Ultimately, he rejects such theories as optical illusions that must be set aside even if there is nothing to replace them, even if one is left in the end with only a *ne to*, "not that." This aporia determines the ontological ambiguity of the space of exception as the object of philosophical, autobiographical, and literary representation to which I now turn.

3. Ontological Ambiguity in the Space of Exception: *Katorga* as Medium

The archetypal function of the sovereign's creation of a state of exception, as both Carl Schmitt and Agamben after him maintain, had been to "trac[e] a threshold" between what is inside the juridico-political order and what is outside, between "the normal situation and chaos," and, as such, it was "essentially unlocalizable," a "zone of indistinction."[47] At the same time, of course, "definite spatiotemporal limits" can be and, in the course of history, have been attached to this zone. Thus, Agamben argues that modernity's ultimate attempt to put the state of exception in "the foreground as the fundamental political structure," "to grant the unlocalizable a permanent and visible location," produced the concentration camp (*HS* 19, 20). Those caught within the camp are not "simply set outside the law and made indifferent to it but rather *abandoned* by it, that is, exposed and threatened on the threshold in which life and law, outside and inside, become indistinguishable" (*HS* 37). The camp thus brings out an obscure truth about the law, that its "originary relation [. . .] to life is not application but Abandonment," by which Agamben means that the law, beneath the applications which have accrued to it over time, is fundamentally "nonrelational" (*HS* 29). Two centuries before the rise of totalitarianism, Kant could celebrate this as "the purely formal character" of the law by which it "founds its claim of universal practical applicability in every circumstance" (*HS* 53). Kafka and Benjamin (and certainly Dostoevsky in 1849), however, had cause to deplore it; Solzhenitsyn condemned the radical emptiness and nonrelationality of Stalinist law in its protean power to claim a referent in any random bodily motion, any unarticulated thought, as expressed in his aphorism, "Where there is law, there is crime" (*Gde zakon, tam i prestuplenie*).[48]

In several of his works, Agamben has offered glimpses of a utopian vision of a "new politics" for which this compulsory relation to the non-relationality of law will have been transcended or otherwise evaded; he speculates, in effect, about the possibility of a politics beyond biopolitics when spaces of exception and the bare life they isolate will have disappeared.[49] What unheard-of ontology might accompany such a politics? As long as his new politics remains a utopian ideal, Agamben is able to discern the lineaments of a "new ontology" only in figures of radical abandonment whose lives are entirely given over to "a thoroughly intransigent state of passivity."[50] Two such figures receive significant analysis in Agamben, one drawn from testimonies of survivors—the so-called *Muselmann* or "Muslim" of the Nazi camps—and the other drawn from literature and exemplified by Herman Melville's Bartleby the scrivener. I'll describe each briefly as exemplars of ontological ambiguity associated with the Agambenian state of exception for the purposes of developing a comparative assessment in relation to the autobiographies of Primo Levi and (in fictional form) of Dostoevsky.

The so-called *Muselmann* or "Muslim" (the epithet apparently signifying unconditional submission) was an inmate of the death camps mentioned in numerous survivor testimonies, a man or woman barely alive, utterly exhausted and apathetic, denuded of self-awareness or any form of human consciousness, the "drowned" for whom, Levi writes, every social habit and instinct is "reduced to silence."[51] In Agamben's lengthy analysis of this figure in *Remnants of Auschwitz*, he situates the *Muselmann* on "the extreme threshold between life and death, the human and the inhuman," in a " 'third realm' " or "central non-place" circumscribed by the selection process for the gas chamber (*RA* 47, 48, 52).[52] The *Muselmann*, we might say, the ultimate *homo sacer*, inhabits a state of exception within the space of exception that is the camp.[53] For Levi, the distinction between the drowned—who "form the backbone of the camp, an anonymous mass, continually renewed and always identical"—and the saved, those who somehow manage to survive, is the distinction between those who "have no story" and those who do have stories, "many, difficult and improbable" stories (*SA* 90).[54] This difference illuminates for Agamben the paradox at the heart of testimony: the *Muselmann*, utterly incapable of bearing witness because he or she is incapable of thought, speech, or reflection, is the camp's only "complete witness." Only he or she, in Levi's words, has "seen the Gorgon"—known and seen, in Agamben's extrapolation of Levi's meaning, "the impossibility of knowing and seeing" (*RA* 54).

Situated at the very threshold of death, the *Muselmann*, "the catastrophe of the subject," may seem an unlikely figure on which to posit a new ontology, as the "cipher of a politics freed from the grasp of the biopoliti-cal."[55] Agamben proposes two aspects of this figure's ambiguity. The first is that the *Muselmann* and the survivor name two asymmetrical compo-nents of a single being, the "subject of testimony":

> To speak, to bear witness, is thus to enter into a vertiginous movement in which something sinks to the bottom, wholly desubjectified and silenced, and something subjectified speaks without truly having anything to say of its own ("I tell of things . . . that I did not actually experience"). Testimony takes place where the speechless one makes the speaking one speak and where the one who speaks bears the impossibility of speaking in his own speech, such that the silent and the speaking, the inhuman and the human enter into a zone of indistinction in which it is impossible to establish the position of the subject, to identify the "imagined substance" of the "I" and, along with it, the true witness. (*RA* 120)

Testimony is thus a novel kind of ventriloquized human utterance whose subject is "constitutively fractured" in "the inseparable intimacy of the *Muselmann* and the witness" (*RA* 151).[56] Without it, the *Muselmann*, a "vegetative life" that had separated itself from the "life of relation," would have slipped without a trace into the radically unthinkable and unsayable, beyond the recuperative powers of history or ethics (*RA* 154). But the *Muselmann* and the witness—"coextensive and, at the same time, non-coincident," "divided and nevertheless inseparable"—accomplish a "dou-ble survival: the non-human is the one who can survive the human being and the human being is the one who can survive the non-human. . . . What can be infinitely destroyed is what can infinitely survive" (*RA* 151).[57] In the event of testimony, the survivor and the *Muselmann* redeem each other (if not the terrible crime perpetrated against them) by making of subjectivity a community of one.

Before turning to the second aspect of the *Muselmann*'s ontological ambiguity, it is worth pausing at this composite subject, this community of one. Levi's testimony, and those of many other survivors including the quasi-fictionalized testimonies of Solzhenitsyn and Dostoevsky of the *gulag* and *katorga*, respectively, record, along with the extraordinary pri-vations of the camps and the terrifying experience of radical abandonment, an account of the extraordinary capacity of human beings to sustain what must be called a culture or community. This distinctive culture, of neces-sity, emerged largely as an activity of exchange suited to "the primordial conditions of camp life"; such exchanges were carried out not in spite of the overwhelming impulse to survive but apparently as an expression of that impulse (*SA* 97). This, perhaps, explains the fact that the *Muselmän-ner* were regarded with such hostility by other inmates of the camp.[58] In any case, survivors both nineteenth- and twentieth-century, of both the

Russian and German camps, provide an abundance of detail about the anthropology of the camps having to do with the nuts and bolts of physical and psychological survival through black market and other illicit exchanges. Levi, for example, writes of exchanging with another inmate German lessons or a spoon for bread and of the prisoner who was able to obtain a newspaper subscription from a "trustworthy German worker" in exchange for a gold tooth (*DS* 97, 114, 102). (Exchanges in *katorga* are examined in more detail in section 5, below.) The *Muselmänner*, in contrast, whose "death had begun before that of their body," who "had already lost the ability to observe, to remember, to compare and express themselves," were not part of this circulation which made possible vital forms of support, including information about or even contact with the outside world in defiance of the Nazis' effort to impose the total isolation that Arendt named as the camp's most horrific feature (*DS* 84, 102). Levi gives pride of place "on the great continent of freedom" to freedom of communication as the touchstone of all other liberties (*DS* 103). We might say, then, that the ontological ambiguity of the *Muselmann* derives from the fact that he or she experiences the *space* of exception precisely as a *state* of exception, and not as the environment Dostoevsky represents and Levi remembers as "an intricate and stratified microcosm," a medium in which all manner of exchanges transpires—of stories, information, food, letters (if rarely), and other forms of material and emotional support (*DS* 20).

The second register in which Agamben explores the ontological ambiguity of the *Muselmann* derives from his very inability to speak about his experience or his condition, an inability to which he ascribes three redemptive functions: the first linguistic (in which "a language that survives the subjects who spoke it," a language "that has no place in the libraries of what has been said or in the archive of statements," finds "a speaker who remains beyond it"); the second historical (in which the impossibility of speech conveyed by the witness's testimony irrefutably proves the existence of Auschwitz which the world might otherwise deny); and the third more properly messianic (in which the witness emerges as the "remnant" through whom "all Israel shall be saved").[59] Here, again, the radical incapacity of the *Muselmann* is revealed as "a special kind of capacity rather than a mere failure," and this capacity is to "maintain [. . .] unsayability" so that the witness testifies to a human experience that surpasses and thus forces a revaluation of everything that had been formerly assumed about the human being itself.[60] Agamben examines the topos of unsayability in tandem with radical ontological ambiguity elsewhere, in Melville's *Bartleby the Scrivener*. In that story, the mysteriously uncooperative member of an antebellum Wall Street lawyer's secretarial staff who, shortly after being hired as a law-copyist, responds to every request his genial employer makes with the phrase, "I would prefer not to," or simply "I prefer not to."[61] Agamben locates Bartleby in a "literary constellation" circumscribed, significantly, by Gogol's Akaky Akakievich at one pole and Dostoevsky's Prince Myshkin at the other (and which includes some characters of Flaubert, Robert Walser, and Kafka). His claim, however, is that only the "philosophical constellation" to which Melville's character also belongs can "contai[n] the figure merely traced by the literary constellation" (*P* 243). What is this figure, generated in literature, but whose truest significance philosophy, not literature (and perhaps not even history), circumscribes and reveals?

Agamben places Bartleby in a constellation comprised of texts from classical philosophy through medieval theology (Jewish, Christian, and Islamic) which examine the nature of potentiality—whose radical ambiguity derives from its relation to that which is done or thought as well as that which is not done or thought—and reads the scrivener's repetitious response to his employer's requests in light of that constellation. The response is irreducible to a moral stance: Bartleby's "preference" is related neither to will (he has no discernible desire or agenda) nor to some unapprehended necessity, the two interpretive possibilities the lawyer initially considers as, in his bewilderment, he consults the works of the Calvinist Jonathan Edwards and the Dissenter Joseph Priestley. Thus, it makes no sense to ask, as the lawyer repeatedly does, what the latter's responsibility to his employee in the face of such mysterious stubbornness might be. In the story, the question of responsibility becomes more fraught as the lawyer is increasingly aware of Bartleby's poverty and solitude, and increasingly anxious about dismissing him. For Agamben, however, there can be no question of ethical content—the man who appears before the lawyer without references and who dies without revealing anything of himself to the lawyer's curiosity is a figure of pure suspense, of radical non-referentiality, "an absolute anaphora, spinning on itself, no longer referring either to a real object or to an anaphorized term: *I would prefer not to prefer not to*" (*P* 255). Bartleby announces, without reason or passion, an ontology that transcends Hamlet's non-decision between Being and non-Being and which is, as pure potential—as something that can be or not be—neither true nor false. He embodies absolute contingency, the refusal of necessity: " 'I would prefer not to,' " Agamben writes, "is the *restitutio in integrum* of possibility, which keeps possibility suspended between occurrence and nonoccurrence, between the capacity to be and the capacity not to be" (*P* 261, 267).[62] It is to keep the integrity of possibility and the freedom of the not-to-be that Bartleby, soon after he is hired as a copyist, stops copying, ending the reproduction of the "what was": "if Bartleby is a new Messiah, he comes not, like Jesus, to redeem what was, but to save what was not" (*P* 270).

Agamben's reading is ingenious, yet it all but ignores the story's witness and first-person narrator (it merely allegorizes him as "the man of the law"), its "remnant," who has not been to the bottom with his cadaverous scrivener, who can offer no information about him, and yet tells his tale (*P* 254). Literature demands that we ask why such a figure as Bartleby should appear before this particular man—Melville's banal if benign lawyer, from whose perspective the scrivener's story is told—to impose the literal rigor (or radical freedom; here they seem indistinguishable) of pure suspense as potential. If we are persuaded that Bartleby is indeed absolute contingency incarnate, "the indifferent truth of the tautology," we must nevertheless ask why he appears in the mechanically harmonious world of his would-be fellow copyists Turkey, Nippers, and Ginger Nut, as well as his would-be employer, and what difference his appearance makes in that world (*P* 267).[63] "Snug" as Poe in their walled-in Wall Street office, doesn't each occupant of the lawyer's chambers evince in his characteristic behavior the inertial ambition of Bartleby's "I would prefer not to" long before they unthinkingly mimic his favorite locution, in fact, long before he enters their world?[64] Such questions suggest that in the literary text the suspense of suspense, so to speak, derives not from an abstraction like absolute contingency; rather, it derives from its relation to that which in literature cannot be absolutely contingent, the givenness or specificity of the literary space (and its inhabitants) in which an embodied and individuated contingency appears.[65]

Agamben finds in Melville's Bartleby, whom he characterizes (as he did the *Muselmann*) as a "figure of abandonment," the "strongest objection" in modern thought "to the principle of sovereignty" and its most significant attempt to go conceptually beyond it, to realize "a constituting power that has definitively broken the ban binding it to constituted power." In this way he adumbrates a new politics grounded in an effort to "thin[k] ontology and politics beyond every figure of relation, beyond even the limit relation that is the sovereign ban" (*HS* 48, 47).[66] It may seem absurd to pair Bartleby and the *Muselmann* (indeed, Agamben does not explicitly do so), and yet they share several characteristics—their apathy, their profound isolation, their absolute indifference to others and to the life around them generally, their extraordinary absence of physical vitality, a level of experience to which no one has anything remotely approaching adequate access.[67] But what definitively brings them together in Agamben's discourse is the radical nature of their abandonment, and the intransigent passivity—whether strategic or not—through which they avoid all relationality and thereby withdraw, to the degree possible, from feeling the abusive effects of an empty but nevertheless binding law, whether in its most extreme or its most mundane manifestations. And yet, for both exemplars of the new ontology, harbingers of a new politics, it is the witness, no matter how self-confessedly inadequate, who allows for the trace of the figure that philosophy constellates anew. True, the *Muselmann* does not seek out the witness he or she requires for redemption from a death that would otherwise signify nothing beyond the production of another corpse (*RA* 74). Nor does Bartleby seek the attention of his employer who, even after he has taken the drastic step of moving out of his own offices in order to get away from his immoveable and unmoving employee, cannot resist the gravitational pull of the "pallid" black hole that is Bartleby: so scrupulously does he continue to make overtures to the one who has as consistently refused them that he is present to close the dead man's eyes after his removal (by the new tenant of the lawyer's former office) to the Tombs. But Agamben's philosophical attention to the ontological and ethical significance of the witness's testimony is nowhere in evidence in relation to Bartleby's "other," the lawyer-witness who returns from the Tombs, from the Dead Letter Office, to tell his admittedly inadequate and, given the depth of his ignorance, quite possibly inaccurate tale.[68]

Agamben concludes *Remnants of Auschwitz* by claiming that a particular structure of witnessing—wherein the witness brings the *Muselmann*'s unsayable experience to speech—offers the sole definitive proof for the existence of Auschwitz, because it articulates an unimaginable truth that is "irreducible to the real elements that constitute it," a reality "that necessarily exceeds its factual elements" (*RA* 164, 12). Testimony—the joint production of the one who speaks for the one who cannot, "an essential duality in which an insufficiency or incapacity is completed or made valid"—is not a matter of asserting or confirming empirical reality (*RA* 150). The authority of testimony "depends not on a factual truth, a conformity between something said and a fact or between memory and what actually happened, but rather on the immemorial relation between the unsayable and the sayable, between the outside and the inside of language":

> Testimony thus guarantees not the factual truth of the statement safeguarded in the archive, but rather its unarchivability, its exteriority with respect to the archive—that is, the necessity by which, as the existence of language, it escapes both memory and forgetting. It is because there is testimony only where there is an impossibility of speaking, because there is a witness only where there has been desubjectification, that the *Muselmann* is the complete witness and that the survivor and the *Muselmann* cannot be split apart. (*RA* 158)

In this principled disjunction of the archive and testimony, there is no ground on which to differentiate the capacities of literature and philosophy to represent the process of a desubjectification that produces a transcript of the unsayable. In fact, to borrow an image from Melville's *Billy*

Budd, in this case we cannot mark the spot at which philosophy, autobiography, and literature "blendingly enter" one another's domain.[69]

One may say generally, however, that whereas the philosopher tends to conceptualize exception as a *state*, the autobiographer and novelist more readily investigate it as an inhabited *space*. More particularly, the latter represents it as a peculiar medium that fosters an equally peculiar culture or community, the community of *homines sacri*, the "threatened and precarious world of the camp inhabitants" (*HS* 185). One may say, further, that whereas the philosopher conceives the state of exception as static in relation to sovereign power, impotent to be anything other than what the sovereign designates it to be with his ban, the autobiographer and novelist explore the kinds of activity and agency elicited by the very stringency of exception and the collective potential of individuated *homines sacri* to forge a dialectical relation to sovereign power. Similarly, whereas the philosopher characterizes *homo sacer* as an unindividuated being without resources, agency, or responsibility—"the catastrophe of the subject," a pure and all but silent victim entirely beyond the purview of ethics—the autobiographer and the novelist reveal forms of communication, discursive and non-discursive, that are peculiar to the space of exception.

Dostoevsky thus portrays the state of exception precisely as a threatened and precarious world, an inhabited if radically isolated space in which men are exposed and expose one another to extraordinary violence. For this reason, the oxymoronic nature of *katorga* as an unlocalizable locale is rendered not abstractly—or "bookishly" (*knizhno*), as Dostoevsky would say—but by the specific feel of the tension it produces in the inmates' minds and bodies:

> Even people who had been sent there for their entire lives were restless or anxious, and certainly every one of them dreamed constantly to himself about something all but impossible. This daily agitation, unspoken but obvious; this strange fever and the involuntary impatience with expressions of hope which were so entirely without foundation that they seemed to come out of delirium and, most striking of all, which often coexisted with the most clearly pragmatic minds—all of this lent an unusual aspect and character to this place, so much so that perhaps precisely these features constituted its most representative quality. One somehow felt, often from the first glance, that this did not exist outside the prison. Everyone here was a dreamer and that was immediately apparent. (*PSS* 4:196/304)

As the novelist portrays it, the specificity of *katorga* as a space of exception is that it is experienced as nightmarishly permanent-provisional, real-fantastic. The malaise of involuntary dreaming prevents the dreamer from settling, from inhabiting the space in which he must live, and yet provides no escape, no transcendence, no resolution. To acquiesce or resist are equally impossible. This allows Gorianchikov to make the existential claim that "all the prisoners lived there *as if not at home*, but as if at a coaching inn, on the road, at some stage or other," and a few paragraphs later make a further social claim, without contradiction, that "every newcomer to the prison within two hours of his arrival [. . .] begins to *make himself at home*," as long as he is of the common classes (*PSS* 4:195–96/304, 198/308; emphasis added).[70] In this way, by providing something like a psychology of the state of exception, Dostoevsky's chronotope circumscribes not just a historically actualized moment (although it is that, too) but a space that the inhabitant, living each moment in a state of agitated immobility, experiences each in his own way as being both inside and outside time, and thus inside and outside history and community as well.

One could plausibly object that the very richness of sensuous, material, and psychological detail attached to the Dostoevskian chronotope of *katorga* disqualifies it as a legitimate realization of Agamben's quintessential space of exception, the Nazi camp. To take one example, the possibility of "making oneself at home" in *katorga* does not seem, by any interpretive stretch, applicable to the Nazi lager, Agamben's telos, nor does one think of the latter's inmates as dreamers, a designation that seems to inject a jarring element of the romantic, both anachronistic and frivolous, into the asperities of the totalitarian death camp. The presence of the dreamer seems to mark an absolute difference between the Dostoevskian and Agambenian assessments of the camp as the state of exception realized. But one must take care to distinguish precisely if and where within the two representations of the space of exception, one philosophical and one literary/autobiographical, that difference and a host of others legitimately obtain.

Dostoevsky's dreamer in the scene invoked above, for example, in no way resembles the conventional romantic dreamer of his own feuilletonistic tales of the forties: in contrast, the inmate's dreaming lent him and most of the prison population a "sullen and threatening" aspect as of a place imbued with "a malice approaching hatred," as one might imagine of caged men (*PSS* 4:196/304).[71] Even given a revised notion of the dreamer, though, one that parts with the romantic convention, the inmates of the Nazi camps as survivors have described them had no energy to spare for the ceaseless swearing, brawling, and quarreling, the constant "gossip, intrigue, cattiness, envy, squabbling, and malice" in which Gorianchikov's dreamers indulge (*PSS* 4:13/14). Nevertheless, one can legitimately ask if another form of dreaming occurred in the Nazi lager, albeit perhaps only for those whom Primo Levi distinguished as the "exiguous minority" of prisoners who "enjoyed some sort of privilege" in the camps as did Levi himself, prisoners who "never fathomed them to the bottom" and thus were more likely to live to write about them.[72] Is it possible to

compare the "pensive and persistent" gaze of the prisoner, who pauses
from his labor to look across the enclosure upon the "unbounded carpet"
of the "free Kirghiz steppe" before returning to work with a "deep sigh,
from the very bottom of the lungs," with the gaze of Levi himself at
the young German women with whom he works for a short time in the
chemistry laboratory adjacent to the camp, who seem "outside this
world," whose desultory singing makes Levi "deeply unhappy," and in
relation to one of whom in particular he dreams of knowing enough German to tell her his plight (*PSS* 4:173/268; *SA* 143, 144)? Irrepressible
hope, increased suffering, and invasive dreaming, both Dostoevsky and
Levi attest, are symptoms of the same affliction. Thus, although Levi
states that his experience has made him immune to hope, the contiguity
of normal life, as when he enters the lab from the camp (as when the
peasant-convict gazes on the unbounded land from his position just inside the enclosure), releases "the pain of remembering, the old ferocious
longing to feel myself a man, which attacks me like a dog the moment my
[consciousness] comes out of the gloom" (*SA* 140, 142).[73] Although Levi
elsewhere asserts that survival required a drastic constriction of one's
mental horizon, he also bears out Dostoevsky's observation that the confined man does dream but that his dreams differ from those of the free:
the prisoner has, "let us assume, also a life—prison life, convict life; but
whoever the convict is and for whatever term he has been exiled, he is
decisively, instinctively unable to accept his fate as something positive and
final, as a part of real life" (*PSS* 4:79/115).

The "stories" that fill the pages of testimony (absent, as Levi noted,
only in the *Muselmann*, Agamben's "perfect witness") reveal from *within*
these spaces of exception the distinctive texture of life in *katorga*, the
Stalinist *gulag*, and the Nazi lager. With astonishing similarities, Levi,
Solzhenitsyn, and Dostoevsky tell us the following about the life beyond
life, the life of the living dead: what was worn and eaten; in what the
labor consisted; what were the routines of the day and night; the process
of habituation to the physical and moral environment; the special environment of the prison infirmary and the challenges of illness; the fundamental distinction between privileged prisoners and the majority; the degrees and forms of privilege or advantage;[74] the liabilities of privilege;
the neutralization of privilege as illustrated by the special plight of "the
cultivated man";[75] the relative burdens of believers and nonbelievers (*DS*
146); the mix of nations and languages; the forms of bearing witness;
biographical details about individual prisoners; characteristic structures
of social behavior; and, as mentioned earlier, an abundance of detail about
the anthropology of the camps in terms of the ways and means of physical
and psychological survival, largely a matter of black market and other
forms of illicit exchange.

Dostoevsky thus apprehends the state of exception as a distinctive space with an equally distinctive temporal dimension—in Bakhtin's literary terminology, a chronotope. He analyzes the complex forms of human relationality through which it is constituted as a historically specific site located at the outer limits of what can be conceived or imagined; something outside the archive and irreducible to the elements which constitute it; and ultimately something for which the mimetic function of language proves inadequate and whose representation therefore demands a novel textual aesthetic. For Dostoevsky, as for his fictional alter ego Gorianchikov, *katorga*, the life beyond life, is not primarily a state but a space, a world so brutal that Gorianchikov claims he could never adjust to it, but in relation to which at every moment he struggles to discover its social logic and its ethical ground. The space of exception emerges not as an inert expanse, silent and featureless, but as a populated medium animated by ceaseless exchange—in some cases consensual, in others coerced—of information, material goods, even fates and identities.[76] Together with the violence imposed by the prison authorities, these exchanges advance the processes of de- and resubjectification characteristic of *katorga*. Collectively, the latter adumbrate what emerges as the central mystery of Gorianchikov's memoir: the connection of crime to personality—what we might call the ontology of crime, the form of ontological ambiguity specific to the Dostoevskian space of exception.

4. The Ontology of Crime: Testimony/Confession

"One wants not to see."
—*PSS* 20:210

Gorianchikov identifies crime as the fundamental mystery of life in the house of the dead in the opening chapter of his memoir. From the outset, it is implicitly but unmistakably a problem associated with the other and with the unintelligibility of the other, primarily the peasant. Even though we have just read the prefatory narrator's account of his crime—"he murdered his wife while still in the first year of marriage, murdered out of jealousy"—Gorianchikov gives no indication in his initial observations of his fellow inmates that the problem of crime they collectively exemplify pertains to him, or that his remarks about how the convicts repress the thought of their crime and prohibit discussion about it are also self-referential (*PSS* 4:6/3). So persuasively and immediately does he establish himself as a privileged observer of an alien and unknown world that we exonerate him from the prefatory narrator's charge of violent crime well before he is identified—although only indirectly and implicitly, by other nobleman-convicts—as a political criminal.[77] As the inmates of *katorga* tacitly agree to suspend their curiosity about one another's crimes, so has Gorianchikov's reader historically suspended his or her curiosity on that score. In the manner of a kind of readerly gentleman's agreement, the autobiographical content of *Notes from the House of the Dead* has been assumed to cover all contingencies, and Gorianchikov's status as a "political" has not been called into question nor has the extent of that term's reference been examined beyond the obvious. However, the text in its entirety—including the prefatory narrator's introduction—affords no basis for uncritically affirming the difference between himself and the peasant-convicts in relation to crime which Gorianchikov's dogged inquiries and perpetual astonishment as well as much of his commentary present as absolute. His observations on crime and the criminal, then, must always be understood as doubly referential. They comprehend both the object of his inquiries, the peasant-convicts of *katorga*, and himself as the self-appointed subject of knowledge who refuses to acknowledge his own crime, and who, for precisely that reason, assumes, but is forced eventually to relinquish, a "spectatorial and intellectualist epistemology based on a subjective self reflecting on an objective world exterior to it."[78]

Crime as "evildoing" (*zlodeianie*) motivated by "baseness" (*podlost'*), in implicit contrast to political crime motivated by conscience, is thus presented from the outset as utterly foreign to Gorianchikov (*PSS* 4:142/218).[79] He describes his shock at finding himself in close quarters with "chance murderers and professional murderers, bandits and bandit chiefs, [. . .] swindlers and vagrants" (*PSS* 4:11/11). The pluralism of the convict population ("every province and every region of Russia had here its own representative") finds its analog in the diversity of crimes—"here there was no crime without its representative" (*PSS* 4:10/9). Yet, Gorianchikov immediately notices that in *katorga* this variety resolves itself into a uniform face of crime, a sharply etched "commonality" (*obshchnost'*, literally "community") or "*artel'* " enforced by a code of behavior to which all convicts conform, no matter how unrestrained their behavior had been in freedom (*PSS* 4:12, 60/12, 86). Compelled to live in this "strange family" or "corporation" (*korporatziia*) without ever being incorporated into it, an outsider on the inside, Gorianchikov immediately assumes the role of objective witness to a radically "singular world," the life of the living dead, with its "own singular laws, its clothing, its morals and customs" (*PSS* 4:12, 57, 9/12, 80, 7). In his isolation and estrangement, he takes up the role of ethnographer-witness of "these degraded ones [*etikh unizhennykh*]" as a kind of project or vocation, just as the prisoners pursue their own crafts and occupations whenever possible, and always at great risk, as a life-saving supplement to the meaningless drudgery of forced labor (*PSS* 4:91/134). In the matter of crime, Gorianchikov works by inclination and necessity from the outside in, beginning his investigation with an account of the prison's categories of punishment and criminal types. He quickly exhausts the informational value of such bureaucratic classifications and turns to crime itself, where, at least initially, he is able to give an account not of the actual transgressions committed by those around him but rather of the obstacles they erect against such an accounting. Instead of recording the straightforward narratives of evildoing he had expected to hear, Gorianchikov describes the peculiar behaviors with which the convicts dissemble or obscure them and which, he is compelled to admit, he lacks the cultural literacy to interpret.

Although each convict "had his own tale [*povest'*]," many factors conspire against their being told or comprehended. When they are told, the tales themselves are "obscure and oppressive, like the fumes from yesterday's drunkenness"; something remains unsaid, outside narrative accountability. Contributing even more directly to the impenetrability of crime is the strong consensus among the prisoners that expressing curiosity about another's story is not simply "not in fashion [*ne v mode*]," but more urgently forbidden: "it was *not necessary* to talk *about that* [*pro eto*] because to talk *about that* was not acceptable" (*PSS* 4:11, 12/11; emphases in original). The "about that," which here refers to without naming the crime, is a variant of the *ne to*—the "not that"—with which the term "democrat" is negatively defined in *The Idiot*; "crime," too, resists positive elaboration. The prohibition against telling the story of one's crime is dramatically illustrated when Gorianchikov describes the convicts' spontaneous and collective response to a drunken convict's attempt to tell the story of how he murdered a five-year-old child by luring him with a toy into an empty shed: "the entire barracks, which up to that point had been laughing at his jokes, cried out like one man, and the bandit was forced to be silent" (*PSS* 4:12/11). Gorianchikov points out that moral indignation has nothing to do with their protest (as no one objects when one convict steals from or informs on another); they object solely to the breach of the unspoken taboo against talking about one's crime.

In those rare cases where such talk is tolerated, apart from the inherent murkiness of the tale, two interpretive impasses emerge, one evinced by the listener and the other, far more troubling, by the teller. The listener invariably listens with "gloomy indifference"—no one tries to draw the narrator out through sympathetic identification or even curiosity (because he uniquely considers himself to be innocent of crime, Gorianchikov is unique in making no effort to hide his curiosity), and no one betrays any feelings about what is being told. The performance of indifference reflects the convicts' commitment to a code of behavior whose central "virtue" (*dobrodetel'*, a good act and thus the antithesis of *zlodeianie*, evildoing) is the suppression of any sign of astonishment (*PSS* 4:12/12). This indiffer-

ent reception of stories of crime partly reflects other stylized behaviors
(Gorianchikov refers to quarrels, petty thievery, drunkenness, and other
quotidian events as more or less skillfully performed "exercises in style")
developed in response to an ordeal harsher than the deprivation of liberty
or compulsory labor: "*compulsory cohabitation*" (*vynuzhdennoe obshchee
cozhitel'stvo*) under constant surveillance (*PSS* 4:25, 22/31, 25; emphasis
in original).[80] In relation to the story of crime, Gorianchikov notices, the
performance of indifference has a socializing function. It domesticates
"even the most caustic, the most original personalities" whose transgressions on the outside had violated all sense of measure and restraint: "they
were immediately put in their places, notwithstanding the fact that some,
up until their arrival in the camp, were the terror of entire villages and
towns. Looking around him, the newcomer soon realized that he had
landed in the wrong place, that here there was no one to astonish, and
imperceptibly he submitted and fell into the general tone" (*PSS* 4:12, 13/
12, 13). By rejecting the stance of indifference, Gorianchikov rejects for
himself the socialization it instantiates.

The corollary to the listener's indifference is the teller's utter lack of
remorse, which Gorianchikov regards as a far more troubling and unreadable sign—stable throughout his years in *katorga*—of the moral valence of
crime for the peasant-convicts. He returns several times in the opening
chapter to the absence of remorse as a central enigma of his new environment: "I have already said that in the course of several years I never saw
in these people the slightest sign of remorse, not the slightest burdensome
thought of their crime, and that the majority of them inwardly considered
themselves to be completely justified." It occurs to him that perhaps their
consciences exist but are deeply buried—"who could say that he had
sounded the depths of these lost hearts and read in them what was secreted
from the whole world?"—but the evidence contradicts such an assumption: "But it should surely have been possible, in so many years, to notice
something, to catch out, to detect in these hearts some sign bearing witness to an inner anguish, to suffering. But it wasn't there, it positively
wasn't there" (*PSS* 4:15/16). The absence of remorse, an outward sign of
an "inner norm, some kind of standard," is particularly distressing with
respect to crimes which humanity unites in condemning: "notwithstanding all possible points of view, everyone agrees that there are some kinds
of crimes which always and everywhere, under every possible code of law,
from the beginning of the world, have been indisputably considered to be
crimes and will be so considered as long as men are men" (*PSS* 4:63,
15/90, 17). If human beings define themselves as such by their universal
condemnation of certain crimes, then what species of man does Gorianchikov encounter in *katorga* where he is hard-pressed to find even one prisoner who "inwardly acknowledges his lawlessness," where he uniquely

hears "stories of the most horrifying, of the most unnatural acts, of the most monstrous murders, told with the most unrestrained, the most childishly merry laughter" (*PSS* 4:13, 15/13, 17)?

The notorious peasant Orlov, whom Gorianchikov encounters in the hospital where the former is brought unconscious after the first of two floggings, becomes for him the embodiment of criminal excess and remorselessness. Despite his reputation as "a rare evildoer who had cold-bloodedly slaughtered old men and children, a man with a terrifying strength of will and with a proud consciousness of his strength"—the peasant as Raskol'nikov's Superman, "the true *sovereign* [*vlastelin*], to whom everything is permitted"—Gorianchikov does not try to hide his "extreme curiosity" stimulated by the "tall tales [*chudesa*]" told about him (*PSS* 4:47/65).[81] As soon as Orlov regains consciousness, he begins to prepare himself for the second half of his punishment (the more quickly to get it over with and plan his escape), and Gorianchikov begins to "acquain[t] myself with him more closely and for a whole week I studied him" (*PSS* 4:47/66). He marvels at his "limitless" self-mastery; his fearlessness despite the fact that he is physically small and weakened by his ordeal; his "infinite energy, thirst for action, thirst for revenge, thirst to attain his intended goal"; and a kind of "strange haughtiness" which convinces Gorianchikov that "there was no being in the world who could have wielded any authority over him" (*PSS* 4:47/66–67). As Gorianchikov becomes friendlier with him, looking specifically for the signs of remorse that will humanize the peasant-convict in his eyes, he finds himself infantilized in Orlov's:

> I tried to talk to him about his adventures. He frowned a little at these interrogations but always answered candidly. When he understood, though, that I was aiming for his conscience to get at whatever kind of remorse it contained, he looked at me with such contempt and arrogance as if I had suddenly become in his eyes some kind of little, stupid boy with whom it was impossible to reason as with an adult. Even something like pity for me was expressed in his face. After a minute he burst out laughing at me with the most simple-hearted laugh, without the slightest irony, and I am sure that once he was alone and recalling my words, he more than once perhaps started laughing to himself. (*PSS* 4:48/67)

Although Orlov shakes hands with Gorianchikov before being released from the hospital for his second round of punishment, the latter surmises that "he couldn't help but despise me and certainly must have looked on me as on a submissive, weak, pitiful creature, in all respects inferior to him" (*PSS* 4:48/68). As the peasant Chekunov tells those on the hospital ward who object to his performing small services for the nobleman, "Look, on their own it's as if they have no hands" (*PSS* 4:133/203). From Orlov's perspective, Gorianchikov's assumption that one's humanity consists in the burden of conscience marks him as an essentially abject creature.

Despite the vivid specificity of his portrait in *House of the Dead*, Orlov's afterlife in Dostoevsky's subsequent works is less of an achieved than of a theoretical and thus ideal selfhood (as in Raskol'nikov's hypothetical Superman who recognizes no authority capable of limiting the realization of his desires). The writer's dark characters—Raskol'nikov, Rogozhin, Svidrigailov, Stavrogin, Piotr Verkhovensky, Ivan Karamazov, Smerdiakov—are far too self-divided, too intellectualized (at times crudely so), to enjoy the pleasure Orlov takes with no trace of ambivalence in the violence attached to his elegant self-mastery. Orlov does not survive the house of the dead—his second round of punishment proves fatal—but the phenomenon he embodies of a sovereign self, uncompromising and formidable, contradicts one of the key interpretive paradigms Gorianchikov develops for understanding the peasant-convicts, the husk and the kernel (*kora i zerno*). Here a repellent and brutal exterior is suddenly, in a chance moment, rent or penetrated, revealing unexpected beauty or goodness within. (This and the other paradigms Gorianchikov develops are discussed in more detail in section 5, below.) This is precisely the effect of Dostoevsky's dream-memory of his father's peasant Marei, according to his 1876 *Diary of a Writer* article, whose unexpected kindness to his master's son, involuntarily recalled, permitted the writer to regard the brawling peasant-convicts around him with new eyes. Marei's gratuitous act of kindness, "in an empty field," with only God and a frightened child as witness, revealed "what profound and enlightened human feeling and what delicate, almost feminine tenderness could fill the heart of a coarse, bestially ignorant Russian serf who at the time did not expect or even dream of his freedom." Dostoevsky claimed that the revelation enabled him to "look on these unfortunates in an entirely different way [because] suddenly, by some sort of miracle, all the hatred and malice in my heart had entirely disappeared [*ischezla*]" (*PSS* 22:49). Orlov's virile integrity, on the contrary, elicits from Gorianchikov not grateful recognition of a familiar good but a powerful fascination with that which refuses to be anything but itself.[82] Hence, what we might call (proleptically, after the Dostoevskian fact) the Nietzschean cast of Gorianchikov's conclusion that crime "cannot be comprehended from an established and ready-made point of view, its philosophy is somewhat more difficult than is supposed" (*PSS* 4:15/16). It is no longer a matter of just the evil deed itself, which one might imagine is committed out of "delirium" or "possession," but of a seamless and unapologetic integrity of act and agent that demands a revaluation of all values and refutes any definition of human beings as such based on the assumption of a universal ethical sensibility (*PSS* 4:12/13).

Gorianchikov relatedly observes the surprising absence in the peasant-convicts of another expected emotional response, resentment toward those who administer punishment in the form of brutal floggings: "Often not even the slightest hint of malice or hatred was heard in stories which at times made my heart heave and start to pound violently. But they would tell stories [of their punishment] and laugh like children," a response that links crime to punishment within the Menippean comedy of abjection itself, no matter whose (*PSS* 4:146/224).[83] In both cases, the laughter denotes a kind of unreasoning pragmatism: some people are fated to be harmed, life is hard, that's the way it is. Like resentment against one's fate, remorse is beside the point, particularly if the crime in question is committed against the authorities:

> The criminal knows and never doubts that he is vindicated in the court of his own native milieu, the common people, who will never—once again, he knows this—judge him once and for all, but for the most part will even completely excuse him, provided that he did not sin against his own, against his brothers, against the common people to whom he belongs by birth. His conscience is at peace, and he is strong in his conscience and is not morally confused, and that's the most important thing. (*PSS* 4:147/225)

If the criminal has transgressed against the authorities (*nachal'stvo*), then this is just part of the "ineluctable fact, which he did not initiate and cannot end, and which will continue for a long, long time, a part of the established, passive, but persistent struggle." But if one can understand that crime against the authorities "isn't worth mentioning," Gorianchikov still sees "no pangs of conscience, even in those cases when the crime had been against their own community [*obshchestvo*]" (*PSS* 4:147/226, 225). The question of conscience, regardless of the class of perpetrator or victim, is ineluctably moot.

Gorianchikov thus finds that the absence of remorse cannot be explained by some theory of the common people's elective affinities and traditional antagonisms; the aporia of crime remains and encompasses both act and agent. In place of an ethics, a theory of internal standards and norms with which all human beings are equipped and which makes crime, when it does occur, comprehensible in terms of the feelings of outrage and remorse it universally elicits, Gorianchikov is able to offer a stark observation which seems to concede to a hopeless relativism at the heart of the problem: "Where there is personality, there is a variation" on crime (*Shto kharakter, to i variatsiia; PSS* 4:43/59). His inquiry into the radical individuation of crime begins with a statement about the mystery not of crime but of punishment, which he claims powerfully impressed him on the first day of his incarceration: "one thought preoccupied me more than any other, which then obsessively haunted me for the duration of my life in prison—an almost insoluble thought, insoluble for me even now: it concerns the inequality of punishment for one and the same crime" (*PSS* 4:42/58).[84] As he unfolds this thought, however, the perception of variation and stability as attached to punishment and crime, respectively, is reversed: variations in punishment, he realizes, are "comparatively few," whereas "the variation in one and the same kind of crime is infinite in number." If the crime in question is murder, it happens that one man kills casually, for no particular reason, whereas another kills only in desperation, as a last resort, perhaps in an attempt to protect an innocent loved one from harm. The contrasts intensify: "One man, pursued by a whole regiment of detectives, kills because he is a vagrant, defending his freedom, his life, often dying of starvation; another slaughters little children for the pleasure of killing, of feeling their warm blood on his hands, of enjoying their terror and their final bird-like trembling under the knife" (*PSS* 4:43/59). In this sense, individual character or personality—comprising an infinite variety of motives, circumstances, and biographies— qualifies crime which loses its status as an absolute act commanding a straightforward philosophy of evaluation and redress: "It was difficult to form even the most rudimentary understanding of some crimes: there was so much that was strange in their execution" (*PSS* 4:87/128).

The fragmentation of "crime" when yoked to individual personality mirrors the larger reality of *katorga* which, as Gorianchikov confesses, defeats all his attempts to systematize and thereby make sense of it: crime, too, appears to be "infinitely diverse, compared with all, even the most subtle, conclusions of abstract thought"; it, too, "does not permit clear-cut and wholesale distinctions"; it, too, "tends toward dis-integration" (*PSS* 4:197/306). The impossibility of adducing a fitting punishment or exacting adequate restitution confirms Gorianchikov's increasingly vertiginous sense that crime is essentially incomprehensible: that is, it cannot be comprehended—redeemed, compensated, or atoned for—by any known form of punishment or restitution, and thus it leaves an unincorporable remainder. His conclusions about the individualization of crime extend inevitably to remorse, vitiating the legal, moral, and (implicitly) social difference between the murderer who "never gives a thought to the murder he committed during his entire stay in *katorga*" and the "educated man, with a developed conscience, with self-awareness, a heart. In advance of any punishment, just the pain in his own heart will kill him with its torments. He condemns himself for his crime more harshly and mercilessly than the most terrible law" (*PSS* 4:43/59, 60).[85] This brief and anonymous characterization begs the question: Is this Gorianchikov's own "variation" on crime? If this is his admission of having transgressed, it is multiply deflected: instead of confession or its preamble, he offers the hypothetical sentiment of a hypothetical criminal type whose act may or may not have been morally defensible and whose subsequent feelings about it, when all is said and done, partake of "an insoluble problem, squaring the circle" (*PSS* 4:43/59). In the final analysis, punishment—which rarely, if ever, fits the crime—must be discarded as a possible key to the solution of crime's mystery, and falls into the vortex created by the absence of remorse. This is especially so, since punishment is meted out in blows, the number ostensibly calibrated to fit the crime, but the pain of these blows—the essence of the punishment—is, as Gorianchikov discovers to his great disappointment, untranslatable, outside of language. No one can tell him what the pain feels like. The "story" associated with crime, on the other hand, is nothing but translation—performance, representation; the crime itself becomes more incomprehensible with each telling and is finally ungraspable.[86] We return to this problem in section 5, below.

Gorianchikov's memoir of life among the convicts, marked by his reticence about his own transgression, contains what may be considered another indirect self-reference, this time in the vein of self-indictment. Here he discusses those members of the medical profession who earn the common people's trust and those who betray it, claiming that their ethical shortcomings are entirely attributable to an unfavorable environment:

> It is time for us to put an end to our apathetic complaining that our environment has consumed us. Let us suppose that it's true that it has devoured much in us—but still, not everything. Often a shrewd and knowing scoundrel will very adroitly cover up and justify not only his weakness but frequently even his mere baseness [*podlost'*] by the influence of the environment, especially if he knows how to speak or write beautifully. (*PSS* 4:142/218)

Gorianchikov's rejection of the environment as an excuse for evildoing, particularly when it is offered by a member of the educated class who exploits his gift of self-expression to promote a lie, returns us to the rejected possibility of internal norms and standards imagined to exist beyond the contingencies of milieu or character. In the vacuum created by an absent conscience, the environment, like individual personality itself, exercises its formative power. Moreover, whereas conscience ensures accountability, its absence guarantees unaccountability—the inadequacy of all narratives or "stories" of crime to comprehend it.

This impasse is at the heart of the crisis of remorse that Gorianchikov registers in his first chapter, the non-appearance of that ultimately redemptive spiritual malaise expected to arise in the wake of crime after the frenzy which motivated it has spent itself. Without remorse as its counter-narrative, crime has the last, unanswerable word. This possibility drives Gorianchikov to abandon his attempt to universalize remorse and to try to democratize it instead by proposing that the peasant-convicts feel remorse only when they transgress against the common people, members of their own class. As we have seen, however, he is forced to conclude, based on his observations, that regardless of the class identity of their victims, the peasant-convicts feel no anguish and rarely reflect on their crimes. Thus, his scattered remarks on class, crime, and manifestations of conscience in *katorga* convey nothing but a tragic mismatching of ethical handicaps: the gentleman-convict does not admit to having done anything wrong and yet is capable of a self-condemnation harsher than any official punishment, whereas the peasant-convict can acknowledge having done something wrong but feels no regret about it. If Gorianchikov is ultimately compelled to abandon his incipient class analysis of conscience, Dostoevsky will stead-ily, if with inconsistent results, pursue this experiment throughout his post-Siberian career, from *House of the Dead* through *The Brothers Kara-mazov*, as well as in polemical venues like his *Diary of a Writer*.

In *House of the Dead*, however, Gorianchikov acknowledges only to re-ject and then reconfirm the vacuum of remorse demonstrated by the peas-ant-convicts of *katorga*. Added to the opacity of crime reinforced by their peculiar culture, it creates the increasingly acute epistemological crisis that is the source of his "terrible, corroding anguish" (*PSS* 4:69/99). In the apparent absence of the ethical touchstone of conscience, how is he to know what manner of men these are and what place, if any, he can secure for himself in their milieu? This question goes to the heart of the estrange-ment that plagues him for the duration of his sentence. To begin to under-stand the peasant-convicts without faulty preconceptions requires that Gorianchikov elaborate a new "philosophy of crime," starting at square one—with the crude, impulsive, and unforeseeable demands of individual "personality" (*lichnost'*) which asserts itself precisely when the efficacy of discipline seemed most secure:

> Sometimes the authorities were astonished when some convict, who had been living for several years with such exemplary submissiveness that they had made him a capo [*desiatochnyi*] for good behavior, suddenly, without any rhyme or reason—precisely as if a devil had entered him—went beserk, started drinking uncontrollably, wouldn't stop brawling, or sometimes even risked a criminal act—either open disrespect to the highest authorities, or he would murder someone, or commit assault, and so on. They would regard him with amazement. Yet perhaps the whole cause of this sudden explosion [*vzryv*] in a man from whom one would have least expected it was an an-guished, convulsive manifestation of personality, an instinctive longing to be his own self, a desire to declare himself and his own abject personality which, having suddenly appeared, reaches the point of fury, madness, the eclipse of reason, paroxysm, and convulsion. So, perhaps, one buried alive and awakening in his coffin, pounds on its lid and tries with all his might to throw it off, although it would seem that reason would convince him of the futility of all his efforts. (*PSS* 4:66–67/96)

Originating in the suffocated personality whose drive to declare itself is comparable in its urgency only to the survival instinct, crime is here revealed as the vehicle for the abject self's (temporary) subjectification.

Abjection is thus at the heart of crime and circumscribes its ontological ambiguity. It describes that state which leads to crime and to which the self will inevitably return after the crime is committed, as well as what must be visited on the other, the victim, if the abject self is to become (for the space of the crime) a full-fledged subject. In the act of crime, subjectification (the acquisition of an empowered selfhood) and its opposite, desubjectification (the obliteration of selfhood) coincide. A typical figure among "our common people," Gorianchikov thus states, is the type of man, perhaps "a peasant, a house serf, a craftsman, or a soldier," who, although he has meekly endured his difficult lot in life, suddenly snaps and commits murder:

> Here is where the strangeness begins: for a time the man suddenly goes way out of bounds. The first one he murdered was his oppressor, his enemy; although that was criminal, it was understandable; there was a motive; but then he kills not enemies but anybody and everybody, he kills for fun, for a rude word, for a look, for a string of beads, or simply: "Get out of the way and don't let me catch you, I'm coming!" He is like a man who is intoxicated, delirious. As if, having once crossed the line that for him was sacred, he begins to revel in the fact that for him there is no longer anything sacred; as if he had an overwhelming urge to transgress all at once against every law and authority, to enjoy the most unbridled and boundless freedom, and to enjoy the sensation of terror which he can't help but feel toward himself. (*PSS* 4:87–88/128–29)

Gorianchikov compares the recklessness of such criminals, who had once been "the most submissive and unremarkable people," to one who looks down into the abyss from a great height and, as if tempted by Poe's imp of the perverse, flirts with the downward tug. The more abject they had been formerly, the more impetuous their violence against others, and the more they court some final reckoning. This mood animates them up to the moment they ascend the scaffold, when all at once it is "cut short":

> Now the man suddenly becomes submissive, is reduced to nothing [*stushevat'-sia*],[87] turns into an old rag. On the scaffold he whimpers and begs the people for forgiveness. He arrives in prison and you see such snivelling, such snuffling, he's so beaten down, that you are astonished at him: "Is this really the same man who murdered five or six people?" (*PSS* 4:88/129)

The vicious circle of violence and abjection to which Gorianchikov attests in his observations of peasant-convicts, whether typical or individual, impedes his efforts to articulate a new philosophy of crime. He does not so much illuminate crime's opacity as transfer it to individual personality. For this reason, "stories" of crime, even when they are told, partake of an infernal circularity antithetical to that of the conversion narrative with its built-in mechanism for transcendence.

Although Gorianchikov is hard-pressed to elaborate a new philosophy of crime based on individual personality, he does have explicit recourse to the common people's own philosophy expressed by the concept of "misfortune" (*neschastnost'*). The idea has two great advantages: first, it originates not in elite society, which, in fact, has "no understanding" of it, as he later claims, but in common culture; and, second, regardless of the nature of the crime, the criminal's personality, or the existence of remorse, it attributes a kind of essence to him via the community at large.[88] Dostoevsky takes up the concept most thoroughly not in *House of the Dead* but in an 1873 *Diary of a Writer* entry entitled "The Environment." It is worth a brief digression here to compare his remarks on the subject in the 1861 novel to those written for polemical purposes more than a decade later.[89]

In "The Environment," his exposition of "misfortune" is offered in refutation of the liberal theory of the influence of the environment on behavior, which defense lawyers had effectively invoked before the new mixed-class juries to excuse or even to deny the fact of crime.[90] Significant in this context is that Dostoevsky introduces "misfortune" in terms of the "*ne to*" or "not that," an unarticulated idea or belief that can only be negatively indicated because it is overshadowed by another, superficially similar but actually antithetical idea, perhaps even a "vile distortion" (*PSS* 21:10/128). In the conclusion to "Old People"—the essay that precedes "The Environment," and which is dedicated to an account of the writer's debut and the powerful influence of his mentor, the radical critic Vissarion Belinsky—Dostoevsky describes his arrival in *katorga* twenty-three years earlier:

> Around me were precisely those people who, according to Belinsky's belief, *could not* refrain from their crimes and, perhaps, were justified and only more unfortunate than others. I knew that the entire Russian people also called us "unfortunates" and I heard this name many times and from many lips. But this was something different, absolutely not that [*ne to*] about which Belinsky spoke and what one hears now, for example, in some of the verdicts of our juries. In this word "unfortunate," in this verdict of the people, a different idea sounded. (*PSS* 21:13/130–31; emphasis in original)

"The Environment" is then devoted to an exposition for the educated reader of this absolutely distinctive popular idea.

The essay begins with an imaginary debate between a narrator and several anonymous interlocutors about the significance of the high rate of acquittals by Russian juries where peasants, "yesterday's insulted and humiliated," had been sitting alongside members of the nobility since the reforms of 1864 (*PSS* 21:13/132). The narrator worries that the high acquittal rate reflects the success of liberal defense lawyers in persuading the common people of their theory of the environment—that a corrupt and oppressive environment makes crime inevitable and thereby justifiable—because of its superficial resemblance to the people's own idea of "misfortune." Although the narrator claims that the people's idea has from time immemorial been "concealed within" them, "unexpressed and unconscious," he is able to articulate it by staging it as an act of speech (*PSS* 21:17/137):

> Briefly, with this word "unfortunate," it is as if the people are saying to the "unfortunate": "You have sinned and are suffering, but we, too, are sinners. If we had been in your place, perhaps we might have done even worse. Were we better than we are, perhaps you might not be sitting in prison. With the retribution for your crime you have also taken on the burden for all our lawlessness. Pray for us, and we pray for you. But for now, unfortunate ones, accept these alms of ours; we give them so that you know we remember you and have not severed our brotherly ties with you." (*PSS* 21:17/138)[91]

Liberal theorists of the environment and their spokesmen, criminal defense lawyers, have substituted for this essentially Christian popular truth a secular update all the more seductive for its deceptive resemblance to the people's instinctively held idea:

> "Society is vile, and therefore we too are vile; but we are rich, we are secure, and it is only by chance that we escaped encountering the things you did. And had we encountered them, we would have acted as you did. Who is to blame? The environment is to blame. And so there is only a faulty social structure, but there is no crime whatsoever." (*PSS* 21:17/138)

In the people's judgment, however, as Dostoevsky represents it, the most unfortunate of all is the criminal who has convinced himself that, since there is no such thing as crime, he cannot be a criminal:

> The people are compassionate, and there is no one more unfortunate than that criminal who has even stopped considering himself a criminal: he is an animal, a beast. And so what if he does not even understand that he is an animal and has strangled his own conscience? He is only doubly unfortunate. Doubly unfortunate, but also doubly criminal. The people feel sorry for him but will not renounce their truth. The people never, having called a criminal an "unfortunate," stop considering him to be a criminal! And there would be no greater calamity for us than if the people themselves agreed with the criminal and assured him, "No, you're not guilty, because there is no 'crime'!" (*PSS* 21:18/138–39)

It is worth noting that the people's idea of misfortune, which Dostoevsky here champions, brought to bear on his fictional alter ego, Gorianchikov, who does not consider himself a criminal, judges him to be doubly unfortunate and doubly criminal. This doubleness follows on the doubleness of self-delusion, examined in part 1, and underwrites the double referentiality of his remarks on the criminal and crime mentioned at the beginning of this section.

Although both *House of the Dead* and "The Environment" share the themes of the convict and the popular idea of misfortune, there are key differences of representation. In *House of the Dead*, as we have seen, Gorianchikov claims repeatedly that, despite his efforts, he never saw the slightest sign of remorse in the vast majority of his fellow convicts, and he concludes that "the criminal, having risen up against society, hates it and almost always considers himself innocent and it guilty." In "The Environment," Dostoevsky draws the opposite conclusion: he insists that, among the many "hardened criminals" he encountered in *katorga*, "not one of them ceased to regard himself as a criminal": "Oh, believe me, in his heart not one of them considered himself justified!"[92] In *House of the Dead*, Gorianchikov repudiates the reformist premise of punishing criminals, "Of course, prison and the system of forced labor do not reform the criminal; they only punish him and ensure society against the villain's further attempts on its peace. In the criminal himself, prison and the most strenuous hard labor develop only hatred, a thirst for forbidden pleasures, and a terrible shallow-mindedness" (*PSS* 21:18/139; *PSS* 4:15/16). In "The Environment," on the contrary, Dostoevsky asserts that, "with strict punishment, imprisonment, and hard labor you would have saved perhaps half [the hardened criminals]." He insists, that is, on the salvific effect of suffering, an opinion that directly contradicts Gorianchikov's statement in *House of the Dead* that the environment of *katorga* itself, which deprives men of meaningful labor and "normal lawful possessions," develops in them "such criminal qualities of which they previously could have had no understanding" so that "they become depraved and turn into beasts" (*PSS* 21:19/139; *PSS* 4:16/18). Finally, in "The Environment," the separation between the elite "us" and the common "them" is taken for granted, as when Dostoevsky points out that "for us" (*u nas*) nothing could be worse than if "they" began to deny the existence of crime—that is, if "they" renounced the inherently disciplinary ethos of misfortune. His assumption of the separation confirms the peasant-convicts' prediction on Gorianchikov's release that he "would go straightaway *to the masters* [*k gospodam*] and would sit down beside these masters as their equal," forgetting his membership in the community of unfortunates (*PSS* 4:231/360; emphasis in original). In *House of the Dead*, although class difference is constantly emphasized both behaviorally and rhetorically, and although

it is strategically asserted by both noble- and peasant-convicts, Gorianchikov, until the moment of his release, is compelled to acknowledge his
equality in abjection. He realizes that outsiders consider him one of
"them," and he is startled to find himself the recipient of charity offered
by peasant civilians to convicts indiscriminately, as unfortunates. The first
chapter of his memoir concludes with his telling how he had been offered
a quarter kopek by a peasant girl and her mother, in Christ's name, when
returning one day from the work site: "I kept that little coin with me for
a long time" (*PSS* 4:19/22).

In *House of the Dead*, then, the people's concept of misfortune, exemplified by the quarter kopek, succeeds in breaking down Gorianchikov's resistance to identifying himself with his new environment and those who
inhabit it. No longer the resolute "I" confronting the "them" of his fellow
convicts across the abyss of class difference, Gorianchikov, startled by the
simple assumption of his criminality in the gesture of alms-giving, finds
himself quite simply cast as a "we," a member of the convict community.
That he accepts and carefully keeps the coin signals his acceptance at some
level of the designation. On the basis of his status as just such a "we,"
Dostoevsky will authorize his representations of the people after 1861 and
distinguish them from those of his peers who had had no such intimate
contact; in "The Environment," for example, he invokes his experience to
authenticate his role as privileged translator of the people's unarticulated,
even unconscious, idea. As for Gorianchikov, following this encounter
with the peasant girl, he uses "we" or "us" in reference to the convict
population, although infrequently and implausibly, and therefore conspicuously.[93] In the hospital, for example, he describes at length another patient, a likeable and easy-going Christian Kalmuck, who relates how he
was beaten daily as a child and whose habit of stealing caused him to be
constantly beaten in prison. Although Gorianchikov complains often
about convict thefts but never himself steals, and although he never reports being the victim of physical violence, he nevertheless asks in the
Kalmuck's defense, "but who among us [*kto zh u nas*] was not sometimes
caught stealing, and who among us was not beaten for it?" (*PSS* 4:146/
224). On another occasion, in a chapter devoted to animals in the prison,
he relates how two convicts illicitly acquired a dog in order to skin it and
make shoes from the hide; Gorianchikov describes how the captive dog
looked uneasily at "us three" (*na nas troikh*) as the preparations for its
demise were being made (*PSS* 4:191/297). In contrast to these examples,
the significance of his use of the first-person plural in referring to himself
and the other convicts as "unfortunates" is immediately apparent. After
he reports receiving alms from the peasant child, he turns in a later chapter
to the relationship of "us," the convict community, himself included, and

those outside the prison who devoted themselves to "brotherly care of the 'unfortunates' " (*PSS* 4:67/97).

Here, Gorianchikov recalls one woman in particular who, for reasons unknown to anyone, "esteemed it a particular happiness to do everything she could for us," so that "we, sitting in prison, felt that there, outside the prison, we had a most devoted friend" (*PSS* 4:67/97). Upon his release, he pays a visit to this woman who, with no apparent motive and no encouragement from him, had supported him in small but significant ways without their ever having personally met:

> She was neither young nor old, neither good-looking nor bad-looking; it was even impossible to tell whether she was intelligent or educated. Only her infinite goodness was noticeable in her at every turn, an insuperable desire to oblige, to make things easier, to do for you something pleasing without fail. [. . .] Together with a friend from my prison acquaintance, I spent almost an entire evening with her. She looked us in the eyes to try to anticipate our wishes, laughed when we laughed, hastened to agree with everything we said; she bustled about offering us what hospitality she could. (*PSS* 4:68/98)

For this woman, the criminal's lack of remorse is not at issue; it is overridden, as it were, by the unmotivated and unconditional attribution to the criminal of a common human essence inherent in the idea of misfortune. The evacuation of personality implicit in her disregard for the contingencies of the criminal's character or the story of his crime is mirrored in her own peculiar quality of being herself without qualities: in addition to the fact that she is physically nondescript, she has emptied herself of personal desires, needs, preferences, and ambitions in order wholly to adopt those of the unfortunate in a gesture of total giving. Crime is for her nothing other than the occasion for this unqualified and voluntary desubjectification, this erasure of the giver's personality, this reduction of the self to nothing—the antithesis of self-reduction as a mark of radical abjection which Gorianchikov had described in the criminal on the scaffold. For this woman, the kinds of judgment Gorianchikov struggled to make throughout his incarceration in order to unravel the mystery of crime and discover its true philosophy is not in question and, implicitly, is left to God. The charitable woman is nothing but charitable, a tautology realized in a process of self-evacuation and investment in the other so completely realized that for Gorianchikov she offers an embodied refutation of the theory (attractive to intellectuals of the early 1860s) that altruism is actually egoism. We have seen how *homo sacer*, abandoned in the space of exception, has been described as a being without qualities. The charitable woman—like the wives of the Decembrists whom Dostoevsky extols for following their husbands into Siberian exile and voluntarily relinquishing their status and wealth—reveals the kenotic positivity of reduction-to-nothing by deliberately placing herself in the space of exception in order to provide a point of contact "outside" for the benefit of the *homines sacri* within.

The character of Sonia in *Crime and Punishment* is a type of the charitable woman who also enacts a voluntary desubjectification or self-effacement for the sake of merging with the other, Raskol'nikov, which Dostoevsky suggests, in the epilogue to that novel, makes her a type of ideal author. Her authorial practice provides access to a hidden (invisible, unarticulated) content and permits it to emerge with its integrity intact—that is, without her interference and absent the traces of her individual personality. Thus, after Sonia decides to follow Raskol'nikov to Siberia despite his indifference to her, she writes letters to his sister and best friend which contain "no account of her own hopes, no guessing about the future, no descriptions of her own feelings." In place of self-representation or her own interpretation of Raskol'nikov's state of mind, Sonia's letters offer:

> only facts—that is, his own words, detailed reports of the condition of his health, of what he had wanted at their meeting on such-and-such a day, what he had asked her, what he had told her to do, and so on. All this news was given in great detail. In the end the image of their unfortunate brother stood forth of itself, clearly and precisely drawn; no mistake was possible here, because these were all true facts. (*PSS* 6:415/541)

Here, through the unlikely example of authorship, the ontological ambiguity inherent in the popular idea of misfortune is evident from its charitable practice: it elides the question of individual personality by disregarding it in the criminal and evacuating it in the alms-giver so that the second-order difference they represent between the good- and evildoer (and, potentially, between the subject who judges and the object who is judged) is resolved in the higher human truth of misfortune and its amelioration through suffering.

Despite his portrait of Sonia's ideal authorship through her practice of a self-effacement associated with the people's idea of misfortune, Dostoevsky, in "The Environment," does not refrain from the kind of interference he implicitly abjures. From the outset, the 1873 essay is at cross-purposes rhetorically. Its ostensible point is to speculate on the high acquittal rate of Russian juries, and, in so doing, to demonstrate the superiority of the people's idea of misfortune in relation to the intelligentsia's theory of the environment, its fraudulent double. But it conspicuously fails to carry out its ideological agenda, a failure similar to that of Belinsky described in the conclusion of the previous essay and which provided the lead-in to "The Environment." Dostoevsky wants the popular concept of misfortune to be and remain a vital one, and the dialogically staged debate on the causes of juries' high acquittal rates is intended to showcase it as such. Instead, it demonstrates that the popular idea, among all those raised in the debate, is the one clearly *not* at play in jury deliberations. Having rejected the possibility, in the name of the principled stringencies of misfortune—its insistence on the salvific power of punishment—that the people are expressing liberal compassion for the criminal at the bar in their acquittals, he is forced to conclude that the liberal hypothesis at least "somehow explains something, at least it provides a way out of the darkness, and without [it] there is only bewilderment, utter gloom inhabited by some madman" (*PSS* 21:20/141). It is as though he is conceding that without the explanations we ourselves concoct, we understand nothing of the people's inner life.

Dostoevsky's apparent concession leads directly and without transition into a lengthy narrative, imaginatively embellished and conspicuously so, of a crime familiar to readers in 1873 through the newspapers and familiar to us as readers of *House of the Dead*: a peasant, in a constant state of drunkenness, abuses his wife so viciously and relentlessly that it ends in her death.[94] This, of course, is the "story" of crime that materializes at the heart of Gorianchikov's memoir, "Akul'ka's Husband," and then again, twelve years later, as the conclusion to "The Environment." The two "stories" differ in certain ways: the abused wife, in "The Environment," goes to the authorities for help but to no avail, and she resorts to suicide. The peasant is tried, a small daughter who had witnessed it all courageously testifies against her father, but the jury, although acknowledging his guilt, recommends clemency. Dostoevsky points out that, instead of Siberia, the husband will face "only eight months in prison and then come home and demand his daughter back, who had testified against him on behalf of her mother. Once again he will have someone to hang by the heels" (*PSS* 21:22/143). Moreover, the suicide had happened recently and, along with the husband's trial, had been reported in all the newspapers. Akul'ka's case, we recall, is somewhat different. Her husband beats and then murders her in a drunken rage; he is sent to Siberia for the crime; there was no one to whom she could appeal for help; the couple had had no children and were, in fact, newlyweds; and her story, never published and unknown outside the benighted village where she lived and died, found an accidental witness in Gorianchikov long after her death.

The similarity uniting the two narratives, however, is more significant than the differences, and it arises from the very nature of the crime in question. Despite the authorizing claim to have, in some sense, borne witness to the crime made explicitly by Dostoevsky ("Have you seen how a peasant beats his wife? I have") and implicitly by Gorianchikov, it escapes the promise of accountability inherent in the claim (*PSS* 21:21/ 142). In other words, in both cases the claim to have "seen" or "heard" how a husband kills his wife, instead of increasing the reader's confidence that we will come to know the meaning of such an event, is revealed to be uncertain, if not downright specious. In place of testimony, the "witness" offers a narrative whose basis in imagination rather than actuality, far from denied, is foregrounded. At the same time, the reader's sensation of seeing the crime unfold before his or her eyes, of partaking voyeuristically in the husband's sadistic rage and the wife's terror, is heightened through the pacing of both narratives and the graphic detail they generously provide. Both these attributes of the narratives—their questionable truth status coupled paradoxically with the sense of immediacy they convey—cast doubt upon the nature of the witnessing that makes them available to us. Insofar as the motive for including the narratives, in both cases, is at least partly pedagogical (intended to convey to the elite reader information intimately related to the twin mysteries of brutal crime and peasant culture), they function as conspicuous stumbling blocks to the objective, which is of pressing and explicit concern to both narrators, of making crime accountable—that is, articulable and thus understandable and thus redeemable. In both texts, however, it is the very graphic quality of the "stories" of crime that ensures their opacity and allows them to escape accountability. They remain, as Agamben would put it, stubbornly outside the archive, and, despite the richness of their unfolding, they remain at some level unsayable, beyond the capacity of language to produce some counter-narrative in which they would clearly appear as elements of some larger system in which they are always already resolved. Let us look more closely at the narratives' representation of the fundamental unspeakability of crime in "The Environment," before concluding this section with an examination of the complex structure of witnessing in "Akul'ka's Husband."

In "The Environment," tapping into the credibility he had long cultivated as a former "unfortunate" with personal experience of the peasant-convicts and their culture, Dostoevsky claims to have "seen" how a peasant beats his wife. He begins by recounting the crime as reported in the newspapers: "Quite simply, the wife hung herself because of her husband's beatings; the husband was tried and found deserving of leniency." Even if accurate to the facts of the case, this is inadequate: "But for a long time thereafter the whole situation would appear to me; it appears to me even now." The narrator begins imaginatively to supplement the newspaper account with a frankly literary richness of detail; if the reports said the peasant was fair-haired, Dostoevsky "would add something more: thinning hair." Witnesses had reported that he was cruel to animals—"a most characteristic trait!" It becomes impossible to know if the flood of detail that follows originates in witness accounts, trial transcripts, the newspaper, or the narrator's understanding, imaginatively fleshed out, of the lineaments of peasant *byt*, or everyday life. The peasant's body is white and bloated;

he moves slowly; he speaks ponderously. If the beatings were constant, the staging and instruments varied. Although violent, they were unmotivated—"I think he himself did not know why he was beating her"—and were supplemented with other tortures, like starvation. So the husband would place bread within reach of the starving wife, but say, " 'Don't you dare touch that bread. That's *my* bread'—another extremely characteristic trait!" (*PSS* 21:20/141). As for the wife, "I can imagine what she looked like"—small and skinny, because "men with white, bloated bodies" of the peasant class often choose to marry such women. She killed herself on what was "probably" a bright spring morning. These details of character, appearance, and setting are not precisely fanciful, because they are not chosen at random but with a strict mimetic fidelity to what is "most characteristic" according to Dostoevsky: "It seems to me that if she had become pregnant by him in her final days it would have been an even more characteristic and essential trait for completing the picture [*obstanovka*; also, a theatrical set], but without which it would seem incomplete" (*PSS* 21:20–21/142).

The fleshing out of the picture requires, too, an anthropologically accurate and psychologically astute account of how the beatings occur and what nuances of enjoyment the husband derives from his choice of weapon, the part of his wife's body on which he chooses to inflict the blows, his chosen method for immobilizing her, the various sounds she makes while being beaten and afterward, when and if she loses consciousness, the pace of the blows, and his routine drink of kvas after his energy is depleted. However, with the reader's attention at its most engaged, in the middle of this imaginative staging of the crime, Dostoevsky undercuts his polemic against environmental theorists. Having just described how the husband listens with delight to his wife's screams, Dostoevsky pauses to speculate on who, given different circumstances, the woman might have been:

> Do you know, gentlemen, people are born in various circumstances: can you really not believe that this woman in other circumstances might have been some kind of Juliet or Beatrice from Shakespeare, or Gretchen from *Faust*? I'm not saying that she was—it would be ridiculous to insist on that—but yet there could have been in embryo in her some kind of nobility of soul, no less, it may be, than in one of noble birth.

Having paused to speculate on the formative effects of the environment, relevant in the victim's case but inadmissable, according to the ideology of the essay, in the evildoer's, the beating recommences: "and here this same Beatrice or Gretchen is beaten, beaten like a cat! The blows pour down faster and faster, harder and harder, innumerable" (*PSS* 21:21/142).

Here, the hero or heroine who exists embryonically in every human being meets the executioner within.

Imaginatively fleshing out the crime on the basis of what is "characteristic," far from providing a clear perspective on the abyssal event, only reenacts the desubjectification of the peasant woman. The woman's plight is both an aesthetically elaborated facsimile that one "witnesses" with excitement and a crime one deplores, part theater and part mundane reality, as she herself is both a human being and a bundle of hypothetically characteristic attributes. Stories such as hers, which Gorianchikov wants to hear so that he will know and Dostoevsky wants to broadcast so that others will know, resurrect the dead only to restage their desubjectification and death. The story of crime thus emerges as a specific form of narrative that represents the diabolical inversion of all narrative dynamism or progress. Unlike the circularity of the conversion narrative that brings about the transition, within the narrator, of pilgrim into poet, of the blind one who suffers into the one with perspective who knows, the story of crime brings its protagonist to life solely in order to kill her. Her status as a full-fledged human being is therefore never securely established: she "lives" only to be slaughtered, like an animal. In "The Environment," the story of the crime of wife-murder represents an internal limit to the paradigm of misfortune wherein desubjectification (of the alms-giver) leads to subjectification (of the unfortunate, the criminal). Likewise, in *House of the Dead,* the story of the crime of wife-murder, "Akul'ka's Husband," can only constitute an unincorporable remainder in a narrative consecrated to conversion, a resurrection from the dead without remainder, and thus represents the limit of the conversion paradigm. In both cases, the crime remains *ne to*— not that—outside all attempts to conceptualize it in such a way as to adduce a meaning that will redeem the crime by removing the stumbling block to understanding that it represents.[95]

The peasant woman—in life, a victim of the daily abuse that inexorably accomplishes her death; in stories, the premise for resurrecting a life in order to recommit it to death— represents one aspect of the ontological ambiguity of crime. We are now in a position to understand another by focusing not on the victim but on the ostensibly untranslatable criminal. His act makes him not just the evildoer but—as many criminal confessions have shown—a potentially privileged witness to evildoing itself, the one most capable of illuminating its obscurity. This consideration returns us to Agamben's analysis of the ventriloquistic structure of witnessing, his account of the relation of the survivor to the non-survivor—the one who returns to tell the tale and the one who perishes. What relevance might it have for reading "Akul'ka's Husband," the central story of crime in *House of the Dead*? This crime, we recall, is the very crime which the prefatory narrator of the ex-convict's memoirs ascribes to Gorianchikov himself and which many of Dostoevsky's contemporary readers ascribed to him. The identification through their crimes of the nobleman Gorianchikov with the brutal peasant Shishkov, established in advance of our reading of the former's memoir, complicates the structure of testimony in the text—testimony regarding the brutal world of penal servitude, a world invisible to the memoirist's readers—by superimposing upon it another form of first-person narration, confession. In the aftermath of a violent event, what normally distinguishes testimony from confession is, of course, that whereas the speaker of testimony suffers the horror to which he or she bears witness (even if not as its ultimate victim), the speaker of confession bears witness to it as an agent of that horror. Of equal relevance for our purposes, confession, in its literary sense, signifies a quest to discover the truth about the self, typically in relation to the commission of some abhorrent act about which one is self-deceived. As we saw in part 1, J. M. Coetzee ascribes to the genre of confession an ontological significance insofar as it accentuates "problems of truth-telling and self-recognition, deception and self-deception."[96] If the violent or abhorrent act engenders both testimony and confession, it is also that which makes them fundamentally incompatible forms of first-person utterance. In order to understand the ontology of crime in *Notes from the House of the Dead*, we must begin by attempting to disentangle the subjects of testimony and confession in order to see more clearly how and why in this text they resist disentanglement—how and why testimony and confession here occupy their own zone of indistinction.

As described in part 1, Gorianchikov gives Shishkov's narrative formal independence as a discrete chapter in his memoir as well as a title that identifies its narrator and perhaps its genre, "Akul'ka's Husband: A Story." The subtitle both relates it to the "stories" of crime told more reluctantly or only partially by other peasant-convicts and also suggests that a fictional component underlies all such narratives. In Formalist terms, Shishkov's story is a classic example of *skaz*, a tale told by a first-person narrator of folk or lower-class origins clearly differentiated by his or her speech from the authorial figure (in cases where the story is embedded in a larger narrative). Shishkov's tale of murdering his wife evinces the integrity of his own uninflected brutality, and it is difficult to detect any sign that he doubts the necessity or even the probity of his act (he is the "doubly unfortunate" criminal, according to the concept of misfortune, who does not acknowledge his wrongdoing). Therefore, there is no indication that he tells his tale in order to bear witness to Akul'ka's otherwise invisible life and death to which he attributes no value. Nevertheless, his tale evinces the structure that Agamben associates with the "constitutively fractured" subject of testimony: Akul'ka is that "something" which "sinks to the bottom, wholly

desubjectified and silenced" in the space of exception of an isolated peasant village, and Shishkov is that "something subjectified" which "speaks
without truly having anything to say of its own"—that is, anything about
Akul'ka's experience of mortal terror (*RA* 151). This speaking without
having anything to say of his own is, in fact, precisely what is so jarring
about Shishkov's tale—he describes at great length how he terrorized and
then murdered his wife without himself registering her terror. (His inability even retrospectively to acknowledge her suffering is amplified by his
interlocutor, the peasant Cherevin, whose laconic responses to the escalating horror and belatedly pragmatic advice about how to enjoy wife-beat-
ing for a lifetime are themselves chilling.) In Shishkov's testimony about
Akul'ka's life and death—a confession without remorse—the "speechless
one," Akul'ka, "makes the speaking one speak," although, in the absence
of remorse or an empathetic identification with her suffering, we, who
overhear Gorianchikov's overhearing, get no insight into or perspective
on this crime but are thrust into the black chaos of a violence wholly
unleashed. The "zone of indistinction" that the criminal and his victim
occupy is registered in the story's title, "Akul'ka's Husband" (*Akul'kin
Muzh*), in which (as noted in part 1) husband and wife seem to struggle
for entitlement: Shishkov is named in the title only as Akul'ka's husband,
and Akul'ka's name is transformed into a masculinized modifier of the
noun "husband."

Gorianchikov's narrative, in which Shishkov's story is embedded, even
more clearly exemplifies what Agamben describes as the "vertiginous"
quality of witnessing in which an "inseparable intimacy" is forged between
two beings, henceforth coextensive but non-coincident, divided but inseparable. This intimacy is evident both in the uncertain status of Shishkov's story (is it Gorianchikov's invention, hallucination, dream, or memory, or an independently existing actuality?) as well as in its supersession
of Gorianchikov's own authorial voice, a process described in part 1 as the
nobleman's disarticulation at the mediate level of his narrative. In other
words, as Shishkov's voice overtakes Gorianchikov's and appropriates his
narrative authority, we might say that some aspect of the nobleman's life
sinks to the bottom, silenced, and, in so doing, allows "something subjectified"—for the space of the narrative, the peasant Shishkov—to speak.
Although this might seem to ally the nobleman with the murdered peasant
woman, the more persuasive allegorical reading to which the expressive
intimacy of the two narrators lends support is that Shishkov's story *is* Gorianchikov's confession (Shishkov, c'est moi): through the story of peasant
murder, the nobleman (the author Dostoevsky and his fictional alter ego
Gorianchikov) tells a truth about himself that he cannot acknowledge.[97]
He did not undertake political activism on behalf of the enslaved peasants
from a conviction of their equality with him. Instead, it was premised on

their silence and on the substitution of their own word with rumors and myths about them (as Shishkov slits his wife's throat in response to rumors of her infidelity and in the absence of a partnership based, if not on equality, then on mutual respect). Despite his intentions, then, the nobleman's activism promoted nothing more than the peasants' further silencing and desubjectification. Guilty in this sense of a crime against the peasants, Dostoevsky/Gorianchikov might be bewildered by their unremitting hostility when he encounters them in *katorga* but knows in his heart that he has earned it, that his actions helped widen the *bezdna*, or abyss, on whose far shore he stands, looking longingly across at the common people's *svoi*, their milieu, but with no means of access. Nevertheless, his memoir reveals that, in the space of exception that is *katorga*, the truth of Gorianchikov's own inadmissable "crime" sinks, unacknowledged, only to be articulated in the speech not of the self but of the anti-self or, rather, in an embodied "zone of indistinction" between self and anti-self which likewise evinces no experiential relation to that which it tells (*RA* 120).

Allegorically considered, then, the emphasis in the story of Akul'ka's murder falls not on the "crime" as transgressive event, an innocent woman's brutal and senseless murder, but as a translation of the nobleman's bad faith. Not only is the allegorical reading of the crime to which Gorianchikov "bears witness" removed from the brutal violence against Akul'ka described at such gruesome length and with such graphic detail. The allegorical reading itself displaces that reality, the life and death of *this* woman, and puts something else—the nobleman's guilty conscience, obscure but finally comprehensible—in its place.[98] This is precisely why the allegorical reading, though plausible in light of Dostoevsky's later critique of his political radicalism, must finally be superseded. The story of this crime cannot be dismissed as some form of mere translation—allegory, nightmare, questionable memory, guilty conscience for bad faith, the empty boasting of an oaf—or rendered insubstantiable as an event that "poetic" justice will one day vicariously redeem. This is so not just on ethical but also on literary-historical grounds. "Akul'ka's Husband: A Story" is the first inside narrative of crime—a crime which in its telling (as in its commission) lacks any outside perspective—in Dostoevsky's oeuvre. It requires the reader to leave the safety of the shore, so to speak, and proceed unaccompanied into a hellish world where nothing prevents the realization of murderous or sadistic impulses. Uniquely in Dostoevsky's oeuvre, no attempt is made in the text to compensate or atone for the crime: it is left entirely unaddressed—neither explained (for example, by the framing commentary we saw in "The Environment") nor redeemed (by conscience, for example, as in Raskol'nikov's case). Shishkov is the exception to the rule cited by Joseph Frank that, "while Dostoevsky does not spare his readers the evil that he so vividly represents, he invariably counterbalances its effects by insisting on the ineradicability of a moral conscience that even the most hardened evildoer will not be able to escape."[99] No sense of conscience or even decency censors Shishkov from within to impede his whiningly self-righteous narrative that catalogues all of Akul'ka's imaginary sins against him: Dostoevsky gives him voice, and that voice has free and unimpeded reign in his story. Although one may read Shishkov's narrative with reference to Gorianchikov's bad faith, the story of Akul'ka cannot, in the end, be regarded as a mere symptom. Structurally unincorporated into the memoir that frames it and unassimilable to its many anecdotes about the peasant-convicts, "Akul'ka's Husband" stands alone and signifies *precisely as crime*, as something that has happened and cannot be expunged, and that has contributed its modicum to the quantity of blood with which, as Ivan Karamazov observes, the earth's crust is soaked.

The "unsayable"—the crime against Akul'ka—is more arcane than the repressed content of the nobleman's consciousness with its multiple if indirect expressive resources. "Akul'ka's Husband" is both authorless and multiply authored, the terminus of a chain of brutally repressive acts extending infinitely into the historical past in which action and reaction have long been indistinguishable. On two levels, then—both the content of what is told and the scene of its telling—the story of Akul'ka's killing exists in an uncertain zone between nobleman and peasant. Whether or not we consider "Akul'ka's Husband" to be "only" allegory, it is manifestly a joint production of nobleman and peasant, the disfigured offspring, perhaps, of their historical relationship. This is the zone of indistinction occupied by crime in the memoir and in the concentric spaces of exception the memoir represents. Fundamentally opaque, the crime against Akul'ka remains essentially unincorporable, the least abstract and yet the most conceptually elusive element in the entire memoir. It is ultimately impossible to attribute this crime to anybody. The question Gorianchikov insistently asks at the conclusion of his memoir—"And who is to blame? That's just it, who is to blame?"—cannot be answered. We cannot know, in the end, the relationship of Gorianchikov to the crime committed against the peasants he encounters in *katorga*, who, he laments, have been condemned to perish "abnormally, unlawfully, irrevocably," nor can we know his relationship to the un-authored or de-authored crime whose narration is situated at the heart of his memoir and which cannot be incorporated into it (*PSS* 4:231/360). All we can say is that crime—and, specifically, the crime against Akul'ka, owned by no one, confessed without remorse, and witnessed without understanding, a *ne to* that lies outside positive identification or accountability—is an integral component of the autobiography's central unconsummated image: the self that is dead to its former life but has not yet been born into the new.

5. The Flesh of the Political

The image [. . .] stood forth of itself.
—*PSS* 6:415/541

In *Notes from the House of the Dead*, Dostoevsky creates an artistic image of a particular experience of selfhood in which the subject finds himself in a space and a time between a former existence that is dead to him and a future existence that has not materialized. He has been rendered a *ne to*—neither this nor that—for an incalculable period, and cannot know positively if he will ever return to what he was or become something else altogether, something inconceivable. His anxiety recalls the scene of mystical loathing that Myshkin described to the Epanchin women. His sentence prolongs and normalizes the state of the man on the scaffold faced with the incontrovertible fact of his own imminent demise and wondering what (not who) he is about to become. Gorianchikov suffers something akin to this elemental terror, and struggles at every moment to guard his former integrity and keep it intact. He feels immediately upon his induction into the prison that the boundary between himself and others in this environment is never secure, and he suffers a disarticulation which he intuits at every moment but of which he is only partly aware. More menacing than the threat of physical violence, about which he is explicitly anxious, is that in the space of exception the self may become indistinguishable from and, in effect, merge with another who, from the perspective of the former life, could not be more antithetical—specifically, the brutal and illiterate peasant-convict. This is how the *ne to* of crime and of the common people with whom Gorianchikov exclusively associates crime are conjoined with the *ne to* of the disarticulated noble narrator: together they constitute the text's central unconsummated image.

The merging of self and anti-self or, put differently, this authorless production of an unconsummated image, can be achieved only in this space of exception or abandonment which the literary text represents as a specific environment, *katorga*. We might expect that this mutation, the merging of antithetical selves, augurs consequences for the world outside *katorga*, the larger social order, but they cannot be and therefore are not realized in the memoir for two reasons. First, as discussed in part 1, the memoir by its very structure returns us to its beginning to reenact the process of Gorianchikov's disarticulation. Resurrection from the dead, although proclaimed, is (on the testimony of the prefatory narrator's introduction) not achieved and its accomplishment remains prospective. If Gorianchikov is not resurrected from the dead and reborn into a new world, nor is he able to go back to a former state, to rejoin the masters as if his sojourn in the Dead House had never happened, as the peasant-convicts imagine him doing. At the conclusion of this novel, the new world has not come into being; we might say, along with the narrator of *Crime and Punishment*, that the new world into which the new man emerges after dying to his former life "might make the subject of a new story—but our present story is ended" (*PSS* 6:422/551).[100] The image is left unconsummated, but in *katorga* its component parts are assembled—the noble and the common subject are brought together in the equality of abjection, around the abyss of class difference, and under the sign of crime.

This brings us to the second reason why Gorianchikov's memoir does not make manifest the consequences for the larger social order of the merging of noble with common subjects in *katorga*. It is committed to representing not the advent of the new man in a newly realized world that could only have been fantastical at the time of Dostoevsky's Siberian exile in the last years of Nicholas's reign, but rather of *katorga* as the only possible, if entirely implausible, site of its mise-en-scène. It is the place where the nobleman is not just permitted an intimate view of, but must also ineluctably partake in, the irreducibility of bare life, the ground of his integration with the common people that, for Gorianchikov, is beyond uncontrollable—it is all but inconceivable. It is the populated medium which, even as it crystallizes the history of the relationship of common to elite (indeed, this is its distinctiveness as a chronotope), forges a new paradigm of relation. As such, it is the medium in which Russian modernity constitutes itself in the space of abandonment, without the benefit of a foundational epistemology and bereft of any certainties other than those established by the facts and needs of bare life. In this final section of part 2, I examine *Notes from the House of the Dead* as the mise-en-scène, never finalized, of an unheard-of democracy.

The Grammar of Katorga

At various points in his narrative, Gorianchikov records the peasant-convicts' own collective self-characterizations: "we are a literate people [*gramotnyi narod*]"; "we are a lost people [*pogibshyi narod*]"; "we are a beaten people [*bityi narod*]"; "we are a people without a tongue [*narod bez iazyka*]" (*PSS* 4:12, 13, 16–18, 181/11, 13, 18, 281).[101] Taken together, they fuel his determination to find the logic or at least the principle of legibility of common culture and then to transcribe it—to position first himself and, by extension, his class in relation to it.[102] But even with the hints these self-characterizations provide, his task is difficult: each one is ambiguous. Does the people's being "lost" mean that they are fallen or abandoned; does their being "beaten" mean that they are abused or defeated; does their being without a tongue mean that they are inarticulate or unrepresented; do we hear in their words confession or protest? The initial self-characterization—"we are a literate people"—seems more straightforward, and Gorianchikov even confirms its literal truth; the context in which it appears, however, complicates the question of its significance.

In its immediate context—Gorianchikov's discussion of the obstacles to the peasant-convicts' telling the stories of their crimes—the statement "we are a literate people" is simply a non sequitur. Having described how the stories of the peasant-convicts' crimes are disfigured either in their remembrance, their telling, or their reception, he suddenly, mid-paragraph and apropos of nothing, cites the people's claim to literacy which is itself characterized, he notes, by a "strange self-satisfaction." Immediately and without transition, the discussion reverts to its original subject; Gorianchikov recounts the horrific details of one story that, counter to the general rule, *was* told, and by the drunken convict who murdered a little boy by luring him into a shed with a toy. Again without transition, the narrator reverts to the topic of peasant literacy, assuring his readers that the claim was "literally" (*bukval'no*) correct—more than half the peasant-convicts were able to read and write—and he briefly disputes the elite perception that "literacy ruins the people," even if it does "develop [their] self-sufficiency" (*PSS* 4:12/11). The switchback pattern of the digression highlights the literacy claim, underscoring its elusive significance by placing it in the context of interpretive crisis and its dubiousness by insisting on its literal truth.[103] This initial and structurally marked self-characterization flags those that follow and links them into a word portrait (literate, beaten, lost, without a tongue); it also establishes literacy as a central topos. From his position as alienated observer, Gorianchikov will in the course of his memoir teach reading, read the convicts for certain revelatory signs (of remorse, for example), and be read by them: in a word, the literacy theme makes the epistemological problem explicit.[104] Moreover, the fact of literacy acquires a penumbra of meanings far beyond the abstractions of its sociological significance. The case of the common convict Petrov provides an example. First mentioned in the inaugural chapter as an instance of unreadable behavior, Petrov emerges later on as a remarkably literate prisoner who routinely discusses a number of bookish subjects with Gorianchikov, from Napoleon and the Countess La Vallière to a tall species of monkey with remarkably long arms rumored to live in America. Most significant about Petrov's bookishness, however, is the incoherence of his interests, which lend a fantastic air to his conversations. He has mastered a purely formal aesthetic of learned discourse—a grave air, a certain politesse, an urgent tone—but the content of conversation amounts to a series of non sequiturs, leaving Gorianchikov baffled and convinced that Petrov is among *katorga*'s most dangerous personalities.[105]

The literacy question develops in tension with, on the one hand, the peasants' self-characterization as a people "without a tongue" and, on the other, the mysterious grammar or logic of their distinctive "life" (*zhit'e byt'e*), which Gorianchikov struggles to discern (*PSS* 4:33/43). Irremediably alone and anomalous by virtue of his class, he realizes that the peasant, the object of his curiosity as well as his hatred and envy, within "two hours of his arrival" in the camp is "*at home . . .* understood by everybody and he himself understands everybody, he is familiar to everyone, and everyone considers him as *one of their own* [*stanovitsia u sebia doma . . . vsem poniaten, i sam vsekh ponimaet, vsem znakom, i vse schitaiut ego za svoego*]" (*PSS* 4:198/308). The nobleman, in contrast, is blinded by the unfamiliarity of his surroundings. Especially in the first year of his sentence, Gorianchiov reports, the "light of reality" was insufficient to the task of sight:

> Even though I looked at everything with such earnest and avid attention, I yet could not distinctly see much of what lay under my nose. Naturally, what struck me at first were the more sharply outstanding aspects, those on a large scale, but even these, perhaps, produced a mistaken impression on me, and they left behind in my soul only a feeling of oppression and hopeless melancholy. (*PSS* 4:62/89)[106]

The simple but baffling point of the nobleman's estrangement from the community of the common people is twice reiterated at the novel's conclusion: "He does not belong to them, and that's that [*Ne svoi chelovek, da i tol'ko*]"; "we were simply not comrades, and that's that [*prosto ne tovarishch, da i tol'ko*]." The stubborn fact strikes Gorianchikov with the unexpected impact and force of revelation. "I suddenly understood what up until then I had only poorly sensed": namely, that an absolute obstacle impedes his efforts and frustrates even his ardent desire to see and understand and, in so doing, to belong to the other—to claim and be claimed, to own and be owned (*PSS* 4:198, 207/308, 322). He is emphatically not, as in Dostoevsky's optimistic remark to his brother in the letter written on the eve of his exile, simply "*a man* among men" (*PSS* 28 [I]: 162; emphasis in original). In place of the expected common ground, the medium, the *mezhdu* of human being, Gorianchikov finds himself standing without any possibility of retreat at an absolute limit, the edge of "the profoundest abyss" of class difference. From that perspective, he sees that he is blind or, perhaps more accurate, he confronts his own illiteracy as he struggles to read the signs in order to know the meanings of the alien world he has no choice but to enter.

Gorianchikov thus looks closely at the peasant-convicts in an effort "to find out from their faces and their movements what kind of people they were and what kind of characters they possessed" (*PSS* 4:69/99).[107] His painful awareness of his own blindness—his inability, as he expresses it, to "penetrate into the inner depths of this life"—spurs him to construct in his memoir an inventory of life in *katorga* in all its aspects (*PSS* 4:197/ 306). The project is a mimetic one: by describing the surface of this alien life while maintaining a rigorous objectivity (in part, by describing his emotional responses to it with the same objectivity), and by trying to organize it into categories, he will finally achieve, if not a total picture, then a critical mass that will yield up the secret of its hidden depths. Gorianchikov's inventory is intended to make manifest the constituent elements of a foreign cultural logic or grammar, and to crack its code by simply recording what he sees and reflecting intelligently upon it. Throughout his incarceration, he thus struggles to perceive the foundational principles of social and moral life in *katorga*, to discern patterns of relationship, signs of an internal order beneath the constant chaos he finds so oppressive. The inventory he compiles—his detailed representations of customs, personalities, and events—is intended to provide the raw materials for a kind of incipient semiotics of *katorga*, its hidden organizing principles.[108]

Over the course of his memoir, Gorianchikov's inventory evinces patterns of relationship between seemingly anomalous elements to which it is possible to assign a provisional significance. These patterns describe unexpected combinations or, alternatively, failures to combine; their epistemological value lies in the shock of unanticipated attractions or repulsions. The dynamics of integration and disintegration produce meaning positively and negatively: the failure of a relationship to develop, for example, between two people or a pair of utterances when Gorianchikov had anticipated or assumed such a relationship can be just as revealing as when a relationship turns out to exist between elements that had seemed utterly disjunct. I turn first to the disintegrative patterns in which an anticipated interaction or relationship is repelled—the sudden explosion (*vzryv*) and the barrier (*peregorodka*)—before looking at integrative patterns of convergence or combination—patterns of nesting or concentricity and, most revealing, the substitution or exchange.

We already encountered the explosion (*vzryv*, or, alternatively, "outbreak" or "outburst") as a paradigm for the revelation or production of meaning in which expected linkages of cause and effect, motive and act, stimulus and response, are torn asunder.[109] Gorianchikov cites the curious case of the convict, apparently peaceful and resigned to his lot, who "suddenly, and for absolutely no rhyme or reason, but as if possessed by a devil, goes off the deep end, goes on a binge, brawls, and sometimes even enters into criminal behavior" (*PSS* 4:66/96). Although "the point is that this is not a question of reason, but of convulsions," still the "sudden outburst" destructive of both the prisoner's mind and his body (he will be punished severely) is of the highest significance. Gorianchikov analyzes the prisoner's "malice, fury, eclipse of reason, paroxysm and convulsion" as "an anguished, convulsive manifestation of personality, an instinctive yearning after one's own self, a desire to declare oneself, to assert one's humbled personality" (*PSS* 4:67/96).[110] Although it appears insane or ridiculous, the sudden outburst, as a manifestation, declaration, and assertion, reveals psychological disintegration to be a sign of the integrity of personality. A similar if less dramatic instance occurs in the case of the meek Sushilov who, having inexplicably devoted himself to serving Gorianchikov, is one day unjustly reproached by the latter for unsatisfactory work. The normally self-effacing Sushilov collapses in a fit of weeping. So unprecedented and impassioned is this demonstration of feeling that, although relations between "master" and "man" eventually return to normal, Gorianchikov understands "by several, almost imperceptible signs that in his heart [Sushilov] would never forgive me for my reproach" (*PSS* 4:62/88).

The meek prisoner's unexpected outburst, his unpredictable response, is one of several that perplex Gorianchikov. He observes that theft elicits no embarrassment and no moral indignation and is not despised. Cheerfulness, on the other hand, is. Beatings and executions provoke not expressions of hatred and resentment against those who carry them out but rather good-natured laughter and childlike chatter. As we have seen, Gorianchikov is dismayed that the occasional narration of the most vicious crime often inspired the same childlike laughter in those listening. Abusive encounters which Gorianchikov expected to end in bloodshed turned out to be "extraordinarily innocuous," "scenes . . . played like a comedy for everyone's pleasure," a mere "exercise in style" (*PSS* 4:23, 25/28, 31). Meek obedience yields to fury, whereas pain produces a peculiar pleasure and reconciliation a deep horror. The discursive manifestation of the *vzryv*, not surprisingly, is the non sequitur, the staple of the prisoner Petrov's conversations. Embodying in his speech and his desultory restlessness the most profound disconnectedness, Petrov is generally perceived, despite his apparent tameness, as the most dangerous—because the most unpredictable—of convicts. For this reason, despite his "sincere attachment" to Gorianchikov, and notwithstanding their nightly chats behind the barracks, the latter suspects that Petrov might well be "the most determined, fearless, and unrestrained of men" (*PSS* 4:84/123). Broadly surveyed, then, the *vzryv*—a more or less violent splitting or rending of a thing, utterance, person, or event from that which should follow, according to logic or custom—demonstrates that the repulsion of (anticipated) significance is itself significant.

The second disintegrative pattern also hinders the manifestation of expected meanings. According to this pattern, elements that seem to be converging on one another stop short of combination or exchange; what one expected to see revealed as a hidden affinity, rapport, or logic ends in mere contiguity. Gorianchikov uses the image of the barrier, literally the roadblock (*peregorodka*), to describe this development which is most compellingly used as a metaphor for the mysterious arrest of the desired, expected rapprochement of nobleman and peasant (*PSS* 4:229/357). Those incidents (including the strike, the delegation of tasks at the worksite, the confrontation in the mess hall with Gazin, and others), which impress on Gorianchikov (never without an accompanying sense of shock and betrayal) that, by virtue of his class and notwithstanding all other behavioral manifestations of his character, he will be forever ostracized by the peasant community, reveal something about Russian class relations to which he had previously been blind. Thus does the barrier fulfill the paradoxical function of removing an obstacle to clearsightedness. He sees that there are things he cannot see or only thought he saw but which turn out to be "optical illusions, and nothing more" (*PSS* 4:199/309). Not only does it reveal the nature of the relationship between Gorianchikov and the peasant-convicts, but it also determines his point of view on that relationship by compelling him to keep his distance. The barrier registers in Gorianchikov's account as instances of blackout or opacity in the topography of *katorga*, marking off whole regions into which he cannot penetrate.

If the barrier can be seen as the functional opposite of the explosion insofar as it announces the existence of a semiotic space by closing it off rather than by blowing it open, the paradigm of the husk and the kernel (*kora i zerno*) represents a combination of these two disintegrative patterns to form an integrative or positive pattern. According to this paradigm, elements (in most cases personalities) that appear utterly repellent to other elements and that, by resisting all intimacy and inquiry, encourage meanings dominated by the fact of the impasse, suddenly undergo a metamorphosis and turn out to be precisely not what they had seemed. Essentially this pattern is a concentric one in which meaning derives from the shock of the contrast invested in its structure: a repellent exterior, functioning in the manner of the barrier (*peregorodka*), inexplicably, in a chance moment, is rent (*vzryv*), revealing something within that could never have been expected:

> In prison, it sometimes happened that you would know a man for several years and you would think of him as more a beast than a man and you would despise him. And then suddenly a chance moment would arrive in which his soul, by some involuntary impulse [*poryv*] would open itself to the outside, and you would see in it such wealth, feeling, heart, such a clear understanding of its own suffering and that of others, that it was as if your eyes had been unclosed, and at first you did not even believe what you were seeing and hearing. (*PSS* 4:197–98/307)[111]

The difference between the *vzyrv* and the paradigm of the husk and the kernel can almost be specified as one of pace and direction, the latter occurring as a centripetal variation of the centrifugal *vzyrv*. Thus, whereas the *vzryv* often astonishes and unsettles Gorianchikov, causing him to flounder for an explanation for its occurrence, the paradigm of the husk and kernel seems to inspire him with a certain calmness, and results not in isolated attempts at tentative explanation but rather in a profound thematic development deployed in this text as the reiteration of an observed truth. Indeed, meditations on the paradigm of the husk and the kernel appear in all of Dostoevsky's subsequent major works, appearing finally as the epigraph to *The Brothers Karamazov*, taken from the Gospel according to John (12:24): "Verily, verily, I say unto you, except a corn of wheat fall into the ground and die, it abideth alone: but if it die, it bringeth forth much fruit." In *House of the Dead*, the paradigm of the husk and the kernel leads to the development of related themes based on the contrast between appearance and essence, and ultimately exceeds its signifying function to acquire a pedagogical one:

> It is necessary only to remove the outer, alien [*nanosnaia*, also "slanderous"] husk and to look more attentively and closely, without prejudices, at the kernel itself—and you will see in the people such things about which you had never suspected. Our wise men cannot teach the people much. I would even state positively that just the opposite is true: they themselves should learn from the people. (*PSS* 4:121–22/184; cf. 197–98/307)

By far, the most productive interaction of elements in Gorianchikov's inventory in terms of meaning, from the most quotidian levels to those informing Gorianchikov's deepest understanding of the philosophy of crime, involves their substitution or exchange. This is the case for two reasons. First, understood simply as a system of barter by which the convict acquires otherwise unprocurable essentials, exchange constitutes the inner life of the "life beyond life." To his amazement, Gorianchikov quickly learns that in *katorga* every rag commands its price. Second, more broadly understood as a transaction whereby one element (a person, object, event, or utterance) converts into or can be substituted for or replaced by another, exchange permits Gorianchikov to deduce some notion of the revaluation of all values that distinguishes peasant-convict life. Activities involving exchange thus materially realize the peasant- convicts' otherwise unarticulated and unsystematic ethical code; in this respect, attentive observation of such transactions yields Gorianchikov more information than do his attempts to plumb the depths of the peasant-convict mind through direct inquiry. For example, the practice of bribing executioners for lighter punishments, or one prisoner's exchanging his good health for a means of avoiding punishment altogether (he drinks a brew of tobacco steeped in wine and subsequently dies), reveal more to Gorianchikov about the pain of corporal punishment than do all his thwarted attempts to understand how it feels, as we will see. The individual exchanges which Gorianchikov documents range from the most quotidian (i.e., those that reveal how a convict survives the deprivations of *katorga* from day to day), to those that, in their unanticipated repercussions, ineluctably determine the course of an individual's life. Unregulated and often leading those who engage in it far beyond the intent of the original undertaking, exchange— the lifeblood of the Dead House—is rarely undertaken with equanimity. Indeed, the illicit and illimitable nature of this secret life is responsible for the atmosphere of surging anxiety and restlessness that the heavy monotony imposed by the constraints of prison routine can barely contain: life in the state of exception of *katorga* is, for the prisoners, both unalterable and radically provisional, "like that of settlers on Mt. Vesuvius" (*PSS* 4:17/20). The exchange, in sum, allows the peasant-convict a peculiar fluidity—in all other respects strictly prohibited—by means of which he may transgress boundaries and conduct regularly, impossibly, a range of prohibited activities.

From Gorianchikov's perspective, the exchange nullifies—by ignoring or denying—barriers that would normally prohibit the admission of two elements into the same conceptual, ethical, or even material arena. Thus, he learns that when money enters the picture, the "normal" reluctance of civilians to associate with convicts dissolves (a squeamishness to which the prefatory narrator testifies does not in any case pertain, at least not in Siberia), and sexual encounters between those on the outside and those on the inside occur, a bribed guard having permitted passage through the fortress walls. Similarly, the executioner can be bribed to administer a lighter punishment (thus the executioner grows fat in prison); conversely, failure to offer something to the executioner can result in excessive punishment. In both cases, the official delimitation of punishments is rendered null and void. These sorts of exchanges are markedly utilitarian in nature and commonly involve the use of money as a medium of exchange: as Gorianchikov observes, in prison "money is coined freedom" (*PSS* 4:17/ 19).[112] Such exchanges include bribes to the guards for allowing a host of illegal activities centered upon forbidden systems of barter involving all manner of goods. These systems, in turn, inform Gorianchikov which objects—and, ultimately, which activities—the convicts consider necessary to their survival (but on which they cannot, finally, get a purchase), including money, work orders from outside the prison and the tools to fill them, pipes and tobacco, food, vodka, and sex. Gorianchikov notes many such exchanges based on utility: the pleasure of a pet dog's company is exchanged for shoe leather; a pet goat is ultimately enjoyed as a pot of stew; hospitalized prisoners on special diets might exchange meals with others whose diets please them better; and so forth.

In his discussion of an "insoluble" problem, that of the profound imbalance in the criminal system created by "the inequality of punishment [received in exchange] for one and the same crime," Gorianchikov suggests that murder itself can constitute just another species of apparently pragmatic exchange. Why is it, he asks himself, that the man who kills to protect the honor of his beloved and the man who kills trivially, "for nothing, for an onion," receive the same sentence? The unacknowledged disparity of motives underlying the commission of what is technically the same crime is reflected in the incommensurate suffering inflicted upon the honorable (educated) man and the casual (peasant) killer by what is technically an identical punishment. Gorianchikov illustrates these dissemblances of motive and suffering housed in apparent semblances of crime and punishment with a "prison legend" based on a dialogue between a pair of (peasant) highway robbers:

> [One of them] goes out on a highway, and kills a passing peasant, only to find that all he has on him is an onion. "What's the deal, man! You send me out for loot so I knife this guy and all I find is an onion." "Moron! An onion's worth a kopek! You kill a hundred you get a hundred onions, and that's a ruble!" (*PSS* 4:42/59)

The exploits of Petrov are consonant with those of the legendary highway robbers in Gorianchikov's estimation; he deduces from Petrov's having unabashedly admitted to the theft of his beloved Bible (in order to exchange it for a drink) that he might "slaughter a man for twenty-five kopeks in order to buy a half-bottle of vodka" (*PSS* 4:86/126). In *The Idiot*, Prince Myshkin reports to Rogozhin (and characterizes as "typically Russian") a similar exchange of a life for a trivial object in the murder of one peasant by his best friend who had long coveted the former's watch. For Myshkin, as for Gorianchikov, outsiders both, such apparently absurd exchanges contain a significance that can be tapped only by indirection. The largely pragmatic motives for exchange do not encapsulate its full significance. What begins as a pragmatic move may possess a significance that goes far beyond the completion of a transaction. For example, the exchanging of one peasant cook for another in the prisoners' galley may signify profound power shifts between groups of convicts, and even between convicts and guards. Most notable, and far removed from the comparatively systematized and customary procedures of utilitarian trading, the exchange underlies the related activities of "changing places" (*smenit'sia*) and "changing one's lot" (*peremenit' uchast'*).

Sushilov, Gorianchikov's self-effacing and self-appointed servant, had on the march to Siberia agreed, out of simplicity, timidity, and drunkenness, "to change places"— that is, to sell his name (and thus his sentence) "for a red shirt and a silver ruble" in exchange for another man's name (and, with it, his immeasurably heavier sentence). Arriving at last among that convict sector designated the "Special Class," desperate criminals all, like the convict who had duped him, Sushilov finds himself the butt of an ongoing joke, not so much because he had changed places but because "he took only a red shirt and a silver ruble: he asked too insignificant a price. Usually, exchanging commanded a higher sum" (*PSS* 4:61/87). Later in his memoir, Gorianchikov discusses a type of exchange marked by a similar disproportion in terms of human cost, again engineered by those desperate to "change their lot." This "technical term," as Gorianchikov characterizes it, describes the commission of some desperate act—a crime, an escape attempt—undertaken solely to bring about a change in the unbearable monotony of daily existence, even a change for the worse. It would occur especially among those who had already served perhaps half a long sentence and, unable to bear the thought of the years that remain, add that much again onto its length when they are, inevitably, apprehended. This group in particular illustrates the appeal of the exchange—from the most trivial to the momentous—as a way of scrambling the sentence in an attempt, albeit illogical, to challenge its monolithic impassivity.[113]

As a nobleman of modest but independent means, Gorianchikov is largely exempt from the life of exchange and observes it as a curious custom peculiar to prison life. He is thus initiated into that life unwittingly when he enters the prison hospital and is made to exchange his convict jacket for a hospital dressing-gown. In so doing, he confronts the limits of the epistemological project represented by his inventory and intended to reveal the hidden grammar—the logic and language—of peasant culture. It is paradoxical that this should occur in the hospital, the place where the normative routines and behaviors of forced labor are suspended and surfaces would seem easier to penetrate. In the ward, the men lie immobile and bored, and their confinement in close quarters encourages conversation and creates opportunities for eavesdropping. Gorianchikov takes full advantage of these conditions: he both eavesdrops on his ward mates and interrogates them directly about matters of almost obsessive curiosity and which occupy the foreground of life in the sick ward, punishment and the pain associated with it. But he is baffled in these efforts to acquire information. We have already seen the results of his eavesdropping in the hospital ward. Despite the fact that he is ideally situated to observe Shishkov and Cherevin unnoticed, and that he is able to hear the voice emanating from the secret heart of peasant culture and, moreover, hear it in the form of the graphic narrative of crime, the story the peasants' reticence had deferred for so long, Gorianchikov finds in "Akul'ka's Husband" the antithesis of revelation.[114] The more detailed Shishkov's narrative, the more obscure it becomes. The peasant's story, which relates the slow, immutable extinction of the iconic image of the woman at its center, is a black hole from which no commentary or reflection escapes; it represents the total eclipse of significance rather than the item requisite to a total inventory of signs.[115] Thus does the voice of the peasant at its purest, unmediated and uncensored, articulate a fundamental nihilism which voids the nobleman's continuous effort to convert the syntagmas of his inventory of peasant-convict life into paradigms of meaning.

Gorianchikov discovers that the "story" of crime, once he has finally heard it in its entirety and without mediation, is mere translation with no core, no portable, comprehensible meaning. The phenomenon of pain appears to offer an alternative inroad into the mind of the peasant-convict, specifically the pain of corporal punishment, but he finds that it, too, has no adequate linguistic equivalent—it is "without a tongue" (*bez iazyka*).[116] The hospital provides an opportunity to conduct interviews on the subject of pain, but Gorianchikov is defeated by the peasants' responses to his direct questions:

> I was agitated, confused, and frightened. I remember that at that time I began suddenly and impatiently to probe into all the details of these new phenomena, to listen to the talk and stories of other prisoners on this subject. I put questions to them myself, and tried to get answers. (*PSS* 4:152/233)[117]

In addition to questions about the various degrees of sentencing and nuances in the execution of punishments, as well as efforts to imagine the psychological state of those going to punishment, he asks the peasants to describe the pain of punishment in such a way that, without having experienced it himself, he might know precisely how it feels:

> I asked a lot of questions about the pain. I sometimes wanted to know definitively how great this pain was and with what, finally, it could be compared. Truly, I don't know why I pursued this. I remember only that it was not from idle curiosity. I repeat that I was agitated and shaken. But whomever I asked, I could in no way get an answer that satisfied me. It burns, it scorches like fire—this was all I could learn, the only answer I received. It burns, and that's it. (*PSS* 4:153–54/235–36)

Here Gorianchikov reveals in its entirety his axiomatic assumption concerning the peasant-convicts: along with their susceptibility to the commission of crime, they are distinguished from the nobility by their experience of pain. For the nobleman, therefore, crime (the act of physical violence) and pain (the suffering of physical violence) admit only a negative or indirect understanding; taken together, they constitute the *ne to* or fundamental unknowability of the people.

From the moment he unthinkingly exchanges his convict jacket for the hospital gown, however, this foundational assumption of his absolute difference from the common people is undermined. Observing an old man on the ward smearing mucus on his own dressing-gown after a fit of sneezing, Gorianchikov reflects that "our simple people are not at all squeamish or prone to disgust," but at the very moment he asserts this difference, not just with his ethnographic observation but also by instinctively shrinking from physical contact with his own gown, he finds that he has already failed to keep his distance:

> At that moment, I flinched and began immediately and unwillingly to inspect with loathing and curiosity the dressing-gown I had just put on. I suddenly realized that it had been attracting my attention for some time with its strong smell; it had by now had time to get warm on my body and smelled more and more strongly of medicines, plasters, and, it seemed to me, some kind of pus— which was not surprising, since from time immemorial it had not been removed from the shoulders of sick men.

His observation of the peasant's difference compels his realization that he has been enrobed in the contaminated gown, its skin against his, that his body heat has released its odors distilled from the bodies of common convicts "who had just run the gauntlet, their backs covered with wounds": the garment has not come to him cleansed of its past. The dressing-gown inspires in him a "fearful mistrust" that the differences upon which the integrity of his identity relies might prove illusory, and the growing certainty that, if they dissolved, he would be compensated by no greater understanding of the other whom he so unexpectedly would have become.

Although he shrinks with revulsion from contact with the gown just when he realizes its significance, that it brings him in contact with the flesh of the peasant in the form of a "lining impregnated with every possible unpleasant fluid," the self-saving gesture comes much too late (*PSS* 4:135–36/207). The instant his skin touches and warms the impregnated lining and he breathes in its odor and absorbs its fluid through his pores, a kind of consummation occurs. His body receives the "knowledge" of pain he had sought through his interviews. Gorianchikov may enjoy some protection from corporal punishment, but he is also no longer a being apart. Neither this nor that, he finds himself enlisted by a susceptibility of his body into the ranks of those "beaten" ones, the "simple people" whose sufferings have deprived them of "a tongue." If it is true that the donning of the hospital gown marks the limits of his ethnographic quest to compile an inventory of the peculiar life of *katorga* as "a sum of facts or a system of ideas," nevertheless he gains by its touch on his skin a compensating (if only negatively intuited) certainty—"the impossibility of meaninglessness or ontological void" in the space of exception.[118] The gown is an instrument of revelation: it is able to bridge the impassable abyss between Gorianchikov and the peasant-convicts because its significance is entirely adequate to and can be immediately apprehended in its materiality, the bodily fluids with which it is saturated and the bodily warmth which distils and releases them.

Corporeality and Intercorporeality in Katorga

Among the often clownishly autocratic authority figures who populate *katorga* and the tsarist disciplinary system generally, Gorianchikov describes one lieutenant-colonel remarkable for what he calls his "instinctive democratism" (*instinktivnyi demokratizm*) (*PSS* 4:90, 215/132, 334).[119] It elicited from the peasant-convicts not an inappropriate familiarity in their dealings with him but the profoundest respect and even "adoration": "there was nothing overbearing" in his behavior, Gorianchikov explains, "no hint of a condescending or purely official kindness. He was their comrade, in the highest degree one of them [*svoj chelovek*]" (*PSS* 4:215/334). This relationship of true belonging is one that Gorianchikov himself does not succeed in cultivating. At first, he does not desire it and strategically performs his estrangement from the peasant-convicts in order to control the relationship by asserting the superiority he is sure they will recognize, even if he is indistinguishable from them in appearance. He resolves to show no "particular desire to get close to them" and "not to thrust myself into their fellowship" (*PSS* 4:76/111). Later on he learns that, with some of his fellow convicts, friendship is possible and even desirable; despite his overtures, however, these potential comrades "never met me on an equal footing [*na ravnuiu nogu*]" and he has no choice but "to acknowledge my isolation and the anomalousness of my position in the prison" (*PSS* 4:199/309). On the one hand, he laments his inability to penetrate the "inner depths" of peasant culture, its "genuine life, the essence [*sushchnost'*] of the life, its very heart" (*PSS* 19: 7). On the other, in his most unambiguously positive use of the first-person plural, he insists that he did share fully in the peculiar existence they lived in common: "Our life was distinctive and it belonged to us, and although it wasn't much, it wasn't merely an official life, but rather an inner life of our very own" (*PSS* 4:197/306).

If we have taken seriously Gorianchikov's estrangement from the common people about which he writes with increasing anguish as his memoir progresses, then his insistence that he nevertheless shared equally with them a distinctive "inner life" must raise several questions. When and how did he become aware of this shared existence? What kind of literacy was required "to read in it the route it followed in becoming a world," a world that did not simply appear before him for his close inspection but to which he found himself "bound [. . .] through all its parts, up against it"? (*VI* 38, 115 n. 2). How do we understand his being simultaneously estranged from and bound to this world? Estrangement is, as we have seen, a reciprocal stance: the peasants too regard with "savage curiosity" the "newcomer from the nobility, who had suddenly appeared in their corporation [*korporatzii*]" (*PSS* 4:57/80).[120] But beyond simply appearing in the people's corporation, the nobleman finds himself incorporated into it by his very physicality: in addition to the oppressive tedium he must endure, he has no choice but to imbibe its "poisonous atmosphere" (*PSS* 4:138/210). He must inhale the "suffocating exhalations" of the hospital ward and the "unspeakable stench" of the barracks, slip in the accumulated filth on the barracks floor, suffer its extremes of heat and cold, hear the constant racket, ingest the soup in which float a "huge number of cockroaches," perform hard labor to the point of complete exhaustion, wash with the water of the bathhouse made filthy by passing over other men's bodies, listen as a consumptive prisoner slowly suffocates to death, observe unwillingly the normally private bodily functions of his fellows and be observed by them. There is no space apart or time alone; the convicts live, Gorianchikov says, like "herring in a barrel" (*PSS* 4:138, 22/210, 26).[121]

Here we find the irreducibility of bare life, naked and abandoned. If by virtue of his class, Gorianchikov is a being irremediably set apart, by virtue of his body he is ineluctably part of what the philosopher Maurice Merleau-Ponty has called "the carnal context of the essence"; his flesh makes up the peculiar "spatial and temporal pulp" of *katorga* which cannot be considered merely "as fact or sum of facts"—the underlying premise of the nobleman's inventory of *katorga*—"but as the locus of an inscription of truth" (*VI* 114, 131 n. 1). The truth in question here has to do with the collective body or "corporation" of *katorga* and its relation to Gorianchikov's own body, whether this relationship may be described as a community and, if so, what the nature of this community is both actually and potentially. It is useful at this point to review briefly Merleau-Ponty's concepts of the "flesh" and of "intercorporeity," including his privileging of literature in his account of how the latter manifests itself on the level of the individual. The concept of intercorporeity illuminates the experiential dimension of common life, which in *katorga* is also bare life, that from which Gorianchikov cannot opt out. It also provides the ground for what the political philosopher Claude Lefort, after Merleau-Ponty, has examined with reference to the formation of modern democracy as "the flesh of the political," a phenomenological concept rendered with sensate particularity on the literary plane in *House of the Dead*, as we will see.[122]

In his last, unfinished work, *The Visible and the Invisible*, Merleau-Ponty elaborated a concept of the "flesh" that permits us to understand how and in what sense the body can become constitutive of a particular "world" or community and, beyond this, to imagine how this community might potentially become, in Agamben's words, "a constituting power that has definitively broken the ban binding it to constituted power" (*HS* 47).[123] The horizontal dynamism of exchange which, as we have seen, subtends the rigid vertical hierarchy of the camp's military authorities (and which they are unable to supervise, let alone contain) provides one model for conceiving of the distinctive fabric of bare life collectively lived. Merleau-Ponty provides another by considering, first, the ways in which corporeality itself might be productive of community; and, second, the ways in which such a community, restricted to bare life, might possess a constituting or, more precisely in this case, an emancipatory power. His concept of the "flesh" provides a way of moving beyond the subject-object impasse in touch, vision, language, and thought by focusing on that which connects one to the other; in so doing, it shows how the material body participates in the same vast web of transactions as language itself.

The "flesh" or "flesh of the world" in Merleau-Ponty is a term he gives to the normally disregarded and therefore invisible medium that contains (without uniting) both subject and object, and that desituates their opposition by recasting them as separate-but-equal partners in any transaction, whether of touch, sight, or language (*VI* 133). Because they are embedded in the flesh as a "fabric" or "tissue," subject and object (animate and inanimate) cannot be considered as atoms, "chunk[s] of absolutely hard, indivisible being," nor is it possible to assign an ontological priority to one over the other (*VI* 132). The toucher cannot be distinguished from the touched insofar as touch itself describes a "crisscrossing" whereby the act of touching "incorporate[s]" those who touch "into the universe they interrogate": "the 'touching subject' passes over to the ranks of the touched, descends into the things, such as the touch is formed in the midst of the world and as it were in the things" (*VI* 133, 134). As Merleau-Ponty rhetorically asks, "Where are we to put the limit between the body and the world, since the world is flesh?" (*VI* 138).[124] Insofar as sight "is a palpation with the look," vision is not exempt from this reciprocal and simultaneous action of its ostensible object on the seeing subject: "every visible is cut out in the tangible, every tactile being in some manner promised to visibility" (*VI* 134). The "thickness of flesh" in which subject and object (or "thing") are contained is "constitutive for the thing of its visibility as for the seer of his corporeity; it is not an obstacle between them, it is their means of communication" (*VI* 135). In short, the body possesses a "double reference," belonging simultaneously both to the order of the object and of the subject (*VI* 137). Not only does the flesh as "Visibility" itself—"a generality of the Sensible"—mandate this "reversibility" of subject and object, it also demotes the seer from his or her self-appointed position of primacy as "knowing subject" by "traversing" and thereby constituting the seer to begin with (*VI* 139, 154, 140).

Merleau-Ponty elaborates the idea of "intercorporeity" to distinguish the "synergy" or reciprocity between subjects and their human objects (*VI* 141, 142). The "anonymous visibility" in which we all appear to one another disallows all claims to ownership or mastery; it is a "primordial property that belongs to the flesh" rather than to any one subject who has claimed for him- or herself a "titular" status in relation to it (*VI* 142, 143). Gorianchikov struggles to claim and maintain such a status for himself in *katorga* but inevitably finds, as Merleau-Ponty expresses it, that he "must plunge into the world instead of surveying it, [he] must descend toward it such as it is instead of working [his] way back up toward a prior possibility of thinking it—which would impose upon the world in advance the conditions for our control over it" (*VI* 38–39). On several occasions, Gorianchikov denies that there could be any prior possibility of thinking *katorga* as an illusion that crumbled before its unmasterable reality. Such mastery is denied not just by the others but because intercorporeality makes it possible to see and demystify seeing itself: "For the first time, the seeing that I am is for me really visible; for the first time I appear to myself completely turned inside out under my own eyes" (*VI* 143). Thus does Gorianchikov realize in *katorga* that his vision of the peasant was simply an optical illusion: just as his vision of them masked his blindness, he suspects that their reciprocal and multiform visions of him are similarly compromised. His vision of himself is also revolutionized. The sneezing inmate leads him to see (smell and then inspect) his own hospital gown and to realize with a shock that it lends his body an unsuspected dimension, which Merleau-Ponty calls the "unfathomable depth" of the visible: his skin appears to him no longer as that membrane which separates him from the world and preserves his difference but as the inner lining of the hospital gown. He experiences a version of what is "inalienable" to the human subject that has nothing to do with abstract right; rather, it is the "interior horizon" of every object (the gown, its lining, and his skin as the lining of the lining) that links it inalienably to the flesh of the world (*VI* 152). The heavy atmosphere of the hospital ward is thick with visions that penetrate and often violate their objects, the self as often as others. Immobilized, Gorianchikov is unable here to evade the angry look or word by walking away; he is forced to see how he sees and is seen and what manner of reaction the promiscuous merging of these visions produces.[125]

Seeing oneself seeing or failing to see, seeing oneself seen, seeing the seen as the product of one's own and others' seeing: vision constitutes in *House of the Dead* an enormously complex web of relations analogous, in

Merleau-Ponty's reading, to language itself.[126] Both language and vision realize "a relation to Being through a being"; the seeing body, like speech (voiced language), is charismatic: "narcissistic, eroticized, endowed with a natural magic that attracts the other significations into its web" (*VI* 118). The image of the web that scrambles fundamental distinctions such as subject and object, primary and secondary, carries echoes of Bakhtin (including Bakhtin on Dostoevsky) and also of Hannah Arendt:[127]

> A discussion is not an exchange or a confrontation of ideas, as if each formed his own, showed them to the others, looked at theirs, and returned to correct them with his own. . . . Someone speaks, and immediately the others are now but certain divergencies by relation to his words, and he himself specifies his divergence in relation to them. Whether he speaks up or hardly whispers, each one speaks with all that he is, with his "ideas," but also with his obsessions, his secret history which the others suddenly lay bare by formulating them as ideas. Life becomes ideas and the ideas return to life, each is caught up in the vortex in which he first committed only measured stakes, each is led on by what he said and the response he received, led on by his own thought of which he is no longer the sole thinker. (*VI* 119)

Like language, vision—neither matter nor a product of mind, and therefore not a representation—can only be described as "a *general thing*, midway between the spatio-temporal individual and the idea, a sort of incarnate principle" (*VI* 139). As with thinking itself, this in-betweenness of vision, its existence between rather than in individual minds as their property, is the ground of its constitutive power. Again, Merleau-Ponty has recourse to language to make the point: "It is by the combination of words (with their charge of sedimented significations, which are in principle capable of entering into other relations than the relations that have served to form them) that I *form* the transcendental attitude, that I *constitute* the constitutive consciousness"—for example, in the distinctive world of *katorga* (*VI* 171; emphases in original). Michel de Certeau, in an essay on Merleau-Ponty, makes use of the same analogy between vision and language: "An invisible reality makes the perception of visible things possible, just as a non-localisable organicism of language permits the successive positivities of particular utterances."[128]

In speaking as in seeing, the individual subject co-produces the consciousness that transcends all individual consciousnesses. This constitutive consciousness can only be the product, formed by everyone and no one, of a combination of visions. This is why only this composite consciousness, and not that of the epistemological subject, the author-prisoner, can bring to consummation an image of the new world which he imagines awaits him on the other side of exile and into which he longs to be resurrected. His consciousness of his inability to see clearly the life around him when he attempts to use prefabricated images as a lens forces him to acknowledge that vision is neither the creation nor the property of a single mind. Instead, it comes to that mind freighted with its sedimented significations contributed by the visions of numerous others, similarly heterogeneous. Dostoevsky's aesthetic achievement in *House of the Dead* is to represent what would seem unrepresentable, an in-betweenness of vision that holds a desired but still inconceivable new world in abeyance, rather than vision as the consummated product of an individual mind. This achievement constitutes a perhaps unrecognized aspect of what Bakhtin described as his polyphonic method. That he represents the in-betweenness of vision by way of autobiographical narration compounds the aesthetic invention of this first of the great novels: the composite vision is not limited, for example, to a depiction of the peasant-convicts' *svoi*, their milieu, which reconstitutes itself anew and is thus reaffirmed with the arrival of each new inmate. Instead, in dynamic counterpoint to such representations, the in-betweenness of vision emerges as the by-product of the representation of the narrator's desubjectification, his merging (variously realized) with other consciousnesses. The primary proof of the constitutive power which the in-betweenness of vision—the community of *katorga*—possesses is the text itself. On this literary ground, the possibility of a more permanent realization—"the possibility of democracy"—takes its first stand.[129] I return to this possibility below.

Bakhtin explained the simultaneous stability and dynamism of language as the result of the centripetal and centrifugal forces within it. The former ensure not just the stability of language—indeed, its very viability—but its tensile strength in the service of hegemonic power, whereas the latter constantly erodes the former through a vitality of the living language that precludes its finalization or appropriation.[130] Merleau-Ponty similarly posits a "central vision that joins the scattered visions" but attributes to each seeing body a receptive and thus generative power, elaborated through an extended metaphor of germination, through which new visions are constantly brought into being and released into the world: "the durable flesh of the world [is] pregnant with many other visions besides my own" (*VI* 145, 123). Using a series of "as thoughs" to illustrate this "pregnancy," he asks us to imagine that the flesh of the world, the medium in which subjects and objects coexist, is infused with visions, as when a seed pod opens and releases its contents (dehiscence) which then permeate the atmosphere or "horizon" and are carried by irresistible currents into circumambient bodies (*VI* 149). Impregnated by these seeds or visions, the bodies, the objects, the seen or "visibles," are converted into subjects, seers. The "labor" of metamorphosis, the making of a seer, is accomplished by the body upon itself; of itself, the body prepares a "hollow whence a vision will come, inaugurates the long maturation at whose term suddenly it will see," and seeing, "will be visible for itself"—will see itself as the seen, the visible (*VI* 147). This "hollow," then, is "the formative medium of the object and the subject" which continually metamorphose into each other without ever coinciding. There is no perfect reversibility of seer and seen, no absolute transcendence of the opposition between seer and seen, no resurrection from the kind of dynamic stalemate of our ontology, our "general manner of being" (*VI* 147). Instead, there is simultaneity without coincidence; one is both subject and object, seer and seen, but those two dispositions never become one. The body remains an "abyss": "I am always on the same side of my body; it presents itself to me in one invariable perspective"; therefore, "I cannot help putting the other, and the perception he has, *behind his body*" (*VI* 148, 9; emphasis in original).

The "hollow," then, is a metaphor for describing the "relations between the visible and the invisible" as an aspect of the relationship of subject to object, where the invisible, the idea, would reveal itself not as the contrary of the visible, "the sensible," but rather as "its lining and its depth" (*VI* 149). This "central cavity" into which visions penetrate, germinate, and from which they emerge into the flesh of the world—the sum total of all incorporeity—as other, new visions, makes it possible to conceive of an authorless image possessed of the aesthetic agency to figure a new world. This, it bears repeating, is the conceptual and aesthetic challenge of Dostoevsky's anxious hope of rebirth on the eve of exile: translation into a new life would require an alternative grammar of creation—indeed, of perception itself.[131] Merleau-Ponty finds this alternative in the inseparability of the idea (music, literature, love, genius, sensibility, etc.) from the body most powerfully demonstrated in Proust:[132]

> It is not only that we would find in that carnal experience the *occasion* to think them; it is that they owe their authority, their fascinating, indestructible power, precisely to the fact that they are in transparency behind the sensible, or in its heart. Each time we want to get at [the idea] immediately, or lay hands on it, or circumscribe it, or see it unveiled, we do in fact feel that the attempt is misconceived, that it retreats in the measure that we approach. The explicitation does not give us the idea itself; it is but a second version of it, a more manageable derivative. (*VI* 150)

This "carnal texture" of the idea which permits us to grasp it—whether of love in Proust, or of crime in Dostoevsky—is acquired through its residence in the embodied "hollow," "a negativity that is not nothing," an "invagination" that produces "not the shadow" of the empirical thing but its "incarnate principle" (*VI* 152).

The "incarnate principle," the idea possessed of a "carnal texture," is—like love for Swann or religious belief for Myshkin or the common people for Gorianchikov or Bartleby's preference—a *ne to*, a powerfully felt reality that is nevertheless inappropriable and untranslatable except as that which is suspended between this partial incarnation and that. To convey all that can be known of Bartleby's preference, the lawyer can only describe the precise feel of his oppressive physical presence in the office and the responsive behaviors of himself and each of his employees. To describe the religiosity of the Russian people, Myshkin creates for Rogozhin a kind of ideo-grammatic parable through the stories of his separate encounters with four peasants.[133] In Proust, the idea of love is captured in the five notes of Vinteuil's sonata, the "little phrase" which involuntarily resurrects in Swann the precise sensation in all its historical complexity of his love for Odette as the madeleine resurrects for Marcel the sensate memories of childhood. For Gorianchikov, the "philosophy of crime" is available only through the countless variations—"perfectly distinct" and "unequal"—of individual personality (*VI* 151). If for no other reason than his need to breathe and eat, see and touch, Gorianchikov involuntarily acquires knowledge not through his inquiries and observations but through his body in which the idea acquires flesh. As Merleau-Ponty articulates it:

> Being no longer being *before me*, but surrounding me and in a sense traversing me, and my vision of Being not forming itself from elsewhere, but from the midst of Being—the alleged facts, the spatio-temporal individuals, are from the first mounted on the axes, the pivots, the dimensions, the generality of my body, and the ideas are therefore already encrusted in its joints. (*VI* 114)

Walt Whitman saw in this encrusting of the American (thus universal) democratic idea in the body the source of all poetry in his famous apostrophe to the American poet: "your very flesh shall be a great poem and have the richest fluency not only in its words but in the silent lines of its lips and face and between the lashes of your eyes and in every motion and joint of your body."[134] In Dostoevsky, the body that incarnates the Russian (thus universal) democratic idea is a merging of poet and convict—a body both brutal and vulnerable, repellent and charismatic.

Dostoevsky's Democratic Aesthetic

If Gorianchikov shares Whitman's intuition of the poetry encrusted in the flesh, he does not share his exuberance. What for Swann or Marcel is "the first vision, the first contact, the first pleasure" (even the first painful plea-sure) is for Gorianchikov the enduring shock of entering the House of the Dead and finding himself assaulted by the inescapable "racket and uproar, guffaws, cursing, the rattle of fetters, fumes and soot, shaved heads, branded faces, clothing made of scraps, everything accursed and dishonor-able" (*PSS* 4:10/9). As with Proust's characters, his initiation involves "not the positing of a content, but the opening of a dimension that can never again be closed, the establishment of a level in terms of which every other experience will henceforth be situated" (*VI* 151). This opening of a dimension that can never again be closed—this "ordeal" of "being held in an opening [one] does not create," as Claude Lefort, one of Merleau-Ponty's ablest readers, expresses it—is powerfully represented in *House of the Dead* in the scene where Gorianchikov stands at the entry to the bath house where the prisoners have been taken en masse and imagines that "we had entered Hell" (*PSS* 4:98/145).[135] The dimension that opens before him, the opening in which he is held, is intercorporeity at its most unadorned, which is to say, bare life: one hundred naked men packed into a room twelve paces by twelve connected by their filth, their animal joy in the sensual pleasure of the bath, and their anxious desire to enjoy it to the fullest.[136] Standing at the entrance to the bath house, wearing only his fetters, subjected to what Merleau-Ponty calls the "complementary vision [. . .] myself seen from without, such as another would see me," Gorianchikov offers an apt example of one "installed in the midst of the visible, occupied in considering it from a certain spot" (*VI* 134).

On this spot, fully exposed to the sight and the touch of others, Gorianchikov must literally plunge into the world of *katorga* with no possibility of surveying it at a remove: upon entering the room he is immediately enveloped in "steam that clouded the eyes, soot, filth, closeness to such a degree that there was nowhere to put one's foot" (*PSS* 4:98/145):

> Everywhere was shouting and roars of laughter, with the sound of a hundred chains dragging on the floor . . . Some, who wanted to pass through, got tangled up in the chains of others, caught their own on the heads of those sitting on the floor, and fell, swearing and dragging after them those they had caught. Filth coursed down on all sides. (*PSS* 4:98/146; ellipses in original)

He wants to flee, but there is no possibility of withdrawal. He must plunge into the "thick, scalding cloud" of steam in which all are enveloped, and discerns "beaten backs, shaved heads, contorted arms and legs," a profusion of body parts (*PSS* 4:98–99/146). The bodies of the "beaten people," made grotesque by their experience of corporal punishment, make his flesh creep:

> The shaved heads and the bodies of the convicts, scarlet with the steam, seemed even more monstrous. On a back that has been steamed, the scars from strokes of the lash and the rod no matter when they were received often stand out clearly, so that now all these backs seemed newly wounded. Dreadful scars! Looking at them, a shiver ran over my skin. (*PSS* 4:98/146)

Petrov, who has undertaken to shepherd the nobleman through his experience, uses the latter's kopek to secure a space for him on a bench and squats underneath it, "where it was dark, filthy and where the sticky moisture had everywhere accumulated to almost half a finger" (*PSS* 4:98/145). Each convict receives a single bucket of water; the water poured over the heads of those standing trickles down on those squatting. United with the others in a single physical mass connected by the streaming water, the filth, chains and the enveloping steam, Gorianchikov does not identify with them; his response to the experience is one in which pleasure and horror are distinct and yet inextricable.

In the bath house, the body appears before him in all its repulsive brutishness, the dead end of significance, and at the same time it evokes a creaturely sympathy with his fellow convicts.[137] Gorianchikov's complex and overwhelmed response to the shockingly literal experience of intercorporeity in the bath house provides a touchstone for seeing what Merleau-Ponty calls "the flesh of the world." Beyond that, it reveals the degree to which he is and is not incorporated into the *korporatsiia* of the peasant-convicts: that is, it raises the question of the flesh of the political. Initially, we might pose the question thus: how and to what degree is it possible to regard this *korporatsiia* of men denuded, beaten, and abandoned as a constituting power, and what kind of power do they constitute? Where do we see evidence of that constitutive consciousness able to break the ban, evidence for *katorga* as the mise-en-scène of an emancipation whose fulfillment lies in an unforeseeable future?

Throughout Gorianchikov's memoir, there are hints, small rumblings which at times resemble eruptions of laughter, of a force poised to overturn normative power relations, if only temporarily and conditionally. For example, the peasant Petrov, the most dangerous convict in the prison according to many, treats Gorianchikov in the bathhouse with a benign and, as it were, natural condescension, as of an adult toward a child.[138] With no servility or expectation of a fee for services rendered, he undertakes to assist the nobleman step by step through the unfamiliar experience, remaining by him throughout, helping him to undress (Gorianchikov is unused to maneuvering around his shackles), taking his kopeks to buy him extra soap and buckets of water, helping him walk through the packed room, and finding a place for him to sit:

> Petrov announced that he would wash me from head to toe, so that "you'll be nice and clean," and he earnestly invited me to steam myself. I refrained from being steamed. Petrov rubbed me all over with soap. "And now I'll wash your little feet," he added in conclusion. I wanted to answer that I could wash them myself, but couldn't bring myself to contradict him and completely gave myself up to his will. In the diminutive "little feet" there decidedly sounded not one note of slavishness; it was simply and plainly that Petrov could not call my feet feet, probably because other people, real people [*nastoiashchie liudi*], had feet and I had as yet only little feet. (*PSS* 4:99/147)

Petrov's behavior toward Gorianchikov is reminiscent of the peasant killer Orlov for whom the nobleman's concern with the question of conscience suggests that he has not in some sense reached his majority. Petrov's determination to serve him unasked is exhibited by several other convicts, most revealingly by Chekunov, his neighbor in the hospital, whose readiness to serve elicits the contempt of the other peasant-convicts on the ward. As we saw in part 1, Gorianchikov complains that his self-appointed servants "in the end completely mastered me, so that they were in reality my lords and I their servant" (*PSS* 4:134/205). This revolutionary reversal of normative power relations between the nobleman and the common people is most explicit in those prison environments where the fact of intercorporeality, this democracy of the flesh, is inescapable: the hospital and the bathhouse, where the *korporatsia* of convicts appears at its most vulnerable, and where Gorianchikov finds himself as repelled as he is bound.

On an individual level, the carnivalesque reversal of roles is most successfully sustained by "our Jew," Isai Fomich, the outcast of outcasts. Like Gorianchikov but without his advantages of caste, Fomich endures upon entering the barracks the savage curiosity of the other convicts who had heard "that they'd brought in a little Yid [*zhidok*] and were shaving him in the guardroom" (*PSS* 4:93/137).[139] Intimidated and mute, "he dared not even lift his eyes to the crowd of mocking, mutilated, and terrifying faces which closed tightly around him" (*PSS* 4:93/138). One inmate approaches him with a mock pledge, a filthy and ragged pair of summer trousers, and asks if Isai Fomich would consider giving him a silver ruble for them. Almost paralyzed with fear and timidity, he yet rouses himself to give the rags a thorough examination. " 'A silver ruble is impossible, but seven kopeks might work out.' And those were the first words produced by Isai Fomich in prison. Everyone roared with laughter" (*PSS* 4:94/138). From this point forward, Isai Fomich is universally liked despite the fact that he is a Jew and that the entire prison is in his debt. He uses the money he earns as prison pawnbroker (and as a jeweler for the town nearby) to pay others to render him services, most notably in the prison bathhouse where, having purchased a spot on the highest shelf, prisoners without even a kopek beat him with birch sticks while he steams himself into a noisy ecstasy (*PSS* 4:99/147). Subjected repeatedly to potentially explosive anti-Semitic taunts, he is permitted to respond to them with impunity in a kind of ritual comic dialogue that regularly entertains the assembled company.[140] Isai Fomich's very abjectness as a Jew both allows him to function as a mediating figure between the outside and inside of the prison (he is permitted to attend the Omsk prayer house weekly in the town from which he returns with news from the capitol and elsewhere) and provides the opening for emancipatory behavior. After his ritualistic verbal sparring with his fellow convicts, for example, he sings an "absurd and funny tune" which, he tells Gorianchikov, "was that same song and precisely the same tune that all six hundred thousand Jews sang, from the least to the greatest, as they crossed the Red Sea, that tune which every Jew is commanded to sing in the moment of triumph and victory over his enemies" (*PSS* 4:95/140).

As the allusion to the exodus of the Jews from slavery under the Egyptian Pharoah suggests, Isai Fomich, through the apparently "simple-hearted comedy" of the religious rituals he scrupulously observes, engages in a revolutionary practice in relation to those who would oppress him (*PSS* 4:94/139). "What was funny," Gorianchikov observes of the Jewish convict's weekly Sabbath prayers, "was that Isai Fomich was as if purposely acting a part before us and showing off with his rituals," which involve various garments, songs, gestures, and the display of a range of hyperbolic emotions from extreme joy to violent distress (*PSS* 4:95/140).[141] Gorianchikov inquires into the meaning of the sudden transition from despair to bliss:

> He hastened to explain that the weeping and sobbing represented the idea of the loss of Jerusalem and that the Law prescribed the most violent possible sobbing and beating of the breast at this idea. But at the moment of the very bitterest lamentations he, Isai Fomich, *must suddenly*, and as if by chance, remember (this *suddenly* is also prescribed by the Law) that there is a prophecy of the return of the Jews to Jerusalem. Then he must immediately burst into rejoicing, songs, laughter, and recite the prayers in such a way that his voice expressed the greatest possible happiness and his face the greatest triumph and nobility. (*PSS* 4:95/141; emphases in original)

The revolutionary subtext of Isai Fomich's "prescribed" religious observances becomes explicit when the dreaded major, escorted by guards and an officer, unexpectedly visits the barracks while he is in the middle of his prayer ritual. All the inmates spring to attention, but Isai Fomich "began to cry out and grimace even more," taking advantage of the fact that his religious observances are protected in *katorga*. The major is barred from interrupting them:

> The major went up to within a step of him: Isai Fomich turned his back to his little table and in a singsong voice began to read directly into the major's face his victorious prophecy while swinging his arms. Since it was also prescribed that at that moment he express in his face the most extreme happiness and nobility, he promptly did so, somehow peculiarly screwing up his eyes, smiling and nodding his head at the major. The major was dumbfounded. (*PSS* 4:96/141–42)[142]

Afterward, when Gorianchikov asks Isai Fomich what he would have done if the major had been angry, the latter claims to have been unaware that the major was present, as "at that point in these prayers he fell into a kind of ecstasy and saw and heard nothing of what was going on around him" (*PSS* 4:96/142). He gives a stellar performance of revolutionary power of which he claims to be entirely unaware. Here Dostoevsky applies the Russian Orthodox tradition of the "holy fool" who speaks truth to power with impunity to the outcast Jew as "prisoner-buffoon," possessed of his higher Law and his own historical tradition of emancipation from illegitimate power.[143]

Although Isai Fomich's subversive activities are the most sustained and explicit in the memoir, other instances of incipient rebellion are worth a brief mention. Gorianchikov overhears a former house serf, Luke Kuzmich, tell the story of his crime, the murder of a prison commandant in the habit of telling the prisoners that he was their tsar and God:

> "No, I says, your honor," and I'm coming closer and closer to him, "no, that can't be, I says, your honor, that you're tsar and God to us."
>
> "What are you saying, what are you saying?" screamed the major. "Rebel! [*Buntovshchik*!]"
>
> "No, I says (and I'm getting closer and closer), no, I says, your honor, how can, you must know yourself, our God, all powerful and everywhere, is one, I says. And our tsar is one, who God put over all of us. He, your honor, I says, is the monarch. And you, I says, your honor, are still just a major—our superior, your honor, by the grace of the tsar, I says, and your own merits."
>
> "How-how-how-how!" that's how he screeched, he couldn't talk, he was choking. He was really amazed.
>
> "That's how," I says; and I suddenly jumped on him just like that and stuck my whole knife right in his stomach. (*PSS* 4:90/132–33)

One of the skits during the prison theatricals contains a scene in which an abject servant, traveling with his master and robbing him at every opportunity, watches him carried away by devils in their haunted room at an inn and, even in his terrible fear, gleefully registers that "The devils have taken my master!" to the delight of the peasant-convicts in the audience (*PSS* 4:127/194).

A key scene of overt revolutionary activity occurs when the peasants, outraged at the poor quality of the prison food, conspire to confront the authorities en masse. They forbid Gorianchikov to join them and, with overt hostility and condescension, compel him to wait out the strike in the kitchen with "your people"—other noblemen, the Poles, and Isai Fomich (*PSS* 4:203/315). The grievance, as all had expected, comes to naught, but Gorianchikov is disturbed by what had been revealed during the protest. Petrov, to whom he has confessed his disappointment at being refused the chance to show solidarity with the peasant-convicts, is genuinely puzzled: "But . . . but how can you be a comrade to us?" In Petrov's question, Gorianchikov detects no "irony, bitterness, mockery," only "genuine naiveté," "simple-hearted bewilderment":

> Now for the first time a certain idea, which had been obscurely stirring in me and haunting me for a long time, was decisively clarified for me and I suddenly understood what up until then I had only poorly made out. I understood that I should never be accepted by them in fellowship, even if I were a prisoner to the end of time . . . . There was nothing to be done about it: I was simply not a comrade, and that was all there was to it. You go your way and we ours; you have your affairs, and we have ours. (*PSS* 4:207/322)

For the moment, the revolution has arrived: in *katorga*, it is the peasants who determine the nature of their relationship with the masters, and it is they who remain steadfast in their refusal to consider any rapprochement on any pretext with (former) members of the nobility.

Such examples of the reversal of the master-slave relationship illustrate the "reversibility" of subject and object accomplished, according to Merleau-Ponty, in the flesh of the world and of language. But when the carnival of reversals and overturnings subsides, two subjects, equal in their abjection, face each other across an impassable divide, each with his own road and his own affairs, and yet compelled to live in a space set apart in conditions of unprecedented physical intimacy. After his term of exile had concluded, Dostoevsky envisioned a new world in which this mandated physical intimacy would have been converted into a consensual national-spiritual unity, the basis of his democratic vision. The lesson of *katorga* was that if the new world was to be brought into being at all, it could only emerge as the co-production of its equally abject inhabitants. Its mise-en-scène is accomplished first (if haphazardly) in the space of exception and from the ground up, and it is (fitfully) visible only from this ground in the images of resistance, powerful in their very fragility, which Gorianchikov registers in his autobiographical confession, and ultimately in its most interior spaces. The democratic ground is literary ground first of all because only literature makes collectively perceptible that which the individual is the first almost to glimpse in the world, almost to know of him- or herself, but not quite: the *ne to*, that which has not fully materialized. Literature does so by representing not the object of perception but the acts of seeing and not seeing carried out by the individual as embodied contingency and by a *korporatsiia* of such individuals.

That he inhabited this democratic ground with no choice but to "become [. . .] one of the common people," their equal in abjection, underlies Dostoevsky's claim to an authoritative knowledge of the people when he returned to his literary career in St. Petersburg on the eve of emancipation (*PSS* 4:65/93).[144] Compared to this experiential knowledge, he argues, the knowledge derived from theoretical abstractions about the people put forward by "our very best 'experts' on the people's life" must be fundamentally false, because, as Merleau-Ponty describes it, bookish knowledge puts "into the things [here, the actual lives of the people] what it will then pretend to find in them" (*PSS* 19:7; *VI* 38). Dostoevsky amplified this point in his journal *Time* [*Vremia*] in a pair of articles of 1861, titled "Bookishness and Literacy," devoted to examining the promise and pitfalls of teaching the people to read. Dostoevsky is deeply committed to mass literacy programs which he claims are uniquely capable of bringing about "our unification with our native soil, with our popular [*narodnye*] origins" (*PSS* 19:6).[145] But in the course of these articles, literacy acquires a meaning other than the obvious one. It refers to the kind of knowledge possessed by the common people, a cultural logic or grammar antithetical to the abstractions of the elite and of which they are largely unaware.[146] In these articles, then, he reconceptualizes the project of reform by denying the inequality of teacher and student, giver and receiver—in fact, he denies the validity of these oppositional roles altogether. The literacy project cannot be a matter of persuading the educated and powerful to help the weak and ignorant rise to their level; rather, it is one of co-education, where the viability of the nation itself is shown to depend on the culture-wide achievement of combining equally important and legitimate forms of knowledge. To draw out this alternative meaning of literacy, he begins by invoking those experts

> who have really studied the people's life, even *lived* with the peasants, that is lived with them not on some landowner's country estate but alongside them, in their huts, *looked on* their indigence, saw all their peculiarities, acutely felt their desires, became familiar with their perspectives, even their cast of mind and so forth and so on. They've eaten together with the people, even their food; others have even *drunk* with them. Finally, there are even those who have worked with them, that is, performed the common people's work. There may not be many of them, but they exist. And what of it? These people are fully convinced that they know the people. They would even start laughing if we contradicted them and said to them, "You, gentlemen, know only the outside; you are very intelligent, you have noticed a lot, but the genuine life, the essence of the life, its very heart, you do not know." (*PSS* 19: 7/140–41, emphases in original)[147]

The experts come equipped on their visits to peasant cottages with their "bookish" idea of the people and seek to confirm it there. (Their peasant counterpart, comically, is Petrov, who assumes in his nightly conversations with Gorianchikov "that it was impossible to talk with me as with other people, that outside of conversations about books I would understand nothing and would even be incapable of understanding, so that there was no point in agitating me" [*PSS* 4:86/127].) But as Gorianchikov learns in his quest to apprehend the ideas of crime and pain in the absence of that bodily experience inseparable from them, it is not that "we" possess the ideas but that the ideas "possess us" and reveal their significance to us: in this situation, meaning cannot be given in advance but arises only when it "antedates itself by a retrograde movement" (*VI* 154). Possession, that is, not of but by the idea—an idea which is the product of a multiplicity of visions and in which constitutive power, the power to bring about community, inheres. Possession by the idea begins not in the analytical mind but in the body, as both Gorianchikov and Dostoevsky assert:

> The peasant will talk with you, tell you about himself, laugh together with you; will, perhaps, cry before you (although not with you), but he will never take you for one of his own. He will never seriously take you for his intimate, his brother, his real *homespun* fellow countryman. And never, never will he trust you. Even if you yourself were to dress (or fate dresses you) in homespun, even if you were to work together with him and perform his labor, he wouldn't put his faith even in that. He withholds his faith unconsciously, that is, he wouldn't believe even if he wanted to believe, because this mistrustfulness has entered into his flesh and blood. (*PSS* 19:7/140–41; emphases in the original)[148]

Precisely this flesh and blood irrevocably divides noble from common convicts, but within the space of exception of *katorga* it as irrevocably joins them in a common body. If distrust is part of the people's flesh and blood, it inheres in that of the nobleman as well, made visible in the wincing, the withholding from physical contact, the constant fretful distress that the less squeamish and pain-tolerant people lack. The historically constituted flesh and blood determines *that* the common flesh of the convict body possesses a constitutive power as well as *what* it can constitute by means of it.

In Gorianchikov's memoir, this constitutive power is only fleetingly glimpsed as a tentative staging or mise-en-scène in *katorga* of an emancipation from bondage to sovereign power, including the structurally central and disfiguring abyss of class difference. Emancipation is briefly realized in the revolutionary reversibility of noble-subject (master) and peasant-object (slave) and inadequately asserted through the practice of exchange. Gorianchikov intuits that in order for it to sustain itself, in order to resist those forces that forbid its fragile instanciations beyond the momentary here and there, emancipatory power requires the consummation of some image or representation through which a new world might come into being. As Lefort writes, "the advent of a society capable of organizing social relations can come about only if it can institute the conditions of their intelligibility, and only if it can use a multiplicity of signs to arrive at a quasi-representation of itself."[149] Gorianchikov's first instinct as a memoirist is to bring the world of *katorga* into representation vertically, by acquiring a perspective that would enable the organization of an inventory of prison life, but he is forced to concede that its reality tends toward a fragmentation in which he participates and so can acquire no privileged, integrative view. Its mise-en-scène requires instead that the author or subject, the would-be creator of the image, stand aside, undergo his own desubjectification, so that the multiplicity of signs through which the quasi-representation is achieved may circulate through him. But once he has in this way become incorporated, enmeshed in the common body, his claim to having been resurrected from the dead, which Gorianchikov identifies with his own release from *katorga,* can only be, as the prefatory narrator exists to show, illusory. Without resurrection, there can be no resolution, and thus no finalization of the ontological and political open-endedness that the novel, fulfilling its Bakhtinian raison d'être, brings into representation.[150] The novel ends in a suspense pregnant with the tension of the *ne to*, the "not that"—the "invisible texture of visible things."[151] The referent for the *ne to* that most fully comprehends its never fully comprehensible instantiations—the nobleman who is no longer a nobleman, crime, pain, the people—is "democracy," the word which stands for that which cannot be named but is not for that reason false or nonexistent.

Conclusion

THE RUSSIAN PEOPLE, THIS UNRIDDLED SPHINX

On the 19th of February the Petrine period of Russian
history definitively came to an end, so that long ago we
entered into a period of absolute uncertainty.
—*PSS* 23:41[1]

Carmen Horrendum

In the passage from "Bookishness and Literacy" cited at the conclusion of part 2, Dostoevsky identifies the populist discourse and practice of the liberal Russian elite as a prime example of "bookishness" (*knizhnost'*), an official discourse of power and knowledge. "Literacy" (*gramotnost'*), in contrast, describes another type of knowledge altogether: unarticulated and unprogrammatic, inseparable from experience and lodged in the flesh and blood, this alternative knowledge underwrites the integrity and vitality of an abject and illiterate culture.[2] Uniquely possessed by the illiterate peasantry, "literacy" is the non-text–based cultural logic of genuine Russianness, that which makes the peasant from Taganrog and the one from Petropavlovsk immediately familiar to each other. It is difficult, if not impossible, to apprehend for educated Russians situated outside the common milieu (*PSS* 4:198/308). In his article, Dostoevsky tries to imagine how these two antithetical forms of knowledge, the elite's bookishness and the people's literacy, might be made to harmonize without sacrificing one or the other. He suggests that the resolution of this epistemological impasse will bring the Russian people into being—not simply "the *people* as a subset and as fragmentary multiplicity of needy and excluded bodies" but, rather, "the *People* as a whole and as an integral body politic." Resolution of the impasse between bookishness and literacy promises to heal what Agamben calls the "fundamental biopolitical fracture" between the "total state of the sovereign and integrated citizens," on the one hand, and "the wretched, the oppressed, and the vanquished," on the other. It is thus the sine qua non of real emancipation. But as Agamben points out, insofar as the concept of the people already contains the primal division of bare life and political existence (*zoe* and *bios*) characteristic of "the original political structure," it must always refer paradoxically to "*what cannot be included in the whole of which it is a part as well as what cannot belong to the whole in which it is always already included.*" The people or *narod* seem inevitably to be "what always already is" but also "what has yet to be realized"—the *ne to* of Dostoevsky's democracy.[3]

Dostoevsky's contemporary, the radical critic Dmitri Pisarev, began his 1866 article on *House of the Dead*, "The Perished and the Perishing" [*"Pogibshie i pogibaiushchie"*], by observing: "The comparative method is as useful and essential to the anatomist of a single individual as it is to social science, which we might call the anatomy of a society."[4] Despite the difference between the race-based slavery of the United States and the class-based slavery of Russia, the autobiographical narratives of Frederick Douglass provide a comparative touchstone for gaining a perspective on Dostoevsky's democracy. Not surprisingly, emancipation is also centrally at stake in Douglass's representation of his escape from slavery, and, more particularly, of an epistemological impasse unique to the institution of slavery which he articulates in terms of the mutually exclusive knowledges that Dostoevsky designates bookishness and literacy.[5] Douglass structures his autobiographies with reference to a spatial poetics of "outside" and "inside," in which the enslaved find themselves abandoned within the exceptional space or " 'tabooed' spot" of the plantation, a "secluded, dark, and out-of-the-way place" unilluminated by public discourse or opinion or even "the glimmering and unsteady light of trade."[6] To have been born "within the circle" is to realize that one is "without an intelligible beginning in the world"—a peculiar challenge for an autobiographer (*MBMF* 99, 60). The acquisition of one's most fundamental knowledge of oneself must be derived from experience rather than genealogy; here, desubjectification is not what happens to the subject who enters the space of exception, it is where one begins. Douglass notes that "to outward seeming," the plantation would appear "a most strikingly interesting place, full of life, activity, and spirit" (*MBMF* 65). But it is a hermetically sealed world. Just as *katorga* had its "own singular laws, its clothing, its morals and customs," so the plantation has "its own language, its own rules, regulations and customs" (*PSS* 4:9/7). It is thus a world whose expressive forms are inaudible or incomprehensible to outsiders; the slave, by definition always the "criminal" here, Douglass says, "is always dumb" (*MBMF* 64).

Yet the slave finds his or her voice in the slave song, which is sung within the innermost circle of exception, the places where the inhuman labor is performed. In Douglass's representation of the slave song, we encounter a powerful instance of the opposition between "literacy" and "bookishness":

> They would compose and sing as they went along, consulting neither time nor tune. The thought that came up, came out—if not in the word, in the sound;—and as frequently in the one as in the other. They would sometimes sing the most pathetic sentiment in the most rapturous tone, and the most rapturous sentiment in the most pathetic tone. [. . .] they would sing, as a

chorus, to words which to many would seem unmeaning jargon, but which, nevertheless, were full of meaning to themselves. I have sometimes thought that the mere hearing of those songs would do more to impress some minds with the horrible character of slavery, than the reading of whole volumes of philosophy on the subject could do.[7]

In lieu of reading, Douglass invites his curious reader to bypass bookish knowledge and accede to "literacy," which requires the flesh, the direct participation of the body as the privileged receiver of meaning:

> If any one wishes to be impressed with the soul-killing effects of slavery, let him [. . .] place himself in the deep pine woods, and there let him, in silence, analyze the sounds that shall pass through the chambers of his soul,—and if he is not thus impressed, it will only be because "there is no flesh in his obdurate heart." (*MBMF* 99)

But the impossibility of such an impression taking on the minds of Douglass's hypothetical eavesdroppers is already suggested here. Although the slaves' "literacy"—the intimate, bodily knowledge of slavery audible in their songs—expresses the character of slavery more powerfully than the philosophers' (or the abolitionists') "bookishness," the transmission of their knowledge is impeded by the fact that listeners with no personal experience of slavery can hear in the songs only "unmeaning jargon." The conversion of readers to listeners does not redress the problem of illiteracy; the meaning of the "*carmen horrendum*" or "horrible song" is exclusive to the millions "*hors la loi*" who sing them.[8]

A further complication develops in Douglass's analysis. Illiteracy, as it turns out, does not differentiate those on the outside from those on the inside. Instead, it extends even to those "within the circle" from whom the meaning of slavery is also withheld:

> I did not, when a slave, understand the deep meaning of those rude and apparently incoherent songs. I was myself within the circle; so that I neither saw nor heard as those without might see and hear. They told a tale of woe which was then altogether beyond my feeble comprehension; they were tones loud, long, and deep; they breathed the prayer and complaint of souls boiling over with the bitterest anguish. (*MBMF* 99)

Although Douglass traces to the slave songs "my first glimmering conceptions of the dehumanizing character of slavery," it is only after his escape, his self-removal from the circle and his acquisition of perspective, that Douglass claims fully to understand the significance of slavery (*MBMF* 99). Yet to be placed outside the circle within which the songs are produced is to lose the "thought" that "came up" out of the body to express itself directly (with no participation by the analytical mind) in song. Bookishness, on the contrary, offers a knowledge gained through various "indirections" (*MBMF* 151). Self-possession excludes possession by the idea or "thought" of enslavement. If "bookishness" entails a mistaken seeing or a hearing without understanding, "literacy" appears to entail an understanding that cannot be owned (objectified, articulated, reproduced, transmitted). The problem the slave song passages in the autobiographies educes is one reinforced by Douglass's early frustrations as a speaker on the abolitionist circuit: slavery is in certain respects a *ne to*, something language can only indirectly represent, for example, in stories "of mere physical cruelties" that fail to convey the invisible reality.[9]

Douglass nevertheless figures his emancipation as having been made possible, first as a state of mind and then as an act, by a coming together of bookishness and literacy. Having been sent as a young boy to the freer environment of Baltimore to serve in the family of one of his master's relatives, Douglass surreptitiously acquires the skills of reading, and at the age of twelve he becomes aware that he is a special class of being who is not a self-reliant subject, "A SLAVE FOR LIFE" (*MBMF* 156). At thirteen, he makes a subversive purchase of a schoolbook titled *The Columbian Orator* that includes a short dialogue between a master and a slave in which the legitimacy of slavery itself is debated and the master, having been bested by the slave, "meekly emancipates" him.[10] Bookishness offers its own mode of possession by the idea: such entries, Douglass writes, "enabled me to give tongue to many interesting thoughts, which had frequently flashed through my soul, and died away for want of utterance"—here the book "gives tongue" (flesh, form) to the thought that otherwise would not have materialized (*MBMF* 158).[11] Using Claude Lefort's analysis of the advent of modern democracy, we might say that what Douglass achieves in his purchase, reading, and ventriloquization of the book is the ability to reflect on power by gaining access to "a place from which it can be seen, read and named," and, in so doing, engendering a self-splitting or "internal-external articulation" which offers at the same time a demystifying "quasi-representation" of his society. The "view" Douglass reports gaining of himself and his situation through reading is thus analogous to "a movement of the externalization of the social which goes hand in hand with its internalization."[12] Although painful, his acquisition of book knowledge constitutes the turning point of the narrative, the creation of a world outside the circle into which he can break free. He represents this outward move as an inward move, as a penetration of the outer world's secret, thereby inverting the spatial poetics operative in that part of his life when slavery had enclosed and defined him (*MBMF* 159).[13]

Several years after Douglass's escape in 1838, the Garrisonians who recruit him to speak for the Massachusetts Anti-Slavery Society attempt to drive the ex-slave's bookishness back into the performance of literacy in the form of a recitation of "the facts" of his personal experience commensurate with his status as a *"brand new fact,"* an *"it"* or *"thing"* that yet can speak (*MBMF* 361, 360). Thus, he is constrained to reiterate at each event the same simple narration of wrongs he had suffered: "we will take care of the philosophy," he is told by his abolitionist agents (*MBMF* 361).[14] Only on the first occasion of public address is his performance of his literacy genuine and therefore "inspired." Significantly, his "speech on this occasion is about the only one I ever made, of which I do not remember a single connected sentence"; he recalls only the embarrassment he suffered on being made to externalize his experience before an audience (*MBMF* 358). Literacy, as we have seen, resists being owned, and as he acquires "new views" from "reading and thinking," Douglass finds himself increasingly unable and then unwilling to dissimulate its possession (*MBMF* 361). Moreover, the performance of his literacy involves for Douglass the aggravated self-alienation imposed by the Garrisonians who in their own speeches take him "as their text," and allude to his body as a type of text, his *"diploma"* proving his matriculation from "the peculiar institution" (*MBMF* 358, 359). When John A. Collins, general agent of the Massachusetts Anti-Slavery Society, urges him once again to tell his "story" and thereby commands him to "be yourself," he finds himself unable to "obey, for I was now reading and thinking" (*MBMF* 362, 361). His bookishness makes him appear fraudulent to his audience for it changes the way he walks, looks, and acts, and he is urged by his handlers to "have a *little* of the plantation manner of speech than not; 'tis not best that you seem too learned" (*MBMF* 362). The *Columbian Orator* had afforded the slave boy the opportunity to imagine himself speaking truth to power, and the self-emancipation for which his reading prepared him leads to his becoming an orator in reality on the abolitionist circuit. But the transition from literacy to bookishness which he envisions as natural intellectual growth is disallowed by the Garrisonians' desire to resurrect his literacy through its performance, on the one hand, and, on the other, to literalize him as an emblem of slavery (*MBMF* 362).

The path Douglass took to complete his emancipation is well known: having honed his skills as an orator of great power, having grown impatient with the limitations the abolitionists placed on his development, and having written his first (1845) autobiography which brought the fugitive slave a possibly dangerous visibility, Douglass liberated himself from "republican slavery" by traveling to "monarchical England" (*MBMF* 360).[15] There, as he writes to Garrison in a letter published by the abolitionist organ *The Liberator* on New Year's Day 1846, he feels that he has "undergone a transformation [into] a new life" (*MBMF* 370). Both in the United Kingdom and after his return to the United States, Douglass comes into his own as a spectacularly successful public figure, speaker, and writer, an exemplary self-fashioner. Bookishness thus liberates Douglass from a literacy that afforded no outlet and no growth; indeed, even as a child, he had "instinctively assented to the proposition" conveyed by his master in forbidding his mistress to teach him to read that " 'knowledge unfits a child to be a slave,' " and he reports that "from that moment I understood the direct pathway from slavery to freedom" (*MBMF* 146, 147). Douglass thus has no sentimental attachment to literacy and does not dream of preserving it, nor does he envision a merging of a knowledge unique to the slave with that of American society at large. At most he may have contemplated, according to historian John Stauffer, an ambition shared with a group of radical abolitionists, both black and white, to heal the abyss of racial prejudice by persuading white America to acquire a "black heart." In order for the "heart of the whites [to] be changed, thoroughly, entirely, permanently changed" (in the words of the black abolitionist James McCune Smith), they must not only renounce their belief in the superiority of whiteness, but also "learn how to view the world as if they were black." But these abolitionists contemplated less a merger of black and white knowledges than a transcendence of their difference in what was fundamentally a religious undertaking, an aspect of spiritual awakening and conversion, and, secondarily, a social-political program.[16] Only a change of heart can bring about that change of perception that will bring about in turn the new world into which the new man will be reborn.

In contrast to Frederick Douglass, Dostoevsky is unwilling to relinquish his conviction that literacy, the knowledge gained by the common people through the experience of abjection itself, possesses an independent value that should not be sacrificed but somehow wedded to the knowledge of the elite if the new world, a unified and thus truly emancipated Russia, is to come into being. But as Douglass affirmed, gaining access to this literacy is impossible not only for those who have never lived "within the circle" but even for those who have, if to gain access to this form of knowledge means to own it. Dostoevsky/Gorianchikov, of course, had lived within the circle and had produced from that milieu powerful representations of the everyday life of a Siberian forced labor camp and the personalities and incidents attached to it. But through the mediate level of narration, the aporia of autobiographical representation examined in part I of this volume, Gorianchikov unwittingly represents his own perceptual blindness in relation to his crime and thus to the common people who provide the focus of his memoir.[17] Through novel techniques of first-person narration developed in this first of the great novels, Dostoevsky reveals not just the moral and political danger but the elusiveness and stubbornness of the nobleman's habitual regard. Specifically, he illuminates that internal force that resists a true acknowledgment of the other as the privileged object of one's efforts to understand despite one's best intentions. In so doing, he also reveals the commonness of the common people in all its strangeness, the alterity of the peasant Other unamenable to the reforming efforts of the liberal elite, the philanthropists, and the sentimentalists. Before the recuperation of one's perception of the Other can occur, Dostoevsky suggests through his auto-biographical alter ego Gorianchikov, one must first see the extent of one's blindness. This is his starting position in the journalistic debates of 1861 on whether and how the soon-to-be emancipated peasants should be taught to read. Just as, in Douglass's case, the opportunities and limits of antebellum America's "solution" to the epistemological impasse of bookishness and literacy offer a view of the "democratic" cast of its culture beyond the institutional or merely rhetorical senses, so, too, does Dostoevsky's post-Siberian meditation on the challenge of "educating democracy" adumbrate the meaning of "becoming democratic" in mid-nineteenth-century Russia, at the inception of its own revolutionary modernity.

Bookishness, Literacy, and Becoming Democratic

"It's as if you . . . as if it's from a book," she said,
and again something like mockery sounded in her voice.
—*Notes from the Underground*

In *Remnants of Auschwitz*, Giorgio Agamben makes reference to the early-twentieth-century Portuguese poet Fernando Pessoa, whose poetic practice involved the invention of heteronyms which he represents as a consummation of self and alter ego:

> An urging of spirit came upon me, absolutely foreign, for one reason or another, of that which I am, or which I suppose that I am. I spoke to it, immediately, spontaneously, as if it were a certain friend of mine whose name I invented, whose history I adapted, and whose figure—face, build, clothes, and manner—I immediately saw inside of me. And so I contrived and procreated various friends and acquaintances who never existed but whom still today—nearly thirty years later—I hear, feel, see.

He comes to regard one particular heteronym—Alberto Caeiro—as his "master," through whom he writes thirty poems in succession in a kind of ecstasy. But then, Pessoa tells us,

> scarcely were those thirty-odd poems written when I snatched more paper and wrote, again without stopping, the six poems constituting "Oblique Rain," by Fernando Pessoa. [. . .] It was the return of Fernando Pessoa/Alberto Caeiro to Fernando Pessoa himself. Or better, it was the reaction of Fernando Pessoa against his nonexistence as Alberto Caeiro.

Agamben concludes of this triple movement—Pessoa yielding to Caeiro who yields to Pessoa—that "a new poetic consciousness, something like a genuine *ethos* of poetry, begins once Fernando Pessoa, having survived his own depersonalization, returns to a self who both is and is no longer the first subject. Then he understands that he must react to his nonexistence as Alberto Caeiro, *that he must respond to his own desubjectification*" (*RA* 118, 119; emphasis in original).

Before Pessoa, Dostoevsky had similarly derived a genuine ethos of poetry from a return to oneself inseparable from the accomplishment in literature of the desubjectification of one's former self and subsumption in another. Pessoa's story recalls Gorianchikov's in *Notes from the House of the Dead*, as well as that of the humble clerk Goliadkin in the 1846 novella *The Double* to which Dostoevsky had returned at the time he was writing the 1861 novel: both the naïve, impoverished clerk and the urbane, incarcerated landowner personify this "urging of the spirit" to create an other "absolutely foreign [to] that which I am, or which I suppose that I am," and to let this alien other speak to them and let it speak for them. Pessoa's and Dostoevsky's narratives of literary creation bear the same triple structure one finds in the conversion narrative (as opposed to the Hegelian dialectic), except that the death of one's former life is figured as an estranged residence *in* or *as* an embodied antithetical other, and one's rebirth is figured as an apotheosis that does not transcend but refers back to this other as the alienated yet inalienable ground of an ongoing transfiguration. In a series of articles written in his journal *Time* in 1861, Dostoevsky will figure the coming-into-being of a genuinely national literature, too, with reference to this tripartite structure. As Joseph Frank observes, at this juncture the writer is

> caught, like Matthew Arnold's traveler in "Stanzas from the Grande Chartreuse," "Wandering between two worlds, one dead, / The other powerless to be born, / With nowhere yet to rest [his] head," in search of a new ideal to replace the old European one in which, like the entire highly civilized society to which he belongs, he is no longer able fully to believe: "For at bottom, his soul is thirsting for a new truth."[18]

The "new truth" of a nation emancipated from its own history of external division (the West's cultural colonization of the Russian elite) and internal division (the Westernized elite's cultural ostracization of the Russian common people), far from representing the transcendence of this history, can only be elaborated from out of its very impossibility. The new truth is one that will not arrive but must be delivered—both emancipated from and brought into existence through the contradictory cultural material at hand.

In contrast to Douglass's case, emancipation here signifies not an individual's liberation but the collective orchestration of a culture's becoming self-identical. This is what Dostoevsky means when he speaks of "becoming democratic"; it is what he intends when he insists, as he does in 1861, that there is no class conflict in Russia even as he describes the "native soil" as deeply fissured by the "ravine," "abyss," or "chasm" of class division.[19] Pragmatically, the project of becoming democratic, he insisted, hinged on resolving the impasse of bookishness and literacy. Its resolution would permit a movement away from reliance on the "idea," the always embattled brainchild of a handful of bookish partisans, so that a truly national culture might emerge (in Merleau-Ponty's formulation) as "a created generality [. . .] come to add to and recapture and rectify the natural generality of my body and of the world" (*VI* 152). The resolution of the bookishness/literacy impasse would eliminate the tragic opposition of *zoe* and *bios* which the European Enlightenment had exacerbated, if not created. As his nationalism became increasingly messianic, Dostoevsky represents the rapprochement of *zoe* and *bios* as Russia's exclusive prerogative, the hallmark of Russianness (*narodnost'*) itself. If the nation had never managed to foster anything resembling the cultural vitality of Europe, as Westernizers from Chaadaev to Turgenev had lamented, it was nevertheless spared its necrosis. Russian culture could not be entirely free of the body, its "native soil": for that reason, its attempts to adopt the culture of European enlightenment had been a tragicomic failure. Yet that failure, once acknowledged by all educated Russians, would free the nation to deliver from out of its own body—revered, despised, but above all unknown—a culture never before seen and in that sense new, whose mise-en-sens would not precede but be simultaneous with its mise-en-scène.[20] It would merge with its indigenous forms a European content first vetted and then naturalized not by the elite but by Russiannness itself, a consummation that would produce "another less heavy, more transparent body": not a liberal Russia based on possessive individualism but a democratic Russia "emancipated but not freed from every condition" (*VI* 153).[21]

The philosopher's oxymoron, "emancipated but not free," fairly describes the situation in 1861 for both the common and elite classes: on the one hand, a formally proclaimed emancipation that would not go into practical effect for years;[22] and, on the other, a privileged class compelled on ethical and pragmatic grounds to take a revolutionary step toward eradicating the inequities of class that it did not know how to take but on which "everything depends" (*PSS* 18:66). The combined forces of the elite and of the "peasantry"—"many millions of Russians [who] will emerge into Russian life [and who] will bring to it their own fresh, untouched powers"—were expected to utter in concert a "new word" they could not articulate (*PSS* 18:35).[23] To the question, "where is the point of contact with the people? How do we take the first step towards rapprochement with them?" Dostoevsky's answer was "literacy and education" (*PSS* 18:37). Russia's self-deliverance through self-education was of paramount importance: "Everything makes way for it; all class privileges, one may say, are subsumed by it" (*PSS* 19:19). Against all argument, he steadily urged the importance of universal literacy as a prerequisite to national unification.[24] But his pragmatic recommendations for achieving this goal and his judgments on the literacy programs devised by others are marked by the familiar contortions produced by the abyss of class difference. He detects sentimentality or condescension in every concrete attempt to extend literacy through the publication of readers, the creation of institutions intended to extend and encourage literacy among the common people, and other formal measures.[25] It is not just that he eschews elite manipulation of the means of acquiring literacy but, beyond that, elite monopoly of the very concept of literacy which must inevitably bear the stigma of bookishness.

The challenge of reconciling bookishness with literacy was a problem of the chicken-and-egg variety. Instead of masterminding the transition to a literate and therefore harmonious society, the elite were to bring the common people into "civilized" (European) culture without Europeanizing them while simultaneously returning to their own Russian roots, from which more than a century and a half of Westernization had alienated them, by somehow intuiting and incorporating (not studying) the people's own unspoken, unpublished truth (*PSS* 18:66). If elite teachers were an inevitability, they must be capable of teaching their (common) students in such a way that they would not be mistaken for and rejected as masters. These (common) students would, on the one hand, submit willingly to the authority of their (elite) teachers because they themselves had authorized their teaching in recognition of their mastery, yet, on the other, they were to be kept by those teachers unaware of their own standing as students. On the collective level, Dostoevsky, on one side, envisioned a transfiguration or conversion unilaterally undertaken by the civilized class — "we must transform ourselves into them completely"[26]—and, on the other, saw a mutually undertaken and synchronized rapprochement in which each class would recognize and concede the unique contribution of the other to a genuinely common and fully representative culture (*PSS* 19:7). As we will see below, Dostoevsky claimed personal experience of the peasants' willingness to defer to the expertise of the nobility when there was a valid reason to do so.

Even if these self-contradictory requirements could be met, a more fundamental issue arose in the form of a simple question: "What, precisely, should the people be given to read?" In the first part of "Bookishness and Literacy," Dostoevsky rejects the seemingly obvious answer, Russian literature:

We haven't yet spoken about the fact that somehow all of us, without a superfluous word, have tacitly acknowledged that everything written by us, all
literature past and present, is not suited for popular reading. Whether or not
this is true is another question; it is evident only that it is as if all of us, with
no discussion, agreed that the people would understand absolutely nothing
in it. (*PSS* 19:6)

What lies behind this tacit consensus? Dostoevsky rejects the commonsensical explanation: it is not simply that we are educated, they are not, and
it will take time to bring them into our interpretive community. As he
unfolds, over the course of several articles, the deceptively straightforward
question of what the people should be given to read, the problem of literacy—the acquisition of the ability to read texts—ramifies in the face of
"literacy" as a historically acquired experiential knowledge.

First and most obvious, because they are illiterate, the people have no
intellectual access to the various literary representations beyond the narrow
folkish range reflected in the conventions of oral literature, a limitation in
both content and form that would be replicated even in print should a
"genuine people's poet" (*nastoiashchii prostonarodnyi poet*) materialize:

> Such a poet, first of all, would give imaginative expression to his own envi-
> ronment, without elevating himself above it, having accepted his sur-
> rounding reality as the norm, the ideal. His poetry would then almost coin-
> cide with folk songs, which are somehow composed as they are sung. He
> might appear in another aspect, that is, not taking his surroundings as the
> norm, but already denying a part of it, and could then portray some moment
> of common life, some popular movement, something of the people's desire.
> Such a poet could be very powerful, could authentically voice [*vyrazit'*] the
> people. But in any case he would not be profound and his horizon would
> be very narrow. (*PSS* 19:16)

As producers and consumers, then, the common people are unable to occupy the capacious ground of modern literary representation. As characters, whether created by elite or common writers, they lent themselves to
the same impoverished forms of expression, as even those radical critics
willing to overlook the artistry in literary texts admitted.[27] Dostoevsky
quotes the utilitarian critic Dobroliubov's 1860 review in the *Contemporary* [*Sovremmenik*] of the peasant tales of Marko Vovchok, particularly
her story of the rebellious peasant girl Masha who, like Frederick Douglass, although enslaved and ignorant, possesses a precocious sense of her
individuality. Determined as he is to celebrate Vovchok's contribution,
Dobroliubov must concede that "the consciousness of the people has still
not reached in our time the point where it can express itself by means of
the poetic image." Beyond that, "it is still impossible to demand from our
stories of peasant life an exacting conclusiveness and thoroughness, it still

has not opened itself to us in all its fullness, and that which is open to us we don't yet know how to or can't yet express well" (*PSS* 18:85).

In addition to such considerations, Dostoevsky reminded his readers throughout these essays that to bring the common people into literature as characters risked reproducing the elite class's bookish illusions about them, whether sentimental or derogatory, and risked the possibility that common readers would take these illusions for the truth about themselves, making literature an instrument of cultural corruption rather than renewal. Moreover, their passivity as literary consumers and their absence as literary producers threatened to replicate the sin of an unauthorized "speaking for" which *Notes from the House of the Dead*, published simultaneously with these essays, had called so forcefully into question.[28] In an 1862 essay titled "Are the Peasant Children to Learn to Write from Us? or, Are We to Learn from the Peasant Children?" Tolstoy attempted to bypass the chicken-and-egg conundrum in which discussion of the future literature of an emancipated Russia had become mired by describing at length his work with peasant children on his estate for whom he had provided the opportunity to write creatively. The "us" of his essay is not so much the elite class, as it is adults generally whose self-expression had been delimited by their factitious social identities; the peasant children, in contrast, exemplify all the imaginative vitality of those Turgenev represented through the eyes of his noble "hunter" in "Bezhin Meadow" with none of their predisposition to the limitations of the folk sensibility. Literacy emerges in Tolstoy's essay as something close to Dostoevsky's figurative understanding of *gramotnost'*: the intuitive sense, neither teachable nor programmable, that ensures one's conformity with one's essential self.[29] Ideally, such intuitive knowledge individually elicited but nationally staged would find its objective correlative in a genuinely comprehensive national literature. As things stood in 1861, the common people might possess but were unable to reproduce their knowledge textually, either as a literature or as a program for authentic nationality. Assuming that they would be taught to read, however, they could uniquely verify the authenticity of such knowledge if the educated classes, despite their bookishness and through their own still unconscious literacy, found a way to make it legible.

Dostoevsky sets the scene for such an eventuality by posing only to dismiss the validity of two vexing questions. First, does national character (*narodnost'*) belong solely to the common people (*prostonarod'e*) or, differently put, "Is it really the case that we, the 'educated,' are not the Russian people [*russkii narod*]?"[30] Relatedly, must the national poet write only in the common people's vernacular? (*PSS* 19:14, 15). These questions must be raised and dismissed because Dostoevsky's candidate for national poet is, and will remain throughout his life, Alexander Pushkin, an aristocrat entirely unknown to the common people whose work engaged the topic of their significance only indirectly. In order to uphold Pushkin as the already arrived national poet of global importance, Dostoevsky redefines nationality as residing not in an external qualifier such as class but in the poetic sensibility itself imagined as a kind of raw material to which all Russians had equal access.[31] It could therefore serve as a reliable index of genuine "Russianness," whether it surfaced in the sophisticated textual representations of Pushkin or the anonymous oral productions of peasant culture. Dostoevsky/Gorianchikov had had the opportunity to verify the intrinsic worth of the latter as occupant of a front-row seat to the peasant-convict Christmas theatricals in *katorga*, a position he explicitly compares—for the press of bodies, for the remarkable view it affords of genuine peasant life—to his experience of the bathhouse.[32]

In this scene, we find Gorianchikov in his usual predicament: concerning the sketches performed so expertly by the peasant-convicts, "however many questions I asked, I could find out nothing beforehand" (*PSS* 4:118/179). He comes to the peasant theatricals a blank slate, entirely ignorant of its origins, conventions, and development. He calls on researchers to look into the subject, to interview "soldiers, factory workers in factory towns, and even small merchants in unknown, impoverished villages," and proposes that popular theater originated in the theatricals staged for members of the landed nobility by their own serfs whom they had formed into private theatrical companies (*PSS* 4:119/180).[33] The peasants particularly seek out Gorianchikov's opinion of their performance. If they escort him to the front row of the makeshift theater because they know he will contribute the extra kopek, it is also partly because "they saw in me a connoisseur, an expert, one who used to frequent such theaters." Class prejudices are for the occasion entirely disregarded:

> The convicts might laugh at me, seeing that I was a poor helper for them at work. Almazov could look contemptuously at us, the nobility, while showing off his expertise in calcining alabaster. But mixed in with their persecution of us and their laughing at us was something else: we had been noblemen; we had belonged to the same class as their former masters, of whom they could not have preserved fond memories. But now, in the theater, they deferred to me. They acknowledged that in this I could judge better than they, that I saw and knew more than they did. Those among them who were least disposed toward me (I know this) now wanted me to praise their theater and without any servility put me in the best seat. (*PSS* 4:121/184)

Gorianchikov finds ample reason to praise everything—the music, the staging, the acting, the content, the audience reception—and describes all aspects of the performance in appreciative detail. He arrives at precisely Tolstoy's conclusion: "Our wise men can teach the people little. I would even insist that the opposite is true: they should themselves learn from the people" (*PSS* 4:122/184).[34] Nevertheless, after the euphoria of the performance has passed and Gorianchikov is locked in the barracks with those whose behavior in the context of art had betokened a (momentary) moral transformation, he rises up from his bunk in terror. Scrutinizing every aspect of his wretched surroundings, including the peasant-convicts themselves, he struggles to convince himself "that all this was not the continuation of an ugly dream, but the actual truth. But it was the truth" (*PSS* 4:130/198). The theatricals offer the quintissential mise-en-scène of emancipation unique to *katorga* in which all are freed temporarily from their enslavement to class difference, an experience euphoric for some, terrifying for others. All the constituent elements for the rapprochement envisioned in the journalism are in place, but, as Gorianchikov's impulse of estranged horror confirms, the moment of consummation has not arrived.[35]

The poetry of Pushkin constitutes another and more enduring opportunity, albeit one generated by the noble class and offered to the common. Dostoevsky offsets the potential problem of Pushkin's elevated content by proposing that the national poem announces itself as such by providing the occasion for just such a process of poetic apprehension as Gorianchikov experienced in the peasant theatricals where the plays were mere fragments, without logic or sense. On such occasions, the reader or spectator immediately recognizes an unfamiliar poetic form to be "in the highest degree Russian," not an imitation (*PSS* 19:15). If the common people at their present stage of development cannot appreciate Pushkin, Dostoevsky confidently asserts that they will "understand him later and from his poetry will come to know themselves" (*PSS* 19:16). Unlike the hypothetical people's poet whose only skill is to become a conduit for the expression of his or her immediate reality, the national poet speaks the truth "directly and simply to the people, without lies and without falsehoods" (*PSS* 16:17). As was the case historically with the reforms of Peter the Great, the people will instinctively, "from the first glance," reject whatever in the new cultural forms is "un-Russian, false and mistaken" (*PSS* 19:18). Meanwhile, the abyss of class difference constrains Dostoevsky's ongoing discussion to the hypothetical—the quintessentially bookish—mode.

Where Have All the Peasants Gone?

> The folk hero has awakened and is stretching his limbs;
> perhaps he will want to go on a binge, to cross the line.
> *PSS* 23:41/168

In his letter of 9 October 1859 to his brother, Mikhail, Dostoevsky boasted that the novel on which he had begun to work, *Notes from the House of the Dead*, would be distinguished by its "representation of personalities *never before heard* [*ne slykhannykh*] in literature" (*PSS* 28 [I]: 349; emphasis in original). The "Siberian Notebook," kept illegally in *katorga* to record examples of peasant conversation, represents a commitment to a new democratic aesthetic in which these silenced voices find representation on the literary if not the political stage.[36] But although he offers his unique knowledge of the people as the guarantor of his authorial legitimacy upon returning to the profession, nothing Dostoevsky writes after *Notes from the House of the Dead* approaches that novel's profound engagement with the common people. A cursory glance through the post-Siberian work suggests that their roles are minor, their often heavily allegorized characters linked to non-ideological crime, gratuitous violence committed for the simple pleasure of brutalizing another, weaker creature. Here we find the village peasant either as perpetrator (the dream-peasant who beats the little mare to death in *Crime and Punishment*; the hypothetical peasant who tortures his wife before their daughter and drives her to suicide in the *Diary of a Writer* article "The Environment") or as victim (the abusive peasant's wife; the peasant child to whose torture Alyosha Karamazov will not hypothetically assent even as the sole condition for eternal paradise). One finds, too, a smattering of peasant characters less remarkably vicious or saintly who play minor roles in a novel's action, such as the ex-convict Fedka in *The Demons* or Smerdiakov's adoptive parents Grigory and Marfa in *The Brothers Karamazov*, whom Dostoevsky's narrator refers to as "auxiliary persons" (*PSS* 14:85/92). Generally, however, notwithstanding the intimate knowledge of the common people that Dostoevsky claimed to have gained through his prison experience, the peasant seems to pose as dire a challenge to novelistic representation as, significantly, characters who exemplify religious truth (such as Zosima) or absolute goodness (such as Myshkin). We might assume that the representational limitations he identified and analyzed in his journalism inhibited his own artistic efforts in this regard. Yet, the question of the peasant in Dostoevsky's oeuvre is worth a closer look: where in his work do we glimpse their still-distant silhouettes?

One answer may lie in his continuing experimentation with the sentimental theme of triangulated romance. In 1859, Dostoevsky wrote several variations of a sketch tentatively titled "Spring Love." All its versions describe the relationship between a wealthy prince, a writer who acts as the prince's companion and dependent, and an innocent young woman, characterized chiefly as being "without her own words" (*bez svoikh slov*), a phrase Turgenev used to describe Liza, his saintly heroine in *Home of the Gentry*, published in the journal *Sovremennik* in January 1859.[37] In these sketches, Dostoevsky experimented with several triangular configurations for representing the shifting dynamics of a sexual/psychological power struggle. The prince and the writer alternately play the villain in relation to the "wordless" young girl, seducing her, bragging to the other about the conquest, and leaving her. Dostoevsky scholars have recognized in these figures the initial appearance of the principal characters in his first post-Siberian novel, *The Insulted and the Injured* (1861), as well as the 1862 tale, "A Nasty Story," in which the shared theme of psychological domination masquerading as love is squarely contextualized within the theme of class oppression. But they also bear a resemblance to the main types of *Notes from the House of the Dead*: the aristocratic prefatory narrator, a man "with convictions"; the writer Gorianchikov, of equal stature to the anterior narrator, yet in some sense diminished; and the figure who exists apart—sexually and discursively—from those who spar for the right to victimize her: the helpless young girl whose capacity for silent suffering, like the peasant's, constitutes a formidable if unrecognized spiritual resource. The apotheosis of the theme of class-based psychological domination occurring in a sexual context is, of course, *Notes from the Underground*, in the naked verbal aggression, at times reciprocal, of the post-coital dialogue of the Underground Man with the prostitute Liza.[38]

A more direct connection to the themes generated by contact with the peasant in *katorga* may be found in Dostoevsky's enduring obsession with crime which he continues to explore through each of the major novels with explicit reference to class. As in his pre-Siberian work, in the great novels the dramatic personae ramify beyond the elite/common opposition into borderline figures, including the urban poor and the non-noble intellectual, or *raznochinets*. The literary focus of Dostoevsky's early career from the publication of his debut novel *Poor People* in 1846 until his arrest in 1849 had been the Petersburg underclass—"the proletariat of the capital," as he apparently referred to them—who occupied the humblest positions in the tsarist bureaucracy.[39] Following the trend initiated by Gogol toward social realism, Dostoevsky's early fiction was celebrated for his complex, if sentimental, portraits of lowly civil servants and other members of the city's literate and/or non-peasant underclass, and for his increasingly acute portrayal of the psychological effects of poverty and social marginalization.[40] His Siberian experience, however, supplements this focus through the intercalated themes of crime, remorse, and the environment.

Dostoevsky most directly continues the investigation of these themes so powerfully initiated in *House of the Dead* in the epilogue to the first of the great novels, *Crime and Punishment*, where the uncharacteristically omniscient narrator states that Raskol'nikov "did not repent of his crime," his murder of the old pawnbroker and her sister.[41] He doubts that "evildoing" (*zlodeianie*) has a meaning apart from its legal definition as "a criminal act" (*ugolovnoe prestuplenie*): "of course, the letter of the law was broken and blood was shed; well, then, have my head for the letter of the law

. . . and enough!"[42] These are his private musings, in advance of his sudden conversion. At his trial, "the ultimate questions of precisely what had inclined him to homicide and what had prompted him to commit robbery," and his response, characterized by "the crudest exactitude," combines as cynical excuse the environment and individual personality: "the cause of it all lay in his bad situation, his poverty and helplessness. . . . He had resolved on the murder as a result of his frivolous and fainthearted nature, further exasperated by hardship and failure" (*PSS* 6:411/536). If Raskol'nikov rejects the environment excuse (a rejection implicit in his glib—"crude"—mention of his destitution), he does not renounce the idea that those who dare to seize power deserve it, nor his belief that his confession proves not his guilt but his weakness. His theoretical bent seems to elicit the contempt of the peasant-convicts in *katorga* who, he suspects, laugh at his crime (" 'You're a gentleman!' they said to him. 'What did you take up an axe for; it's no business for a gentleman' ") and are outraged at his apparent atheism. Like Gorianchikov, he senses "the terrible and impassable abyss [*propast'*] that lay between him" and the common people, "as if he and they belonged to different nations" (*PSS* 6:418/546, 545). The crisis of remorse, though recognized, is not resolved in *Crime and Punishment,* where Raskol'nikov's regeneration is marked not by the "burning repentance" he longs to feel "that breaks the heart, that drives sleep away" but by a newfound ability to love Sonia; the effect of love on his assessment of his crime, however, is left unspecified as is the class significance of remorse (*PSS* 6:417/544).[43] The peasant-convicts themselves are distant and undifferentiated figures.

In *The Idiot,* Prince Myshkin and the elegant Evgenii Pavlovich discuss the problem of crime in contemporary Russia as part of a conversation about whether the liberal sentiments of the landowning classes and the intelligentsia bespeak a love or a hatred for the nation. Within this context, Evgenii Pavlovich refers to a recent and widely publicized trial of a young man for murdering six people, and asks Myshkin what he thinks of the liberal defense lawyer's assertion that "given the destitute condition of the criminal, it *naturally* had to occur to him to kill those six people": "In my personal opinion," Evgenii Pavlovich says, "the defense attorney, in voicing such a strange thought, was fully convinced that what he was saying was the most liberal, the most humane and progressive thing that could possibly be said in our time. Well, what would you say: is this perversion of notions and convictions, this possibility of such a warped and extraordinary view of things, a particular case or a general one?"[44] Myshkin's view is that the case is general, and he supports it by telling how, in a visit to Russian prisons, he encountered terrible murderers who felt no remorse whatever for their crime. Even so, Myshkin observes, such criminals fell into two distinct groups: on the one hand, "the most inveterate and unrepentant murderer [who] still knows that he is a *criminal*, that is, in all conscience he considers that he has done wrong, though without any repentance," and, on the other, convicts who "do not even want to consider themselves criminals and think to themselves that they had the right and . . . even did a good thing, or almost."[45] Myshkin adds of the latter group: "And note that they're all young people, that is, precisely of an age when they can most easily and defenselessly fall under the influence of perverse ideas" (*PSS* 8:280/339).

The distinction here is not between those who feel remorse and those who do not—the two groups are united in their lack of repentance. It is, rather, between those who are unrepentant but who "never accept, never will accept, and have no wish to accept their sin as truth," as Dostoevsky maintains of the people in 1880, and those who, like Raskol'nikov, are motivated by an idea, and recognize their criminality merely in a legal sense (*PSS* 26:152).[46] The allusion to the influence of ideas makes the latter group recognizably affiliated with the educated (Westernized) rather than the common class.[47] This difference between elite and common is borne up in the novel's only explicit discussion of the peasant (examined in section 2 of the introduction), when Myshkin relates to Rogozhin four anecdotes that encapsulate what he learned about Russia and its people during his travels through the country. The first anecdote involves Myshkin's conversation on a train with an educated man, an atheist, whose well-developed views of religion and irreligion bespeak a profound conceptual alienation from both. In contrast, the three anecdotes that follow describe brief encounters with common people for whom mundane and religious realities seamlessly coexist across a spectrum of acts from murder to maternal love. The allegorical significance of the people is here at its most concentrated and the individual peasants most removed from the novel's action or, indeed, any narrative context.

In an 1873 *Diary of a Writer* article titled "Vlas," however, Dostoevsky exerts critical pressure—variously characterized as sociological, psychological, and historical—on this seamlessness of religious to profane realities in the peasant mind, and, in so doing, discovers the basis for a novelizable peasant internally resistant to the straightforward significations of allegory. Like another article focused on peasant life in the 1873 series, "The Environment" (discussed in part 2 above), "Vlas" offers a speculative elaboration on what purports to be a real event, in this case a "fantastic story" told to him by an elder in a remote monastery about a repentant young peasant whose confession he had personally received (*PSS* 23:33/ 158). Dostoevsky contrasts this peasant whom he calls Vlas—and who actually comprises two "Vlases," boyhood friends who conspire to commit blasphemy—to the "ultraliberal" and thus bookish Nekrasov's "poetical Vlas," the eponymous subject of his 1855 poem about an aged peasant who undertakes a lifelong pilgrimage through Russia to atone for the murder of his wife.[48] Although Dostoevsky finds much to admire in Nekrasov's poem, he accuses him of sentimentalizing the Russian peasant by making him a kind of "everyman" (*obshchechelovek*) (*PSS* 23:33/ 158). Yet, he gives both his young peasants the name Vlas while insisting on the "exceptionality" of their characters and their story which, he claims—precisely as he had claimed fourteen years earlier of the peasant-convicts' stories in the letter to his brother—has "never been heard until now" (*neslykhannykh docele*).[49]

This story, "an amazing tale from the life of the people," tells of two village boys, one of whom challenges the other to swear on his own salvation to perform "the most daring" thing the first can think up (*PSS* 23:33, 34/159). The dare accepted, he orders his friend not to swallow the Eucharist given to him at Holy Communion but to reserve it, bring it to a garden, place it atop a stick driven into the ground, load a gun procured for the occasion, and then shoot the communion wafer. The young peasant coolly loads the weapon, raises it, takes aim, but just as he is about to fire he sees a vision of the crucified Christ and falls to the ground unconscious.[50] The scene may be considered a remarkable re-envisioning of Dostoevsky's own mock execution; it recalls the story of a drunken peasant, a "Christ-seller," who tries to sell his cross to Myshkin to buy more vodka (*PSS* 8:183/220); and with its themes of hallucination, mystical horror, and loss of consciousness, it counts, too, as a variant of the epileptic seizure in all its ambiguity as a symbol of death and sometimes resurrection.[51] Upon regaining consciousness, the young peasant crawls on his knees to the elder's monastery to confess and do penance; the story of the other Vlas, the friend who tempts the penitent, is unknown and a particular object of Dostoevsky's speculation.

Dostoevsky judges of this incident that "these same, sundry 'Vlases,' repentant and unrepentant," will determine the fate of Russia, and he identifies them—as against Chernyshevsky's radical intellectuals—as the "new men" of the future: "It is not Petersburg that will finally decide Russia's destiny. And therefore every, even the slightest, *new* trait of these 'new people' may be worthy of our attention" (*PSS* 23:34/160). "Vlas" insists, through a series of images, on an unstoppable power of cataclysmic force gathering just beneath the skin of the present and whose trajectory cannot be predicted. This imminence and unpredictability are conveyed in the wild vacillation between belief and negation he observes in the behavior of the peasant boys, a superimposition of the antithetical peasant types of Marei and Gazin so that the extremes of tenderness and debauchery they represent coexist—not seamlessly but in a constant and extraordinary tension. They are conveyed, too, in Dostoevsky's sense of how in peasant culture unconscious knowledge—here, a "heartfelt knowledge of

Christ" that far exceeds anything attainable through religious instruction—may be realized with stunning amplitude in something as trivial as an adolescent dare (*PSS* 23:38/164). Just as Myshkin marveled that a peasant woman's reaction to her infant's first smile expressed "the main thought of Christ," "the whole essence of Christianity," so Dostoevsky discovers in the peasant boys' dare an equally acute but unconscious understanding of the essence of evil: "the Russian Mephistopheles couldn't have thought up anything more audacious!" (*PSS* 8:184/221; *PSS* 23:38/164). The triviality of its occasion only reinforces for Dostoevsky the breadth of its power, and of the present as the penultimate moment before this deep knowledge, both psychological and religious, breaks into the vast consciousness of the Russian people to sever it from its past and initiate its unforeseeable future.

In his elaboration of what transpired in the minds of the two Vlases as they assumed the roles of tempter and victim, Dostoevsky pays particular attention to the penultimate moment before the shot never fired and to the unbidden "mystical terror" by which the young peasant was instantly overcome. How to account for a visitation that comes unbidden to the soul but which derives from one's own imagination or unconscious knowledge (Christianity's essence, Christ's reality), and which propels one across barriers to understanding of such magnitude that one did not even realize they were there? (*PSS* 23:38/165) In his reading, Dostoevsky approaches the phenomenon of mystical terror by structuring the story in terms of two sequential splittings: first, the splitting of agency in relation to the commission of a great sin into two symbiotic personalities, the two Vlases, tempter and victim, one of whom leads the other to the actual commission of an act; and then an internal splitting of the one led, the "victim," at the very moment of action when he takes aim at the Eucharist.

In the first, Dostoevsky assumes that some prior relationship must have existed to produce such a pact, a childhood friendship that fostered a "suppressed enmity." This "tension of mutual hatred" broke out unexpectedly at the "moment of the challenge," that moment when an unthinkable idea—literally, an "unheard-of" (*neslykhannaia*) idea, that negative descriptor of popular culture to which Dostoevsky again resorts—had "developed almost to the point of a conscious idea" in the terms of the dare (*PSS* 23:37/163, 164). But in the days before its realization in the dare—the form in which the idea begins its assault on the barrier of consciousness—he imagines that their mutual hatred must have ceded to a mutual need: only by spurring each other on "to lean over the abyss [*propast'*] and peer into it" could they bring an affair grown psychologically and spiritually oppressive to an end (*PSS* 23:39/166). Everything Dostoevsky posits here about the two Vlases—that they have known each other since childhood; that they are linked as tempter and victim by a long-standing but concealed enmity; that this feeling issues in a dare expressive of a profoundly criminal but unacknowledged idea that has developed almost but not quite to the point of consciousness—is equally applicable to another pair, the half-brothers Smerdiakov and Ivan Karamazov of Dostoevsky's last great novel, one a peasant lackey and the other a nobleman intellectual. I return to this likeness below.

The subsequent, internal splitting of the victim-Vlas occurs at "the very last moment" before the fulfillment of the unthinkable act. The truth, which coexists in his soul with the false idea (recognizably of the "all-is-permitted" variety), at this moment detaches itself as "judgment," "tear[-ing] itself suddenly in an instant from his heart [to stand] before him in terrible denunciation." Before this vision, although he had been cool enough a moment before to load his gun, raise it, and aim, the young peasant is instantly disarmed and loses consciousness. Why, Dostoevsky asks, did the peasant's own truth "manifest itself in an image, as if completely external, a fact independent of his soul?" (*PSS* 23:40/167). The question is a variant of one he had posed earlier, in *The Idiot*, which serves as the opening epigraph to this book—"Can something that has no image appear as an image?" (*PSS* 8:340). In "Vlas," he seems to offer an answer that nevertheless, in the last analysis, is deferred: the phenomenon of something that has no image appearing as an image is, on the one hand, a "hallucination," an "enormous psychological problem" (referred to earlier in the article as the complexity of the two "national types" that comprise the Russian people), but it is also a "vision" and therefore an "act of God" (*PSS* 23:35, 40/161, 167). For Vlas-victim, only the last is real: "For him, for the criminal, it undoubtedly was an act of God. Vlas became a beggar and demanded suffering" (*PSS* 23:40/167). Like Raskol'nikov before him, if not as conscientiously, Vlas-victim had attempted to be a certain kind of "new man," the kind of modern subject that seizes the freedom of the secular to see the communion wafer as an inert thing rather than as the body of Christ. But the latent significance of the wafer reveals itself in Christ's crucified body despite the peasant's determination, and, before this revelation, he is helpless. His vision imposes a return to the conditions of the truth by which he is possessed. It may be, Dostoevsky wants to conclude, that this Vlas will lead the nation as one body back to its foundational truth so that "salvation will come radiating up from below" (*PSS* 23:168). But for Vlas-tempter, it may be otherwise.

As we have seen, images of imminent revelation, unpredictable and potentially cataclysmic in its consequences, saturate this article. The images are temporal (the penultimate moment before firing), psychological (the idea materializing just under the theshold of consciousness), medical (the shocking hallucination that in an instant shatters expectations of self-mastery), theological (the unbidden vision that converts one thing into something else), and finally national, an image that orchestrates by historicizing the others and that Dostoevsky calls "February 19":

> The contemporary Vlas is quickly changing. Beginning with February 19, precisely the same seething turbulence that exists above with us exists below with him. The folk hero [*bogatyr*] has awakened and is stretching his limbs; perhaps he will want to go on a binge, to cross the line. They say that he's already gone on a binge. Horrors are spoken of and published: drunkenness, banditry, drunken children, drunken mothers, cynicism, destitution, dishonorableness, godlessness.

Dostoevsky enjoins his readers to remember "Vlas" (whether the quotation marks indicate the article or victim-Vlas is ambiguous) and, even as they await the impact of February 19 (an impact building at this point for more than a decade), to stay calm: "at the last moment everything false, if it is false, will jump out of the people's heart and stand before them with the incredible force of denunciation [*oblichenie*, denoting also an unmasking or exposure]" (*PSS* 23:41/168).

Despite this reassurance, "Vlas" ends by invoking the enduring and absolute "uncertainty" produced by abolition, which brought the Petrine period to a definitive end and unmasked the "bankruptcy" of the elite, but without as definitively initiating the reign of those new people destined to forge a new path leading out of the national-cultural dead end to which Russia had arrived. The unresolved anxiety of this conclusion cannot therefore be attributed to the fact that the rapprochement of the common with the elite classes had not yet been realized despite the atmosphere of "seething turbulence" that characterizes their respective worlds "above" and "below." Rather, it is that Vlas-tempter is not securely rehabilitated in "Vlas," has perhaps not judged himself as Vlas-victim had so definitively done, and thus is left an unincorporable remainder and refutation of the article's final vision of national salvation from below. The legend (*legenda*)—for this is how Dostoevsky now characterizes the story he claimed the elder had related to him as fact—is silent about his fate, which engenders another, anxious possibility:

> What if he really is a genuine village nihilist, a homegrown denier and intellectual, an unbeliever who thought up the object of the contest with arrogant mockery, who didn't suffer and didn't tremble together with his victim as we suggested in our sketch, but who followed with cold curiosity his tremblings and convulsions solely from the need of another's suffering, of another human being's humiliation—perhaps, the devil knows, for scholarly research? (*PSS* 23:40/168)

If Vlas-victim sees in his extremity an act of God, Vlas-tempter might indeed see his friend's extreme spiritual suffering as an "enormous psychological problem"—and, moreover, a fascinating one that might be tested and examined in the ultimate laboratory of the soul. Dostoevsky muses, "If such qualities really exist even in the people's character (and anything is possible these days) and even in our villages, then this really is a new revelation, something really unexpected. In former times qualities such as these were something unheard of [*ne slykhano*]" (*PSS* 23:40–41/168).

Precisely this uncertainty is restaged in the character of the peasant-lackey Smerdiakov in *The Brothers Karamazov*. Unlike his adoptive parents who are types of Dostoevsky's good and simple peasants, Smerdiakov is a hybrid character (literally: he is the bastard son of Stinking Lizaveta and Karamazov *père* who rapes and impregnates the retarded peasant woman) who exceeds his status in the novel as an "auxiliary person." Fond of hanging cats, a dandy strangely "inaccessible" to both men and women and contemptuous of both, a casuist at once skilled and feeble, seething with resentment of his alleged betters and with bitter admiration for his half-brother Ivan's brilliance and his atheism, Smerdiakov engages with the latter in a tacit pact to kill their father. His role in the novel is to carry out the crime which he claims Ivan has masterminded and then, perhaps more crucial, to convince him in the course of three dialogues marked by Ivan's fearful contempt and Smerdiakov's mocking deference that the former had, in fact, virtually murdered his father although their brother, Dmitri, had been the one indicted.

An adequate analysis of the relationship of Smerdiakov and Ivan is beyond the scope of this book, but it provides a fitting image of the limits of Dostoevsky's democracy, particularly as a religious phenomenon. Smerdiakov first appears in the novel playing the ass to Ivan's Balaam: serving at table, he outrages his adoptive father, Grigory, and delights his biological father, Fyodor, by offering the philosophical grounds of a rebellion against religion which Ivan will later transform into his great poem of tragic refusal, "The Grand Inquisitor." At the conclusion of this initial appearance, the narrator tries to elucidate Smerdiakov's significance by invoking Kramskoi's portrait of a peasant standing alone in a forest, *The Contemplator*, who "stands as if he were lost in thought, but he is not thinking, he is 'contemplating' something" whose content, if asked, he will not know, although he "keep[s] hidden away in himself the impression he had been under while contemplating":

> These impressions are dear to him, and he is most likely storing them up imperceptibly and even without realizing it—why and what for, of course, he does not know either; perhaps suddenly, having stored up his impressions over many years, he will drop everything and wander off to Jerusalem to save his soul, or perhaps he will suddenly burn down his native village, or perhaps he will do both. There are plenty of contemplators among the people. Most likely

Smerdiakov, too, was such a contemplator, and most likely he, too, was greedily storing up his impressions, almost without knowing why himself. (*PSS* 14:116, 117/126, 127)[52]

With Smerdiakov, Dostoevsky succeeds in restaging the drama of Vlas in a social milieu far more complex than the peasant village, on a psychological terrain far richer than that which exists between two simple peasant boys, and on a literary canvas far more encompassing than the journalistic "étude."

Unlike the other three Karamazov brothers, Smerdiakov's involvement in the novel's central crime delimits his importance, and, in that sense, he remains "auxiliary": he hasn't Ivan's intellectuality, Alyosha's spirituality, or Dmitri's vitality. Even in his critical afterlife, he has not been accorded equivalent significance to his three legitimate brothers, and perhaps this indicates a shared judgment that the mystery of the Russian peasant, however imminent its revelation might be, was invulnerable even to the novel's representational powers. Still, it is Smerdiakov whose image or shadow prevents Ivan from escaping not so much his family as his acknowledgment of his complicity in his father's murder; it is Smerdiakov who reveals the moral bankruptcy of Ivan's vision of entering a new world:

> "Away with all the past, I'm through with the old world forever, and may I never hear another word or echo from it; to the new world, to new places, and no looking back!'" But instead of delight, such darkness suddenly descended on his soul, and such grief gnawed at his heart, as he had never known before in the whole of his life.[53]

We may say, then, that in *Notes from the House of the Dead*, through the chronotope of *katorga* and the adventure therein of the unconsummated image, Dostoevsky initiates a career-long examination of that which remains insusceptible both to novelistic elaboration and moral resolution: an ontology of crime for which the peasant is his most visible representative.

In *Notes from the House of the Dead*, the ethical mystery of *katorga* entails less the subtleties of collaboration or complicity than the brute fact of crime. Gorianchikov notes with distress and wonder the convicts' commission in *katorga* of an array of specific crimes from rampant theft to gratuitous violence against fellow prisoners. He also reports at length on the peasant-convicts' stories of their former lives—"the time-before"—and their unreadable attitudes toward the crimes they had committed.[54] His focus on crime, and through others' his own, leads him to seek to understand crime from a perspective beyond guilt and expiation, as fundamentally an ontological category rather than a social or moral one.[55] Whereas for Arendt, crime (by definition against the concentration camp inmates by their persecutors) led irrevocably to the disintegration of personality, for Dostoevsky crime (committed by persecutors but also inmates both before and during their incarceration) leads to the assertion of personality.[56] Crime thus acquires at the inception of Dostoevsky's mature work a kind of ontological priority and is thus inextricably bound up with the possibility of community and the qualified restoration of agency. More specific to *Notes from the House of the Dead*, it is inextricably bound up with the mystery posed by bare life in the state of exception and thus with the meaning of emancipation and the reconstitution of the nation. Counterintuitively, Dostoevsky understands crime as that impulse which aims to bring *zoe*, bare life, to *bios*, the "qualified" life of culture and community, and of language (*HS* 1).

Gorianchikov, as we have seen, seeks to distance himself from crime, a circumstance that becomes evident in the usurpation of his prerogative as an autobiographical narrator, first by the anterior narrator who identifies his crime as wife murder and then by the brutal peasant Shishkov who tells the story of how he murdered his wife. This evasion makes him unable to understand the grammar, or cultural logic, which for the peasant-convicts makes it possible to regard bare life as constitutive of a distinctive community immediately recognizable as such to the initiate but opaque to Gorianchikov. It is only superficially true to state that Dostoevsky/Gorianchikov speak the same language as the peasant-convicts, as Dostoevsky's careful record of peasant speech in his "Siberian Notebook" attests. For this reason, and by virtue of the process of desubjectification made evident in the eclipse of his narrating voice, Gorianchikov cannot render a transparent report of his experience of the dead house. He does not figure in his memoir as a subject of knowledge in the Cartesian sense, provided first and foremost with the self-certainty of his own thought. Far from being the subject of knowledge, the Virgil who leads the reader unscathed through the House of the Dead, Gorianchikov appears in his own memoir as something of a tragic lexicographer forced to ponder in isolation the meaning contained in the peasant-convicts' contradictory self-characterization as "a people without a tongue" who are yet a "literate people" possessed of their own impenetrable grammar (*PSS* 4:12, 13, 16, 181).[57]

Gorianchikov remains throughout his memoir a figure of suspense, one who is dead to his former life but who has not yet been reborn, in part because the "new world" in which he is to emerge as a new being has not itself been fully constituted. The figuration of this new world both does and does not depend on Gorianchikov, *homo sacer* as literary artist. Its constitution or figuration, its consummation as an artistic image, can only be the collaborative project, masterminded by no one, of men in extremity: this is the writer's "conviction," gained from experience, of the ontological ambiguity of the space of exception. Likewise, Gorianchikov's re-birth as a "new man" into this new world must also be the product of a collaboration. It depends on the coming into being—the emergence into cultural visibility—of the common convicts, the community of *homines sacri*, which requires that he is able to see them. That depends, in turn, on his ability to see the obstacle to sight, the optical illusion which had always stood in for the common people and which allowed him to speak for them without having either seen or heard them truly. *Katorga*, then, is the medium in which the illusion of sight is itself seen and rejected even if it leaves the seer epistemologically groundless, and in which the potential exists for that doubly negative gesture to produce, uniquely, a novel insight into one's own blindness. The chronotope of *katorga* represents that milieu in which one sees not *what* but *that* one does not see, a feat we might understand as the initial step in the rebirth of the new man as the subject of a compound knowledge. But if that resurrection is truly a collaborative project, a mutual rescue from cultural death, then the object of sight—the peasant-convicts—must play a vital role in the sighted subject's rebirth: as Sartre put it, " 'Being-seen-by-the-Other' is the *truth* of 'seeing-the-Other.' "[58] Accordingly, the question repeatedly posed in *Notes from the House of the Dead* and then linked to the nation held in the opening of its own modernity: who is this Other whose seeing is constitutive of one's own sight and thus of the new world into which the new man will be reborn and the new word spoken?

Notes

~

Introduction

1. F. M. Dostoevskii, *Polnoe sobranie sochinenii v tridtzati tomakh* [The complete works in thirty volumes] (Leningrad, 1972–90), 8:340. Cited hereafter in the text as *PSS* followed by volume number, (book number), and page number(s). Unless otherwise indicated, all translations in this book are my own. For the reader's convenience, however, page numbers to available English translations of Dostoevsky's works, fully cited in the bibliography, appear after those for *PSS*.

2. Cited in Joseph Frank, *Mantle of the Prophet*, 497. On the nineteenth-century development of the idea of civil society (*obshchestvo*), and its relations to the autocratic state on the one hand and the common people (*narod*) on the other, see Nicholas V. Riasanovsky, *A Parting of the Ways*, and W. Bruce Lincoln, *The Great Reforms*.

3. The journalist I. F. Vasilevsky is quoted in Marcus C. Levitt, *Russian Literary Politics*, 9–10. For a brief history of the Russian intelligentsia's response to government censorship from the nineteenth-century reforms through the prerevolutionary period in the early twentieth century, see Aileen M. Kelly, "The Intelligentsia and Self-Censorship," in idem, *Toward Another Shore*, 133–54.

4. Cited in Levitt, *Russian Literary Politics*, 2.

5. Alexander's assassination was the fourth such attempt; the first occurred in 1866. For an account of the political climate surrounding the 1880 celebration, see Levitt, *Russian Literary Politics*, chap. 3, which, in addition to describing events directly related to the Pushkin festival, gives a brief account of the growth of a nascent public sphere in Russia between 1860 and 1880.

6. On Alexander II's reforms, see Lincoln, *The Great Reforms*; Terence Emmons, "The Peasant and the Emancipation"; and Daniel Field, "The Year of Jubilee." For an excellent account of the symbolic dimension of the emancipation, see Irina Paperno, "The Liberation of the Serfs as a Cultural Symbol." For translations of documents relevant to the emancipation and associated peasant uprisings, see Daniel Field, *Rebels in the Name of the Tsar*.

7. The classic history of nineteenth-century Russian radicalism is Franco Venturi, *Roots of Revolution*. See also Isaiah Berlin, "Russia and 1848," in his *Russian Thinkers*, 1–21.

8. Dostoevsky's early political radicalism and its consequences are discussed in part 1 of this volume (sections 1–5). On the development of a noble and then non-noble intelligentsia, see Berlin, "The Birth of the Russia Intelligentsia," in idem, *Russian Thinkers*, 114–35; Kelly, "Carnival of the Intellectuals: 1855," in idem, *Toward Another Shore*, 37–54; and Elise Kimerling Wirtschafter, *Social Identity in Imperial Russia*, esp. chap. 3, which places the growth of the non-noble intelligentsia, or *raznochintsy*, in the context of a developing Russian middle class.

9. I. S. Turgenev to A. I. Herzen, cited in Joseph Frank, *Miraculous Years,* 213. On the Slavophile-Westernizer debate, see Andrzej Walicki, *A History of Russian Thought from the Enlightenment to Marxism,* chaps. 6–14, and *The Slavophile Controversy,* esp. chaps. 7–9; and Kelly, "The Nihilism of Ivan Turgenev" and "Liberal Dilemmas and Populist Solutions," in idem, *Toward Another Shore,* 91–118, 119–33, respectively.

10. See Levitt, *Russian Literary Politics,* 2; and Frank, *Mantle of the Prophet,* chaps. 27–29.

11. "Pushkin, Lermontov, and Nekrasov," in *Diary of a Writer* (December 1877), *PSS* 26: 113–19, esp. 116. English translation available as *A Writer's Diary Vol. 2: 1877–1881,* trans. Kenneth Lantz, 1248–56, esp. 1251; page numbers hereafter provided in the text following those in *PSS.* For an analysis of Dostoevsky's views on Pushkin expressed elsewhere in his *Diary of a Writer,* see *PSS* 26:445–51.

12. "Pushkin (A Sketch)" in *Diary of a Writer* (August 1880), *PSS* 26:136–49, esp. 144/1290.

13. Frank, *Mantle of the Prophet,* 520. Dostoevsky described his triumphant reception as a prophet in a letter to his wife (*PSS* 30 [I]: 184–85). English translation available in Joseph Frank and David I. Goldstein, eds., *Selected Letters of Fyodor Dostoevsky,* 503–5; page numbers hereafter provided in the text following those in *PSS.*

14. On Russian political theology, see Michael Cherniavsky, *Tsar and People*; see also Field, "Myth of the Tsar," introducing his *Rebels in the Name of the Tsar,* 1–29.

15. In a letter to A. N. Maikov of May 15/27, 1869, Dostoevsky defined "nostalgia" as perhaps a "spontaneous feeling" of "Russianness," of "oneness with the Russian root" (*PSS* 29 [1]: 42/311). In *The Future of Nostalgia,* Svetlana Boym characterized Dostoevsky as a "modern nostalgi[c]" who, following his 1862 European tour (written up in 1863 as "Winter Notes on Summer Impressions"), translated European modernity "back into the language of religious prophesy, opposing the Western fall from grace to the Russian 'eternal spiritual resistance' " (23).

16. For disparate views on the Slavophilic cast of Dostoevsky's utopian socialism, see *PSS* 28 (II): 471 n. 25.

17. On Dostoevsky's nationalism, see Robert L. Belknap, "Dostoevsky's Nationalist Ideology and Rhetoric." Belknap and others note the idiosyncratic nature of Dostoevsky's nationalism which disallows our placing him squarely in any ideological camp; even his insistence on Orthodoxy as the core of Russian nationality is superseded by an all-embracing universalism which, from 1861, he considers the quintessential Russian trait (98–99). Frank observes that in 1861, the era most at issue in this book, Dostoevsky's "instinctive democratic populism" made him more an ally of Chernyshevsky and other radical socialists affiliated with the journal *The Contemporary* (*Sovremmenik*) than of Mikhail Katkov and advocates of Western bourgeois liberalism and laissez-faire economics at *The Russian Messenger* (*Russkii Vestnik*). See Frank, *Stir of Liberation,* 97, 107; idem, *Miraculous Years,* 50, 250; and Pierre Pascal, *Dostoïevski, l'homme et l'oeuvre,* chap. 14, 331–62. As Julia Kristeva has said of the ways in which the novels complicate the cruder rheto-

ric of Dostoevsky's correspondence, "With and beyond ideology, writing remains" (*Black Sun*, 187).

18. Here and throughout, I use the Pevear and Volokhonsky translation of *The Idiot*; page numbers hereafter provided in the text following those in *PSS*.

I do not elaborate on the first instance when, at Myshkin's initial meeting with the Epanchin women, Aglaia calls him a "democrat" when she learns that he has told their valet about an execution he had witnessed (*PSS* 8:54/63).

Dostoevsky first mentions his intention to portray a "wholly beautiful man" in a letter to Maikov of 31 December 1867/12 January 1868, and shortly thereafter (on 1/13 January 1868) to his niece, S. A. Ivanova. See *PSS* 28 (II): 239–45/ 260–7 and 249–53/268–72 respectively. Letters such as those to S. A. Ivanova on 30 March/10 April 1868 and Maikov of 26 October/7 November 1868 suggest Dostoevsky's anxieties about the novel's viability.

19. Lizaveta Prokofevna's ambivalence here mimics Dostoevsky's early uncertainty about his hero's character as expressed in his notebooks for *The Idiot*: "*An enigma*. Who is he? A terrible villain or a mysterious ideal?" (*PSS* 9:195).

20. Turgenev's heroine in *Smoke* (*Dym*, 1867), Irina Pavlovna, notes the aristocracy's combination of "tact and cunning" (*Polnoe sobranie sochinenii i pisem v dvadtzati vos'mi tomakh*, 9:227).

21. Dostoevsky expresses similar convictions in several letters written at the time he was writing *The Idiot*: see, for example, the letters to Maikov on 31 December 1867/12 January 1868 and 15/27 May 1869; and to N. N. Strakhov on 18–30 March 1869.

22. In *Miraculous Years* (199–201), Frank notes that Lebedev articulates Dostoevsky's response to Alexander Herzen's memoirs (*PSS* 8:311–12/375–76).

23. The dignitary's investment in "service" marks him as a nobleman of the old school in relation to what the historian Orlando Figes describes as "the Russian cultural renaissance of the nineteenth century" which, beginning with the Decembrist uprising of 1825, entailed a revolt against the service ethic of the earlier generation. According to the latter, to be a nobleman "was to take one's place in the service of the state, either as a civil servant or as an officer; and to leave that service, even to become a poet or an artist, was regarded as a fall from grace." (Pushkin was among the first to make this move.) Pavlishchev's religious conversion is, in this sense, analogous to the poet's self-reinvention. The Russian cultural renaissance replaced the ethic of state service with the liberal-democratic belief in the nation and "the people"—the peasant as exemplary future citizen. See *Natasha's Dance: A Cultural History of Russia*, 78–79, and, more generally, chap. 2, "Children of 1812."

24. Dostoevsky expressed similar sentiments in a letter to Maikov of 31 December/12 January 1868 shortly after having sent the first chapters of *The Idiot* to Katkov from Geneva. For further expressions of his Russian messianism, see *PSS* 28 (II): 459 n. 16.

25. Aspects of Myshkin's unintentionally caustic characterization of the Russian aristocracy may have been suggested by Turgenev's representation of that class in *Smoke*, published in April 1867 in Katkov's *Russian Messenger* to which Dostoevsky had promised *The Idiot*. Turgenev's friend, P. V. Annenkov, informed him after its publication that the agitated readers of St. Petersburg were "frightened by

a novel inviting them to believe that all of the Russian aristocracy, yes, and all of Russian life, is an abomination." Quoted in Frank, *Miraculous Years*, 214. In his first letter to Maikov from abroad, written on 16/28 August 1867, Dostoevsky described his meeting with Turgenev in Baden Baden and the latter's chagrin at learning that Russians of all political persuasions were vilifying him. He registers his own disgust with Turgenev not only for his alleged hatred of Russia and his cosmopolitanism but for his atheistic pride which Dostoevsky felt typified Turgenev's class (*PSS* 28 [II]: 210/254).

26. In a letter to his wife of 8/20 May 1867, Dostoevsky wrote, "Form, gesture I don't possess" (*Formy, zhesta ne imeiu*). See *PSS* 28 (II): 189. Myshkin says, "I don't possess gesture" (*Ia ne imeiu zhesta*). Dostoevsky gave Myshkin many of his own characteristics, including the burden of epilepsy.

27. M. M. Bakhtin, *Problems of Dostoevsky's Poetics*, 232 (hereafter, *PDP*). See Harriet Murav's insightful critique of the Bakhtinian "loophole" in *Holy Foolishness*, 11. Murav's excellent reading of this scene in the context of the narrator's estrangement from and ultimate loss of control over Myshkin appears on pages 84–88. Also see her analysis of Dostoevsky's use of the confessional mode in "Dostoevsky in Siberia: Remembering the Past."

28. See Robert Lord's discussion of Myshkin's name in relation to the Underground Man in *Dostoevsky: Essays and Perspectives*, 99–100.

29. On the contemporary significance of this epithet in the contexts of holy foolishness and epilepsy, see Murav, *Holy Foolishness*, 88–98. She helpfully reminds us that "scandal is more than a breach of decorum. It is that which cannot be mastered. It is a temptation, that which leads us astray or causes a fall, and it is an essential part of the message of the cross" (96).

30. On the epileptic seizure as a metaphor for "the well-known *ambivalence* of Dostoevsky's heroes, which led Bakhtin to postulate a 'dialogism' at the foundation of his poetics"—the "opposition, without a synthetic solution" structurally central to his novels—see Kristeva, "Dostoevsky, the Writing of Suffering, and Forgiveness," in *Black Sun*, 173–217, esp. 185–86.

31. Dostoevsky expressed similar sentiments against the Russian liberals throughout this period; see, for example, his letter to Maikov of 18 February/1 March 1868 (*PSS* 28 [II]: 259, esp. 258/274–76). Here Evgeny Pavlovich resembles Myshkin in the fateful scene at the engagement party—he speaks unstoppably and in an oddly "pleased and excited state of mind," making others uneasy by his inappropriate emotional affect (*PSS* 8:275, 276/332, 333).

32. On the establishment of jury trials in Russia, see Murav, *Russia's Legal Fictions*. "As in carnival," she notes, referring to the suspension of the normative hierarchy of social power which Bakhtin famously explored in literature and culture, "the central actor at a jury trial may be said to be the people. The power of judgment, which had formerly inhered in the tsar or his officials, is now dispersed to a corporate body that mingles social classes: merchants, civil servants of all ranks, nobles, and peasants sat together and were sequestered together" (61).

33. Dostoevsky elaborated further on this in the 1873 *Diary of a Writer* article entitled "The Environment [*Sreda*]" (*PSS* 21:13–22). English translation available as *A Writer's Diary Vol. 1: 1873–1876*, trans. Kenneth Lantz, 132–45.

34. Evgeny Pavlovich's indignation is especially ironic given his introduction as an extraordinarily promising young man who had, however, a "somewhat ticklish" reputation as a ladies' man (*PSS* 8:155/187).

35. For a fascinating narratological analysis of the ethical significance of the relationship of the novel's two heroines, see Sarah Young, *Dostoevsky's "The Idiot,"* esp. 28–74.

36. Donald Fanger, *The Creation of Nikolai Gogol*, 257, 214. As far as I am aware, Fanger was the first to observe the literary importance of the "not that" or "*ne to*"; certainly his analysis of the *ne to* in Gogol made Dostoevsky's use of the phrase visible to me. The *ne to* functions as Gogol's "central principle" because it produces his hallmark "free-floating" and "normless" irony (220, 107). As Fanger shows, art was for Gogol a "quasi-religious" enterprise—a "creation out of nothing"; nevertheless, although meaning is "a fundamental thematic concern in the Gogolian text," it is "identifiable only negatively via the principle of *ne to* [as] a potential presence" (23, 68, 244).

37. Ippolit observes that "in any ingenious or new human thought, or even simply in any serious human thought born in someone's head, there always remains something which it is quite impossible to convey to other people, though you may fill whole volumes with writing and spend thirty-five years trying to explain your thought; there always remains something that absolutely refuses to leave your skull and will stay with you forever; you will die with it, not having conveyed to anyone what is perhaps most important in your idea" (*PSS* 8:328/394–95). Cf. passages on 351/423 about the "thought that refused to take shape" and on 378/452.

38. See Kristeva's meditation on Dostoevsky and Holbein in "Holbein's Dead Christ," in her *Black Sun*, 105–38.

39. Cf. Robin Feuer Miller's analysis of this scene and Myshkin's "parabolic narrative" which "represents [Myshkin's] own rejection of rational discourse" in *Dostoevsky and "The Idiot,"* 184–87, esp. 184. Miller notes the operation in the narrative of a "double irony": that "one must successfully use words to express an idea that cannot be expressed by words" (185). I explore a related irony in *Notes from the House of the Dead* (in part 1, section 3, below): the autobiographer's attempt to deliver a non-bookish conviction to his reader by means of the book.

40. Venturi points out that political ideologies such as liberalism, populism, and radicalism which are elsewhere and at other historical moments quite distinct are not easily separated out in Russia in the 1860s where they arose "in the same social world, the world of the intelligentsia." Proponents of what would seem to be opposed beliefs "were not cold adversaries and enemies, but passionate friends who suffered deeply in the conflicts, clashes, and differences that arose between them." See "Revised Author's Introduction, Russian Populism," in *Roots of Revolution*, lxxiii. See also Marc Raeff's similar conclusions in "Some Reflections on Russian Liberalism," *Political Ideas and Institutions in Imperial Russia*, 32–41.

41. So, for example, Frank observes that Dostoevsky, ambitious to create a character who would "represent his positive moral ideal," originally imagined a character described by others as a "socialist." An early notebook for *The Idiot* registers both the idea and its modification: "he is not a socialist; on the contrary; he finds in socialism little besides an unrealizable ideal. Economic redistribution, the problem of bread." Quoted in Frank, *Miraculous Years*, 260.

42. Fanger, *Creation of Nikolai Gogol*, 23.

43. That Myshkin cannot lie would suggest that he is also impervious to shame except that, as Deborah A. Martinsen shows in her fascinating study of Dostoevsky's liars, *Surprised by Shame*, he is ashamed not before others but of his own critical thoughts.

44. On the difficulties of credibly assigning Dostoevsky to any political camp, see note 17, above.

45. The early work begins with Dostoevsky's first novella *Poor People*, in 1846, and ends with the unfinished novel *Netochka Nezvanova*, the last installment of which appeared a month after the writer's arrest in April 1849. The first of the "great novels" is, by general consensus, *Crime and Punishment*, completed at the end of 1866. Neither *Notes from the House of the Dead* (1861) nor *Notes from the Underground* (1864) is normally included in that phrase.

46. Preparation began in earnest, as the ongoing journalistic polemic makes evident, despite the fact that the emancipation legislation of 19 February 1861 specifically guarded against an exodus to the city and the subsequent creation of a landless proletariat by establishing a lengthy (nine-year) "temporary-obligatory" period requiring peasants to stay on the land in the allotments given to them (and for which they paid either quitrent or labor for their use) even after emancipation. After that period had passed, it remained almost impossible for them to redeem their allotments, first, because the entire community had to do so, and, second, because redemption was voluntary for the estate owner. For a concise account of these requirements and of the peasant disorders which followed emancipation, see Emmons, "The Peasant and the Emancipation," esp. 45ff. See also note 6 above, and the conclusion, note 23.

47. Andrei Bitov writes that "OUR Dostoevsky came out of *House of the Dead*," not just his entire cast of future characters but more generally the crucial link between his literary passion and his own experience of suffering. See Bitov, "Novyi Robinzon," 16; emphasis in original.

48. The page number following *PSS* refers to *Memoirs from the House of the Dead*, trans. Jessie Coulson, and is cited hereafter in the text.

49. Giorgio Agamben, *Homo Sacer: Sovereign Power and Bare Life*.

50. Although it was clearly in common use in the nineteenth century, the word "*demokratizm*" did not enter the dictionary until 1935, where it was defined as an "abstract noun for *democratic*. Democratism is a way of life" (*otvlechennoe suschestvitel'noe k demokraticheskii. Demokratizm v obraze zhizni*). See *Tolkovyi slovar' russkogo iazyka pod redaktsiei D. N. Ushakova*, 1:684. "Democracy" (*demokratiia*), on the other hand, appears in Vladimir Dal's *Tolkovyi slovar' zhivogo velikorusskogo iazyka; gosudarstvennoe izdatel'stvo inostrannykh i natsional'nykh slovarei*, 1:427. It was defined as "people's governance, popular sovereignty, popular power" (*narodnoe pravlenie, narododerzhavie, narodovlastie*).

51. The 22 February 1854 letter to Mikhail M. Dostoevsky contradicts one written two years later to Maikov on 18 January 1856 (*PSS* 28 [I]: 208), often cited to support the conversion hypothesis: here Dostoevsky claims to have rejected French utopian socialism and embraced the religiosity of the Russian common people. Contrary to the hostility of the peasant-convicts he reports to Mikhail, he describes them as his brothers in adversity. This evidence for Dostoevsky's ideologi-

cal revision of his encounter with the people in prison continues through the 1873 *Diary of a Writer* article (*PSS* 21: 134/289), in which he describes not how he and fellow noble convicts crafted an attitude of moral superiority toward them but rather their "awareness that we ourselves had become as they, equal to them, and even placed on the very lowest of their levels."

52. Cf. Dostoevsky's discussion in another 1861 article, " 'Svistok' i 'Russkii Vestnik,' " in *PSS* 19:105–16.

53. The critical response to the patriotic odes Dostoevsky wrote from Siberia in the mid-1850s on the occasion of the Crimean War exemplifies the power of foregone conclusions to blunt interpretive analysis. Within months of his release, in an attempt well documented in his letters to be permitted to return to St. Petersburg and his profession, Dostoevsky began to disseminate the odes, xenophobic and national-messianistic in tone (and his only foray into this genre), to certain sympathetic and politically well-placed recipients. These were accompanied by letters in which he insisted that he had recognized the error of his youthful ideals, accepted the judiciousness of his punishment, and thus no longer represented a political danger. Several influential critics, while acknowledging his motive, nevertheless insist that they testify, in Leonid Grossman's words, to the " 'rebirth of [Dostoevsky's] convictions' (that is, his repudiation of the utopian socialism of the forties and his return to the religious-patriotic views of his early period)" (*Dostoevskii*, 174–76). Frank concurs: if the odes were "a means of attracting attention, or of trying to do so, and should not be taken too seriously," still they indicate that "Dostoevsky had now begun to look on his arrest and conviction as a providential act of God," a shift in perspective that elicited "some of those conclusions of his prison-camp meditations that we search for elsewhere in vain" (*Years of Ordeal*, 181, 199, 206). See also Pascal, *Dostoïevski, l'homme et l'oeuvre*, 92, 94.

Part I
Building Out the House of the Dead

1. On Dostoevsky's crime, see Joseph Frank, *Seeds of Revolt*, chaps. 17–19; and Frank, *Years of Ordeal*, chaps. 1–5. In Russian, see N. F. Bel'chikov, *Dostoevskii v protsesse petrashevtzev*, 2nd ed.; and V. R. Leikina, E. A. Korolchuk, and V. A. Desnitsky, eds., *Delo petrashevtsev*, 3 vols. For Dostoevsky's testimony, declarations, and final statement to the examining commission, see his *Polnoe sobranie sochinenii v tridtzati tomakh* [The complete works in thirty volumes], 18:117–95, 306–65; cited hereafter in the text as *PSS* followed by volume number, (book number), and page number(s). Unless otherwise indicated, all translations in this study are my own. For the reader's convenience, however, page numbers to available English translations of Dostoevsky's works, fully cited in the bibliography, will appear after those for *PSS*. For an English translation of selected documents related to Dostoevsky's arrest and imprisonment with an excellent introductory essay, see Liza Knapp, ed. and trans., *Dostoevsky as Reformer*.

2. A full account of this episode may be found in Frank, *Years of Ordeal*, chap. 5. Frank relies on the description of the incident provided by a fellow prisoner of Dostoevsky's, D. D. Akhsharumov (see A. Dolinin, ed., *F. M. Dostoevskii v vospomi-*

naniiakh sovremennikov, 1:222–234). Akhsharumov's memory of the order of events differs from Dostoevsky's account in his letter to his brother, Mikhail, written just hours after the mock execution occurred on 22 December 1849, on which I rely here.

3. In "Crime and Punishment in the House of the Dead," the historian Alan Wood writes that the tsarist authorities regarded those condemned to Siberian exile as "legally dead, in the sense that they were stripped of all personal, civil, and property rights pertaining to their social class, children could 'inherit' their goods, and remaining spouses were free to remarry. Indeed, after the *de facto* abolition of capital punishment in Russia during the reign of Empress Elizabeth, it was replaced by the practice of 'civil execution' (*grazhdanskaya kazn'*) and the concept of 'political death' (*politicheskaya smert'*)" (216). On civil death in mid-nineteenth-century Russia, see also Pierre Pascal, *Dostoïevski*, 75; Leonid Grossman, " 'Grazhdanskaia smert' F. M. Dostoevskogo" [The "civil death" of F. M. Dostoevsky], esp. 684; and Abby M. Schrader, *Languages of the Lash*, 29, 78–83, 109. The details of the tsar's public performance of Chernyshevsky's punishment in 1864 before his exile demonstrate how the emphasis in the mid-nineteenth century in the ceremony of civil death shifted from *lishenie prav*—the deprivation of class privilege and identity—to a more modern understanding of the prerogatives of civilians once the *raznochintsy* or non-noble intelligentsia began to be convicted of political crime in the 1860s. See M. N. Gernet, *Istoriia tsarskoi tiur'my*, 3rd ed., 2:285–89.

4. In " 'Civil Death,' " Grossman characterizes Dostoevsky's ordeal as an "unconsummated" execution, putting quotation marks around the word without attribution (683). On the extent of Nicholas I's personal involvement in setting up the mock execution, see also Konstantin Mochulsky, *Dostoevsky*, 140.

5. The Military-Judicial Commission deprived Dostoevsky "of ranks, of all rights concomitant to his social estate" and recommended "the death penalty by shooting." This sentence was commuted by the High Military Court to deprivation "of all rights concomitant to his social estate" and exile to "a hard-labor prison camp for eight years." Nicholas I then reduced the eight years to four and ordered that he be made a private (Gorianchikov, in contrast, serves a ten-year sentence followed by permanent resettlement in Siberia). He served in the Seventh Line Battalion at Semipalatinsk and was promoted in 1856 to commissioned officer; in March 1859, he was given permission to retire from military service and return to Western Russia, though not to Petersburg or Moscow. By December 1859, however, precisely ten years after his departure into exile, he made his return to Petersburg. See Knapp, *Dostoevsky as Reformer*, 91, 93–94, 127 nn. 31, 33.

6. On the class background of Dostoevsky's family, see Frank, *Seeds of Revolt*, 8–10, 14–15; Grossman, *Dostoevskii*, chap. 1. The family was originally from the Lithuanian nobility. Mikhail A. Dostoevsky, the writer's father, was the son and grandson of non-monastic clergymen who was promoted to a legal title of nobility for his service as a military surgeon. Mikhail purchased—probably with his wife's money, the daughter of a Moscow merchant with pretensions to a noble lineage—a small estate (Grossman estimates fourteen hundred acres) of two villages with (Grossman's figure) one hundred serfs, a source of both pride and impoverishment (14). After his father's death, when Dostoevsky was eighteen, he lived on a monthly stipend from the estate. Frank writes that in 1845 he legally

renounced all claims to the estate in exchange for a thousand rubles in ready cash. From that time forward, he lived solely on the income generated by his writing (*Seeds of Revolt*, 116 n.).

7. English translation available in Joseph Frank and David I. Goldstein, eds., *Selected Letters of Fyodor Dostoevsky*, 50–54, esp. 51; page numbers hereafter are provided in the text following those in *PSS*.

8. This passage in the letter of 22 December 1849 has supported a long and widely held view of the mock execution as producing, if not a spiritual conversion, then a state of beatitude necessary for conversion (see, for example, Grossman in *Dostoevskii*, 174, 176). Two remarks made decades after the experience have been marshaled to support this view. In *Mantle of the Prophet*, Frank cites an 1874 remark to Vsevolod Soloviev of the "great happiness" of Siberia: "I understood myself there. . . . I understood Christ. . . . I understood Russian man and felt that I was a Russian myself, that I was one of the Russian people" (62). Although Frank reminds us that Dostoevsky's words to Soloviev "cannot be taken as even a remotely adequate account of the reality of Dostoevsky's experiences," he nevertheless claims that Dostoevsky's letter to his brother indicated that he emerged from the ordeal of the mock execution "with an ecstatic sense of the infinite value of life" (62). Grossman cites a passage in Dostoevsky's notebook written thirty years after the event: "Never before had a man more filled with hope, a thirst for life and faith, entered the prison" (*Dostoevskii*, 164). See also the Symbolist poet Viacheslav Ivanov's account of the mock execution as "a beatified death" (*Freedom and the Tragic Life*, 34); André Gide's emphasis on the writer's unshakeable optimism (*Dostoevsky*, 67); and László F. Földényi's account of how Siberia engendered the redemptive suffering which eventually "led him to the experience of the limitless—God" ("Dostoevsky Reads Hegel in Siberia," (102, 101). To the degree that such readings of the event revert to a vocabulary of transcendence (albeit rhetorical rather than explanatory), they obscure Dostoevsky's own aesthetic elaboration of an experience of radical suspense. The focus on transcendence thus diminishes the exceptional nature of the mock execution and the exceptional quality of the state of mind it engendered, a state in which Dostoevsky is no longer in his former life.

9. At least as early as the 1846 story "The Landlady," Dostoevsky used the trope of "embodiment" to describe artistic creation (see note 103, below). In a letter to his brother while incarcerated in the Peter and Paul Fortress, he describes how "constant thinking," without the input of any external impressions, feels "oppressive!" "as though I were under an air pump from which the air is being sucked out. Everything in me has gone to my head, and from my head to thought, everything, absolutely everything" (*PSS* 28 [I]: 160–61). Almost twenty years later, in a letter written while he was working on *The Idiot*, he describes how, although "in my head and my soul" he always glimpses "many embryonic artistic ideas," he requires "a full embodiment" (*polnoe voploshchenie*) (*PSS* 28 [II]: 239). The root of this noun is *plot'*—flesh.

10. On the influence on Dostoevsky of Hugo's *The Last Day of a Condemned Man*, and to which he apparently referred as he awaited his turn at the stake, see V. V. Vinogradov, *Poetika russkoi literatury*, 63–75.

11. Julia Kristeva suggests that his support later in life for both liberal innovation and reactionary figures such as the tsar's henchman, Pobedonostev, may reflect the psychic consequences of the mock execution: "a great surge of reconciliation with the deserting power, which has again become a desirable ideal, is doubtless necessary for the life given again to continue and for contact with newly found others to be established. Below this surge, however, there remains the often unquenched melancholy anguish of the subject who has already died once, even though miraculously resurrected . . . The writer's imagination is then beset with an alternation between the unsurpassability of suffering and the flash of forgiveness, and their eternal return articulates the whole of his work" (*Black Sun*, 194–95; ellipses in original).

12. The epilogue to *Crime and Punishment* explicitly locates the peculiar spiritual-aesthetic territory of the forced-labor camp between the life to which one has died and the still unrepresentable life to come. The narrator thus concludes the novel by announcing the deferral of that representation: "here begins a new account, the account of a man's gradual renewal, the account of his gradual regeneration, his gradual *transition from one world to another, his acquaintance with a new, hitherto completely unknown reality.* It might make the subject of a new story—but our present story is ended" (*PSS* 6:422; my emphases). Here and throughout, I use the Pevear and Volokhonsky translation of *Crime and Punishment*; page numbers hereafter are provided in the text following those in *PSS* (here, 551). The narrator's choice of words to describe Raskol'nikov's new environment echoes the prefatory narrator in *House of the Dead* who characterizes Gorianchikov's experience of the camp as a "completely new world, hitherto unknown" (*PSS* 4:8/6).

13. Frank, *Miraculous Years*, 320. Despite my quarrel with some aspects of his interpretation of *Notes from the House of the Dead*, it is impossible to overstate the importance of Frank's work to this study, as my footnotes already have made amply clear.

14. Primo Levi, *Drowned and the Saved*, 149.

15. See note 96, below.

16. Jacques Catteau provides a powerful counterargument to this supposition in the evidence he cites for the onset of Dostoevsky's epilepsy in *katorga* (*Dostoevsky and the Process of Literary Creation*, 102–8). James L. Rice, however, in his definitive study of Dostoevsky's epilepsy (*Dostoevsky and the Art of Healing*), refutes this view (which Dostoevsky himself promoted) and argues for an earlier inception. See also M. M. Gromyko, *Sibirskie znakomye i druz'ia F. M. Dostoevskogo*, 49–51.

17. Despite their *mort civile* having annulled their marriages, the Decembrists were accompanied by their wives into Siberian exile. Dostoevsky met them on his journey to *katorga*, where they routinely provided Bibles and small sums of money to exiled political convicts, and celebrated their martyrdom in his 1873 *Diary of a Writer* article "Old People" (*PSS* 21:8–12). English translation available in *A Writer's Diary Vol.1: 1873–1876*, trans. Kenneth Lantz, 126–31. Page numbers hereafter are provided in the text following those in *PSS*. See also Orlando Figes's account of the Decembrist conspiracy in *Natasha's Dance*, 72–146, esp. 90–101. Five hundred conspirators were arrested; 121 were sent as convict laborers to Siberia; 5 were hanged.

18. There is significant dissent about whether and how this letter provides evidence for religious conversion. Aileen M. Kelly reads it not as proof that Dostoev-

sky had definitively placed faith above reason but rather as "the beginning of a struggle whose outcome was never assured" (*Toward Another Shore*, 59). Grossman interprets it as a confession of "a lack of faith, that was mitigated only by a philosophical interest in Christianity" (*Dostoevskii*, 175). Mochulsky considers the letter as evidence for what Dostoevsky later called the regeneration of his convictions in prison but concludes that "his religious thought still bore little resemblance to the faith of the Orthodox Church." His was not so much "faith in the God-man Christ, but *love for Christ the man*. . . . Here is the direction in which Dostoevsky's convictions were regenerated" (*Dostoevsky*, 153; cf. 157). Catteau claims that Dostoevsky's post-Siberian task was "the reconstruction of his religious culture" which "took place in parallel with the remodelling of his philosophical, historical and economic culture. He was not trying to reinforce his beliefs but to reconstruct a cultural heritage, to remake a basis even of antinomic ideas," a process completed only "after five years of journalism, towards 1864–5" (*Dostoevsky and the Process of Literary Creation*, 70, 82). He points out that Stavrogin (anti-hero of *The Demons*) expresses the same conviction about preferring to remain with Christ even if it were proven that he was outside truth (69–70).

19. See the preceding entry, "Old People," in which Dostoevsky describes the change in his outlook generated by incarceration and exile (*PSS* 21:8–12/ 126–31).

20. P. Ia. Chaadaev had famously characterized all of Russian society in similar terms in the first of eight "philosophical letters" written in 1829 whose publication in 1836 resulted in his arrest: "We live in the most narrow present, without a past and without a future, in the middle of a dead calm" ("Lettres sur la philosophie de l'histoire. Lettre première," 74–93, esp. 79). See part 2, note 11.

21. Mochulsky finds that Gorianchikov begins as "an external observer" but, in the end, "penetrates into the mysterious depths of this world" (*Dostoevsky*, 186; also 188–89). In the penultimate chapter, however, Gorianchikov doubts his success in creating a "clear and vivid picture" of life in *katorga*, partly because of failures of memory: "The earliest years have somehow been effaced in my memory. Many circumstances, I am convinced of this, have been completely forgotten" (*PSS* 4:220/342).

22. Unlike Gorianchikov's first reader, the prefatory narrator, Dostoevsky's actual readers were highly laudatory. Alexander Herzen and Ivan Turgenev explicitly compared Dostoevsky to Dante, the former in an 1864 article in *The Bell* titled "A New Phase in Russian Literature," and the latter in a December 1861 letter of congratulations to Dostoevsky (see part 2, note 138). In an early review of the novel, A. Miliukov referred to him as a "Virgil" as well as a "Livingstone" (V. A. Zelinskii, ed., *Kriticheskii kommentarii* 2:38). Dostoevsky felt that *Notes from the House of the Dead* resurrected the literary reputation which he feared ten years of imprisonment and exile had obliterated (letter to A. E. Vrangel' of 31 March/14 April 1865, in *PSS* 28 [II]: 115). For a review of the novel's critical reception in the nineteenth century, see I. I. Zamotin, *F. M. Dostoevskii v russkoi kritike*. For a briefer discussion of its twentieth-century reception, including information on translations, see *PSS* 4:294–300. Frank discusses its immediate reception in *Stir of Liberation*, 215–16.

23. Mikhail M. Bakhtin, in *Problems of Dostoevsky's Poetics*, claims that the Dostoevskian hero "is not an objectified image but an autonomous discourse, *pure voice*; we do not see him, we hear him; everything that we see and know apart from his discourse is nonessential and is swallowed up by discourse as its raw material, or else remains outside it as something that stimulates and provokes" (53). Far from pure voice, though, the prefatory narrator's introduction highlights the textuality of the memoir, an anticipatory offensive against the reader's tendency to identify with the narrator, Gorianchikov, and thus to imagine him as in some sense present and speaking directly to the reader. On the "conversion" of autobiographical discourse from the trope of speech (understood as a purging of narrative from discourse, according to Gérard Genette's distinction), see Geoffrey Galt Harpham, "Profit and Loss in the Ascesis of Discourse," in idem, *The Ascetic Imperative in Culture and Criticism*.

24. On the tradition of holy foolishness (of which Gorianchikov's post-*katorga* behavior is suggestive) in Russian religious culture, see Harriet Murav, *Holy Foolishness*.

25. To see the extent to which this is true, compare the prefatory narrator's discourse on Gorianchikov to Sonia's on Raskol'nikov in the camp (in *Crime and Punishment*): "Instead of attempts to explain his psychological condition and his inner life in general, there were only facts, that is, his own words, detailed reports on the state of his health, what he expressed a desire for at their meetings, the questions he asked her, the errands he entrusted to her, and so on. All this information was communicated in extraordinary detail. In the end, [Raskolnikov's image] emerged unembellished, precisely and clearly drawn; there could be no mistake because everything was simple fact" (*PSS* 6:415/541).

26. For the publishing history of *Notes from the House of the Dead*, see *PSS* 4:275–78. The introduction and first chapter were published in *Russkii mir* (Russian world), no. 67 (1 September 1860); the second, third, and fourth chapters appeared in issues 4, 11, and 25 January 1861 in that journal; the introduction and the first four chapters then appeared in Dostoevsky's own journal, *Vremia* (*Time*), in April 1861, and separately in January 1862. The novel was published in full during Dostoevsky's lifetime in 1862 (minus the chapter "Comrades"), in 1865 (in Dostoevsky's first *Complete Works*), and in 1875 (where he titled the introduction, made several stylistic corrections, and omitted the "Comrades" chapter; see James L. Rice, "Psychoanalysis of 'Peasant Marei,' " 253). For an account of Dostoevsky's decision to write his memoirs and publish them in *Russkii mir*, see the 4 March 1882 letter from the journal's editor, A. S. Gieroglifov, to Dostoevsky's first biographer, O. F. Miller, reprinted in A. P. Mogilianskii, "K istorii pervoi publikatsii 'Zapisok iz mertvogo doma,' " 179–81. Frank discusses the unusual publication history of the text, including run-ins with the censor, in *Stir of Liberation*, 28–30. For a discussion of critical accounts of the discrepancy between the prefatory narrator's explanation of Gorianchikov's crime and his own implication that he was a political prisoner, see note 116 below.

27. For an account of Dostoevsky's ambitions concerning his literary comeback, as well as cultural-literary developments during the decade of his exile, see Frank, *Years of Ordeal*, esp. chaps. 17–20; the phrase cited appears at 266. See also Frank, *Stir of Liberation*, chaps. 1–3, for a detailed account of Dostoevsky's literary

activities upon his return to western Russia. G. M. Fridlender notes that the combination of artistic, autobiographical, and essayistic forms in a single work was typical
of Russian works in the 1850s and 1860s. This resulted from the "desire to tell
the reader of things and events (usually experienced by the author himself) that
. . . by their very nature required that the author employ [for their expression]
artistic devices other than those provided by the novel with its invented subjects
and characters" (Fridlender, *Realizm Dostoevskogo*, 95). V. A. Tunimanov characterizes the publication of such works in those decades as amounting to a "flood":
"Complaints were even heard that the 'literature of reminiscence' had prevailed
over literature itself." He quotes one mid-century critic as writing "with obvious
disapproval, 'All these memoirs, all these autobiographies, all these notes!' "
(*Tvorchestvo Dostoevskogo*, 74 n. 10).

28. For Gary Saul Morson, the introduction marks the beginning of a purely
Dostoevskian convention, a technique for the text's "formal self-characterization"
which Dostoevsky will utilize in *Notes from the Underground* (1864), *A Raw Youth*
(1876), "The Meek One: A Fantastic Story" (1876), and *Diary of a Writer* (*The
Boundaries of Genre*, 12–13). Viktor Shklovsky argues that the prefatory narrator
represents the renewal of a convention associated with the "old European novel"—
Dostoevsky's introduction, exaggeratedly light in tone compared to the text it
introduces, allows for "a new [novelistic] unity" of artistically arranged fragments
which Shklovsky describes as a "new, unique, and artistically unified docu-novel"
(*Za i protiv*, 99, 101, 123).

29. For the importance to Dostoevsky of representing life "on the threshold,"
see Bakhtin, *Problems of Dostoevsky's Poetics*. Bakhtin attributes the prevalence of
"threshold situations" in Dostoevsky's work to its dialogism and, relatedly, to his
ethical commitment to the representation of consciousness as "unfinalizable."

30. The prefatory narrator's attempts to approach Gorianchikov in the spirit of
friendship confirm the latter's reputation as a "terrible misanthrope"—he notes
the ex-convict's "insane mistrust," his "looks of alarm" and suffering, and his
"terrified" response to social overtures, all suggesting that, almost like a wild animal (to which Dostoevsky himself was compared by those who knew him in *katorga*; see note 98, below), he anticipates some form of violence from the advances
of others. His "most important concern," the prefatory narrator concludes, was to
"hide himself away as far as possible from all of society" (*PSS* 4:6, 7/3, 4, 5).

31. In a letter to his brother of 1 October 1859 Dostoevsky announced his plan
to rewrite *The Double*, but he did not publish a redacted version until 1866 (*PSS*
28 [I]: 339–41). For a complete account of the history of the text's composition
from the 1840s to the 1860s, the complete 1846 and 1866 versions and a summary
of the differences between the two, as well as an English translation of the entries
related to the reworking of *The Double* in notebooks from 1860 to 1864 (in *PSS*
1:432–36), see Evelyn Jasiulko Harden's introduction to her translation, *The Double: Two Versions*. In his article "Novyi Robinzon," Andrei Bitov points out that
the notebooks show that Dostoevsky had envisioned a reworking of Goliadkin's
character in particular but that *House of the Dead* allowed him to realize his specific
ambitions for *The Double* and so "the ring of 'The Double' was broken" (16). In
my view, two items in the notebooks support this point. First, in Notebook 1 for
1860–62, Dostoevsky wrote, "Junior, it turns out, knows all of Senior's secrets, as

if he were the personification of Senior's conscience [*olitsetvorennaia sovest' starshego*]" (*PSS* 1:434). The relationship of the prefatory narrator to Gorianchikov is arguably analogous; see section 4, below. Second, in Notebook 2 for 1862–64, Dostoevsky has Goliadkin Senior go to Petrashevsky's where, of course, Junior turns up, outshines him by taking an active role, and ends up telling Petrashevsky that Senior is an informer (*PSS* 1:435). Senior's conscience is also his executioner within: see my discussion of this figure later in part 1.

32. See John Freccero, "Logology: Burke on St. Augustine," 64.

33. The pilgrim is the author's textual persona, the experiential subject of a text's linear evolution, and the poet is the transcendent, "resurrected" authorial voice that tells the pilgrim's tale from the perspective of its conclusion. Whereas many commentators uncritically collapse the pilgrim/poet distinction by referring interchangeably to Gorianchikov and Dostoevsky, Robert Louis Jackson invokes it as an opposition between "Gorianchikov the memoirist" and "Gorianchikov the convict." According to his reading, however, far from the narrative itself documenting the rapprochement of one aspect of the self with the other, consummated in the "central syntactic moment," "the convict" is from the outset subordinated to "the memoirist" in the interests of rendering the "poetic," if not the literal, truth of Dostoevsky's prison experience. See Jackson, *Art of Dostoevsky*, 41–54, esp. 45; hereafter, cited in the text as *AD*. Cf. William C. Spengemann's *Forms of Autobiography*, esp. chap. 1.

34. Wood notes that the institution of *katorga* or penal servitude introduced by Peter the Great "was retained, after Elizabeth's abolition of the death penalty, as the harshest form of punishment in the tsarist Criminal Code right until the Revolution of 1917 when it was abolished by the Provisional Government" ("Crime and Punishment in the House of the Dead," 221).

35. This antagonism of discursive modes and conversional motives and meanings is also central to Harpham's reading of Augustine's *Confessions*, where he argues against the "metaphysical prejudice" that, by attributing "at once too much security and too little productive capacity" to the autobiographical narrator of the conversion narrative, mandates an affirmation of textual closure as the achieved transcendence of life's problems. I discuss in section 6 below how this perfectionist impulse so pervasive in the text's critical reception requires the suppression of the prefatory narrator's contribution to the text. As antidote to the sacrificial gesture required by perfection, Harpham offers "a shadow-reading [of *The Confession*] that takes its place *within* the canonical reading, completing it without contradicting it." See Harpham, "The Language of Conversion," in idem, *The Ascetic Imperative*, 92, 93.

36. Grossman maintains that the nobleman's redemptive conviction regarding the necessity of being turned into or merged with the common people "became the programme of [Dostoevsky's] writing once he was free again" (*Dostoevskii*, 171).

37. An important subset of the novel's critics has lauded its "documentary accuracy" and thus its ethnographic value as an objective representation of a nineteenth-century Siberian hard-labor camp. The Soviet scholar V. I. Etov, for example, wrote: "Thanks to the emphasis on documentary accuracy [*dokumentalizm*], the population of the Siberian prison appears before the reader as a world apart

[*kak osobyi mir*], distinct from the ordinary, civilized world to the same degree as the life of exotic peoples is distinct from the European. The documentary accuracy of *Notes from the House of the Dead* is to a certain degree the documentary accuracy of ethnographic studies. And, as is the case with all ethnographic research, the goal of *House of the Dead* is a similar study of a population" (*Dostoevskii*, 108). Frank notes that the novel stimulated an immediate interest in prison reform (*Stir of Liberation*, 215–16).

38. Tunimanov also notes this recuperative discursive shift characteristic of the second part of *House of the Dead*, describing it as "distinguished from the first by a sharp ideologization of the narration, by the tragic emphasis of nearly all the fundamental motifs, and by the intensification of the polemics" (*Tvorchestvo Dostoevskogo*, 121).

39. Mochulsky describes the tripartite structure of *House of the Dead* thus: "The upper stratum of the *Notes* is an *artistic description* of the facts; the middle is their psychological explanation with the help of the idea of freedom and of personality; the lower is a *metaphysical* investigation of good and evil in the soul of man" (*Dostoevsky*, 192). Grossman envisioned it in terms of three components: the first, "wonderful genre paintings, daguerrotypes, episodes, scenes, dialogues—physiological sketches from the world of the outcast"; second, character studies of the "social types" contained in the prison, guided by the sentiment of respect for their inner strength; and, third, inserted stories of the prisoners themselves about their pasts, "convict folklore" (*Dostoevskii*, 249–50).

40. Catteau locates the chronotopic integrity of *katorga* in "le chiffrage, le nombre inhumain, le billion parfaitement 'indécent' dont parle le diable d'Ivan Karamazov, bref *la transcription numérique de la répétitivité*," [the accounting, the inhuman number, the perfectly 'indecent' billion of which Ivan Karamazov's devil speaks, in sum, *the numeric transcription of repetition*]," which ensures "la correlation entre l'espace de l'enfermement et le temps de l'enfermement" [the correlation between the space of incarceration and the time of incarceration]" (*"De la structure de La maison des morts* de F. M. Dostoevskij," esp. 70–71); see also note 46, below. Catteau refers particularly to Gorianchikov's daily counting off the remaining days of his sentence on the fifteen hundred pales of the stockade. Shklovsky similarly notes the spatio-temporal significance of the stockade "not only as a barrier between the world and the prison, but also as a calendar in which each log is a day": "the stockade *is* the sentence [*srok*]" (*Za i protiv*, 108). For another view of the disbursement of spatial and temporal representations in *katorga*, see I. P. Smirnov, "Otchuzhdenie-v-otchuzhdenii."

41. Gorianchikov/Dostoevsky had, of course, lost the nobleman's protection from corporal punishment but enjoyed some unofficial (hence unreliable) protection from those prison authorities who, since the time of the Decembrists, hesitated to flog members of the nobility, especially political prisoners.

42. The abyss of class difference is, of course, patrolled on both its borders, a circumstance not addressed by the conversion hypothesis (nor in "The Peasant Marei"). The nobleman's voluntarily undertaken turn (in)to the common people clearly occurs within the context established by the *mutual* exception of the other from one's proper class milieu; that is, the nobleman's unilateral turning does not rehabilitate the milieu the antagonistic classes only physically share, as if the ques-

tion of the other's reception of this gesture is irrelevant. On the history of the "democratic" impulse to turn into the common people dating from the Napoleonic invasion of 1812, see Figes, *Natasha's Dance*, 72–83.

43. Cf. Mochulsky, who identifies the epilogue of *Crime and Punishment* as the missing pages of *Notes from the House of the Dead*. In that epilogue, Raskolnikov, as Gorianchikov before him, suffers from the hostility of the peasant-convicts without understanding the reason for their animosity. In response, Raskolnikov expresses "that which was left not fully expressed in the letter [to Mikhail Dostoevsky] of [22 February] 1854 and in the *Notes from the House of Death*" (*Dostoevsky*, 154).

44. For the importance of what Burke calls "the *vert*-series" to the conversion narrative, see his *Rhetoric of Religion*, esp. 62–65.

45. Without denying the sincerity of his conviction, it is possible to detect in Gorianchikov's character (as Jackson suggests in *AD*, 65) the faintest adumbration of Mme Khokhlakova (a minor character in the *The Brothers Karamazov*) who was prepared to love humanity, even to kiss its festering wounds, as long as humanity kept its distance—a posture incompatible with "active love" which Father Zosima calls "love in dreams."

46. Catteau describes the novel's "structure cyclique où l'esprit s'englue," the chronotopic combination of "enclosed space and cyclical [as opposed to "spiral"] time" providing the "perfect form with which to signify inertia, immobility, death, the loss of liberty" ("De la structure de *La maison des morts*," 67, 72). Frank offers an alternative account of the text's repetitiveness in *Stir of Liberation*, 221.

47. Both meanings of the word *bezdna* as Dostoevsky uses them appear in the story of the Gerasine demoniac (Luke 8:30–31): "Jesus then asked him, 'What is your name?' And he said, 'Legion,' for many demons had entered him. And they begged him not to command them to depart into the abyss [*Iisus sprosil ego: kak tebe imia? On skazal: "legion"; potomu chto mnogo besov voshlo v nego. I oni sprosili Iisusa, chtoby ne povelel im idti v bezdnu*]." The apocalyptic significance of the *bezdna* derives from its appearance in Revelation where it designates the bottomless pit in which Satan, bound by an angel of God, is to be sealed for a thousand years. See Revelation 9.1–11; 11.7; 17.8; 20.1–3. In the *Polnyi pravoslavnyi bogoslovskii entsiklopedicheskii slovar'*, Vol. 1, "*bezdna*" is defined as a "dungeon or place of eternal torment for the condemned, devils and sinners *who have been turned away by God* [*otverzhennykh Bogom*]" (298; my emphasis).

48. Bakhtin, *Problems of Dostoevsky's Poetics*, 32.

49. The classic discussion of defamiliarization or estrangement (*ostranenie*) is Viktor B. Shklovsky's "Art as Technique." For a discussion of Shklovskian estrangement in relation to *House of the Dead*, see Nancy Ruttenburg, "Dostoevsky's Estrangement" (720–23).

50. On the "God-term," see Burke, *Rhetoric of Religion*, 24–27. Burke's discussion of the perfection principle appears (in disguise) in the same volume, 295–304.

51. Freccero, "Logology," 63.

52. Jackson, *AD*, 34, 39.

53. Apart from an initial brief account of how he came to overhear Shishkov's narrative and a brief description of him, Gorianchikov's voice is heard in the narrative proper only in a handful of attributive discourse tags.

54. Jackson, *AD*, 136, 96.

55. This remains true even though later in his reading in *AD*, Jackson insists that "Dostoevsky's central effort in *House of the Dead* is not to idealize the suffering of the Russian people, that is, to extract a compensatory virtue from their miseries"; it is, rather, to direct the reader's attention to "the terrible social, moral, and spiritual consequences of that suffering" (137).

56. Catteau, "De la structure de *La maison des morts*," 66.

57. Jackson, *AD*, 96. Sarah Hudspith makes a similar argument in *Dostoevsky and the Idea of Russianness*, 181.

58. Jackson, *AD*, 40.

59. Ibid., 68, 39.

60. Ibid., 40, 41.

61. Tunimanov suggests this notion of accuracy when he characterizes *House of the Dead* as a series of vivid illustrations that do not add up to the remote ideological conclusions of *Diary of a Writer* (*Tvorchestvo Dostoevskogo*, 92).

62. Cf. Gorianchikov's statement at *PSS* 4:195/303, where he claims that he did finally "accustom himself" (*osvoit'sia s*) to his situation in the camp (the verb suggests that he was able to make it *his own*, as a kind of second nature); he adds, "and there were also other prisoners who were not able *to become accustomed* to this life [*privyknut'* k]" (Gorianchikov's emphasis). His search for the proper verb to render the convicts' relation to the life around them underscores the specificity of the verb used in the passage considered here: "*primirit'sia s*," or "to be reconciled with," "to make peace with." The statements are not contradictory: he could become accustomed to the life (in particular, the routine) without becoming reconciled with it.

63. In "Autobiography as De-facement," Paul De Man questioned the assumption that autobiography represents "a simpler mode of referentiality" than the novel and characterized it otherwise, as a figure for reading the self (920–21). Recent studies of autobiography particularly suggestive in relation to *House of the Dead* include Gerhard Richter, *Walter Benjamin and the Corpus of Autobiography*, which examines the subject "perpetually caught between construction and dispersal in the act of self-portraiture" and the tension "between the impetus to construct the subject through the act of writing and the narrative renunciation of such a project" (14, 34); and the relational account of (narrated) identity offered by Adriana Cavarero, *Relating Narratives*.

64. See the entries for "raskaianie" and "pokaianie" in *Slovar' tserkovo-slavianskogo i russkogo iazyka*, vol. 2, 4:41 and 3:303, respectively. Cf. the entries for "attrition" and "contrition" in Van A. Harvey, *A Handbook of Theological Terms*, where he invokes the Roman Catholic tradition.

65. In *Problems of Dostoevsky's Poetics*, Bakhtin notes that in Dostoevsky's works "the hero very often hides from himself what he knows, and pretends to himself that he does not see what in fact is constantly before his eyes" (239).

66. There is ample bibliography on the phenomenon of the "as if," beginning perhaps with Hans Vaihinger's 1911 study, *The Philosophy of "As if."* Wolfgang Iser has most interestingly extended the philosophical discussion into the category of fiction as that which, far from attempting to mask, purposely discloses its own fictionality, thereby realizing the imaginary. See his "Feigning in Fiction" and *The*

Fictive and the Imaginary, esp. 130–52. The prefatory narrator, too, repeatedly uses the phrase "as if" in his efforts to account for Gorianchikov's odd behavior.

67. For a discussion after Freud of the peculiar disavowal represented here, see Octave Mannoni, "Je sais bien, mais quand même. . ."; cited in D. A. Miller, *The Novel and the Police*, 16 n. 5, 206–7.

68. P. K. Martianov, who interviewed those with whom Dostoevsky had had contact in *katorga*, remarked upon the success of his strategies for holding himself apart. "*Katorga* didn't like him, but admitted his moral authority; somberly, not without hatred toward his superiority, it looked at him and silently kept away from him. Seeing that, he himself kept away from everybody" ("V perelome veka," 237).

69. Syzmon Tokarzewski, a Polish nobleman incarcerated in the Omsk prison, remembered Dostoevsky thus: " 'Nobility,' 'nobleman,' 'nobility,' 'I am a nobleman,' 'we, the nobility,' he [Dostoevsky] would constantly repeat. And when he would turn to us, Poles, saying: 'We, the nobility,' I would always interrupt him: 'Excuse me, sir, I think that in this prison there are no gentry, there are only men deprived of rights, only convicts.' Then he would foam with anger: 'And you, sir, are evidently pleased that you are a convict,' he shouted with anger and irony. 'That I am just such a convict as I am, I am happy,' I would answer quietly" (cited in Jackson, *AD*, 42). Tokarzewski is one of the novel's many readers who considered it straightforward autobiography clumsily masquerading as fiction. According to Jackson, Tokarzewski resented Gorianchikov's portrayal of the "humanitarian views of the ordinary Russian convict against the background of the Poles' alleged 'exclusiveness' " insofar as it dissembled "the inner content of his attitude toward the ordinary Russian convict in prison" (42–43). Tokarzewski's memoir reverses the roles Dostoevsky assigned to Russian and Pole in "The Peasant Marei." On Dostoevsky's relationship to the Polish noblemen-convicts, see Frank, *Years of Ordeal*, 110–14.

70. Mary Louise Pratt notes that "the image of the castaway is an evocative and utopian self-image for the ethnographer." The captive or castaway, because he does not exploit the culture that holds him against his will, retains an innocence that the ethnographer as scientist must relinquish along with his utopian fantasies of an encounter with a "virgin" people. In this regard, the castaway and captive "realize the ideal of the participant-observer" ("Fieldwork in Common Places," 38). Similarly, Renato Rosaldo notes that the ethnographer's plight, told as the "story of how [he] suffered as he crossed cultural boundaries," may provide him with authority: "as lone heroic victim [he] establishes his innocence from colonial domination and validates his credentials as a disinterested scientist" ("Fieldworker and Inquisitor," 89, 93). On the problem of ethnographic authority as one of self-fashioning, see also James Clifford, "On Ethnographic Self-Fashioning."

71. The Underground Man perceptively observes, "In every man's memories there are such things as he will reveal not to everyone, but perhaps only to his friends. There are also such as he will reveal not even to friends, but only to himself, and that in secret. Then, finally, there are such as a man is afraid to reveal even to himself, and every decent man will have accumulated quite a few things of this sort. That is, one might even say: the more decent a man is, the more of them he will have" (*PSS* 5:122). I use here the Pevear and Volokhonsky translation of *Notes from Underground*, 39.

72. In "The Memory of the Offense," Primo Levi's meditation on the self-exculpatory testimony of men and women who were complicit in perpetrating the Nazi atrocities, he observes that the distinction between good faith and bad faith "is optimistic and smacks of the Enlightenment." The self-deceptive stance partakes of both. His ensuing comments on the complex progress of self-deception in self-narration are relevant here. See *Drowned and the Saved*, 26–27.

73. In *Dostoevsky and "The Idiot"*, Robin Feuer Miller describes the peculiarities of the Dostoevskian "narrator-chronicler" as combining the advantages of first- and third-person narration: "He lives in the town where the action occurs, has access to minute details of that action, but does not participate in it. He does not shrink, however, from judging or interpreting the people and events around him. In spite of the narrator-chronicler's general reliability, his point of view often differs from Dostoevsky's" (2). Although Miller traces the development of the narrator-chronicler from *The Idiot* to its perfection in *The Demons* and *The Brothers Karamazov* (2–3), I would argue for Gorianchikov as its first instanciation: at the first and third narrative levels, he maintains an in-it-but-not-of-it stance toward the camp and an ethnographer's or chronicler's distance from its inhabitants, along with the will (if all too often not the ability, he concedes) to interpret and even judge what he observes. Moreover, despite the autobiographical content of the novel, his is "a separate consciousness with its own inherent contradictions" and therefore cannot be considered Dostoevsky's textual representative (258 n. 11). Murav suggestively situates Dostoevsky's systematic undermining of the narrator's authority, particularly evident in *The Idiot*, within the context of "the poetics of holy foolishness" which unfolds on the shifting threshold of sacred and profane (*Holy Foolishness*, 13, 71–98).

74. This suggests that the "space of exception," the Agambenian paradigm with which I explore *katorga* as a distinctive type of chronotope in part 2, may be metaphorically associated with the place from which one narrates.

75. "Desubjectification" is a concept I borrow and adapt from Giorgio Agamben's *Remnants of Auschwitz* in order to examine (in part 2) the implications of the disarticulation of the narrating voice.

76. Raskolnikov similarly refuses to see: "In prison, in his surroundings, he did not notice much, of course, and really did not want to notice. He lived somehow with lowered eyes: it was repulsive and unbearable to look." The narrative continues, "But in the end many things began to surprise him, and he somehow involuntarily began to notice what he had not even suspected before" (*PSS* 6:418/545). See also Jackson, *AD*, 354 n. 28 on the connection in Dostoevsky's aesthetics between sight and understanding.

77. Throughout his career, Dostoevsky pondered the relationship of the upper class to the lower; see section 2 of the conclusion to this volume. He is particularly blunt in the February 1876 *Diary of a Writer* (directly preceding "The Peasant Marei"), where he notes that the question on everybody's lips is "Who is better—we or the people? Do the people follow us or do we follow the people?" Dostoevsky's reply is unequivocal—"It is we who should bow before the people and await everything from them, both ideas and their expression . . ."—but he qualifies it immediately: "on the other hand, we should bow only on one condition, and this one *sine qua non*: that the people receive from us much of that which we bring

with us. We absolutely cannot destroy ourselves completely before them, and even before whatever may be their truth; let ours remain ours, and we won't give it up for anything in the world, even, in the most extreme case, for the happiness of uniting with the people" (*PSS* 22:44, 45/349).

78. Cf. Alexander Herzen's portrayal of the executioner within in *From the Other Shore*, written in Paris in the wake of the failed 1848 Revolution: "Within every man there is a permanent revolutionary tribunal, there is a merciless Fouquier-Tinville [prosecutor of Robespierre's Revolutionary Tribunal] and, above all, there is a guillotine. Sometimes the judge may nod, the guillotine grow rusty, and then all that is false, obsolete, romantic, weak raises its head, until suddenly some wild shock rouses the dormant court, the slumbering hangman. Then rough justice begins. The slightest concession, act of compassion, mercy, lead back to the past and leave the chains intact. There is no choice—one must either slaughter and go forward or pardon and falter half-way" (49). In Herzen's vision of July 1848, it is one's cherished convictions and beliefs that must be eradicated in the wake of their negation by the historical event.

79. This was not the case, however, for many of Dostoevsky's contemporary readers who assumed that he had been imprisoned for the murder of his wife. See notes 102 and 112, below.

80. On the significance of the question of the prefatory narrator's publishing or editing function or both, see note 122 below.

81. See note 31, above. Frank argues that the pre-Siberian story provided Dostoevsky "with a psychological paradigm that he would later constantly re-employ," most famously in his Underground Man. Frank attributes the "new ideological richness" of the paradigm in the post-Siberian work to Dostoevsky's greater awareness of the socially subversive implications of Goliadkin's insanity (*Stir of Liberation*, 3, 70).

82. On the significance of parody as "perverse imitation," see Burke, *Rhetoric of Religion*, 44.

83. From 1861, Dostoevsky extended that chain of misapprehension binding the powerful and powerless to Europe's reading of Russia. In the "Introduction" [*Vvedenie*] to *Time*, for example, he writes how, "at various times, enormous efforts were expended by our inquisitive neighbors to understand us and our way of life; materials, figures, facts were collected; research was undertaken. . . . But all imaginable attempts to deduce from these materials, figures, facts something fundamental, sensible and to the point about Russian man, something synthetically true—all these efforts always smash up against some sort of fatal impossibility, as if predestined by someone for some reason." The same inability to grasp the culture is evident in individual foreigners who come to live in Russia and who, even after many years, are unable to gain a perspective that will reveal to them its "main idea" (*PSS* 18:41–42).

84. Robert Lord notes Rogozhin's technique for committing bloodless murder (of Nastasia Filippovna) at which Myshkin marvels in *The Idiot*'s shocking final scene. The crude and illiterate but enormously wealthy son of a rich merchant and Old Believer, Rogozhin thus combines the aristocratic skill of killing cleanly with "impulsive, uncontrolled emotion, life at its rawest, like the superhuman convicts Dostoevsky knew intimately in Siberia." In contrast to Rogozhin, the "ontological

predicament" of Myshkin, who also haunts the abyss between the classes, is that his epilepsy prevents him from following through on his own "criminal" (in society's view) convictions and impulses (*Dostoevsky*, 98, 100). The difficulty of owning one's own crime is a theme most fully realized in the character of Ivan in *The Brothers Karamazov* where Dmitri—whose crude impulsiveness resembles Rogozhin's—is persuaded to accept responsibility for a murder he did not commit.

85. In the context of a discussion about Gorianchikov's and Dostoevsky's views on the existence of conscience in the peasant criminal, Jackson writes of the "shock and disbelief" of their shared "discovery" that the peasant seems not to feel remorse (*AD*, 119). Jackson reads the problem of conscience and crime in *House of the Dead* as almost exclusively focused on the peasant. The state of Gorianchikov's own conscience (and his own crime) is at issue only insofar as "the educated convict typically experiences his crime in an especially acute way," and his hardships are therefore greater than the peasant's, not because he is more sensitive but because he is estranged, because "he has been plunged into a primitive environment" (132, 131).

86. The term "iron beak" appears in the letter Dostoevsky wrote to his brother upon his release from hard labor on February 22, 1854 (*PSS* 28 [1]: 169/59).

87. Shklovsky maintains that "Akul'ka's Husband" "enters the novel as a separate novella" (*Za i protiv*, 119–22).

88. Cf. Grossman's discussion of an "organic link" between form and content in Stavrogin's confession in *The Demons* where he notes the "continual disintegration of word and image" in "the confession of the terrible sinner," a theme that demanded new narrative devices. Like *The Demons*, *House of the Dead* devises verbal analogues for a "decadent and criminal consciousness" attempting confession, whose primary trait is that the act confessed (the object of the discourse) is only obliquely present in the confessional text ("Dostoevskii-khudozhnik," 384). In this regard, *House of the Dead* is most assuredly " 'confession' in the style of the Underground Man" and not "prophecy," as Jackson maintains in "The Narrator in Dostoevsky's *Notes from the House of the Dead*," 213. Tunimanov's analysis, in *Tvorchestvo Dostoevskogo*, indicates the extent to which, despite the prefatory narrator's allegations, the link between Gorianchikov and the crime of wife-murder remains "unspoken" in the criticism. Although he brings into his ninety-page discussion of *House of the Dead* figures from Balzac to Nietzsche, he is silent about the figure at the text's very center, the wife-murderer Akul'ka's husband.

89. Shklovsky, *Za i protiv*, 104.

90. Cf. Robert Belknap's concept of associational clusters in *Structure of the Brothers Karamazov*.

91. Burke, *Rhetoric of Religion*, 24–27.

92. Frank, *Stir of Liberation*, 227. Frank's remarks refer to another painfully detailed account of the slow torture of a peasant woman by her husband contained in the 1873 *Diary of a Writer* piece, "The Environment" (*PSS* 21:13–23/132–45), discussed in more detail in part 2, section 4.

93. Frank, *Years of Ordeal*, 114, 115. Although he provides a detailed hypothesis of Dostoevsky's conversion through a reading of "The Peasant Marei," Frank also warns against taking it "too literally" and "confus[ing] his skillful rendering of an incident from his biography with the actual contours of his spiritual evolu-

tion" (128). His view of the writer's spiritual "regeneration," finally, is that it was a protracted process. His interpretation of *Notes from the House of the Dead*, however, relies on the Augustinian model (inflected by a reading of William James on pages 116–19) of a sudden and complete awakening.

94. Frank, *Years of Ordeal*, 206, 114.

95. Jackson, *Dostoevsky's Quest for Form*, 77; *AD*, 7 n. 10; 355.

96. Pascal, *Dostoïevski*, 85. The date refers to Pascal's calculation of the day on which Dostoevsky must have had the conversion experience based on "The Peasant Marei." Cf. Figes's reference to the "vision of redemption" that restored Dostoevsky's faith while in the depths of despair in the prison, a "revelation" that appeared "as if by a miracle, at Easter time" (*Natasha's Dance*, 330). As is the case with Frank, Pascal's position on the meaning of the conversion experience is somewhat contradictory. On the one hand, he flatly states that "Il n'y a pas eu chez [Dostoevsky] de conversion" (331). Here Pascal denies a reversal of Dostoevsky's ideology between his revolutionary youth and his reactionary maturity. On the contrary, he argues for a continuity between his earlier and later beliefs insofar as he was less a disciplined ideologue or philosopher than a writer who drew from multiple disciplines throughout his life in the service of an art that was anything but programmatic. On the other hand, however, Pascal does maintain, in an attempt to shed light on Dostoevsky's religious beliefs, that the writer "rediscovered Christ" in prison. As is the case with Frank, Pascal's sources are *Diary of a Writer* entries published between 1873 and 1880 (331–34, 350–55). Frank disputes Pascal's chronology of the conversion event in *Years of Ordeal*, 119–20.

97. Catteau dates the Marei incident in August 1831 based on his analysis of Dostoevsky's epilepsy (*Dostoevsky and the Process of Literary Creation*, 101).

98. The Russian word for "wolf" and the German word for "people" are homonyms (see note 106, below). There is thus some irony in the fact that Dostoevsky was apparently characterized by fellow inmates as "fierce, withdrawn, unfriendly" to all, like a "wolf in a trap," according to interviews conducted by the biographer P. K. Martianov ("V perelome veka," 240). This characterization of Dostoevsky recalls Gorianchikov's description of the wounded eagle found within the walls of the stockade: "All the time I was near him he used to stare intently in my face with his savage, piercing eyes. Fierce and solitary he awaited death, mistrustful and hostile to all" (*PSS* 4:194/301). Respected and left unharmed by the convicts because he maintained a fierce independence and refused to curry favor (precisely Gorianchikov's strategy for handling the unpredictable peasant-convicts), the eagle is finally thrown over the wall to freedom, accompanied by the same bittersweet commentary Gorianchikov's release will elicit. Gromyko, in *Sibirskie znakomie i druz'ia F. M. Dostoevskogo*, 29–31, questions the accuracy of some of Martianov's claims.

99. Frank, *Years of Ordeal*, 119. For another view of the relevance to Dostoevsky of James's work on conversion in *Varieties of Religious Experience*, see Robin Feuer Miller, "Adventures in Time and Space: Dostoevsky, William James, and the Perilous Journey to Conversion." She observes that *anhedonia*, that state of despair which James noted often precedes conversion, is essentially defamiliarizing. Miller shows how Dostoevsky's presentation of conversion in "The Peasant Marei" is

itself paradigmatic insofar as it contains a set of elements reworked in subsequent fictional representations of the experience.

100. Gromyko discusses evidence that Dostoevsky and Durov were disciplined for writing in *katorga* (*Sibirskie znakomye i druz'ia F. M. Dostoevskogo*, 32–33). See also note 107, below.

101. In *House of the Dead*, Gorianchikov notes that Miretsky was a "man of culture" but not a nobleman, and had suffered corporal punishment; his disdain for the brawling Russians is therefore, implicitly, a matter of nationality rather than class (*PSS* 4:216/336–37). See also note 69, above.

102. Included among those who were persuaded that Dostoevsky was exiled for somebody's murder, and, in fact, for the murder of his wife, was his future second wife, Anna Grigorevna Snitkina, and her family. Her diary is quoted on this subject in *PSS* 22:345–46. See also note 112, below.

103. Cf. Dostoevsky's early description of the psychology of literary creation as a kind of resurrection in his novella "The Landlady" (1846), where the narrator describes how the febrile hero's fear comes to life: "He saw everything, beginning with his vague childish reveries, all his thoughts and dreams, everything that he had experienced in life, everything that he had read in books, everything that he had forgotten long ago, all this was coming to life, acquiring shape, putting on flesh and rising before him in colossal forms and images" (*PSS* 1:279).

104. Frank, *Years of Ordeal*, 122.

105. For a discussion of the indistinguishability of dream, memory, hallucination, and fiction in "The Peasant Marei," see Rice's fascinating "Psychoanalysis of 'Peasant Marej.'" Rice discusses the "creative embellishment" Dostoevsky gave to the figure of Marei (and possible sources for the peasant's unusual name) in several reissues of *House of the Dead*, in drafts and the final text of *A Raw Youth*, and in notes and drafts for *Diary of a Writer* (249, 254–57). On the link between dreaming and "bare life," the life lived by those who have been abandoned and cast out of the normative cultural domain (according to Giorgio Agamben's conception), see Thomas Carl Wall, "Au Hasard," esp. 32.

106. On the relation between the German term for "the people" (*volk*) and the Russian term *narod*, Franco Venturi tells us that the word *narodnost'* "derived from *narod*, meaning both 'people' and 'nation' (like the German *Volk*), had been taken from *Volkstum*, and had a similar political intonation, one of reaction against the French Revolution, against the subsequent national and at the same time liberal movements." Thus, under Nicholas I, the "official trinity of autocracy, orthodoxy and *narodnost'* " was proclaimed, "whose natural synthesis [. . .] lay in the first of these—autocracy." See Venturi, *Roots of Revolution*, 19–26, esp. 19. Cf. Richard Pipes, "*Narodnichestvo*: A Semantic Inquiry," esp. 441–43, who documents the equivalence of the adjective "*narodnyi*" and "democratic."

107. While a prisoner in the Omsk fortress, Dostoevsky managed, with the aid of a sympathetic prison doctor, to keep surreptitiously a "Siberian Notebook" in which he jotted down fragments of peasant speech (as well as Polish, Ukrainian, Jewish, and Tartar expressions)—overheard bits of dialogue, legends, anecdotes, proverbs, catchwords and catchphrases, and so on. The "Siberian Notebook" (*Sibirskaia tetrad'*), containing 486 entries, is reprinted in *PSS* 4:235–47. The editors note of "Akul'ka's Husband" that its source "was unquestionably a

real story told by one of the convicts," a view supported by entries 326 and 384 (275). (For alternative accounts of the literary genesis of the story, see Serman, "Tema narodnosti," 122–24; and Galina Kogan, "Zabytyi roman.") The inclusion of such material in the novel helped stimulate a subgenre of Dostoevsky scholarship on the author's relation to folklore, and has contributed to a prevalent view of the text as especially valuable for its ethnographic content. On the notebook's value to Russian and Soviet ethnographers, to later Russian writers of the prison memoir subgenre, as well as to Dostoevsky himself in composing his subsequent novels, see the editors' comments at *PSS* 4:311–12. For a discussion of the oral poetry (as peasant song) contained in the text, see N. K. Piksanov, "Dostoevskii i fol'klor." For a discussion of the exiled revolutionaries' ("the would-be liberators of the Russian peasant") particular interest in folk culture, and especially the minority folk cultures of the empire, see Yuri Slezkine's fascinating study, *Arctic Mirrors*, esp. 123–29.

108. For a historical overview of the executioner in seventeenth- through nineteenth-century Russia, and particularly the ruling class's growing dependence on executioners (increasingly drawn from the convict class) to maintain the "spectacle of punishment" which made manifest the former's authority, see Schrader, *Languages of the Lash*, esp. 38–46. Schrader shows how, in the early nineteenth century, official defenses of the knout as a form of punishment appropriate to commoners (the people, or *narod*) depended on a view of the lower classes as lacking a sense of shame or honor. Common criminals, however, proved so resistant to recruitment as executioners on the grounds of moral opposition, even when offered material improvement of their own situations (and even after Nikolai I abolished use of the knout in 1845), that a revision of ideas concerning lower-class interiority was under way by mid-century. Schrader quotes Baron Modest Korf, for example, who summarized a Ministry of Internal Affairs investigation in the late 1850s of convicts' unwillingness to perform the service of the executioner, even if offered exemption from flogging, by saying, "convicts' reluctance . . . demonstrates that criminals manifest a vivid sense of shame. This suggests that they evince a lower level of moral decrepitude [than we once believed]. Sentencing a man to be an executioner for the rest of his life therefore constitutes inhumane moral torment. For some people, this is far worse than the harshest flogging" (quoted on 44 [emphases removed]; see also 49, 30).

109. The peasant-convicts' self-characterizations may be found at *PSS* 4:16, 181/18, 281; these are discussed at greater length in part 2. This identification of Gorianchikov with Shishkov is supported, too, by details of character: Shishkov also habitually displaces his own wrongdoing onto others against whom he nurtures a constant sense of grievance, and there is a distinct resemblance between the prefatory narrator's description of Gorianchikov's "other narrative" and Shishkov's tendency, in the midst of telling something, to "break off abruptly or wander off on to something else, be carried away by the details of the new subject and forget what he had begun to speak about" (*PSS* 4:166/255).

110. See Grossman, *Dostoevskii*, 248–49. Gary Rosenshield, in "Akul'ka: The Incarnation of the Ideal," follows Grossman's interpretation in speculating that "Akul'ka's Husband" represents an aborted romantic theme.

111. Frank, *Stir of Liberation*, 277, 228–29, 218. In *Through the Russian Prism*, Frank compares it in similar terms to the interpolated narrative of Jim Trueblood in Ralph Ellison's *The Invisible Man* (39–40).

112. See note 102, above. That this rumor was so tenaciously and widely credited (despite her own initial credulity, Dostoevsky's wife would complain that "this absurd rumor was very much believed by the Russian colony at Dresden during our stay there in 1869–1871") undermines the hypothesis that Dostoevsky meant for the prefatory narrator's charge of wife-murder to function as a transparent fiction whose very transparency would signal to the sophisticated reader the political nature of Gorianchikov's crime (*PSS* 22:345). Dostoevsky complained of his readers' "instinct" to confuse him with his fictitious personae from his first publication, the novella *Poor People*; see, for example, his letter of 1 February 1846 to his brother, M. M. Dostoevsky (*PSS* 28 [I]: 117–18). Pascal, in *Dostoïevski*, 291–94, discusses the tendency of the writer's first biographer, N. N. Strakhov, to identify Dostoevsky with his characters.

113. Mochulsky, *Dostoevsky*, 185.

114. See note 27, above.

115. Miliukov is quoted in Mochulsky, *Dostoevsky*, 185; his 1868 review is reprinted in Zelinskii, *Kriticheskii kommentarii*, 38. A. P. Mogilianskii, in "K istorii pervoi publikatsii *Zapisok iz mertvogo doma*," although he notes that initially Dostoevsky did express apprehension about censorship, claims on the evidence of statements made by A. S. Gieroglifov, editor of *Russkii mir*, that he experienced no significant problem with it; see, esp., 180.

116. Frank, *Stir of Liberation*, 218–20. In discussing the interpretive problem posed by the discrepant information offered by the prefatory narrator and Gorianchikov, he cautions that, since it can probably be explained by "the pressure [on Dostoevsky] of external circumstances," there is no reason "to impose more of an 'artistic' pattern on the narrative structure of *House of the Dead* than the evidence supports" (219). Tunimanov corroborates this view in *Tvorchestvo Dostoevskogo*, 75, 84. As Jackson points out, given that Gorianchikov's political crime becomes obvious in the course of the narrative, concern for censorship does not explain the discrepancy. He suggests that the introduction demonstrates that his narrative, "controlled and objective," must be "incomplete as an expression of Gorianchikov's whole personality." Moreover, the prefatory narrator's assertion that Gorianchikov murdered his wife, Jackson says in agreement with Grossman and Frank, represents an avenue that Dostoevsky "obviously abandoned." He also maintains, however, that these facts do not preclude Dostoevsky's regarding the introduction as "central to his artistic and spiritual design." He does not return in the course of his argument to clarify how the introduction can be both central and obsolete. See Jackson, *AD*, 34, 35. In an earlier article, however, he suggested that the introduction serves to purge the text of that part of Dostoevsky which heartily detested the peasant after his release from prison. I have been arguing, on the contrary, that the introduction foregrounds the part of Dostoevsky that heartily detested the peasant, specifically in the "person" of the prefatory narrator and through his claim that Gorianchikov murdered his wife.

117. Frank refers here to Turgenev, Aksakov, Tolstoy, and Herzen; see *Stir of Liberation*, 217. In my view, the important question relative to the role of censor-

ship is whether it had any decisive and productive influence (in actuality or only through Dostoevsky's anticipation) on the form of the text. For a discussion of the "positive" aspects of the Russian censorship in relation to Russian literary production, see Gary Saul Morson's introduction to Morson, ed., *Literature and History*, 20–21.

118. Arguing for the "intermixing" (*vmeshatel'stvo*) of art and documentary or autobiography, Shklovsky notes that the critical tendency to either/or generic determinations has produced diametrically opposed interpretations extending from the text's mood (pessimistic or optimistic?) to its structure (static or dynamic?) (*Za i protiv*, 101). This lack of consensus may be traced to the question: who emerges from prison, Gorianchikov (art) or Dostoevsky (autobiography)? If one concludes that it is Dostoevsky, then the prefatory narrator's words can be disregarded, and the critical reading will be optimistic. If, as Shklovsky believes, the aesthetic is privileged over the autobiographical, then the outcome is pessimistic: thus Shklovsky maintains that "a dead man was unfettered" at the novel's end (*Povesti o proze*, 197; Shklovsky includes in this volume entire sections from his earlier study, *Za i protiv*). Elizabeth Anne Cole, in a study of conversion and its relation to genre in Dostoevsky, reads *House of the Dead* as establishing a context for subsequent works of Russian prison literature, particularly with reference to autobiographical texts in which "the self is not the primary object" ("Towards a Poetics of Russian Prison Literature," 11). See also Leona Toker, "Toward a Poetics of Documentary Prose—from the Perspective of Gulag Testimonies." Toker examines the writings of Varlam Shalamov about his experience in the Soviet gulag as (quoting Shalamov) a "new prose [. . .] not the prose of the document but the prose of the ordeal borne out as a document." Toker explains that the phrase intends "a rejection of the therapeutic effect that writing may have on the author" (writing is intended to reopen rather than close wounds); "the preservation of evidence despite the psychological and social pressures to forgive and forget"; and a retrospective "processing of experience" as "a *form of art*" (188).

119. Tunimanov, *Tvorchestvo Dostoevskogo*, 83, 80. Serman also downplays the importance of Gorianchikov as an independent character and of the prefatory narrator as well. He states that Dostoevsky gave himself the role of discoverer and publisher of Gorianchikov's notes (that is, Dostoevsky is the prefatory narrator), which were always intended to be the notes of an "unknown" so that the focus could remain squarely on the people. He bases his claim that Dostoevsky meant to keep the memoir impersonal on the writer's discussion of his ideas for the book in the letter to Maikov of 18 January 1856 and to his brother Mikhail on 9 October 1859. Serman does concede that Dostoevsky breaks his own rule immediately, only following it to the extent that he makes no mention of his own "crime," the Petrashevsky affair; see "Tema narodnosti," esp. 122, 140.

120. Marius Teofilov, "Pererastanie dokumental'nogo materiala v khudozhestvennyi v *Zapiskakh iz mertvogo doma* F. M. Dostoevskogo." Through Gorianchikov, however, Dostoevsky does represent himself in a "mediated" (*oposredstvovanno*) fashion, combining his own traits with those of a fictitious narrator (16).

121. Jackson, at times, seems to reverse the association of Gorianchikov with fiction and Dostoevsky with autobiography, as when he appears to consider Gorianchikov to be simply Dostoevsky purged of his ambivalence for the sake of an

accurate representation of *katorga* (*AD*, 355 n. 10); see also "The Narrator," 197–211. Miller is the critic who most successfully navigates these waters. In *Dostoevsky and "The Idiot,"* she writes that "Dostoevsky carefully separated himself from his narrator's point of view: autobiographical material must pass through the filter of a fictional character's personality" (24).

122. Frank, *Stir of Liberation*, 214, 218–19; *Years of Ordeal*, 114. The perceived necessity of containing Gorianchikov's personality in order not to compromise the objectivity of his representations is allied to a widespread critical assumption that the prefatory narrator, who describes himself only as the text's "publisher" (*izdatel'*), actually assumed the role of editor (*PSS* 4:195/303). (Vladimir Dal' differentiates the functions of "editor" [*redaktor*] and "publisher" [*izdatel'*] in his nineteenth-century *Tolkovyi slovar' zhivogo velikorusskogo iazyka*, 4:90 and 2:16–17, respectively.) Although he never claims to have engaged in the selection and ordering of the original notebook, many critics have insisted that he purged material from the published version. Shklovsky, for example, conjectures that the prefatory narrator deleted those sections of the original that he describes as "uneven and spasmodic," "strange" and "awful reminiscences"; merely by mentioning them in his introduction, he is able to suggest what underlies the "extraordinary restraint" with which Gorianchikov narrates even the most terrifying events (*Za i protiv*, 101). Tunimanov hypothesizes that the prefatory narrator excised the memoir's real ending, artificially concluding the published text with Gorianchikov's cry of victory upon his release (*Tvorchestvo Dostoevskogo*, 80). Neither critic acknowledges the degree to which pruning the manuscript must be tantamount to pruning the character and experience of Gorianchikov. Even if we find such conjectures about excised material plausible, we must inquire into the formal and ideological consequences of a relationship that allows the prefatory narrator to gainsay, appropriate, modify—to all appearances, misrepresent—the words of the memoirist. Relatedly, what critical purposes are served by assuming the editorially managed sanitation of an autobiographical manuscript?

123. Jackson, *AD*, 220; *PSS* 28 [1]: 169. For a discussion of how Dostoevsky's post-incarceration attitude toward the peasant differed from his pre-Siberian, romantic phase, see Frank, *Years of Ordeal*, 125–27. Tunimanov cautions against simplifying or telescoping Dostoevsky's spiritual-ideological evolution, and, in particular, his idealization of the peasants. Even scenes in *House of the Dead* such as those that depict the peasant-convicts' piety at the Lenten service must be regarded as "one vivid illustration in a series of others" and "for which the attempt at a single explanation is extremely unsatisfactory" (*Tvorchestvo Dostoevskogo*, 92, 90). See also Dale E. Peterson's ground-breaking comparative study, *Up from Bondage: The Literatures of Russian and African American Soul*, which notes how this text has been used to "buttress tendentious notions suggesting that [Dostoevsky] occupies a stable ideological position" (61). Cf. Malcolm Jones's conclusions, reasserted throughout his study, regarding Dostoevsky's religiosity in the biographical introduction to *Dostoevsky and the Dynamics of Religious Experience*, esp. 10, 23. See, finally, the indispensable James L. Rice, "Dostoevsky's Endgame."

124. Hudspith, for example, attributes Dostoevsky's use of multiple narrators to tell Gorianchikov's story to the necessity of "selective processing by a more objective personality" in the interests of producing "the wider picture of a people

transfigured" rather than the portrait of an embittered autobiographer (*Dostoevsky and the Idea of Russianness*, 179, 178). Smirnov argues that Dostoevsky makes use of a narrator in his prison memoirs as the sign of his self-estrangement, but as the narrative moves toward its conclusion, the narrator becomes increasingly identified with Dostoevsky—this is why Gorianchikov's crime is transformed from murder to political crime ("Otchuzhdenie-v-otchuzhdenii," 44).

125. J. M. Coetzee, "Confession and Double Thoughts," 194. See also Robin Feuer Miller, "Dostoevsky and Rousseau: The Morality of Confession Reconsidered." For an analysis of Miller's understanding of the confessional mode in Dostoevsky in relation to Bakhtin's, as well as a further look at Dostoevsky's view of Rousseau through a comparison of *House of the Dead* with "The Peasant Marei," see Harriet Murav, "Dostoevsky in Siberia: Remembering the Past."

126. Coetzee notes that, in the case of a "hyperconscious" narrator like the Underground Man who examines the modern disease of hyperconsciousness, every motive to confession conceals another motive making it impossible for the confessant to know why he wants to tell the truth about himself: "We are now beyond all questions of sincerity. The possibility we face is of a confession made via a process of relentless self-unmasking which might yet be not the truth but a self-serving fiction, because the unexamined, unexaminable principle behind it may be not a desire for the truth but a desire to *be a particular way*," a desire to be "perverse" ("Confession and Double Thoughts," 220–21). Robert L. Belknap's essay, "The Unrepentant Confession" is relevant here for its reading of a passage in *Notes from the Underground* against one in *The Brothers Karamazov* which draws out the difference between confession and apologia encapsulated by the term "unrepentant confession." See also the conclusion to this volume, note 45.

127. On the philosophical views of the Petrashevsky circle, see Andrzej Walicki, *History of Russian Thought from the Enlightenment to Marxism*, 152–61. Relevant here is Joseph Frank's discussion in *Stir of Liberation* of Dostoevsky's response to the program of "Young Russia" in 1862. This movement's widely disseminated pamphlet urged "a bloody and pitiless revolution" exceeding the French Terror in order to establish, first, a revolutionary dictatorship and, ultimately, a "Russian Social and Democratic Republic." Frank writes that the pamphlet and its rhetoric reminded Dostoevsky of his own revolutionary aspirations in the late 1840s as a member of a secret society that "had also coolly contemplated the possibility of mass slaughter" and dictatorial control. The particular shock Dostoevsky felt was in "seeing all this *openly* expressed; it was as if his buried past had risen up to confront him, and the secret he had so carefully guarded all these years—and would continue to guard for the remainder of his life—had finally been brought to light"; see 145–48, esp. 148. My point is that Dostoevsky did not keep the secret; instead, it provides the inside narrative of *House of the Dead*.

128. See my discussion of the gentrification of crime in part 2, section 4. Martinsen also locates Dostoevsky's unmasking of complicity at the heart of his narrative ethics. In *Surprised by Shame*, she traces the way in which, through the evocation of characters' experiences of shame, Dostoevsky implicates in their downfall the reader who colludes by uncritically accepting the conventions of social shaming (46–50).

129. Jackson suggests the propriety of characterizing the peasant as the nobility's "female" helpmate by pointing out that Akul'ka exemplifies "the most terrible kind of slavery" for Dostoevsky, where the "husband"—whom I identify with the master—plays the role of "property owner, executioner, and debauchee" (*Art of Dostoevsky*, 104).

130. See Frank's discussion of propagandistic texts written and translated by members of the Speshnev group, possibly including Dostoevsky, which were "couched in terms that peasants would understand and calculated to appeal to their mentality and values." Such texts, in the words of A. N. Pleshcheev (in whose home the Palm-Durov circle met), were intended "to stir up self-consciousness in the people [by] adapting them to the speech-style of the simple people" (*Seeds of Revolt*, 280; Speshnev quoted on 282). A particularly egregious form of such cultural arrogance and ignorance, Dostoevsky came to feel, was his concurrence with his mentor Vissarion Belinsky's representation of the religiosity of the peasant in his 1847 "Letter to Gogol." He begins in his journalistic polemics of the early 1860s to explore the link between this error and a false politics. On the course of this and other journalistic debates in which Dostoevsky avidly participated, see Nechaeva, *Zhurnal Vremia* and *Zhurnal Epokha*; and Kirpotin, *Dostoevskii-khudozhnik* and *Dostoevskii v shestidesiatye gody*.

131. Thus does Dostoevsky define the verb "*stushevat'sia*," a neologism he introduced in his early novella *The Double*, for which he claimed: "I have never advanced in literature anything more serious." See the November 1877 *Diary of a Writer* piece, "The History of the Verb *Stushevat'sia*," in *PSS* 26:65/1184. See also Evelyn Josiulko Harden's introduction to her translation of *The Double*, esp. xviii–xix and xxxv, nn. 46, 47, and 48.

Part II
Building Out the House of the Dead

1. Here and throughout, I use the Pevear and Volokhonsky translation of *The Idiot*; page numbers hereafter are provided in the text following those in *PSS*. Of just such a moment, Giorgio Agamben writes: "Like the fence of the camp, the interval between death sentence and execution delimits an extratemporal and extraterritorial threshold in which the human body is separated from its normal political status and abandoned, in a state of exception, to the most extreme misfortunes. In such a space of exception, subjection to experimentation can, like an expiation rite, either return the human body to life (pardon and the remission of a penalty are, it is worth remembering, manifestations of the sovereign power over life and death) or definitively consign it to the death to which it already belongs" (*Homo Sacer*, 159; hereafter, cited as *HS* in the text). The "experimentation" to which Agamben refers is that practiced by Nazi doctors on inhabitants of the concentration camps; in the present context, one thinks of the tsar's experimentation with the effects of a whimsical application of the death penalty.

2. Cf *PSS* 8:21/23 and 55/64. For an excellent reading of the temporality of this interval, see Sarah Young, *Dostoevsky's "The Idiot,"* 81–85. Dostoevsky explored the possibilities for the last moments of consciousness quite differently in

his 1873 story for *The Citizen* [*Grazhdanin*], "Bobok," in which the narrator, having fallen asleep in a graveyard, overhears not expressions of mystical terror but the hilariously unseemly conversation of the newly buried as they struggle to deal with their petty frustrations upon discovering that consciousness outlives (for a time) the body—ennui, the difficulties of asserting one's class status (or one's revolutionary fearsomeness) when one is decomposing, the impossibility of avoiding unpleasant social situations or making important social contacts when one lies immobile, and so forth (*PSS* 21:41–54). English translation available as *A Writer's Diary, Vol. 1: 1873–1876*, trans. Kenneth Lantz, 170–85; page numbers hereafter are provided in the text following those in *PSS*.

3. See part 1, notes 3 and 5. In "Crime and Punishment in the House of the Dead," Alan Wood notes that the Penal Code of 1845 [*Ulozhenie o nakazaniiakh*] divided criminal punishments into four grades, "all of which were accompanied by complete loss of the personal rights pertaining to one's social rank"; the first grade, the death penalty, could be pronounced by special supreme tribunals under extraordinary circumstances (222). The second grade was exile to penal servitude (*katorga*), for a minimum of four to six years followed by perpetual exile. Siberian exiles lived not under a civilian penal code but rather the brutal Exile Regulations [*Ustav o ssyl'nykh*]; see 222–24.

4. A member of the court that tried the Petrashevtsy put it otherwise: the tsar had staged the mock execution in order to demonstrate mercy: "the sovereign likes to pardon," the official explained. Quoted in John L. Evans, *The Petrasevskij Circle*, 103.

5. On nineteenth-century Russian Orientalism, see Orlando Figes, *Natasha's Dance*, chap. 6, 355–430; Mark Bassin, *Imperial Visions*; and Susan Layton, *Russian Literature and Empire*. Post-1865 Orientalism is compellingly analyzed by Yuri Slezkine, *Arctic Mirrors*. For eighteenth-century antecedents to Russian Orientalism and the literary-historical consequences of imperial expansion, see Harsha Ram, *The Imperial Sublime*.

6. See his 6 November 1854 letter to his brother, Andrei: "Those four years seem to me a time in which I was buried alive and shut up in the grave. It is not in my power to tell you what a terrible time that was, my friend. The suffering was inexpressible, interminable, because every hour, every minute weighed like a stone on my spirit. In the entire four years there was not one moment when I didn't feel that I was in *katorga*. But what a thing to talk about! Even if I were to write you a hundred pages, even then you wouldn't be able to understand what my life was then. One has to see it for oneself, at the very least—not to say to experience it. But that time has passed and is now behind me, like a bad dream, just as my release from *katorga* seemed to me before like a radiant awakening and resurrection into a new life" (*PSS* 28 [I]: 181).

7. Dostoevsky used such expressions frequently to describe his state and that of his fellow convicts throughout the years of penal servitude and exile. See, for example, the letters to his brother, Mikhail, of 6 November 1854 (*PSS* 28 [I]: 181) and 21 August 1855 (*PSS* 28 [I]: 193).

8. Agamben cites Roman lexicographer Sextus Pompeius Festus's treatise *On the Significance of Words*—"*At homo sacer is est, quem populus iudiavit ob ma-*

leficium"—in which "the character of sacredness is tied for the first time to a human life as such."

9. Agamben develops the concept of "bare life" from the appearance of the term in Walter Benjamin's "Critique of Violence" and from a close parallel ("real life") in Carl Schmitt's *Political Theology*; see *HS* 63–67.

10. Agamben, in his discussion of how the juridico-political order is constituted by what it excludes, writes of the "exception that defines the structure of sovereignty": "Here what is outside is included not simply by means of an interdiction or an internment, but rather by means of the suspension of the juridical order's validity—by letting the juridical order, that is, withdraw from the exception and abandon it" (*HS* 18). As Julia Kristeva argues (see part 1, note 11), Dostoevsky strongly felt his abandonment as the withdrawal of order and represents *katorga* as the place where law and violence, joined by sovereign decree, become indistinguishable. See note 13, below.

11. P. Ia. Chaadaev specified the place of composition for his "First Philosophical Letter" ("Lettres sur la philosophie de l'histoire. Lettre première") as "Necropolis," marking all of Nicolaen Russia as a space of exception. The letter conveys a powerful sense of Russia's chronotopic specificity: a vast space abandoned by culture where time has stopped. See also part 1, note 20.

12. Dostoevsky's letter to his brother Mikhail (30 January/22 February 1854) continues: "They would have devoured us if given the chance. But you can imagine for yourself how protected we were when we had to live, sleep, eat, and drink side by side with these people for several years" (*PSS* 28 [I]: 169–70/59). Whether Dostoevsky was flogged (and this precipitated his epilepsy) has been long debated. Konstantin Mochulsky cites it as "legend": "the prisoners thought that he had died—from this came his nickname 'the corpse' " (*Dostoevsky*, 149). Although Mochulsky notes that the story was refuted, he dates Dostoevsky's first epileptic seizures to his imprisonment. Jacques Catteau (*Dostoevsky and the Process of Literary Creation*, 105) cites two sources linking the emergence of Dostoevsky's epilepsy to the threat of being flogged. A Dr. Riesenkampf who visited Omsk in 1851 was told by the prison doctor that "one day, Dostoevsky, ill, was lying on his bunk instead of working like the other convicts and the terrible major of the fortress, Krivtsov, the wild beast in human form depicted in *House of the Dead*, burst into the cell and threatened him with flogging. This flogging is supposed to have taken place and caused the first fit of epilepsy." The second source, P. K. Martianov, who interviewed cadets serving at Omsk, claimed that "Dostoevsky, according to a marine guard who was discreetly looking after him, had stayed in his bunk because he had previously been the victim of an epileptic fit, and for this reason the flogging had been prevented by General de Grave, commander of the fortress of Omsk, and Krivtsov had been reproved." Catteau points out, however, that Dostoevsky's first letter to Mikhail mentions only Krivtsov's numerous threats of flogging. Cf. M. M. Gromyko, *Sibirskie znakomye i druz'ia F. M. Dostoevskogo*, chap. 3, "Oshibka Rizenkampfa [Rizenkampf's mistake]," 40–51. Irina Reyfman analyzes Dostoevsky's anxieties about corporal punishment in *Ritualized Violence Russian Style*, 133–34, 196–99.

13. Grossman (*Dostoevskii*) writes that the "prison authorities received 'the instructions' to consider 'the political convict Dostoevsky' a prisoner in the fullest

sense of the word without any leniency whatsoever," and quotes a Soviet historian of the tsarist prisons, M. N. Gernet, who wrote, "It is astounding that the writer did not perish there. The precept of prison administrations of that time required making the prison a place of nothing but deprivation and suffering," adding that prisoners survived only through a "persistent struggle to live" (169). Grossman notes that Sergei Durov, Dostoevsky's fellow Petrashevets who was also incarcerated in Omsk, and who had "arrived there "young and cheerful," was released "decrepit, grey-haired, short-winded, and barely able to walk" (176).

14. I have in mind characters from Raskolnikov—Dostoevsky's first theorist of the "all is permitted" doctrine, who wants to see his victim as "the most utterly useless louse" (*PSS* 6:211/275) whom he has the right to kill—to the peasant boy whimsically, brutally killed by his master for accidentally wounding his favorite hunting dog's paw and whose death persuades Ivan Karamazov to reject a future divine harmony. For Agamben, the Jew is the twentieth century's ultimate *homo sacer*, whom Hitler killed "as lice" and whose "extermination took place [in] neither religion nor law but biopolitics" (*HS* 114). The Nazi and Stalinist camps are "pure" materializations of the "space of exception" in which (quoting a survivor cited by Hannah Arendt) " 'everything is possible' " (*HS* 134, 170).

15. The unique spatio-temporal character of *katorga* is strongly marked in the novel's opening chapters. Gorianchikov notices, for example, how a convict mastered time by counting off pales in the hexagonal stockade so that "he could see at a glance how many days still remained for him to spend in prison"; he "was genuinely happy when he came to the end of any of the sides of the hexagon" despite the remaining years of incarceration (*PSS* 4:9–10/8). M. M. Bakhtin's classic presentation of his neologism "chronotope" as a formally constitutive literary category appears in "Forms of Time and of the Chronotope in the Novel," in *Dialogic Imagination*, 84–258.

16. Agamben clarifies the relationship of abandonment to captivity in the life of *homo sacer* (as incarcerated exile): "What has been banned is delivered over to its own separateness and, at the same time, consigned to the mercy of the one who abandons it—at once excluded and included, removed and at the same time captured" (*HS* 110).

17. "Siberian Notebook" [*Sibirskaia tetrad'*], no. 411.

18. Richard S. Wortman describes the reign of Nicholas I as "a last effort to make good on the absolutist promise" (*Development of a Russian Legal Consciousness*, 42). On Nicholas I's reign, see also Nicholas Riasanovsky, *Nicholas I and Official Nationality in Russia*, and W. Bruce Lincoln, *Nicholas I: Emperor and Autocrat of All the Russias*. Abby M. Schrader warns against drawing "whiggish interpretations of modernization" from Alexander's reforms: "the potential for reform was not exclusively linked to the emergence of structures related to capitalism and so-called modernity but was also rooted in official political culture" (*Languages of the Lash*, 7).

19. Alexander first announced his intention to abolish serfdom in March 1856 in a speech to the landed gentry of Moscow and, after a period of five years in which the legislation was prepared, signed the emancipation statutes into law on 19 February 1861. See the introduction to this volume, note 46.

20. See the introduction, note 6.

21. Wood, "Solzhenitsyn on the Tsarist Exile System: A Historical Comment," 41. Solzhenitsyn, "The History of Our Sewage Disposal System," in *Gulag Archipelago*, 24–98.

22. Agamben explains that he is not advancing the "idea of an inner solidarity between democracy and totalitarianism" as "a historiographical claim, which would authorize the liquidation and levelling of the enormous differences that characterize their history and their rivalry. Yet this idea must nevertheless be strongly maintained on a historico-philosophical level" (*HS* 10). See also note 45, below. Cf. Claude Lefort's account of the contiguity between democracy and totalitarianism in "The Logic of Totalitarianism" (*Political Forms of Modern Society*, 273–92) and "The Question of Democracy" (*Democracy and Political Theory*, 9–20). See also Jacob L. Talman, *Origins of Totalitarian Democracy*.

23. Agamben here responds to Walter Benjamin's dictum in the eighth of his "Theses on the Philosophy of History": "The tradition of the oppressed teaches us that the 'state of emergency' in which we live is not the exception but the rule. We must attain to a conception of history that is in keeping with this insight" (*Illuminations*, 257).

24. On the history of the Russian camp, see Gernet, *Istoriia tsarskoi tiur'my*.

25. Agamben's analysis in *Homo Sacer* begs this question, since he invokes instances of the politicization of bare life much farther beyond the West's orbit than Russia which, at least since Peter the Great, has developed in explicit dialectic tension with Europe. In his most recent book, *State of Exception*, Agamben states unambiguously that "the modern state of exception is a creation of the democratic-revolutionary tradition and not the absolutist one," but this does not clarify things, for the "democratic-revolutionary tradition" is itself fractured, as Arendt demonstrates in *On Revolution* (5). See also Talman, *Origins of Totalitarian Democracy*.

26. The bibliography on the history of Russian slavery is vast. I have found Peter Kolchin's *Unfree Labor* particularly useful.

27. Quoted in Richard Wortman, "Property Rights, Populism, and Russian Political Culture," in Olga Crisp and Linda Edmondson, eds., *Civil Rights in Imperial Russia*, 13–32, esp. 16.

28. The cited phrase is Herzen's quoted in Venturi, *Roots of Revolution*, 21.

29. Pearson continues, "To the tsarist functionary, 'legal' continued to mean (to quote clause 47 of the Fundamental Laws) 'on the firm basis of positive laws, institutions and charters established by autocratic authority.' As a consequence, the tsarist government never relinquished its view of total authority over its 'subjects' [*poddannye*], implicitly scorning the notion of 'citizens' [*grazhdane*] with their inalienable 'rights' and therefore conditional loyalty." See "Privileges, Rights, and Russification," in Crisp and Edmondson, *Civil Rights in Imperial Russia*, 92–93. Relatedly, Marc Raeff observed that "Russian reality and historical heritage were those of arbitrary autocracy and bureaucratic tyranny; introduction of real legality could only mean the overthrow of the existing regime, the abolition of traditional state power and political authority" (*Political Ideas and Institutions in Imperial Russia*, 35). Lincoln offers a history of the slow and incomplete transition from the "unchecked power" of the autocracy (*proizvol*) to the concept of

lawfulness (*zakonnost'*) from the time of Catherine to the mid-nineteenth-century reforms in *Great Reforms,* esp. chaps. 1 and 4.

30. See part 1, note 41.

31. Cf. the observations of Solzhenitsyn's character, Shukhov, on the equality of camp inmates in *One Day in the Life of Ivan Denisovich.*

32. I cite Thomas Carl Wall's provocative essay on Agamben, "Au Hasard," 40.

33. Wood, "Crime and Punishment in the House of the Dead," 217, 221. See part 1, note 34.

34. Grossman's account of Dostoevsky's pre-exile, eight-month incarceration (four in solitary confinement) is resonant here. He was kept in the " 'secret' " house or dungeon of the Peter and Paul Fortress, the Alexeevsky Ravelin, reserved for the most dangerous political prisoners (the Decembrists were also put there, along with the eighteenth-century abolitionist Alexander Radishchev and the tsarevich Alexis, Peter the Great's son whom he executed). Here "prisoners lost their first and family names, receiving a cell number instead. Life here was entirely regulated by the Tsar's orders. The arbitrariness of the prison administration knew no limits. They permitted no inspections and no controls. The inmates were considered to be buried alive" (*Dostoevskii,* 135–36). Frank ameliorates this picture somewhat (*Years of Ordeal,* 12–15, 19–21), noting that after several months the Petrashevtsy were permitted to receive books and journals and to write letters.

35. Levi, *The Drowned and the Saved,* 21 (cf. 19), 131; hereafter, cited as *DS* in the text.

36. In *Essays in Understanding,* Arendt writes of the "extraordinary difficulty which we have in attempting to understand the institution of the concentration camp and to fit it into the record of human history" (234). The phrase "fabrication of corpses" appears in her 1964 interview with Günter Gaus (1–23, esp. 13–14). Subsequent citations appear in an article in the same volume entitled "Social Science Techniques and the Study of Concentration Camps," 238, 243.

37. Arendt, *Essays in Understanding,* 233; hereafter, cited in the text as *EU.* Although Arendt footnotes the Boer War as the occasion of the first concentration camps, she does not argue that they constitute the first stage (245 n. 12). Agamben claims that if "the essence of the camp consists in the materialization of the state of exception and in the subsequent creation of a space in which bare life and the juridical rule enter into a threshold of indistinction, then we must admit that we find ourselves virtually in the presence of a camp every time such a structure is created, independent of the kinds of crime that are committed there." In this sense, the Nazi camps are not unique; Agamben lists subsequent lesser manifestations of this "essence," including "the *zones d'attentes* in French international airports in which foreigners asking for refugee status are detained" and, in his recent book, *Spaces of Exception,* in the American prison at Guantánamo Bay (*HS* 174).

38. Levi, *Survival in Auschwitz,* 138, 143. Hereafter, cited in text as *SA.* Gorianchikov notes in *House of the Dead* that although prison authorities were not permitted to show prisoners from the nobility any indulgence, they did so once in sending him and another gentleman-convict for three months "as clerks into the Engineers' office" (*PSS* 4:214/333).

39. *Homo sacer* was not always divorced from crime. Agamben notes that the Roman lexicographer who brought the figure forward from ancient Roman law

described him as "one whom the people have judged on account of a crime," and he remarks that, in Pompeius Festus's treatise, "the character of sacredness is tied for the first time to a human life as such" (*HS* 71). That the character of sacredness is tied to one associated with crime is of no interest to Agamben; the aporia of *homo sacer*'s existence has nothing to do with the crime he was judged to have committed and everything to do with the a priori crime of sovereignty. Biopolitics reaches its apotheosis in modernity with the totalitarian camps of the twentieth century where, generally speaking, there can be, of course, no question of the inmates' criminality: *homo sacer* in this case is the pure and absolute victim of the pure and absolute state of exception.

40. Wood, "Crime and Punishment in the House of the Dead," 221, 228.

41. Ibid., 224.

42. Herzen discussed this scene in an article in *The Bell* [*Kolokol*] (15 May 1863), titled "What are they so afraid of?" [*"Chego oni tak ispugalis'?"*]. He cites a conservative Moscow journal which recommended that if Polish insurgents were not responding to administrative forms of coercion, Russia should initiate indiscriminate killing. Zherebiatnikov personifies the casual brutality of Russia's disregard for the law (*Sobranie sochinenii v tridzati tomakh*, 17:141).

43. On *katorga* as a "prison of nations" and the religious significance of this metaphor for Dostoevsky, see V. V. Borisova, "O natzional'no-religioznykh aspektakh *Zapisok iz mertvogo doma* F. M. Dostoevskogo."

44. On the distinction between phenomenal and historical, see Wall's discussion of Robert Antelme's *The Human Race*, particularly his interpretation of Antelme's account of the survivor's inability to speak: "From the anonymity of surviving in the camps to the personality of living in the world, one must take on the first person. . . . The experience they [the survivors] had had, Antelme says, 'was still going forward in our bodies.' Their bodies were still phenomenal, not yet historical" ("Au Hasard," 33).

45. Indeed, Agamben identifies this last vision as "modern democracy's specific aporia." He continues: "To become conscious of this aporia is not to belittle the conquests and accomplishments of democracy. It is, rather, to try to understand once and for all why democracy, at the very moment in which it seemed to have finally triumphed over its adversaries and reached its greatest height, proved itself incapable of saving *zoe*, to whose happiness it had dedicated all its efforts, from unprecedented ruin. Modern democracy's decadence and gradual convergence with totalitarian states [. .] may well be rooted in this aporia, which marks the beginning of modern democracy and forces it into complicity with its most implacable enemy" (*HS* 10).

46. Power (cultural and even political) through abjection, however, is not foreign to Western culture, particularly when the liberal ethos was not yet consolidated. For an analysis of this dynamic in colonial American culture and its translation in the course of the revolutionary period into a foundational national-literary paradigm, see Nancy Ruttenburg, *Democratic Personality*.

47. It should be noted that Agamben here, as elsewhere, borrows concepts from Schmitt but changes their significance.

48. Solzhenitsyn, *Gulag Archipelago* (67, 60). He refers specifically to Article 58 of the nongeneral division of the Criminal Code of 1926, whose "broadest dialectical interpretation" made its sphere of reference virtually limitless (71).

49. In his essay "Form-of-Life," Agamben defines that term as "a life that can never be separated from its form, a life in which it is never possible to isolate something such as naked life," in contrast to political power "as we know it [which] always founds itself [. .] on the separation of a sphere of naked life from the context of the forms of life" (*Means without End*, 3, 4).

50. Kalliopi Nikolopoulou, review of *Homo Sacer*, 128.

51. Levi, *SA* 87. Levi says of the epithet *"Muselmann"* that it was used for reasons unknown to him "by the old ones of the camp to describe the weak, the inept, those doomed to selection" (88 n.). In *Remnants of Auschwitz*, Agamben provides a selection of survivor testimonies and other texts in which the term appears, and concludes that it probably referred to the literal meaning of the Arabic word "muslim—the one who submits unconditionally to the will of God," although "the *Muselmann* of Auschwitz is instead defined by a loss of all will and consciousness" (45); hereafter, cited in text as *RA*. Perhaps the limit that exists between the *Muselmann* and the other inmates of the camps—the limit between the experience of being human and the experience of not being human—is articulated in Gorianchikov's definition of man after he surveys the horrific life of *katorga*'s inmates: "Man is a creature who can get used to anything" (*PSS* 4:10/9). It makes no sense to say that the *Muselmann* has gotten used to his or her life.

52. Agamben attributes the phrase "the third realm" to Wolfgang Sofsky in *Order of Terror*, 294.

53. Agamben writes that the space of the camps "can even be represented as a series of concentric circles that, like waves, incessantly wash up against a central non-place, where the *Muselmann* lives. [. .] The entire population of the camp is, indeed, nothing other than an immense whirlpool obsessively spinning around a faceless center" (*RA* 51–52).

54. Agamben concludes *RA* by differentiating the drowned, the saved, and the witness: "the remnants of Auschwitz—the witnesses—are neither the dead nor the survivors, neither the drowned nor the saved. They are what remains between them"; they are, therefore, the human corollary of messianic time, which is neither historical time nor eternity but their disjunction (164).

55. See Josh Cohen, review of *Homo Sacer* and *Remnants of Auschwitz*, esp. 385. Agamben describes the *Muselmann* as "catastrophe of the subject" (*RA*, 148).

56. It is worth noting that the survivor combines in this way and to this purpose with non-survivors who are not *Muselmänner*, a point Agamben develops in connection with the theme of shame. He cites the testimony of Robert Antelme concerning a young student from Bologna who blushes—"a mute apostrophe flying through time to reach us, to bear witness to him"—in the instant he realizes he is about to be shot by an SS guard (*RA* 103–4).

57. This claim is proven in the excerpts of testimony from survivors who had been *Muselmänner* and lived to write about it, testimonies with which Agamben concludes *RA*.

58. Levi writes that the *Muselmann* "accept[ed] the eclipse of the word," "an ominous symptom" that "signaled the approach of definitive indifference." But a small minority, "solitary by nature, or already habituated to isolation in their 'civilian' life, gave no sign of suffering from it" (*DS* 101).

59. Agamben discusses the redemptive aspects of the incapacity to speak, in *RA* 159–65.

60. Cohen, review of *Homo Sacer*, 383.

61. See Agamben, "Bartleby, or On Contingency," in *Potentialities*, 243–71. Daniel Heller-Roazen's introduction to this volume is notable for its lucid exposition of the terms and stakes of Agamben's argument which contextualize his reading of "Bartleby."

62. Agamben unfolds the specific significance of contingency to testimony in *RA*, 145–46.

63. The narrator of "Bartleby" claims that "it is fit I make some mention of myself, my *employés*, my business, my chambers, and general surroundings; because some such description is indispensable to an adequate understanding of the chief character about to be presented." Yet that description does not allow the reader to understand Bartleby himself but only how irremediably alien he is. See Melville, "Bartleby," 40.

64. This includes the lawyer, who describes himself as immune from the "proverbially energetic and nervous" spirit of the legal profession, as one of "those unambitious lawyers" happy to settle in to "the cool tranquillity of a snug retreat" in order to "do a snug business among rich men's bonds" (Melville, "Bartleby," 40).

65. Nowhere is this more powerfully dramatized than in Melville's novella *Benito Cereno*. See Eric Sundquist's brilliant essay, "Suspense and Tautology in *Benito Cereno*."

66. Nikolopoulou describes Agamben as driven "to imagine a completely uncharted horizon of politics, a politics outside its most essential prerogative: the existence of relations" (128).

67. Melville's narrator says of Bartleby, "While, of other law-copyists, I might write the complete life, of Bartleby nothing of that sort can be done. I believe that no materials exist, for a full and satisfactory biography of this man" (39).

68. The lawyer, in fact, resembles the prefatory narrator of *Notes from the House of the Dead*, who also vainly attempts a relationship with the eccentric Gorianchikov but whose "kindness" goes unappreciated by the one whose death alone puts an end to these overtures. Like the prefatory narrator, the lawyer's "curiosity" about his eccentric acquaintance cannot ultimately be satisfied (Melville, "Bartleby," 73).

69. Melville, *Billy Budd*, 97.

70. Cf. *PSS* 4:48/68, where Gorianchikov describes how the prisoners make themselves at home in the barracks at night once the doors are locked. Solzhenitsyn's Schukov also remarks on the oddity of the convicts reference to the barracks as "home," but he explains that "their days were too full to remember any other home" (*One Day in the Life of Ivan Denisovich*, 132).

71. Frank discusses Dostoevsky's treatment of the dreamer and of dreaming (*mechtatel'nost'*) as a symptom of the social malaise characteristic of Nicolaen Russia (*Seeds of Revolt*, 234–38).

72. Levi, *DS* 17; see also 84, where Levi notes the Russian term for the privileged in the Stalinist gulag cited by Solzhenitsyn, the *pridurki*.

73. I have changed the Italian word *la coscienza*, rendered as "conscience" in the Woolf translation of *SA*, to "consciousness," because Levi clearly alludes here to self-awareness rather than self-judgment. See *Se questo è un uomo*, 178. Thanks to my colleague, Daniel Javitch, for confirming my sense of the word's meaning. Prisoners of the Stalinist gulag also comment in their testimonies on the particular torment of memories of "the world outside prison bars" evoked without warning (E. S. Ginzburg, *Journey into the Whirlwind*, 248).

74. Gorianchikov reports that the Engineers who oversaw the convicts' labor were willing to lighten the labor performed by noble convicts but had to keep their actions a secret from the higher authorities (*PSS* 4:80). He maintains, further, that in practice noble convicts continued to receive some protection despite the formal deprivation of their caste privileges largely because of the influence of the Decembrists, which continued to be felt twenty-five years after their Siberian exile (*PSS* 4:212). See part 1, note 41.

75. Levi discusses the special difficulties for the cultivated man in the camp in "The Intellectual in Auschwitz" (*DS*) and in "The Canto of Ulysses" (*SA*).

76. Agamben briefly considers the possibility of casting the space of exception as a space of knowledge, grounded in mediation, rather than as an absolute space— "the pure immediacy of a juridical power" in Schmitt's words—created by the sovereign ban (*HS* 32–33).

77. The first indication of Gorianchikov's status as a "political" comes from Akim Akimovich, who informs him early on that the peasant-convicts "don't like the noblemen, especially the politicals" (*PSS* 4:28/35). Later, during the peasant-convicts' grievance from which they bar the noblemen, a disgruntled Gorianchikov is told by one of his peers, "Remember why we were sent here. They'll simply be flogged, but we shall be tried" (*PSS* 4:203/316).

78. Martin Jay, *Downcast Eyes*, 263.

79. Raskol'nikov, in the epilogue to *Crime and Punishment*, rejects the view of his crime as evildoing (*zlodeianie*), although he realizes he has broken the law. His crime, in his view, was that he could not sustain his commitment to his right to take power, and his remorse is restricted to the weakness that drove him to break down and confess (*PSS* 6:417). On crime as "baseness," see *PSS* 4:142/218.

80. Such stylized behavior is at times positively motivated, as when Gorianchikov interprets the solemn mood of the convicts at Christmas as evincing an unconscious awareness that it brought each of them "into contact with the whole world, that therefore he was not completely an outcast, a lost soul, a severed fragment, that even in prison it was the same as with regular people. They felt this; it was visible and understood" (*PSS* 4:105/157). Dostoevsky identified the most difficult aspect of his incarceration as the constant company of others in a letter to Natalia D. Fonvizina of late January/20 February 1854 (*PSS* 28 [1]: 175–77).

81. See *Crime and Punishment* (part 3, chap. 6), *PSS* 6:211; emphasis in original.

82. For Gorianchikov, the noble-convict Aristov negatively embodies the all-is-permitted ethos by exemplifying "how far the corporal side of a person could go, unrestrained by any internal standard or any lawfulness." Gorianchikov judges him to be simply a "piece of meat, with teeth and a stomach, and with an unquenchable thirst for the grossest and most bestial physical pleasures, and for the satisfaction of the least and most capricious of these pleasures he was capable of the most cold-blooded imaginable murder, mutilation, in a word, anything, as long as he could hide the results" (*PSS* 4:63/90).

83. On the genre of Menippean satire, its history and its contribution to the novel and associated genres from antiquity, see M. M. Bakhtin, *Problems of Dostoevsky's Poetics*, chap. 4, esp. 126–30 on carnivalistic laughter.

84. Wood supports Gorianchikov's observation ("Crime and Punishment in the House of the Dead," 215–33).

85. The dawning on the nobleman's consciousness of the fact of his crime and its consequences is the subject of Tolstoy's last novel, *Resurrection* [*Voskresenie*] (1899). On the ideological and thematic closeness of *Notes from the House of the Dead* and *Resurrection*, see M. P. Nikolaev, *L. N. Tolstoi i N. G. Chernyshevskii*, 51–59. On the closeness of Gorianchikov's sentiments here to the official rationale for protecting the nobility from corporal punishment, see the conclusion to this volume, note 47.

86. In a discussion of Socrates and the problem of understanding evil and ugliness, Hannah Arendt writes that they are "excluded by definition from the thinking concern, although they may occasionally turn up as deficiencies, as lack of beauty, injustice, and evil [*kakia*] as lack of good. This means that they have no roots of their own, no essence of which thought could get hold. Evil, we are told, cannot be done voluntarily because of its 'ontological status,' as we would say today; it consists in an absence, in something that is not. If thinking dissolves normal, positive concepts into their original meaning, then the same process dissolves these negative 'concepts' into their original meaninglessness, into nothing" ("Thinking and Moral Considerations" in *Responsibility and Judgment*, 159–89, esp. 179).

87. See part 1, note 131. Dostoevsky's neologism connects the abjection of the peasant criminal on the scaffold to the abject and mad civil servant Goliadkin of "The Double."

88. Gorianchikov notes that, among members of the educated class, only doctors share the common people's instinctive and unconscious understanding of "misfortune" and are thus beloved by prisoners throughout Russia even though they identify the doctors as "gentlemen" (*PSS* 4:46, 142/64, 217).

89. See Gary Saul Morson's useful introduction to *A Writer's Diary, Vol. 1: 1873–1876*, trans. Kenneth Lantz, 1–117. The 1873 essays appeared that year as a regular column in the conservative journal *Grazhdanin* [*The Citizen*], edited by Dostoevsky.

90. On the jury reforms, particularly the mixed-class juries, see Murav, *Russia's Legal Fictions*, chap. 2; for a slightly later period, see Alexander K. Afanas'ev, "Jurors and Jury Trials in Imperial Russia, 1866–1885." On the development of a legal consciousness among the people, see Joan Neuberger, "Popular Legal Cultures: The St. Petersburg *Mirovoi Sud*."

91. The paradoxical logic of the popular concept of "misfortune"—as agency becomes less assignable, responsibility becomes more universal—receives its fullest expression in *The Brothers Karamazov*, where Dmitri willingly takes responsibility for the death of his father even though he did not actually kill him.

92. Sarah Hudspith accounts for this difference by proposing that "as the painful memory of the prison camp faded, and as Dostoevsky's views of the Russian people crystallized, he came to readjust his former pessimistic opinion" of the people. My point here is that we abet the fading of memory by allowing our perception of this crystallization to obscure the complex evolution of the writer's populist ideology; Hudspith suggests as much when she cautions against the assumption that Dostoevsky emerged from *katorga* with "a fully formed new set of beliefs" (*Dostoevsky and the Idea of Russianness*, 31, 37).

93. Cf. John Jones's account of the aesthetic advances Dostoevsky realized from the "I/We/They/Everybody flexibility" of narration in *House of the Dead* (*Dostoevsky*, chap. 5). Jones describes the "extreme restlessness" in the stories of the 1840s "over straightforward first-person and third-person narrative" which led to the narratological experimentation in the 1861 novel.

94. The actual case on which Dostoevsky based his article was that of the peasant N. A. Saiapin in September 1872. Murav points out that, whereas in *House of the Dead*, "the narrator's need to know is insatiable, but never satisfied, and the work ends without the closure even of a figurative brotherhood between the narrator and the ordinary prisoners," in *Diary of a Writer*, Dostoevsky represents himself through the persona of the diarist as knowing more than the experts and thus "uncertainty, fear, and even longing are spent" (*Russia's Legal Fictions*, 140–41). For her account of Dostoevsky's representation of the Saiapin case in relation to two other notorious cases, see 125–55.

95. William Mills Todd III shows how, in *Brothers Karamazov*, characters "emphatically reject" the finalizing components of stories of the self, positively in the cases of Zosima and Alyosha. The relationship of "self" to "story" in the context of crime as elaborated in both *House of the Dead* and "The Environment" is perhaps the ultimate example of what Todd calls Dostoevsky's "*negative* poetics for stories of the self": the story that exists only to reiterate the accomplishment of a death represents the literal finalization of character ("Storied Selves," 278, 279). As Homi Bhabha puts it in *Location of Culture*, "the subject is graspable only in the passage between telling/told, between 'here' and 'somewhere else,' and in this double scene the very condition of cultural knowledge is the alienation of the subject" (150).

96. Coetzee, "Confession and Double Thoughts," 194. See also Robin Feuer Miller, "Dostoevsky and Rousseau: The Morality of Confession Reconsidered."

97. See Gerhard Richter's discussion of "allegorical enactment" in Benjamin, whose "abiding interest in reevaluating the theory of allegory" is reflected in his effort "to read political concepts according to the disruptive force of allegorical figuration itself" (*Walter Benjamin and the Corpus of Autobiography*, esp. 21, 22).

98. Akul'ka has been described by critics as an iconic figure—an allegory for the Christian value of unconditional forgiveness situated at the heart of peasant life. But her desubjectification in a remote Russian village—the empire's ubiquitous space of exception, internal and invisible, abandoned by law—is strongly indi-

viduated. Thus, her sole prerogative in her story is to declare not just her forgiveness of but also her love for the liar who has gratuitously destroyed her life, sending her abusive and jealous husband into a murderous rage. There is nothing beatific about her self-sacrifice. Cherevin's wife, too, although her role is brief, is individuated. Cherevin tells Shishkov that when he beat her she would scream, " 'I'll wash your feet and drink the water.' " If she qualifies as the narrative's most abject character, she is nevertheless named—"They called her Avdotya"—and this naming, which both acknowledges the singularity of this sufferer and heightens our sense of her anonymity, concludes "Akul'ka's Husband" (*PSS* 4:173/267). The topos of feet washing is bizarrely reversed when, in the bathhouse, the peasant-convict Petrov, whom Gorianchikov considers perhaps the most dangerous man in the prison and who has taken it upon himself to cultivate a friendship with the nobleman, offers to "wash your little feet"; see section 5, below.

99. Frank, "Dostoevsky and Evil," 272.

100. See also part 1, note 12. One finds the "unconsummated image" elsewhere in the great novels, for example, the image of the "wholly beautiful man" in *The Idiot*.

101. Murav notes that Solzhenitsyn claimed to write *The Gulag Archipelago* "for Russia that has no tongue" and interprets this to mean that "he is referring to those Russians who did not and could not write their own memoirs and testimonies," but also that he is "concerned with the issue of the restoration of self," particularly through the process of bearing witness to one's own suffering: "It restores the reality of suffering to the victim, whose suffering the regime appropriates for its own purposes, that is, to affirm its power. Testimony of suffering recontextualizes the suffering as suffering for the individual" (*Russia's Legal Fictions*, 173). Solzhenitsyn's phrase appears in *Arkhipelag GULag*, 3:331. Two of these self-characterizations are echoed or suggested in titles for two contemporary essays on *House of the Dead*: N. A. Dobroliubov's 1861 "*Zabitye Liudi*" (reprinted in his *Literaturnaia kritika*, 678–725); and D. I. Pisarev's 1866 "*Pogibshie i pogibaiushchie*" (*Polnoe sobranie sochinenii i pisem v dvenadtsati tomakh*, 8:284–336).

102. Dostoevsky transcribed examples of peasant speech in his "Siberian Notebook" (*PSS* 4:235–48); see also part 1, note 107.

103. Dostoevsky featured the problem of peasant literacy in his introduction to the first issue of *Vremia*. I return to this article and the series of which it is a part in the conclusion to this volume (*PSS* 18:61–66). The polemic surrounding the uses and abuses of peasant literacy is examined in *PSS* 4:293.

104. The theme begins with the anterior narrator who reports how, on his first visit to the ex-convict, he surprises Gorianchikov teaching his landlady's young daughter to read. He "was as disconcerted as if I had caught him committing a crime" (*PSS* 4:7). Like his ostensibly murdered wife, the little girl's name is Katya, suggesting the conversion of the inherently guilty gift of literacy to an act of repentance and mutual redemption.

105. Petrov is an example of the kind of "exceptional personality" Dostoevsky claimed were found among literate peasants who demonstrate their sense of superiority to their peers partly by an odd formality of behavior (*PSS* 18:64). In *Notes from the Underground* to *The Brothers Karamazov*, Dostoevsky develops the theme of the exceptional personality that considers itself exempt from the

conventions and rules governing ordinary people: Smerdiakov, whose absurdly pompous behavior and locutions are reminiscent of Petrov, concludes the roster of such characters.

106. Cf. *PSS* 4:197/306: "I have already made some mention of the fact that at the beginning of my stay in prison I did not penetrate into the inner depths of this life, and indeed was incapable of doing so, and therefore all of its outward manifestations were then an unutterable torment and anguish to me." Here Gorianchikov claims that this was equally true for those he assumed were at home, "among their own kind": in fact, though, "each one kept the eyes of his mind averted from the others." In addition to the insufficiency of the light of reality to his desire to see what and who surrounded him, Gorianchikov also faults his anguish, which made him unwilling to see: "I did not notice many of the things around me. I covered my eyes and refused to look" (*PSS* 4:178/276). Dostoevsky revisits this psychology of vision in connection with class difference in *Crime and Punishment*. The narrator describes how, in prison, Raskol'nikov "really did not want to notice [his surroundings]. He lived somehow with lowered eyes: it was loathsome to him and unbearable to look. But in the end many things began to surprise him, and he somehow involuntarily began to notice what he had not suspected before. In general, he came to be surprised most of all by the terrible and impassable abyss (*propast'*) that lay between him and all these people. It was as if he and they were from different nations" (*PSS* 6:419/545).

107. In his first letter to his brother, Mikhail, of 22 February 1854, Dostoevsky spoke similarly of how he "distinguished, at long last, human beings [*otlichil nakonetz liudei*]." See *PSS* 28 (I): 172.

108. Dostoevsky's semiotics of *katorga*, which would evolve into a semiotics of the largely unarticulated and yet manifestly preeminent spiritual life of the Russian peasant, is sufficiently complex to warrant a full-scale analysis of its own; what appears here is a possible platform for such a project.

109. In *Kul'tura i vzryv* [*Culture and explosion*], Iu. M. Lotman defines *vzryv*, or "explosion," as a form of unpredictable cultural change as opposed to the gradual or continuous pace of cultural evolution. The foreignness of "genius" as opposed to "talent" (in Belinsky's formulation) or "inspiration" may generate such volatility in an otherwise stable cultural system.

110. Catteau (with a nod to Roland Barthes) links Dostoevsky's compositional style to his epilepsy. The novels are marked by episodes of "violent convulsions": "Certainly the feverish incandescence of the verb, the brutal discharge of the action in scenes of high tension, is not merely a mimicry of the epileptic storm in writing, but their violent and convulsive tenor indicates that the writer had a secret inclination for the *noble* form of excess: aesthetic excess which is a metaphor for 'what goes beyond bounds' and so weighs heavier and penetrates more deeply. It is the *explosion* which reveals the truth" (*Dostoevsky and the Process of Literary Creation*, 131).

111. As James L. Rice points out, however, this pattern is susceptible to an inversion whereby the outwardly gentle peasant suddenly reveals "the Tatar within," as Dostoevsky observed in his notebooks for 1875–76. Cited in the epigraph to Rice, "Psychoanalysis of 'Peasant Marej' "; cf. 252. Also pertinent is Rice, "Dostoevsky's Endgame."

112. Elsewhere, Gorianchikov relates how "the prisoner passionately loves money and values it above everything, almost equally with freedom [. .] and is ready to steal or do whatever he can to get it" (*PSS* 4:33/43). The symbolic value of money as "coined freedom" as long as it is in circulation may be contrasted with the coin Gorianchikov receives as "an unfortunate" from the peasant girl and which he is careful to keep for the duration of his sentence.

113. L. V. Zharavina suggests that the exchange of names bespeaks a desire for conversion. See "Filosofsko-religioznoe obosnovanie psikhologizma F. M. Dostoevskogo (*Zapiski iz mertvogo doma*)," esp. 117–18.

114. Cf. Turgenev's noble hunter of *A Sportsman's Sketches* who, in the tale "Bezhin Meadow," eavesdrops on a group of peasant children and gains an otherwise inaccessible view of their lives.

115. Jackson discusses Akul'ka's iconic features in *Art of Dostoevsky*, 92–95. See also note 98, above.

116. The now classic study of pain and inarticulateness is Elaine Scarry, *Body in Pain*.

117. A witness, A. I. Ivanov, described Dostoevsky's distress when a prisoner coming from corporal punishment was brought into the hospital ward: he would frantically implore others to "save" the "unfortunate": "*Detushki, detushki! rodnye, spasite ego . . ., spasite neschastnogo*" (cited in Gromyko, *Sibirskie znakomye i druz'ia F. M. Dostoevskogo*, 35). See also Schrader's remarkable research on the psychological trauma suffered by noblemen who participated professionally in the process, including physicians (*Languages of the Lash*, 175–82).

118. The cited phrases are taken from Maurice Merleau-Ponty's discussion of Being and the "flesh of the world" in *The Visible and the Invisible* (117), discussed in more detail below. Cited hereafter in the text as *VI*.

119. On "democratism," see the introduction, note 50.

120. Gorianchikov also uses the words *obshchnost'* and *artel'*—a cooperative association of workmen or peasants—to describe the peasant collective. This association exerts a real force on individual convicts: for example, the "*artel'*" determines that Sushilov may not renege on "changing places" with Mikhailov or protest that their agreement is void because he was drunk: if he tries to do so, "they will chew him up. Beat him to a pulp, perhaps, or simply kill him, at least terrify him" (*PSS* 60/86).

121. Dostoevsky's first letter to his brother Mikhail (30 January/22 February 1854) powerfully describes the physical and psychological stress of living in *katorga* (*PSS* 28 [I]: 166–74/55–65).

122. Bernard Flynn provides excellent accounts of the philosophies of Merleau-Ponty and Lefort in *Political Philosophy at the Close of Metaphysics* and *Philosophy of Claude Lefort*. Lefort, a student of Merleau-Ponty's and one of his most insightful readers, is responsible for extending Merleau-Ponty's distinctive phenomenological vision into the realm of social and political theory, particularly democratic theory. Although the phrase "flesh of the political" clearly describes Lefort's adaptation of Merleau-Ponty's notion of the flesh to the domain of power, and although he specifies a "flesh of the social" (for example, in his essay "The Permanence of the Theologico-Political?"), I can find the actual phrase "flesh of the political" only in Flynn's *Philosophy of Claude Lefort*. Flynn defines it with a citation drawn

from Lefort's study of Machiavelli, *Le travail de l'oeuvre Machiavel* as "the space of an 'entre-deux' which announces itself as the place of the real (*'réel'*) which pre-exists the action of the political subject" (10). This expresses my own understanding of Lefort's concept and the sense in which I see *katorga* as a "political" space.

123. Lefort discusses Merleau-Ponty's concept of the flesh (*chair*) in his *Sur une colonne absente*, esp. 130–39. See also Judith Butler, "Merleau-Ponty and the Touch of Malebranche," which examines the limits to which he took the idea of the primacy of sentience over the knowing subject in his final work.

124. Chapter 94 of Melville's *Moby-Dick* ("A Squeeze of the Hand") power-fully illustrates this identity of touching and touched. Here, with several other men, Ishmael's task is to squeeze congealed spermaceti back into its "sweet and unctuous" liquid form: "I squeezed that sperm till a strange sort of insanity came over me; and I found myself unwittingly squeezing my co-laborers' hands in it, mistaking their hands for the gentle globules." So blissful is the sensation that he wants to exhort the world, "Come; let us squeeze hands all round; nay, let us all squeeze ourselves into each other; let us squeeze ourselves universally into the very milk and sperm of kindness."

125. As Jones puts it in *Dostoevsky*, the "effluvium" of the gown blends with the "psychic stink" of the Dead House, "another smell and yet also the same smell because the life of the dead house is one as well as manifold" (163).

126. Dostoevsky's representation of the nobleman's encounter with the com-mon people in *katorga* is illuminated by Michel de Certeau's comments on vision in *VI*: "The seeing subject is a particular being that tries to reach, in what it distin-guishes, the very being from which it is detached. The objects it sees, therefore, make up the representation of what it had to separate itself from in order to know them. Those objects tell of a broken solidarity—a lost origin—and a return toward things via the paths of consciousness. They are therefore, for the seeing subject, the legend of his own history (the 'legend' that must be read, *legendum*), a history without words, of which the vision is already the thought, played out within the interval that makes of seen things both *objects* toward which knowledge *goes* and quasi-mythological *signs* of the reality whence knowledge comes. [. .] From that point of view, vision could be considered the myth of the 'ontological' narrative, a myth that structures the successive levels of knowledge, from the local, mute account of each particular perception, to the long narration of philosophical inter-rogation which brings about the same return and the same detour." Dostoevsky's later national messianism may be seen as growing out of this reciprocal vision so understood which "posits the principle of an 'ontological history' " ("The Mad-ness of Vision," 26, 27).

127. See Bakhtin, *Problems of Dostoevsky's Poetics*, 283–304; and Hannah Arendt's discussion of "how freedom and non-sovereignty can exist together" in "What is Freedom?" esp. section 4, 165–71 (cited phrase at 164), and *Human Condition*.

128. De Certeau, "The Madness of Vision," 29. He continues, in a passage that bears directly on the mystery of a constitutive consciousness: "Hence, to see is already an act of language. This act makes of seen things the enunciation of the invisible texture that binds them. It is the perception of an invisible solidarity by and in the 'terms' of seen objects. It is word, but silent still. It is already of the

order of language; it represents a mute stage of language, which precedes its verbal stage. Thought is born with this silent 'pact' between things that is the infrastructure of vision."

129. On the "possibility of democracy," see Thomas Docherty, *Aesthetic Democracy.* Docherty's notion of democracy involves the coming-into-being of community through an aesthetic experience that, far from resolving alterity, both requires and reproduces it. He examines this possibility less with reference to any particular aesthetic event occurring in or for a particular culture than to contemporary aesthetic theory.

130. See Bakhtin, *Dialogic Imagination*, esp. 269–75.

131. De Certeau traces the taking shape of "a new aesthetics" to a revolution in perception which institutes a new history. When the normative visual relation between subject and object is reversed, and the subject feels him- or herself looked at by the object, the ensuing "disturbance that 'turns' vision 'inside out' has the force of a beginning and therefore *creates* for aesthetic perception a time of its own. Thus the principle of a history of the visible is posited, which no longer consists in accommodating experience within a pre-established chronological framework, but in revealing within experience the very invention of temporality" ("The Madness of Vision," 28). There are two places, I would argue, where one sees Dostoevsky's ambition to invent temporality in this manner: first, in the chronotope of *katorga* for which he claims a specific temporality; and, second, in his hopes for the coming-into-being of a new world evident in the letter to his brother written on the eve of his Siberian exile, and in his later ideological writings about Russia's messianic destiny.

132. On Merleau-Ponty's literary turn, see de Certeau, "The Madness of Vision," 30.

133. Cf. Merleau-Ponty's concretization of the abstraction of "red" as a "punctuation in the field of red things" including rooftops, terrains, garments, and so on (132). His discussion here is reminiscent of the nineteenth-century Orientalist Ernest Fenollosa's account of the way that the Chinese written character as ideograph conveys abstraction through a constellation of material objects in *The Chinese Written Character as a Medium for Poetry.*

134. Whitman, "Preface" to *Leaves of Grass, 1855*, 11.

135. Lefort, "Permanence of the Theologico-Political?" in *Democracy and Political Theory*, 223.

136. Gorianchikov stresses the common convicts' familiarity with the communal ritual. The public baths for the gentry, to which the prisoners have no access, is divided into private rooms, whereas theirs is "dilapidated, filthy, crowded" (*PSS* 4:96/142).

137. Cf. the hospital scene, where the tubercular convict Mikhailov, unable to bear the weight of his shirt or his cross on his suffering body, dies exposed and in chains. His "long, long body" lies naked but for his fetters which the authorities refuse to remove, even though, as Gorianchikov observes indignantly, "he could by now have pulled his wasted leg" through them (*PSS* 4:140/214). A peasant-convict protests to the sergeant who removes the body, saying, "He too had a mother!"—Gorianchikov describes himself as unexpectedly "pierced" by these

words, conveying both his fear of and identification with the body's pathetic vulnerability (*PSS* 4:141/216).

138. Turgenev famously praised Dostoevsky for the "Dantesque" quality of his portrayal of the bath house, and singled out his representation of Petrov for its psychological insight (*Polnoe sobranie sochinenii i pisem v dvadtsati vos'mi tomakh*, 4:319–20).

139. David Goldstein, in *Dostoevsky and the Jews*, observes that Gorianchikov always refers to Isai Fomich as a Jew (*evrei*) rather than as a Yid (*zhid*), a word he notes was not used by the educated classes, except derogatorily, in Dostoevsky's time (21, 169 n. 5). Dostoevsky himself, in a *Diary of a Writer* (March 1877) response to educated Jews who accuse him of anti-Semitism titled " 'The Jewish Question,' " wonders whether he stands accused "because I sometimes call the Jew a 'Yid' " and proceeds to explain his practice: "in the first place, I didn't think that this was so offensive, and in the second place, as far as I can recall, I always used the word 'Yid' to denote a well-known idea: 'Yid, Yid-ism, the Kingdom of the Yids,' etc." (*PSS* 25:75). English translation available as *A Writer's Diary Vol. 2: 1877–1881*, trans. Kenneth Lantz, 901–18, esp. 902. The March 1877 issue is devoted to the problem of the Jew and proves the writer's anti-Semitism beyond doubt; Dostoevsky's point, essentially, is that the Jew is the enemy of the Russian people. See also Frank's account of his final trip to Germany in 1879 to take the waters at a spa and his impression that the Jews were destroying the German national spirit (*Mantle of the Prophet*, 443–48).

140. Dostoevsky included some of the dialogue contained in this scene in his "Siberian Notebook," which suggests strongly that such conversations did occur between the prisoners and the real-life model for Isai Fomich Bumstein, a Jewish prisoner in Dostoevsky's barrack named Isai Bumstehl (*PSS* 4:238, entries 91, 92). On Bumstehl, see Goldstein, *Dostoevsky and the Jews*, 14, 169 n. 4. Dostoevsky's " 'The Jewish Question' " (cited above) provides an alternative account of his experience with Jews in *katorga* to that in *House of the Dead*. In the 1877 article, he claims that several Jews were in the camp rather than one, and that the Russian common people never taunted them with anti-Semitic remarks or abusive behavior but exhibited tolerance and respect for their religious difference.

141. Goldstein enumerates Dostoevsky's errors in reporting Isai Fomich's Sabbath ritual which he attributes not to weaknesses of observation but to his desire to heighten the comic role he assigns to the Jew and his ridiculous character (*Dostoevsky and the Jews*, 24–25).

142. Goldstein cites the *Ustav o soderzhashchikhsia pod strazheiu* which at the time of Dostoevsky's incarceration guaranteed that incarcerated Jews could remain in their quarters for prayer and could refrain from work on Saturdays (ibid., 171 n. 24). The major's toleration of Isai Fomich's provocative behavior seems to suggest a greater degree of legal protection, though I know of no law guaranteeing freedom of conscience or religion, especially to prisoners.

143. Leonid Grossman refers to Isai Fomich as a prisoner-buffoon (*katorzhny shut*) in "Dostoevskii i iudaizm" (*Ispoved odnovo evreia*, 174).

144. On the changes in the realities of professional authorship between the pre-Siberian and post-Siberian phases of Dostoevsky's career, see Todd, "Dostoevskii as a Professional Writer."

145. English translation of "Bookishness and Literacy: Part I" available in *Dostoevsky's Occasional Writings*, trans. David Magarshack, 138–60, esp. 139. Page numbers hereafter cited in the text following those in *PSS*.

146. The topos of grammar so conceived has for some time been the focus of theoretical development, beginning perhaps with Kenneth Burke's postwar attempt to use the concept of "grammar" metaphorically to identify the essential constituents of all acts, anterior to any philosophic system, and to trace their formal interrelationships in order ultimately to disclose the common ground of all human motive—again, in advance of all the subsequent "casuistry" of philosophy or ideology. The founding question of his *Grammar of Motives* (1945) is also Gorianchikov's vis-à-vis the common people: "What is involved, when we say what people are doing and why they are doing it" (xvii, xv).

147. Cf. Pisarev, who denies any difference between the relationship the Russian common people might have with a Russian writer and with a "tourist from Paraguay," apart from a common language and birthplace: "We love the people or at least imagine that we love them, because it is difficult really to love what we almost don't know, but the people don't love us and don't believe us. We have up until now done virtually nothing for them, we have been living off their labor for centuries [. .]. Who can blame our peasant for the fact that in every gentleman dressed like a European he sees a man in whose presence one has to keep a sharp lookout and with whom one should not allow oneself to be sincere under any circumstances?" ("Narodnye Knizhki," 217).

148. Cf. " 'Svistok' i 'Russkii Vestnik,' " published in the third issue of *Vremia* (*PSS* 19: 113), in which Dostoevsky rejects an understanding of "democratization" favored by the aristocracy during the Napoleonic invasion of 1812 through the Decembrist movement. Figes cites Denis Davidov and the Decembrist poet Alexander Bestuzhev, who urge the gentry to assume the people's outward appearance and speak "the common tongue" to express their common cause (*Natasha's Dance*, 76, 83).

The question of whether social progress would come from the top down or from the bottom up was intensely debated throughout the last half of the nineteenth century. As Berlin notes, "The first enthusiastic adherents of radical Populism—the missionaries who went 'to the people' in the famous summer of 1874—were met by mounting indifference, suspicion, resentment and sometimes active hatred and resistance, on the part of their would-be beneficiaries who, as often as not, handed them over to the police." Two years later, with the Populist movement on the wane, the revolutionary Stepnyak Kravchinsky complained that "Socialism bounced off people like peas from a wall," and that the people listened to their would-be mentors " 'as they do to the priest'—respectfully, without understanding, without any effect upon their actions" (introduction to Venturi, *Roots of Revolution*, xii–xiii, xxvi). Mikhail Butashevich-Petrashevsky, the committed Fourierist whose political meetings Dostoevsky attended from 1847 until his arrest in 1849, built a phalanstery for the serfs on his estate which was apparently then burnt down by the peasants themselves (Venturi, *Roots of Revolution*, 83). Dale E. Peterson suggests that "Dostoevsky intuited that the alienated and ironic self-consciousness of Russia's Westernized intelligentsia was analogous to the alienated and mistrustful consciousness of the denigrated Russian peasantry" (*Up from Bondage*, 113).

149. Lefort, "Permanence of the Theologico-Political?" in *Democracy and Political Theory*, 218–19.

150. If there is no resurrection from the dead for Gorianchikov, Dostoevsky credits his memoir with having resurrected (*vozobnovil*) his authorial career after his return from Siberian exile. See his letter of 31 March/14 April 1865 to A. E. Vrangel' in *PSS* 28 [II]: 115–17, esp. 115.

151. De Certeau, "The Madness of Vision," 29. Insofar as a " 'void' of consciousness" must attend what Merleau-Ponty characterizes as a "fold" in the invisible texture of visible things, de Certeau connects the *ne to* (or "fold") both to belief and to beauty.

Conclusion
The Russian People, This Unriddled Sphinx

The conclusion title echoes the epithet Dostoevsky used for the people, in the introduction to his journal *Time* (*PSS* 18:66), attributing it to "one of our poets," whom the editors identified as Alexander Herzen from *My Past and Thoughts* (*PSS* 18:268). Dostoevsky developed the idea in the February 1876 *Diary of a Writer* essay, "On Love of the People. Essential Contact with the People."

1. An English translation is available in *A Writer's Diary Vol. 1: 1873–1876*, trans. Kenneth Lantz, 156–69, esp. 169. Page numbers hereafter provided in the text following those in *PSS*.

2. See part 2, note 146.

3. Giorgio Agamben, "What Is a People?" in *Means without Ends*, 29–36, esp. 31, 32. Agamben is skeptical of the dream of eradicating the constitutive division of the concept: "What Marx calls class struggle [. . .] is nothing other than this internecine war that divides every people and that shall come to an end only when *People* and *people* coincide, in the classless society or in the messianic kingdom, and only when there shall no longer be, properly speaking, any people" (31–32). On the use of the term *narod* to encompass both "the people" and "the nation" in a trinity with autocracy and orthodoxy during the reign of Nicholas I, see Nicholas Riasanovsky, *Nicholas I and Official Nationality*, esp. chap. 3. The Slavophiles were widely credited for developing the non-official significance of *narodnost'*; see Franco Venturi, *Roots of Revolution*, 19–26. The classic study of the Slavophile movement is Andrzej Walicki, *Slavophile Controversy*.

4. Dmitri I. Pisarev, "*Pogibshie i pogibaiushchie*," in *Polnoe sobranie sochinenii i pisem v dvenadtsati tomakh*, 8:284.

5. For a comparative account of slavery in Russia and the United States, see Peter Kolchin, *Unfree Labor*; see also Dale E. Peterson, *Up from Bondage*.

6. I cite Douglass's second (1855) autobiography, *My Bondage and my Freedom* (62, 63). Citations hereafter appear in the text as *MBMF*.

7. This passage appears in Douglass's first (1845) autobiography, *Narrative of the Life of Frederick Douglass*, 57, hereafter cited in text as *NLFD*. The last sentence of the passage cited appears in *MBMF* slightly amended: "I have sometimes thought that the mere hearing of those songs would do more to impress truly spiritual-minded men and women with the soul-crushing and death-dealing character of

slavery than the reading of whole volumes of its mere physical cruelties. They speak to the heart and soul of the thoughtful" (98). Bookishness here is exemplified not by volumes of philosophy but by volumes delineating slavery's physical cruelties.

8. Herzen described the enslaved Russian peasantry as "twelve million people *hors la loi . . . Carmen horrendum*" (cited in Venturi, *Roots of Revolution*, 21). Herzen also referred to *Notes from the House of the Dead* as a "*carmen horrendum*": "This epoch left us a frightening book, in its way a *carmen horrendum*, which will always adorn the exit from the dark reign of Nicholas, like Dante's superscription over the entrance" (cited in V. Ia. Kirpotin, *Dostoevskii v shestidesiatye gody*, 330).

9. For a classic critique of such "stories" that ignore and therefore betray what is "resolutely indefinable, unpredictable" in the human being as personification of "a Cause," see James Baldwin, "Everybody's Protest Novel," esp. 15.

10. Douglass notes that *The Columbian Orator* also contained "one of Sheridan's mighty speeches, on the subject of Catholic Emancipation, Lord Chatham's speech on the American war, and speeches by the great William Pitt and by Fox" (*MBMF* 158).

11. In the 1855 autobiography, Douglass uses "soul" to replace "mind" which he had used in 1845 (*NLFD*, 83). The substitution emphasizes the ethereality of the thought before given tongue—materialized—by the book.

12. Lefort, "Permanence of the Theologico-Political?" in idem, *Democracy and Political Theory*, 225. Douglass speaks of the "view" of his condition provided by his reading in *NLFD*, 84.

13. Nevertheless, the question remains: Does the condition and the proof of self-possession—emancipation followed by the textual representation of the new man—require a kind of self-digression in which "literacy" is a variant of the scarred body, a powerful signifier, but which nevertheless must be left behind? Or, on the contrary, is self-digression the dominant feature of Douglass's autobiography? Is the representation of self-digression—the self deviating from the self—itself the mark of the text's conservation of the author's "literacy"? There is no opportunity here to compare Douglass's and Dostoevsky's autobiographical writings on the subject of bondage and emancipation from the house of the dead. Nevertheless, it is worth considering Dostoevsky's unique value in helping us understand the difficulties of an autobiographical text like Douglass's where liberation is figured as an act of self-translation made possible by negotiating the divide between bookishness and literacy. By what he would call "the force of external circumstances," Dostoevsky became Douglass's white witness in the woods, and he registers in his autobiography the enduring trauma of what he heard there in his analysis of the sounds that passed through the chambers of his soul.

14. See note 7 above.

15. On black abolitionist Anglophilia, see Elisa Tamarkin, *Anglophilia*, chap. 3.

16. John Stauffer, in *Black Hearts of Men* (1; cf. 18), analyzes the performative dimension of acquiring and/or displaying a "black heart" in the lives and careers of four abolitionists, two white (John Brown and Gerrit Smith) and two black (James McCune Smith and Frederick Douglass), and the limitations of this endeavor in the raid on Harper's Ferry.

17. This acknowledgment of the nobleman's blindness distinguishes Dostoevsky's view of the rapprochement of the classes from Herzen's faith in those he designates "apostles—men who combine faith, will, conviction and energy;

men who will never divorce themselves from [the people]; men who do not necessarily spring from them, but who act within them and with them, with a dedicated and steady faith. The man who feels himself to be so near the people that he has been virtually freed by them from the atmosphere of artificial civilization; the man who has achieved the unity and intensity of which we are speaking—he will be able to speak to the people and must do so" (cited in Venturi, *Roots of Revolution*, 35).

18. Frank, *Stir of Liberation*, 101. For an overview of the journalistic battles in which Dostoevsky participated, see 94–109.

19. On "becoming democratic," see *PSS* 23:28. In his journal *Time* [*Vremia*] in 1861, Dostoevsky declared that "for a long time we've had a neutral soil, on which everyone is merged into one, harmonious, integral, unanimous, all the classes merge peacefully, consensually, and fraternally" (*PSS* 18:49; see also 57; *PSS* 19:19). At the same time, he described that soil as marked by the great faultline of class division: it is a "ravine," an "abyss," a "chasm" (*PSS* 19:6, 20).

20. On the shaping or *mise-en-forme* of a novel social-political entity as a simultaneous giving meaning to (*mise-en-sens*) and staging of (*mise-en-scène*) social relations, see Lefort, *Democracy and Political Theory*, 218–19.

21. C. B. Macpherson first elaborated the theory of possessive individualism as the basis of Western liberal democracy in *Political Theory of Possessive Individualism*. See also Joseph H. Carens, ed., *Democracy and Possessive Individualism*. On the difficulties of defining Russian liberalism in this era and distinguishing it from both radicalism and conservatism, see Mark Raeff, *Political Ideas and Institutions*, 32–41. On Herzen's polemical engagement with Russian liberals in the years immediately before and after emancipation, see Aileen Kelly, "Historical Diffidence: A New Look at an Old Russian Debate."

22. See the introduction, note 46.

23. Field writes that more than twenty million people were liberated in 1861 ("Year of Jubilee," 41). Kelly cites twenty-three million, "almost three-quarters of the inhabitants of the central Russian provinces" ("Historical Diffidence," 498).

24. V. Kirpotin points out that "Dostoevsky polemically affirmed that emancipation [*osvobozhdenie*] would be achieved by itself, without class struggle, without coerced interference, if the people first become literate methodically and gradually" (*Dostoevskii v shestidesiatye gody*, 63–72, esp. 69).

25. See, for example, "Bookishness and Literacy, Second Article," in *PSS* 19:21–57. Cf. Pisarev, "Narodnye knizhki" [People's readers], who acknowledged both the importance of popular education and the "complete abyss [*bezdna*]" which lay "between the theoretical and practical resolution of this question" (213).

26. Dostoevsky attributes precisely this achievement to the aristocratic poet Pushkin in his 1880 Pushkin speech when he praised him as "a man who was reincarnated by his own heart into the common man, into his essence, almost into his image." See the introduction to this volume, note 11.

27. Donald Fanger confirms both "the almost complete absence of works depicting peasant life from the inside," and the no doubt related fact that peasant characters were typically "mute, inexpressive, minimally individualized" ("Peasant in Literature," esp. 231, 246). For an overview of the peasant in artistic representation, including literary, see Orlando Figes, *Natasha's Dance*, 220–87. For an ac-

count of the educated class's antipathy to popular literature when it did develop later in the century, see Jeffrey Brooks, *When Russia Learned to Read*, 295–352.

28. For a comparative analysis of Dostoevsky/Gorianchikov's efforts "to invent the means to recover [a] subliterate alternative culture in a readable narrative" with those of W. E. B. DuBois in African-American culture, see Peterson, *Up from Bondage*, esp. chap. 3, 60–80. See 109–14 for Peterson's discussion of Dostoevsky's efforts in *Vremia* to address the abyss of class difference in the context of the literacy debates.

29. Tolstoy, "*Komu u kogo uchit'sia pisat', krestianski rebiatam u nas, ili nam u krestianskikh rebiat.*" On *Vremia*'s positive response to the article, see Kirpotin, *Dostoevskii v shestidesiatye gody*, 66.

30. On the changing meanings of the term "*narod*" and its derivatives beginning in this period, see part 1, note 106.

31. Although Dostoevsky and Pisarev concur on this point, Pisarev does not consider Pushkin (or Lermontov, Gogol, or Turgenev) to have penetrated beneath the purely external aspect of popular life ("Narodnye knizhki").

32. On the religious-aesthetic significance of the theatricals, see Julie de Sherbinin, "Transcendence Through Art." Noting Gorianchikov's observation that the theatricals engender a temporary moral awakening in the people, Sherbinin writes: "It is the *intelligent* who is able to articulate the value of this brief metamorphosis, although only the 'people' themselves are capable of bringing it about" (349). As I discuss below, precisely this relationship between the intellectual and the people obtains in the commission of crime in *The Brothers Karamazov*, where Ivan (without acknowledging it) articulates the rationale for parricide, but Smerdiakov alone is capable of bringing it about.

33. Figes confirms Gorianchikov's supposition in *Natasha's Dance*, 38–42.

34. See part 1, note 77.

35. The chapter on prison theatricals illustrates Homi Bhabha's point: the tension between pedagogy and performance adumbrates that "conceptual territory where the nation's people must be thought" (*Location of Culture*, 145–54, esp. 145).

36. See part 1, note 107.

37. *PSS* 3:443–46; see also Frank, *Years of Ordeal*, 295–97. In his famous Pushkin speech, Dostoevsky singled out Tatiana, the heroine of *Evgenii Onegin*, as the culmination of Russian spiritual beauty. A noblewoman whose values proved her rootedness in the people, Tatiana is comparable, Dostoevsky claimed, only to Turgenev's heroine "without her own words," Liza (*PSS* 26:140/1285). For the significance of the Pushkin speech and its presentation in 1880, see section 1 of the introduction to this volume. Herzen, too, features such a triangle in his 1847 novel, *Who Is to Blame?* [*Kto vinovat?*].

38. On the Underground Man's pointed refusal to suffer in silence as, paradoxically, a strategy for control, see Deborah A. Martinsen, "Of Shame and Human Bondage: Dostoevsky's *Notes from Underground*," esp. 162–63.

39. Quoted in Frank, *Seeds of Revolt*, 131. Frank identifies both the Russian and the French sources of *Poor People*: Karamzin, Pushkin, and Gogol; and Balzac, Sue, Souvestre, Soulié, Hugo, and particularly George Sand.

40. Frank explores the literary-historical significance of Dostoevsky's relationship to Gogol (*Seeds of Revolt*, chaps. 9 and 10). See also Donald Fanger, *Dostoevsky and Romantic Realism*.

41. Fanger states that, "with the story of Raskolnikov, crime enters Dostoevsky's world"—a common assumption. He excludes *House of the Dead* as the novel which initiates that theme because, with the exception of Orlov, Dostoevsky "treats his fellow convicts by and large in the traditional Russian way, as 'unfortunates.' What they have done anyone, in principle, might do; their crimes are frequently crimes of passion; their common humanity is only too evident" (*Dostoevsky and Romantic Realism*, 207–8). As I have argued, however, Dostoevsky does not immediately or uncritically appropriate the people's idea of the criminal as an "unfortunate" but instead works through the concept and his own relationship to it throughout his fictional and polemical work. Nor does he underestimate the fearsome mystery of crime by linking it to "passion" (that Shishkov murders his wife out of passion does not assuage our sense of the horror of the crime) or portray Gorianchikov as secure in the "common humanity" he ostensibly shares with the peasant-convicts.

42. *PSS* 6:417. I cite the Pevear and Volokhonsky translation of *Crime and Punishment* (544). Hereafter, page numbers to this translation are cited in the text following those to *PSS*.

43. In contrast to the autobiographical staging of Gorianchikov's self-delusion, however, the narrator of *Crime and Punishment*, before describing his conversion, states that Raskol'nikov "may have sensed a profound lie in himself and his convictions." His spiritual crisis engenders not remorse for his crime but rather love for the prostitute Sonia which enables his resurrection, "his gradual transition from one world to another, his acquaintance with a new, hitherto completely unknown reality" (*PSS* 6:422/551).

44. *PSS* 8: 279. I cite the Pevear and Volokhonsky translation of *The Idiot* (337). Page numbers to this translation are hereafter cited in the text following those to *PSS*.

45. Robert L. Belknap, in "The Unrepentant Confession," identifies the difference between these two groups as the difference between "unrepentant confession" and apologia.

46. English translation available in *A Writer's Diary, Vol. 2: 1877–1881*, trans. Kenneth Lantz, 1296–1303, esp. 1300–1301. Cf. Zosima: "God will save Russia, for though the simple man is depraved, and can no longer refrain from rank sin, still he knows that his rank sin is cursed by God and that he does badly in sinning. [. . .] Not so [his] betters" (*PSS* 14:286/315).

47. By the 1860s, the "educated class" could no longer be taken to refer exclusively to the nobility but prominently included "people of various ranks," or *raznochintsy*. See Elise Kimerling Wirtschafter, *Social Identity in Imperial Russia*, esp. 63–71; and Derek Offord, "Dostoevskii and the Intelligentsia." On the complex growth in the last half of the nineteenth century of a Russian middle class, see Edith W. Clowes, Samuel D. Kassow, and James L. West, eds., *Between Tsar and People*. Dostoevsky's claim, developed through the great novels, that the common people were better able to understand the ethico-religious significance of their actions than the elite, reversed the official rationale that had protected members

of the nobility from corporal punishment. According to this rationale, because the nobility possessed a stronger sense of right and wrong as well as an understanding of the intrinsic value of the law, their sense of shame at having committed a crime along with the loss of class privileges was sufficient punishment. See Abby M. Schrader, *Languages of the Lash*, 21–26.

48. *PSS* 23:33, 32/158, 157. Serman, in "Tema narodnosti" (122–24), suggests Nekrasov's "Vlas" as a source for "Akul'ka's Husband."

49. *PSS* 23:33/158; *PSS* 28 [I]: 349. Dostoevsky's objection here to Nekrasov's "loving the universal man" in the guise of the peasant anticipates Zosima's response to Mme Khokhlakova (*PSS* 14:52–53/56–57) as well as Ivan's lead-in to "Rebellion" (*PSS* 14:215–16): "Don't you see that to love the universal man really means not just to have contempt for, but even to hate the actual human being standing beside you?" See *PSS* 23:398 for an account of Dostoevsky's evolving relationship to Nekrasov.

50. The editors of *PSS* cite a number of scholars who attribute this tale to Russian folklore; see 23:397–98.

51. See James L. Rice, *Dostoevsky and the Healing Art*, by far the most thorough and far-ranging study of his epilepsy, in its metaphorical, religious-historical, and medical-historical contexts. On mystical terror as an aspect of Dostoevsky's seizures, see 88–89.

52. See Rice's powerful reading of Smerdiakov as the epileptic-contemplator in *Dostoevsky and the Healing Art*, 252–59; see also 87–89. Rice notes that Kramskoi had become familiar with "Dostoevsky's explosively contemplative types" through *House of the Dead* (254) and traces the evolution of his art through his relationship with Dostoevsky and the painter Tret'iakov.

53. I cite the Pevear and Volokhonsky translation of *The Brothers Karamazov* (*PSS* 14:255/280).

54. The phrase "the time-before" is taken from J. M. Coetzee's discussion of Augustine's *Confessions* and refers to that which occurred before his conversion ("Confession and Double Thoughts").

55. "Beyond Guilt and Expiation" is the title of a book by the Holocaust survivor Jean Améry, cited by Primo Levi in *Drowned and the Saved* (58).

56. For Agamben in *Homo Sacer*, crime is not at issue. The aporia of *homo sacer*'s existence has nothing to do with the crime he was judged to have committed and everything to do with the a priori violence of sovereignty. See part 2, note 9.

57. Cited by Martin Jay in *Downcast Eyes*, 287.

Bibliography

~

Afanas'ev, Alexander K. "Jurors and Jury Trials in Imperial Russia, 1866–1885." In *Russia's Great Reforms, 1855–1881,* ed. Ben Eklof, John Bushnell, and Larissa Zakharova, 214–30. Bloomington: Indiana University Press, 1994.

Agamben, Giorgio. *Homo Sacer: Sovereign Power and Bare Life.* Translated by Daniel Heller-Roazen. Stanford: Stanford University Press, 1998.

———. *Potentialities: Collected Essays in Philosophy.* Edited and translated by Daniel Heller-Roazen. Stanford: Stanford University Press, 1999.

———. *Remnants of Auschwitz: The Witness and the Archive.* Translated by Daniel Heller-Roazen. New York: Zone Books, 1999.

———. *Means Without End: Notes on Politics.* Translated by Vincenzo Binetti and Cesare Casarino. Minneapolis: University of Minnesota Press, 2000.

———. *State of Exception.* Translated by Kevin Attell. Chicago: University of Chicago Press, 2005.

Arendt, Hannah. "What Is Freedom?" *Between Past and Future: Eight Exercises in Political Thought.* New York: Penguin Books, 1993 [1954].

———. *On Revolution.* New York: Penguin, 1977 [1963].

———. *Essays in Understanding, 1930–1954: Formation, Exile, and Totalitarianism.* Edited by Jerome Kuhn. New York: Schocken Books, 1994.

———. *The Human Condition.* Chicago: University of Chicago Press, 1998 [1958].

Bakhtin, M. M. *Problems of Dostoevsky's Poetics.* Edited and translated by Caryl Emerson. Introduction by Wayne C. Booth. Minneapolis: University of Minnesota Press, 1984 [1963].

———. *The Dialogic Imagination: Four Essays.* Edited by Michael Holquist. Translated by Caryl Emerson and Michael Holquist. Austin: University of Texas Press, 1981.

Baldwin, James. "Everybody's Protest Novel." In *Notes of a Native Son,* 13–23. Boston: Beacon Press, 1984 [1955].

Bassin, Mark. *Imperial Visions: Nationalist Imagination and Geographical Expansion in the Russian Far East, 1840–1865.* Cambridge: Cambridge University Press, 1999.

Bel'chikov, N. F. *Dostoevskii v protsesse petrashevtzev,* 2nd ed. Moscow: Nauka, 1971 [1936].

Belknap, Robert L. *The Structure of the Brothers Karamazov.* The Hague: Mouton, 1967.

———. "Dostoevsky's Nationalist Ideology and Rhetoric." In *Russia: The Spirit of Nationalism,* ed. Charles A. Moser, 89–100. Jamaica, N.Y.: St. John's University, 1972.

Belknap, Robert L. "The Unrepentant Confession." In *Russianness: Studies on a Nation's Identity. In Honor of Rufus Mathewson, 1918–1978,* ed. Robert L. Belknap, 113–23. Ann Arbor: Ardis, 1990.

Benjamin, Walter. *Illuminations.* Edited and with an introduction by Hannah Arendt. Translated by Harry Zohn. New York: Schocken Books, 1969 [1950 (completed 1940)].

Berlin, Isaiah. *Russian Thinkers.* Edited by Henry Hardy and Aileen Kelly. Introduction by Aileen Kelly. New York: Penguin Books, 1978 [1948].

Bernstein, Michael André. *Foregone Conclusions: Against Apocalyptic History.* Berkeley: University of California Press, 1994.

Bhabha, Homi. *The Location of Culture.* London: Routledge, 1994.

Bitov, Andrei. "Novyi Robinzon (k 125-letiiu vykhoda v svet *Zapisok iz mertvogo doma*)." In *Novyi Gulliver: aine kliaine arifmetika russkoi literatury,* 7–18. Tenafly, N.J.: Hermitage, 1997 [1987].

Borisova, V. V. "O natzional'no-religioznykh aspektakh *Zapisok iz mertvogo doma* F. M. Dostoevskogo." In *Dostoevskii i sovremennost': Materialy IX mezhdunarodnykh starorusskikh chtenii 1994 g.* Novgorod: Novgorodskii Gosudarstvennyi Ob"edinennyi Muzei-Zapovednik: Dom Myzii F. M. Dostoevskogo, 1995.

Boym, Svetlana. *The Future of Nostalgia.* New York: Basic Books, 2001.

Brooks, Jeffrey. *When Russia Learned to Read: Literacy and Popular Literature, 1861–1917.* Princeton, N.J.: Princeton University Press, 1985.

Burke, Kenneth. *A Grammar of Motives.* Berkeley: University of California Press, 1945.

————. *The Rhetoric of Religion: Studies in Logology.* Berkeley: University of California Press, 1961.

Butler, Judith. "Merleau-Ponty and the Touch of Malebranche." In *The Cambridge Companion to Merleau-Ponty,* ed. Taylor Carman and Mark B. N. Hansen, 181–205. Cambridge: Cambridge University Press, 2005.

Catteau, Jacques. "De la structure de *La maison des morts* de F. M. Dostoevskij." *Revues des Etudes Slaves* 54, nos. 1–2 (1982): 63–72.

————. *Dostoevsky and the Process of Literary Creation.* Translated by Audrey Littlewood. Cambridge: Cambridge University Press, 1989.

Cavarero, Adriana. *Relating Narratives: Storytelling and Selfhood.* Translated by P. A. Kottman. London: Routledge, 2000.

Cavell, Stanley. "Being Odd, Getting Even: Threats to Individuality." In *Reconstructing Individualism: Autonomy, Individuality, and the Self in Western Thought,* ed. Thomas C. Heller, Morton Sosna, and David E. Wellbery, 273–312. Stanford: Stanford University Press, 1986.

Chaadaev, P. Ia. "Lettres sur la philosophie de l'histoire. Lettre première." In *Sochineniia i pis'ma,* 2 vols., ed. M. Gershenzon, 1:74–93. Oxford: Oxford University Press, 1972 [1913–14].

Cherniavsky, Michael. *Tsar and People: Studies in Russian Myths.* New York: Random House, 1969.

Clifford, James. "On Ethnographic Authority." *Representations* 1, no. 2 (1983): 118–46.

———. "Introduction: Partial Truths." In *Writing Culture: The Poetics and Politics of Ethnography*, ed. James Clifford and George E. Marcus, 1–24. Berkeley: University of California Press, 1986.

———. "On Ethnographic Self-Fashioning: Conrad and Malinowski." In *Reconstructing Individualism: Autonomy, Individuality, and the Self in Western Thought*, ed. Thomas C. Heller, Morton Sosna, and David E. Wellbery, 140–62. Stanford: Stanford University Press, 1986.

Clowes, Edith W., Samuel D. Kassow, and James L. West, eds. *Between Tsar and People: Educated Society and the Quest for Public Identity in Late Imperial Russia.* Princeton, N.J.: Princeton University Press, 1991.

Coetzee, J. M. "Confession and Double Thoughts: Tolstoy, Rousseau, Dostoevsky." *Comparative Literature* 37, no. 3 (summer 1985): 193–232.

Cohen, Josh. "Review of Giorgio Agamben, *Homo Sacer* and *Remnants of Auschwitz.*" In *Textual Practice* 15, no. 2 (summer 2001): 379–85.

Cole, Elizabeth Anne. "Towards a Poetics of Russian Prison Literature: Writings on Prison by Dostoevsky, Chekhov, and Solzhenitsyn." Ph.D. dissertation, Yale University, 1991.

Crisp, Olga, and Linda Edmondson, eds. *Civil Rights in Imperial Russia.* Oxford: Clarendon, 1989.

Dal', Vladimir. *Tolkovyi slovar' zhivogo velikorusskogo iazyka.* 4 vols. Moscow: Izdatel'stvo "Russkii Iazyk," 1955 [1880–82].

de Certeau, Michel. "The Madness of Vision." *Enclitic* 7, no. 1 (spring 1983): 24–31.

de Man, Paul. "Autobiography as De-facement," *Modern Language Notes* 94, no. 5 (1979): 919–30.

de Sherbinin, Julie. "Transcendence Through Art: The Convicts' Theatricals in Dostoevskij's *Zapiski iz mertvogo doma.*" *Slavic and East European Journal* 35, no. 3 (1991): 339–51.

Dolinin, A. ed. *F. M. Dostoevskii v vospominaniiakh sovremennikov*, vol. 1. N.p.: Izdatel'stvo khudozhestvennaia literatura, 1964.

Dostoevskii, F. M. *Polnoe sobranie sochinenii v tridtzati tomakh* [The complete works in thirty volumes]. Edited by V. G. Bazanov, V. V. Vinogradov, F. Ia. Priima, et al. Leningrad: Akademiia Nauk, 1972–90.

Dostoevsky, Fyodor. *Memoirs from the House of the Dead.* Edited by Ronald Hingley. Translated by Jessie Coulson. New York: Oxford University Press, 1983.

———. *Notes from Underground.* Translated by Richard Pevear and Larissa Volokhonsky. New York: Vintage, 1993.

———. *Crime and Punishment.* Translated by Richard Pevear and Larissa Volokhonsky. New York: Vintage, 1992.

———. *The Idiot.* Translated by Richard Pevear and Larissa Volokhonsky. New York: Vintage, 2001.

———. *The Brothers Karamazov.* Translated by Richard Pevear and Larissa Volokhonsky. New York: Vintage, 1990.

———. *Dostoevsky's Occasional Writings.* Translated by David Magarshack. Evanston, Ill.: Northwestern University Press, 1963.

Dostoevsky, Fyodor. *A Writer's Diary. Volume 1: 1873–1876.* Translated by Kenneth Lantz. Introduction by Gary Saul Morson. Evanston, Ill: Northwestern University Press, 1994.

———. *A Writer's Diary. Volume 2: 1877–1881.* Translated by Kenneth Lantz. Evanston, Ill.: Northwestern University Press, 1994.

———. *Selected Letters of Fyodor Dostoevsky.* Edited by Joseph Frank and David I. Goldstein. Translated by Andrew R. MacAndrew. New Brunswick, N.J.: Rutgers University Press, 1987.

Douglass, Frederick. *The Narrative of the Life of Frederick Douglass, An American Slave, Written by Himself.* Edited by Houston A. Baker, Jr. New York: Penguin Books, 1982.

———. *My Bondage and My Freedom.* Introduction by Philip S. Foner. New York: Dover, 1969.

Eikhenbaum, Boris M. "The Theory of the Formal Method." In *Readings in Russian Poetics: Formalist and Structuralist Views.* Edited by Ladislav Matejka and Krystyna Pomorska. Cambridge, Mass.: Harvard University Press, 1971.

Eklof, Ben, John Bushnell, and Larissa Zakharova, eds. *Russia's Great Reforms, 1855–1881.* Bloomington: Indiana University Press, 1994.

Emmons, Terence. "The Peasant and the Emancipation." In *The Peasant in Nineteenth-Century Russia,* Wayne S. Vucinich, 41–71. Stanford: Stanford University Press, 1968.

Engelstein, Laura, and Stephanie Sandler, eds. *Self and Story in Russian History.* Ithaca, N.Y.: Cornell University Press, 2000.

Etov, V. I. *Dostoevskii: ocherk tvorchestva.* Moscow: "Prosveshchenie," 1968.

Evans, John L. *The Petrasevskij Circle, 1845–1849.* The Hague: Mouton, 1974.

Fanger, Donald. *Dostoevsky and Romantic Realism: A Study of Dostoevsky in Relation to Balzac, Dickens, and Gogol.* Chicago: University of Chicago Press, 1965.

———. *The Creation of Nikolai Gogol.* Cambridge, Mass.: Harvard University Press, 1979.

Fenollosa, Ernest. *The Chinese Written Character as a Medium for Poetry.* Edited by Ezra Pound. San Francisco: City Lights, 1968.

Field, Daniel. *Rebels in the Name of the Tsar.* Boston: Unwin Hyman, 1989.

———. "The Year of Jubilee." In *Russia's Great Reforms, 1855–1881,* ed. Ben Eklof, John Bushnell, and Larissa Zakharova, 40–57. Bloomington: Indiana University Press, 1994.

Figes, Orlando. *Natasha's Dance: A Cultural History of Russia.* New York: Picador, 2002.

Flynn, Bernard. *Political Philosophy at the Close of Metaphysics.* Englewood Cliffs, N.J.: Humanities Press, 1991.

———. *The Philosophy of Claude Lefort: Interpreting the Political.* Evanston, Ill.: Northwestern University Press, 2005.

Földényi, László. "Dostoevsky Reads Hegel in Siberia and Bursts into Tears." *Common Knowledge* 10, no. 1 (2004): 93–104. Journal of Duke University Press.

Foley, Barbara. *Telling the Truth: The Theory and Practice of Documentary Fiction.* Ithaca, N.Y.: Cornell University Press, 1986.

Frank, Joseph. *Dostoevsky: The Seeds of Revolt, 1821–1849.* Princeton, N.J.: Princeton University Press, 1976.

———. *Dostoevsky: The Years of Ordeal, 1850–1859.* Princeton, N.J.: Princeton University Press, 1983.

———. *Dostoevsky: The Stir of Liberation, 1860–1865.* Princeton, N.J.: Princeton University Press, 1986.

———. *Through the Russian Prism: Essays on Literature and Culture.* Princeton, N.J.: Princeton University Press, 1990.

———. *Dostoevsky: The Miraculous Years, 1865–1871.* Princeton, N.J.: Princeton University Press, 1995.

———. *Dostoevsky: The Mantle of the Prophet, 1871–1881.* Princeton, N.J.: Princeton University Press, 2002.

———. "Dostoevsky and Evil." *Partisan Review* 70, no. 2 (Spring 2003): 262–73.

Freccero, John. "Logology: Burke on St. Augustine." In *Representing Kenneth Burke,* ed. Hayden White and Margaret Brose, 52–67. Baltimore: Johns Hopkins University Press, 1982.

Fridlender, G. M. *Realizm Dostoevskogo.* Moscow: Nauka, 1964.

Gernet, M. N. *Istoriia tsarskoi tiur'my.* 5 vols. Moscow: Gosudarstvennyi izdatel'stvo iuridicheskoi literatury, 1951–60.

Gide, André. *Dostoevsky.* 1923; New York: New Directions, 1961.

Ginzburg, Evgeniia Semionovna. *Journey into the Whirlwind.* Translated by Paul Stevenson and Max Hayward. New York: Harcourt, 1967.

Goldstein, David. *Dostoevsky and the Jews.* Foreword by Joseph Frank. Austin: University of Texas Press, 1981.

Gromyko, M. M. *Sibirskie znakomye i druz'ia F. M. Dostoevskogo. 1850–1854 gg.* Novosibirsk: Izdatel'stvo Nauka, 1985.

Grossman, Leonid. *Ispoved odnovo evreia.* Moscow-Leningrad, 1924.

———. "Dostoevskii-khudozhnik." In *Tvorchestvo F. M. Dostoevskogo,* ed. N. L. Stepanov, 330–416. Moscow: Akademiia Nauk, 1959.

———. " 'Grazhdanskaia smert' F. M. Dostoevskogo." In *Literaturnoe nasledstvo* 22–24 (1935): 683–92. Vaduz: Kraus Reprint, 1963.

———. *Dostoevskii.* Moscow: Molodaia gvardiia, 1963.

———. *Dostoevsky: His Life and Work.* Translated by Mary Mackler. New York: Bobbs-Merrill, 1975.

Harden, Evelyn Josiulko. Introduction to Fyodor Dostoevsky, *The Double: Two Versions.* Translated by Evelyn Jasiulko Harden. Ann Arbor, Mich.: Ardis, 1985.

Harpham, Geoffrey Galt. *The Ascetic Imperative in Culture and Criticism.* Chicago: University of Chicago Press, 1987.

Harvey, Van A. *A Handbook of Theological Terms.* New York: Macmillan, 1964.

Herzen, Alexander I. *From the Other Shore and The Russian People and Socialism, an Open Letter to Jules Michelet.* Introduction by Isaiah Berlin. New York: Meridian Books, 1963.

Herzen [Gertsen], Alexander I. *Sobranie sochinenii v tridzati tomakh.* Moscow: AN CCCP, 1954–66.

Hudspith, Sarah. *Dostoevsky and the Idea of Russianness: A New Perspective on Unity and Brotherhood.* London: RoutledgeCurzon, 2004.

Iser, Wolfgang. "Feigning in Fiction." In *Identity of the Literary Text*, ed. Mario J. Valdés and Owen Miller, 204–28. Toronto: University of Toronto Press, 1985.

———. *The Fictive and the Imaginary: Charting Literary Anthropology*. Baltimore: Johns Hopkins University Press, 1993.

Ivanov, Viacheslav. *Freedom and the Tragic Life: A Study in Dostoevsky*. Translated by Norman Cameron. New York: Noonday, 1952.

Jackson, Robert Louis. "The Narrator in Dostoevsky's *Notes from the House of the Dead*." In *Studies in Russian and Polish Literature, in Honor of Waclaw Lednicki*, ed. Zbigniew Folejewski et al., 192–216. The Hague: Mouton, 1962.

———. *Dostoevsky's Quest for Form: A Study of His Philosophy of Art*. New Haven: Yale University Press, 1966.

———. *The Art of Dostoevsky: Deliriums and Nocturnes*. Princeton, N.J.: Princeton University Press, 1981.

Jay, Martin. *Downcast Eyes: The Denigration of Vision in Twentieth-Century French Thought*. Berkeley: University of California Press, 1993.

Jones, John. *Dostoevsky*. Oxford: Clarendon, 1983.

Jones, Malcolm V. "Dostoevskii and Religion." In *The Cambridge Companion to Dostoevsky*, ed. W. J. Leatherbarrow, 148–74. Cambridge: Cambridge University Press, 2002.

———. *Dostoevsky and the Dynamics of Religious Experience*. London: Anthem, 2005.

Kelly, Aileen M. *Toward Another Shore: Russian Thinkers between Necessity and Chance*. New Haven: Yale University Press, 1998.

———. "Historical Diffidence: A New Look at an Old Russian Debate." *Common Knowledge* 8, no. 3 (2002): 496–515. Journal of Duke University Press.

Kirpotin, V. Ia. *Dostoevskii-khudozhnik*. Moscow: Sovetskii pisatel', 1960.

———. *Dostoevskii v shestidesiatye gody*. Moscow: Khudozhestvenaia Literatura, 1966.

Knapp, Liza. *The Annihilation of Inertia: Dostoevsky and Metaphysics*. Evanston: Northwestern University Press, 1996.

———, ed. and trans. *Dostoevsky as Reformer: The Petrashevsky Case*. Ann Arbor, Mich.: Ardis, 1987.

Kogan, Galina. "Zabytyi roman XIX v. v tvorcheskikh iskaniiakh Dostoevskogo." In *Al'manakh* 1, part 11 (St. Petersburg: Izdatel'stvo Akademii Nauk, 1993).

Kolchin, Peter. *Unfree Labor: American Slavery and Russian Serfdom*. Cambridge, Mass.: Harvard University Press, 1987.

Kristeva, Julia. *Black Sun: Depression and Melancholia*. New York: Columbia University Press, 1989.

Layton, Susan. *Russian Literature and Empire: Conquest of the Caucasus from Pushkin to Tolstoy*. Cambridge: Cambridge University Press, 1994.

Lefort, Claude. *Sur une colonne absente: Ecrits autour de Merleau-Ponty*. N.p.: Editions Gallimard, 1978.

———. *The Political Forms of Modern Society: Bureaucracy, Democracy, Totalitarianism*. Edited by John B. Thompson. Cambridge, Mass.: MIT Press, 1986.

———. *Democracy and Political Theory*. Translated by David Macey. Minneapolis: University of Minnesota Press, 1988.

Leikina, V. R., E. A. Korolchuk, and V. A. Desnitskii, eds., *Delo petrashevtsev.* 3 vols. Moscow-Leningrad: Akademiia Nauk, 1937–51.

Levi, Primo. *The Drowned and the Saved.* Translated by Raymond Rosenthal. New York: Summit Books, 1988.

———. *Survival in Auschwitz.* Translated by Stuart Woolf. 1958; New York: Simon and Schuster, 1996.

Levitt, Marcus C. *Russian Literary Politics and the Pushkin Celebration of 1880.* Ithaca: Cornell University Press, 1989.

Lincoln, W. Bruce. *Nicholas I: Emperor and Autocrat of All the Russias.* Bloomington: Indiana University Press, 1978.

———. *The Great Reforms: Autocracy, Bureaucracy, and the Politics of Change in Imperial Russia.* DeKalb: Northern Illinois University Press, 1990.

Lord, Robert. *Dostoevsky: Essays and Perspectives.* Berkeley: University of California Press, 1970.

Lotman, Iurii M. "Concerning Khlestakov." In *The Semiotics of Russian Cultural History,* ed. Alexander D. Nakhimovsky and Alice S. Nakhimovsky, intro. Boris Gasparov, trans. Louisa Vinton, 150–87. Ithaca: Cornell University Press, 1985.

Macpherson, C. B. *The Political Theory of Possessive Individualism: Hobbes to Locke.* Oxford: Clarendon, 1964.

Mannoni, Octave. "Je sais bien, mais quand même . . .," In *Clefs pour l'imaginaire.* Paris: Éditions du Seuil, 1969.

Martianov, P. K. "V perelome veka." In *F. M. Dostoevskii v vospominaniiakh sovremmenikov,* 2 vols., ed. A. Dolinin, 1:235–43. N.p.: Izdatel'stvo khudozhestvenaia literatura, 1964.

Martinsen, Deborah A. *Literary Journals in Imperial Russia.* Cambridge: Cambridge University Press, 1997.

———. *Surprised by Shame: Dostoevsky's Liars and Narrative Exposure.* Columbus: Ohio State University Press, 2003.

———. "Of Shame and Human Bondage: Dostoevsky's *Notes from Underground.* In *Dostoevsky on the Threshold of Other Worlds: Essays in Honour of Malcolm V. Jones,* ed. Sarah Young and Lesley Milne, 157–69. Ilkeston, Derbyshire: Bramcote, 2006.

Maslan, Susan. *Revolutionary Acts: Theater, Democracy, and the French Revolution.* Baltimore: Johns Hopkins University Press, 2005.

Melville, Herman. "Bartleby, the Scrivener: A Story of Wall-Street." In *Great Short Works of Herman Melville,* ed. Warner Berthoff, 39–74. New York: Harper and Row, 1969.

———. *Billy Budd, Sailor: An Inside Narrative.* Edited by Milton R. Stern. Indianapolis, Ind.: Bobbs-Merrill Education Publishing, 1975.

Merleau-Ponty, Maurice. *The Visible and the Invisible.* Edited by Claude Lefort. Translated by Alphonso Lingis. Evanston, Ill.: Northwestern University Press, 1968.

Miller, Robin Feuer. *Dostoevsky and "The Idiot": Author, Narrator, and Reader.* Cambridge, Mass.: Harvard University Press, 1981.

Miller, Robin Feuer. "Dostoevsky and Rousseau: The Morality of Confession Reconsidered." In *Dostoevsky: New Perspectives*, ed. Robert Louis Jackson, 82–97. Englewood Cliffs, N.J.: Prentice Hall, 1984.

———. "Adventures in Time and Space: Dostoevsky, William James, and the Perilous Journey to Conversion." In *William James in Russian Culture*, ed. Joan D. Grossman and Ruth Rischin, 33–58. Lanham, Md.: Lexington Books, 2003.

Mochulsky, Konstantin. *Dostoevsky: His Life and Work*. Translated by Michael A. Minihan. Princeton, N.J.: Princeton University Press, 1967.

Mogilianskii, A. P. "K istorii pervoi publikatsii 'Zapisok iz mertvogo doma.' " *Russkaia literatura* 3 (1969): 179–81.

Morson, Gary Saul. *The Boundaries of Genre: Dostoevsky's Diary of a Writer and the Traditions of Literary Utopia*. Austin: University of Texas Press, 1981.

———, ed. *Literature and History: Theoretical Problems and Russian Case Studies*. Stanford: Stanford University Press, 1986.

Murav, Harriet. "Dostoevsky in Siberia: Remembering the Past." *Slavic Review* 50, no. 4 (winter 1991): 858–66.

———. *Holy Foolishness: Dostoevsky's Novels and the Poetics of Cultural Critique*. Stanford: Stanford University Press, 1992.

———. *Russia's Legal Fictions*. Ann Arbor: University of Michigan Press, 1998.

Nechaeva, V. S. *Zhurnal M. M. i F. M. Dostoevskikh Vremia*, 1861–1863. Moscow: Nauka, 1972.

———. *Zhurnal M. M. i F. M. Dostoevskikh Epokha*, 1864–1865. Moscow: Nauka, 1975.

Neuberger, Joan. "Popular Legal Cultures: The St. Petersburg *Mirovoi sud*." In *Russia's Great Reforms, 1855–1881*, ed. Ben Eklof, John Bushnell, and Larissa Zakharova, 231–46. Bloomington: Indiana University Press, 1994.

Nikolaev, M. P. *L. N. Tolstoi i N. G. Chernyshevskii*. Tula: Priokskoe knizhnoe izdatel'stvo, 1969.

Nikolopoulou, Kalliope. Review of Giorgio Agamben, *Homo Sacer*. In *Substance* 93 (2000): 124–31.

Norris, Andrew, ed. *Politics, Metaphysics, and Death: Essays on Giorgio Agamben's Homo Sacer*. Durham: Duke University Press, 2005.

Offord, Derek. "Dostoevskii and the Intelligentsia." In *The Cambridge Companion to Dostoevskii*, ed. J. W. Leatherbarrow, 111–30. Cambridge: Cambridge University Press, 2002.

Paperno, Irina. "The Liberation of the Serfs as a Cultural Symbol." In *Russian Review* 50, no. 4 (October 1991): 418–36.

Pascal, Pierre. *Dostoïevski, L'homme et l'oeuvre*. Lausanne: Slavica, 1970.

Peterson, Dale E. *Up from Bondage: The Literatures of Russian and African American Soul*. Durham: Duke University Press, 2000.

Piksanov, N. K. "Dostoevskii i fol'klor." *Sovetskaia etnografiia*, nos. 1–2 (1934).

Pipes, Richard. "*Narodnichestvo*: A Semantic Inquiry." *Slavic Review* 23, no. 3 (September 1964): 441–58.

Pisarev, D. I. "Narodnye Knizhki." In *Polnoe sobranie sochinenii i pisem v 12 tomakh*, vol. 2, *Stat'i i retsenzii, 1860–1861 (Ianvar'–Mai)*, 213–29. Moscow: Nauka, 2000.

———. "*Pogibshie i pogibaiushchie.*" In *Polnoe sobranie sochinenii i pisem v dvenadtsati tomakh*, 8:284–336. Moscow: "Nauka," 2004.

Polnyi pravoslavnyi bogoslovskii entsiklopedicheskii slovar'. London: Varorium Reprints, 1971 [1913].

Pratt, Mary Louise. "Fieldwork in Common Places." In *Writing Culture: The Poetics and Politics of Ethnography*, ed. James Clifford and George E. Marcus, 27–52. Berkeley: University of California Press, 1986.

Raeff, Marc. *Political Ideas and Institutions in Imperial Russia*. Boulder, Colo.: Westview, 1994.

Ram, Harsha. *The Imperial Sublime: A Russian Poetics of Empire*. Madison: University of Wisconsin Press, 2003.

Reyfman, Irina. *Ritualized Violence Russian Style: The Duel in Russian Culture and Literature*. Stanford: Stanford University Press, 1999.

Riasanovsky, Nicholas. *Nicholas I and Official Nationality in Russia, 1825–1855*. Berkeley: University of California Press, 1959.

———. *A Parting of the Ways: Government and the Educated Public in Russia, 1801–1855*. Oxford: Clarendon, 1976.

Richter, Gerhard. *Walter Benjamin and the Corpus of Autobiography*. Detroit: Wayne State University Press, 2000.

Rice, James L. *Dostoevsky and the Healing Art: An Essay in Literary and Medical History*. Ann Arbor, Mich.: Ardis, 1985.

———. "Psychoanalysis of 'Peasant Marej': Some Residual Problems." In *Russian Literature and Psychoanalysis*, ed. Daniel Rancour-Laferriere, 245–61. Amsterdam/Philadelphia: John Benjamins, 1989.

———. "Dostoevsky's Endgame: The Projected Sequel to *The Brothers Karamazov*." *Russian History. Histoire Russe* 33, no. 1 (Spring 2006): 45–62.

Rosaldo, Renato. "From the Door of His Tent: The Fieldworker and the Inquisitor." In *Writing Culture: The Poetics and Politics of Ethnography*, ed. James Clifford and George E. Marcus, 77–97. Berkeley: University of California Press, 1986.

Rosenshield, Gary. "Akul'ka: The Incarnation of the Ideal in Dostoevskij's *Notes from the House of the Dead*." *Slavic and East European Journal* 31, no. 1 (1987): 10–19.

Ruttenburg, Nancy. *Democratic Personality: Popular Voice and the Trial of American Authorship*. Stanford: Stanford University Press, 1998.

———. "Dostoevsky's Estrangement." *Poetics Today* 26, no. 4 (Winter 2005): 719–51.

Scarry, Elaine. *The Body in Pain: The Making and Unmaking of the World*. New York: Oxford University Press, 1985.

Schrader, Abby M. *Languages of the Lash: Corporal Punishment and Identity in Imperial Russia*. DeKalb: Northern Illinois University Press, 2002.

Seleznev, Iurii. *Dostoevskii*. Moscow: Molodaia Gvardiia, 1981.

Serman, Ilya. "Tema narodnosti v *Zapiskikh iz mervogo doma*." *Dostoevsky Studies* 3 (1982): 101–44.

Shklovskii, Viktor. *Za i protiv: zametki o Dostoevskom*. Moscow: Sovetskii pisatel', 1957.

Shklovskii, Viktor. "Art as Technique." In *Russian Formalist Criticism: Four Essays.* Translated by Lee T. Lemon and Marion J. Reis, 5–24. Lincoln: University of Nebraska Press, 1965.

Slezkine, Yuri. *Arctic Mirrors: Russia and the Small Peoples of the North.* Ithaca, N.Y.: Cornell University Press, 1994.

Smirnov, I. P. "Otchuzhdenie-v-otchuzhdenii (o 'Zapiskakh iz mertvogo doma')." *Wiener Slawistischer Almanach* 7 (1981): 37–48.

Solzhenitsyn, Alexander. *The Gulag Archipelago, 1918–1956: An Experiment in Literary Investigation.* Vols. 1–2. Translated by Thomas P. Whitney. New York: Harper and Row/Perennial Classics, 1973.

Solzhenitsyn, Aleksandr. *Arkhipelag GULag, 1918–1956, opyt khudozhestvennogo issledovaniia.* Vols. 1–3. Paris: YMCA Press, 1973.

Spengemann, William. *The Forms of Autobiography.* New Haven: Yale University Press, 1980.

Stauffer, John. *The Black Hearts of Men: Radical Abolitionists and the Transformation of Race.* Cambridge, Mass.: Harvard University Press, 2002.

Sundquist, Eric. "Suspense and Tautology in *Benito Cereno.*" *Glyph* 8 (1981): 103–26.

Talman, Jacob L. *The Origins of Totalitarian Democracy.* New York: Norton, 1970.

Tamarkin, Elisa. *Anglophilia: Deference, Devotion and Antebellum America.* Chicago: University of Chicago Press, 2007.

Teofilov, Marius. "Pererastanie dokumental'nogo materiala v khudozhestvennyi v *Zapiskakh iz mertvogo doma* F. M. Dostoevskogo." *Bolgarskaia rusistika* 4 (1988): 11–18.

Todd III, William Mills. "Storied Selves: Constructing Character in *The Brothers Karamazov.*" In *Self and Story in Russian History,* ed. Laura Engelstein and Stephanie Sandler, 266–79. Ithaca, N.Y.: Cornell University Press, 2000.

———. "Dostoevskii as a Professional Writer." In *The Cambridge Companion to Dostoevskii,* ed. W. J. Leatherbarrow, 66–92. Cambridge: Cambridge University Press, 2002.

Toker, Leona. "Towards a Poetics of Documentary Prose—From the Perspective of Gulag Testimonies." *Poetics Today* 18, no. 2 (Summer 1997): 187–222.

Tolstoy, Leo. "Are the Peasant Children to Learn to Write from Us? or, Are we to Learn from the Peasant Children?" In *The Complete Works of Count Tolstoy: Pedagogical Articles,* trans. Leo Wiener, 191–224. Boston: Dana Estes, 1904.

Tolstoy, L. N. "*Komu u kogo uchit'sia pisat', krestianski rebiatam u nas, ili nam u krestianskikh rebiat?*" In *Polnoe sobranie sochinenii,* Vol. 8, *Pedagogicheskie stat'i 1860–1863,* 301–24. Moscow: Gosudarstvennoe izdatel'stvo khudozhestvennoi literatury, 1936 [1862].

Tunimanov, V. A. *Tvorchestvo Dostoevskogo.* Leningrad: Nauka, 1980.

Turgenev, I. S. *Polnoe sobranie sochinenii i pisem v dvadtsati vos'mi tomakh.* Moscow/Leningrad: Nauka, 1961–68.

Venturi, Franco. *Roots of Revolution: A History of the Populist and Socialist Movements in 19th Century Russia.* Rev. ed. Introduction by Isaiah Berlin. London: Phoenix, 2001 [1960].

Vinogradov, V. V. *Poetika russkoi literatury.* Moscow: Nauka, 1976.

Volgin, Igor'. *Koleblias' nad bezdnoi: Dostoevskii i imperatorskii dom*. Moscow: Izdatel'stvo "Tsentr gumanitarnogo obrazovaniia," 1998.

———. *Propavshii zagovor: Dostoevskii i politicheskii protsess 1849 g*. Moscow: Izdatel'stvo Libereia, 2000.

Vucinich, Wayne S., ed. *The Peasant in Nineteenth-Century Russia*. Stanford: Stanford University Press, 1968.

Walicki, Andrzej. *A History of Russian Thought from the Enlightenment to Marxism*. Translated by Hilda Andrews-Rusiecka. Stanford: Stanford University Press, 1978.

———. *The Slavophile Controversy: History of a Conservative Utopia in Nineteenth-Century Russian Thought*. Translated by Hilda Andrews-Rusiecka. Notre Dame, Ind.: University of Notre Dame Press, 1989.

Wall, Thomas Carl. "Au Hasard." In *Politics, Metaphysics, and Death: Essays on Giorgio Agamben's Homo Sacer*, ed. Andrew Norris, 31–48. Durham: Duke University Press, 2005.

Whitman, Walt. Preface to *Leaves of Grass*. In Walt Whitman, *Complete Poetry and Collected Prose*, 5–26. New York: Library of America, 1982 [1855].

Wirtschafter, Elise Kimerling. *Social Identity in Imperial Russia*. Dekalb: Northern Illinois University Press, 1997.

Wood, Alan. "Solzhenitsyn on the Tsarist Exile System: A Historical Comment." *Journal of Russian Studies*, no. 42 (1981): 39–43.

———. "Crime and Punishment in the House of the Dead." In *Civil Rights in Imperial Russia*, ed. Olga Crisp and Linda Edmondson, 215–34. Oxford: Clarendon, 1989.

Wortman, Richard. *The Development of a Russian Legal Consciousness*. Chicago: University of Chicago Press, 1976.

Young, Sarah. *Dostoevsky's "The Idiot" and the Ethical Foundations of Narrative: Reading, Narrating, Scripting*. London: Anthem, 2004.

Zamotin, I. I. *F. M. Dostoevskii v russkoi kritike*. Warsaw: Tipografiia okruzhago shtaba, 1913.

Zelinskii, V. A., ed. *Kriticheskii kommentarii k sochineniiam F. M. Dostoevskogo. Sbornik kriticheskikh statei*. Vol. 2. Moscow: Tipografiia vil'de, 1901.

Index

~

abandonment: Bartleby and *Muselmann* as figures of abandonment, 110; castaways, 214n70; *homo sacer* and, 25, 105–7, 130, 228n16; *katorga* and, 95, 99–100, 140–41, 227n10; modernity and, 110, 141; punishment as radical, 99–100, 105–6

abjection: and absence of remorse or resentment, 121; crime and, 124–25; freedom or emancipation linked to, 104–5; *katorga* and equality of, 100, 104–5, 129, 141, 166; literacy and, 141–42, 175; power and, 231n46; subjectification and, 124–25, 166

abyss of class difference, 23, 27–28, 46–47, 49, 53–54, 60, 64–65, 104, 138, 143, 175, 211n42, 238n106, 246n19

accuracy of inventory, 51, 57–60, 169, 210–11n37

Agamben, Giorgio, 40–41, 244n3; on bare life, 94–96; on biopolitical fracture, 170–71; on community as constituting power, 155; democracy and totalitarianism as continuity, 97, 229n22; "Form-of-Life," 232n49; on Nazi lagers as state of exception, 113–14; on totalitarian camps, 97–98, 100; Western modernity and, 97–98, 100, 104, 141; witnessing as intimacy, 137. *See also homo sacer* (sacred man); state of exception

Aglaia Epanchina *(The Idiot)*, 8–9, 10, 17, 18, 199n18

Akim Akimich *(Notes from the House of the Dead)*, 103, 234n77

"Akul'ka's Husband," 52–53; as allegory, 89, 236–37n98; as confession narrative, 71–72, 75, 81–82, 89; desubjectification and, 75–76, 79, 136–37, 236–37n98; "The Environment" as companion text for, 132–35; framing devices and, 71; Jackson's reading of, 52; as love story, 83; prefatory narrator's focus on, 82; publication as separate work, 89; as ritual sac-

rifice, 81–82; Shiskov as narrator, 52, 71–72, 75–76, 79–83, 136–39

Alexander II, Tsar of Russia, 1–2, 7, 16, 84, 96–97

Aley *(Notes from the House of the Dead)*, 67

alterity, perception of the Other, 176. *See also* abyss of class difference; subject / object dichotomy

apology, 87, 224n126

Arendt, Hannah, 97, 98, 100–102, 108, 157, 193–94, 230nn36–37, 235n86

aristocracy. *See* elites

Aristov *(Notes from the House of the Dead)*, 235n82

atheism, 13–14, 19–20, 35, 187, 192

audience, 165; Gorianchikov as, 80; as indifferent, 117–18; Myshkin's relationship to his, 12. *See also* reader(s)

autobiography, 214n69, 245n13; autobiographical readings of *House of the Dead*, 40–41, 83–88, 94, 95, 115–16, 132–33, 137–38, 175–76, 214n69, 219n102, 221n112, 222nn118–19; Dostoevsky and fiction as filter for, 222–23n121; Gorianchikov as Dostoevsky's alter ego, 41, 84–86, 94, 115–16, 132–33, 137–38, 175–76, 214n69, 219n102, 221n112, 222n119; memoir as confession, 87; Russian tradition of integrated genres, 208–9n27, 222n118

auxiliary persons, fictional characters as, 184–85, 192–93

Bakhtin, M. M., 11–12, 51, 115, 157, 158, 200n30, 200n32, 208n23, 209n29, 213n65

bare life, 94–99, 104–5, 106, 141, 154–55, 161, 229n25; slavery and, 98–99; *zoe / bios* dichotomy, 97, 104–5, 170, 178, 194

barriers as pattern of disintegration, 144–46

desubjectification (*cont'd*)
"negative poetics for stories of the self,"
236n95; of peasants by Gorianchikov,
137–38, 181; personality and, 103; slavery and, 171, 173; space of exception
and, 140; of victim, 136–37; of the witness, 111, 135
Diary of a Writer, 4–5, 25, 36, 120, 124,
236n94, 242nn139–40; "The Peasant
Marei" in, 36, 48, 76–80, 86, 120;
"Vlas" in, 187–92
disintegration: barrier as pattern of disintegration, 144–46; explosion as pattern of,
144–47; of Gorianchikov's personality,
24–25, 42, 47–48, 60; Nazis and disintegration of personality as goal, 100–101;
and resistance of meaning, 144, 145–46
dissembling, 13–14, 70
Dmitri Karamazov *(Brothers Karamazov)*.
See Karamazov, Dmitri *(Brothers Karamazov)*
Dobroliubov, N., 180–81
Dostoevsky, Andrei (brother), correspondence with, 226n6
Dostoevsky, F. M.: autobiographical readings of *House of the Dead*, 40–41, 83–88,
94, 95, 115–16, 132–33, 137–38, 175–
76, 214n69, 219n102, 221n112,
222nn118–19; conservative ideology of,
21–22; death of, 2, 97; estrangement of,
32–33, 101; exile and imprisonment of,
2, 26, 31, 95, 230n34; explosion linked
to creativity by, 238n110; family and biographical information, 6; on fellow inmates of *katorga*, 95; Gorianchikov as
alter ego for, 41, 78, 84–86, 94, 115,
132–33, 137–38, 175–76, 214n69,
219n102, 221n112; loss of class privileges as punishment of, 95, 227–
28nn12–13; religious faith of, 36, 206–
7n18, 218n96; speech at Pushkin celebration, 3–4; Turgenev and, 3–4. *See also specific works of*
Dostoevsky, Mikhail (brother), 204–5n6;
correspondence with, 27, 28, 32, 77, 94,
143, 183–84, 202–3n51, 227n12
The Double, 68–69, 177, 209–10n31,
225n131
doubling: in *Brothers Karamazov*, 87, 190,
193; Gorianchikov and, 68–69, 128; prefatory narrator as double for Gorianchi-

kov, 68–69; Shishkov as double for Gorianchikov, 86–90; in "Vlas," 187–90
Douglass, Frederick, 171–76, 178, 180,
245n13
dreaming, 112–14, 219n105; "Akul'ka's
Husband" as dream or hallucination, 79,
120; memory and, 36, 76, 79, 120
dressing gown incident, 72, 74–75, 150–53
The Drowned and the Saved (Levi), 91

Edwards, Jonathan, 109
elites: Aristov as representative of, 235n82;
democracy and Russian, 4–5; Dostoevsky
on democracy and, 25–26; Dostoevsky's
identity with, 214n69; Dostoevsky's portrayal of, 4–5; "educated class" as part of,
248–49n47; executioner within and, 66;
gentrification of crime, 88; peasants as
theoretical or sentimentalized by, 6, 27–
28, 105, 167
emancipation: equality and, 104, 183; of
Frederick Douglass, 171–76, 245n13;
modernity and, 100; of peasants, 2, 23,
26, 31, 66, 97, 191, 202n46; as reconciliation, 170; revolutionary reversal
and, 168
embodiment: artistic creation as, 32–33,
205n9, 219n103; the body and bare life,
161–62; body as both subject and object,
155–56, 159; corporation and, 25, 154,
160–62, 169; democracy as "flesh of the
political," 154–60; dressing gown incident as experience of body, 152–53; Eucharist in "Vlas," 188–89; "flesh of the
political," 239–40n122; Holbein's
Christ's Body in the Tomb, 19; ideas as inseparable from body, 159–60, 168; *katorga* and reduction to body, 103–4;
Merleau-Ponty on "flesh of the world"
and, 154–62, 239–40n122; phenomenal
vs. historical body, 103–4, 231n44; slavery and literacy of the body, 171–72,
245n13
emphysema, 2
"The Environment" *(Diary of a Writer)*,
126–29, 131–35, 236n95; "Akul'ka's
Husband" as companion text for,
132–35
Epanchin women, 8–9, 16–17, 140,
199n18
epilepsy, 7, 13, 18–19, 200nn29–30,
227n12, 238n110